Palgrave Studies in Risk, Crime and Society

Series Editors
Kieran McCartan
Department of Criminology
University of the West of England
Bristol, UK

Beth Weaver
School of Social Work and Social Policy
University of Strathclyde
Glasgow, Lanarkshire, UK

Risk is a major contemporary issue which has widespread implications for theory, policy, governance, public protection, professional practice and societal understandings of crime and criminal justice. The potential harm associated with risk can lead to uncertainty, fear and conflict as well as disproportionate, ineffective and ill-judged state responses to perceived risk and risky groups. Risk, Crime and Society is a series featuring monographs and edited collections which examine the notion of risk, the risky behaviour of individuals and groups, as well as state responses to risk and its consequences in contemporary society. The series will include critical examinations of the notion of risk and the problematic nature of state responses to perceived risk. While Risk, Crime and Society will consider the problems associated with 'mainstream' risky groups including sex offenders, terrorists and white collar criminals, it welcomes scholarly analysis which broadens our understanding of how risk is defined, interpreted and managed. Risk, Crime and Society examines risk in contemporary society through the multi-disciplinary perspectives of law, criminology and socio-legal studies and will feature work that is theoretical as well as empirical in nature.

Geoff Pearson • Clifford Stott

A New Agenda For Football Crowd Management

Reforming Legal and Policing Responses to Risk

palgrave
macmillan

Geoff Pearson
School of Law
University of Manchester
Manchester, UK

Clifford Stott
School of Psychology
University of Keele
Keele, Staffordshire, UK

Palgrave Studies in Risk, Crime and Society
ISBN 978-3-031-16297-8 ISBN 978-3-031-16298-5 (eBook)
https://doi.org/10.1007/978-3-031-16298-5

This Palgrave Macmillan imprint is published by the registered company Springer Nature Switzerland AG.
The registered company address is: Gewerbestrasse 11, 6330 Cham, Switzerland

Acknowledgements

The work we cover in this book draws from decades of collaborative research involving many people and organisations to whom we owe a debt of gratitude. There are too many for us to list individually, so we have decided to focus on those who have made particularly important contributions. Given the numbers involved and the passage of time, there will be several whose names we have inadvertently neglected and for that oversight when it occurs, we apologise.

While this book is about policing football crowds, throughout their evolution the theoretical ideas on crowd psychology that we draw upon have been formed in partnership with John Drury and Steve Reicher and their theoretical contributions in that regard need to be acknowledged from the outset. For the early years of the research work on football crowds that we set out in this book, we would also like to thank David Bohannon, who at that time was working within the Home Office Public Order Unit. Without his confidence, political manoeuvring, and financial investment, it is arguable that much of the latter stages of our work on football crowd policing would not have had the impact that was achieved. Key contributors during this period also include Bryan Drew and Tony Conniford, then of the UK Football Policing Unit (UKFPU), David Swift and the late Michael Harrison from Staffordshire Police, as well as Otto Adang and Martina Schreiber from the Police Academy of the Netherlands. For the work connected to Euro2004, we would also like to thank the various students, officers, and commanders of Public Security Police in Portugal, including Jose Carlos Neto, whose roles in informing and adoption of the research were the first major milestone in 'stress testing' the otherwise theoretical ideas and translating them into research-led police practice. The study on the policing of Euro2004 was enabled by a grant from the ESRC-RES-000-23-617 *Crowd dynamics, policing, and 'hooliganism' at Euro2004*. As the work subsequently developed in the European context, we would also like to acknowledge the key support received from, among others, Kenny Scott, Marc Otten, Marc Timmer, and Steve Frosdick from UEFA.

During the development of the ENABLE project in Scandinavia we would like to extend our thanks to the various police officers of the Swedish and Danish Police, the *Allsvenskan* and the various clubs, organisations and individuals that hosted, supported, populated, and funded our observations. In the early stages, funding was provided by Djurgårdens IF and the UK's ESRC 'Celebrating Impact Prize'. In March 2015, additional funding was obtained from *Länsstyrelsen* Stockholm and the charitable foundation *Gålöstiftelsen* that allowed for further fieldwork between 2015 and 2017. Among others, we also extend our gratitude to our Danish colleagues including Jonas Havelund, Kristian Rasmussen, Tom Carstensen, and Lasse Bauer. In Sweden we would like to thank and acknowledge the important contributions of, among others, Jens Lindgren, Carsten Alven, Philip Lundberg, Sammyh Khan, Neil Williams, Sara Vestegren, Mark Goodyear, Mikael Berkesand, Lena Borg, Lars Ekstrand, Martin Fredman, Kent Tillberg, Jerker Mohlund, Lena Matthijs, and Thomas Delerud.

During the subsequent ENABLE phase in the UK and Switzerland, we would like to thank the N8 Policing Research Partnership, the ESRC Celebrating Impact prize, and the English Football League (in particular John Nagle and Bob Eastwood) for funding our work. We would like to thank the KPAC Centre Manager, Debbie Tallent, as well as the multiple police forces and football clubs that hosted us, in addition to the many police officers, club security officials, fan organisations, and academics that joined our observation teams and informed our analyses. These include, among others, Ravi Sharma, Rob Killingworth, Wayne Nash, Chris Patzelt, Sue Watson, and Phil Mayer, as well as several other club safety officers who allowed or participated in our observations and otherwise supported our work. We would also like to thank our many observers and contributors to analysis including Owen West, Marcus Beale, Leanne Savigar-Shaw, Matt Radburn, Ian Leach, and James Hoggett. There are then the hundreds of police officers and several police forces who supported, populated, and contributed to our observations. While the forces need to remain nameless, we would like to thank, among others, Richard Cawkwell, Dan Greenwood, John Arrowsuch, Bryn Stokes, Mick Cheetham, Julian Platt, Paul Elliot, Kev Evans, Tony Cornwell, Phil Hutchinson, Mike Hope, Vicky Howell, Wayne Palmer, Joe Jones, Nick Lyall, Steve Furnham, Howard Lewis Jones, Mark Goodyear, Nick Rowe, Stewart Bladen, Stuart Bill, Andy Bridgewater, Jenny Richards, Nigel Sarling, Chris Wilkins, David Mapp, Beth Bridges, Lizzie Lewandowski, Mark Reilly, Wayne Jones, Martin Brereton, Jonathan Staite, Matt Derek, Craig Wagstaff, Stephen Smith, Sharon Cooney, Lesley Wheatley, and Steve Neil. We would like to acknowledge the importance of the support we have received from the UKFPU including Paul Foley, Tim Gant, Chad Heuston, Adrian Roberts, and Mick Johnson. We also extend thanks to Mark Holland and Martyn Henderson of the Sports Grounds Safety Authority (SGSA) and, for our work in Switzerland, our close collaborators of Alain Brechbühl and his colleagues at the University of Bern, as well as the police forces of the Cantons of Bern and Zurich.

On the law, human rights, and football banning order aspects of this book, we would like to extend our gratitude to those academics and practitioners that have helped to clarify understandings on some of the complex and constantly evolving areas, including Martin Browne, Melanie Cooke, Mark James, David Mead, and Charmian Werren. Any errors and oversights, however, remain ours and ours alone!

Finally, as we argue in this book, engagement with football supporters is essential for achieving positive outcomes in this field. We have therefore tried to practice what we preach and would like to thank, in particular, Amanda Jacks, Kevin Miles, Gwyn Davies, Paul Corkrey, 'Big Sam', Macca, Adam Gilliatt, Vince Alm, Dave Rose, Andrew Hird, Kevin Rye, Daniela Wurbs, and Endi Endemann for their contributions and support. We also extend our thanks to the other (anonymous) fan group supporter representatives who contributed to our work in Chap. 5 and elsewhere.

Contents

About the Authors

Geoff Pearson is Professor of Law at the University of Manchester and Academic Director of the N8 Policing Research Partnership. He has conducted research on football crowd behaviour, and legal and policing responses to football-related disorder since the 1990s, mostly utilising ethnographic methods. He completed a PhD on 'Legal Responses to Football Crowd Disorder' at Lancaster University in 1999 and was then Director of Studies of the MBA (Football Industries) programme at the University of Liverpool 2003–2014, before joining the University of Manchester's Law School. Geoff has been engaged in research with numerous police forces (both domestically and abroad), the UK Home Office, the English Football League, the European Commission, FIFPro, and the Sports Grounds Safety Authority (SGSA), and has advised the Organisation for Security and Cooperation in Europe, FIFA, UEFA, the UK Football Policing Unit (UKFPU), the Independent Office for Police Conduct, the College of Policing, the Law Commission, and the Security and Policing sub-group of Scientific Advisory Group in Emergencies (SAGE). He has published extensively in peer-reviewed journals on football crowd law, regulation, and management and is author of *Football Hooliganism* (2007, with Clifford Stott), *An Ethnography of English Football Fans* (2012), *Legal Responses to Football Hooliganism in Europe* (2016, with Anastassia Tsoukala and Peter Coenen), and *Police Street Powers and Criminal Justice* (2020, with Mike Rowe).

Clifford Stott is Professor of Social Psychology and Research Centre Director of the Keele Policing Academic Collaboration (KPAC) at Keele University in Staffordshire, England. He has been researching football crowd behaviour and policing since his PhD on the *Intergroup Dynamics of Crowd Behaviour* which he completed in 1996 at the University of Exeter. Since then, he has published widely on the relationships between crowd psychology and public order policing. His research has had high-level impact at a national and international level informing policy, guidance, and practice in the management of crowds for a range of government and police organisations across the world. As a reflection of the impact and importance of his research, in 2014 he was awarded the Economic and Social Research Council's '*Celebrating Impact*' First Prize and in 2015 his work was acknowledged by the ESRC as one of its 'Top 50' achievements in its 50-year history. During the Covid-19 pandemic, he was co-chair of the Security and Policing sub-group of the UK Government's Scientific Advisory Group in Emergencies (SAGE) and is currently a member of the National Police Chief Council Scientific Advisory Council. In 2021 he was awarded an MBE for services to crowd psychology and the Covid-19 response.

List of Figures

1

Introduction

'Euro Sunday'

At 20.00 on Sunday, 11 July 2021, England made their first appearance in a UEFA European Championship final, and their first final in any major football tournament since the 1966 World Cup. The match, and indeed the entire 'Euro 2020' tournament, took place under the shadow of the UK's second wave of the Coronavirus pandemic, and although the original 'stay at home' restrictions been lifted, strict constraints limiting public gatherings were still in place. So-called Freedom Day, when the majority of Covid-19 public health restrictions in England were due to be lifted, had been delayed and was still over a week away. The whole multi-country tournament had already been delayed by a year due to the pandemic, and as such was still labelled 'Euro 2020' even though it was taking place in the summer of 2021. However, as the tournament progressed, levels of infection in England reduced and levels of vaccination increased. Consequently, the limits on the number of tickets sold for matches started to be relaxed, from under 20,000 for the first England match at Wembley in the group stages to 65,000 for the team's extra-time semi-final victory over Denmark. Yet, as a reflection of the surrounding conditions even for the final, although 67,000 tickets were sold, this was still well short of Wembley's normal capacity of 90,000.

G. Pearson, C. Stott, *A New Agenda For Football Crowd Management*, Palgrave Studies in Risk, Crime and Society, https://doi.org/10.1007/978-3-031-16298-5_1

As a result of the pandemic, football fans had been starved of being able to attend live matches for all but a few weeks since the first 'lockdown' started in March 2020, and despite the restrictions on public assembly, thousands of fans descended on London, and Wembley in particular, for the day of the final, both those with tickets and those without. All hoped to party like it was 1966. It was estimated by the independent review conducted into the events of that day, led by the Conservative peer Baroness Casey, that around 33,000 ticketless fans found their way to the environs around Wembley stadium, where they gathered from around 10.00 to celebrate *en masse*: chanting, displaying flags, drinking alcohol, and some consuming cocaine. As is normative for crowds of England fans, many were engaging in transgressive behaviour such as setting off pyrotechnics, climbing on street furniture, blocking roads, and throwing beer in the air as they raucously celebrated England reaching the final. Crowds started to build up in the open spaces around the stadium, including outside the 'White Horse' public house. Coincidently, the pub was named after a famous crowd control measure utilised by police after disorder and mass unlawful entry took place at the first ever Wembley FA Cup Final nearly a century before. As the afternoon progressed, crowd density increased and the transgressive and carnivalesque celebration started to become ever more 'anti-social' and 'disorderly'. Vehicles were climbed onto, several incidents of vandalism took place, and bottles were thrown into the air causing several injuries.

Despite the early gathering crowds, the main police deployment was only planned to begin at 15.00, and by late morning it was already clear that this was far too late. As a result of the increasingly difficult situation that was developing, police deployment was brought forward by half-an-hour, but by that point much of the crowd was already too dense and disorderly for the police to enter without fear of creating an escalation, possibly even a riot. Concerns were also starting to be expressed by the stadium authorities about what would happen when the turnstiles opened. A temporary Outer Security Perimeter (OSP) had been constructed with the intention of keeping ticketless fans away from the turnstiles, but this was merely of weak rickety, crowd control barriers, and

'Heras fencing'. By early afternoon, the crowd was already dense near the OSP, causing justifiable fears that it would be breached by the thousands of ticketless fans who might try to gain entry, the practice known in many football fan circles as 'jibbing'.

Once the OSP and the turnstiles opened, fans started to enter, and the congestion and density eased. However, within minutes, security officials began reporting the first attempts at 'jibbing' into the stadium itself, as ticketless fans who had already breached the OSP 'tailgated' fans with tickets. Other methods of entry by subterfuge were also reported, including the bribing of stewards to allow entry through the turnstiles. Some ticketless fans were reported to have photographed the barcodes of tickets of other fans on their mobile phones and were using these to enter through the electronic turnstiles. This also meant that the fans with those genuine tickets were then unable to gain access to the stadium. Adding to the issues, other fans found that their digital tickets had not been activated when they arrived at the turnstiles and would not work. All these problems meant that crowd density also started to build at the turnstiles as well as the OSP, the confusion and congestion further frustrating ticket holders and assisting the ticketless in equal measure.

News of successful 'jibs' then started to be disseminated through the ticketless crowd by social media and word-of-mouth, and the OSP came under sustained assault from large groups of ticketless fans working collectively to force access. These fans would have been aware of the thousands of empty seats in the stadium due to the Covid-19 restrictions. As a result, shortly before 17.30, a group of around 100 ticketless fans collectively broke through the OSP, assaulting several stewards in the process. In response to this breach, the Wembley stadium authorities locked down the stadium, preventing anyone passing through the turnstiles, but after 20 minutes, in which time crowd density and frustration outside the turnstiles had further increased, the turnstiles were re-opened. Soon afterwards, groups of ticketless fans who had successfully breached the OSP started to target the disabled gates, executive entrances, and fire exits to try to gain entry.

On the other side of the OSP, pubs and bars in the vicinity of the stadium were full, and several made the decision to close their doors to new customers or even closed altogether. Due to the risks of Covid-19 transmission, there were no 'fan zones' with a big screen near the stadium, and only one reported in the whole of London, already at capacity in Trafalgar Square, and as kick-off loomed, the only place for the thousands of ticketless fans to go, if they wanted to watch the match, was Wembley itself. By 18.00, only two hours before kick-off, there were still between 10,000 and 20,000 ticketless, and mostly highly intoxicated, fans immediately outside the OSP of the stadium. Given the density, the crush of both ticket holders and ticketless fans in the area at the end of Wembley Way at the start of the crowd control barriers at the bottom of the Olympic Steps, was becoming increasingly dangerous. According to Pearson's review of the CCTV stills for the Casey Review, there was at this time an imminent risk of progressive crowd collapse and potentially severe injuries and fatalities. Crowd Safety Expert Eric Stuart also concluded in the same review that "a series of incidents occurred that were a sequence of very near misses and any one of these could have led to significant injuries or death(s) occurring" (Casey, 2021, p. 54). Unable to intervene into the crowd, or attempt to disperse it, without risking loss of life, the Metropolitan Police judged they had no choice but to deploy the bulk of their resources behind the OSP to try and protect the stadium entrances from further 'jibbing'.

Meanwhile, on the stadium side of the OSP, 16 'mass breaches' of disabled and fire gates occurred between 18.29 and 19.46, several involving over 100 individuals. In the most serious incident, a fire door was deliberately opened from the inside and nearly 700 fans entered. Police, including mounted- and dog units, were deployed to support security at the perimeter and turnstiles, but events were quickly overtaking both police and stadium security operations. The decision was made to increase the power on the electromagnetic locks on the doors from 25% to 100%, but with some door-locking mechanisms already broken, security staff sometimes had to improvise solutions to block emergency entrances, including in one case using "a heavy-duty forklift truck" (Casey, 2021, p. 44). Had a rapid evacuation of the stadium been required at this time, the consequences could have been utterly horrific and on a par with the worst stadium disasters in history.

Two minutes before kick-off there were further mass breaches of the OSP at the foot of the Olympic Steps. These were likely triggered by either the noise of the teams entering the field or the national anthems being played, and the realisation that those ticketless fans outside were about to miss probably the most significant England match of their lifetimes. Whatever the cause, dozens of fans climbed over the walls either side of the steps, dropping down behind the security cordon. Others attempted to rush the middle of the OSP barriers. A 'baton push' by a line of police against fans rushing up the stairs caused them to retreat, but this was only into other crowds of fans coming up the stairs behind them. The situation was what the Casey Review subsequently judged to have been another "significant threat to life" (Casey, 2021, p. 60). A few minutes later there was further major breach of the OSP, when Luke Shaw put England into the lead after only two minutes.

With nowhere to go to watch the match and wishing to be as close as possible to the potential England tournament victory, around 6000 fans waited outside the stadium, listening to the cheers and groans of the crowd inside as news filtered through of Italy's second-half equaliser and then the start of extra-time. Throughout the match, there were repeated attempts by some of these ticketless fans to break into the stadium, with the final attempt reported midway through the penalty shoot-out. Evidence provided to the Casey Review suggested that it was only England's highly predictable failure in the inevitable penalty shoot-out that prevented potentially more serious breaches, as exit gates would have opened to release (mainly Italian) fans, potentially leading to a rush by ticketless fans through these departing fans to try and enter the stadium to celebrate England's victory inside.

Throughout the afternoon and evening, it was estimated that between 1776 and 1964 fans gained entry to Wembley, either through 'tailgating' or taking part in a mass breach. Of these, around 1254 to 1386 gained entry to the stadium bowl with only approximately 400 subsequently ejected by stewards (Casey, 2021). Despite footage of these incursions being posted on social media at the time, Wembley initially denied any security breaches, before stadium officials and the Metropolitan Police ultimately acknowledged the following day that "a small number" of fans without tickets had broken in (BBC News Online 12/7/21). It was only the subsequent Casey Review that revealed the scale and intensity of the substantive failures that took place. Inside the stadium, there were continued small-scale incidents of violence, with fights breaking out in the concourse, and in one case several fans attacking 'jibbers' as they broke in. The concourses inside the stadium were reported as being congested and dangerous, littered with plastic glasses and spilt beer. Disputes arose as many fans found others sat in the seats allocated to them. Others reported seeing Italian supporters abused and threatened both inside the stadium and outside after the match had ended.

It is our view that the Casey Review correctly identified most of the key failings of 'Euro Sunday'; a failure to construct a more robust OSP, breakdowns in communication and planning across the organisations involved in the final, and a deployment of police resources over four hours after the first incidents of disorder and criminality were reported. The Review appropriately concluded that the unusual factors present on the day led to a "perfect storm". However, the Casey Review's conclusions, reflecting the media narrative in the aftermath of the disorder, ultimately blamed the behaviour of a large minority of fans on the day, for their use of alcohol and cocaine, and the way they and their behaviour recklessly endangered their fellow fans. While we do not dispute this was a major contributing factor, we would argue that it cannot, and should not, be seen in isolation and to do so fundamentally degrades our understanding of why events developed as they did.

Correspondingly, the recommendations of the Review were that a new risk category for "football matches of national significance" should be created, with key partners setting out what steps should be taken for such events, including increased police resources, the creation of a sterile area around the stadium restricted to ticket holders, and "enhanced enforcement" of bans on alcohol consumption on public transport and public spaces. With specific focus on the national stadium, the review also called for the establishment of a more secure OSP to filter out ticketless fans, and a "joined up approach between Wembley and the MPS". More generally it proposed all partners (the Sports Grounds Safety Authority [SGSA], governing bodies, stadium owners, police, and local government) establish accountability for what is referred to as 'Zone Ex'; the area around the stadium where jurisdiction, responsibility, and accountability for security matters are currently opaque. It recommended a thorough review of stewarding and an FA-led national campaign, "to bring about a sea-change in attitudes towards supporter behaviours". Finally, the Review recommended, "strengthening the penalties for football-related disorder, particularly behaviours which recklessly endanger lives", and making 'tailgating' a criminal offence. It argued that the "existing enforcement mechanisms available to the police and other enforcement officers do not offer enough deterrent against those determined to use the cover of football matches to commit criminal offences". It further supported calls for the Football Spectators Act 1989 to be reformed to include convictions for possession of drugs or engaging in racist abuse online in their category of qualifying offences (Casey, 2021, Recommendations).

Knee-Jerk Reactions and Panic Law

It was unfortunate that after such a thorough and forensic analysis of what happened on 'Euro Sunday', the recommendations fell into the same trap as many of the responses to other high-profile incidents of football-related violence, disorder, or tragedy, in football in England and Wales since the 1980s. Many of the recommendations, including joined-up planning, liaison, and accountability, and the creation of better physical infrastructure to manage crowds, should be welcomed. However, as we will argue in this book, calls for new football-specific offences, 'tougher' enforcement, and increased sentences characterise much of what we describe as the early piecemeal and 'knee-jerk' attempts to mitigate football crowd disorder. As we will see in Chap. 2, the recommendations replicated the failures of earlier attempts to manage football crowds from the late 1950s until the turn of the century, as well as overlooking the value of the positive steps that have been taken since then. Rather than learning the valuable historical and scientific lessons of the past half century, the legislative proposals can be described as falling foul of what Jeremy Bentham, over 250 years ago, considered to be the two characteristics of British legislation, "never move a finger till your passions are inflamed, nor ever look further than your nose" (Lieberman, 1988). It is worth mentioning that at no point did the Review consider any empirical research or data about how such new laws or enforcement mechanisms might work in practice, what (if any) deterrent effect they might have, and whether there were any concerns of unintended consequences upon levels of disorder and the operational effectiveness of the police. Ultimately, all the violent and disorderly behaviour considered above, including 'jibbing' by subterfuge, already falls under either existing criminal offences, breaches bylaws that could lead to fixed-penalty notices, would be sufficient for an arrest on the grounds of breach of the peace or could lead to a Football Banning Order on Complaint. In other words, the Casey Review merely suggests we do more, in much the same way of what largely we already try to do, but which so clearly failed at Wembley on that day.

There is no doubt to us that 'Euro Sunday' was indeed a "perfect storm", in that a connection of highly unusual factors came together to produce an unprecedented challenge to public order, and that whatever steps were taken at the time, there would, as a result, have been some criminality, disorder, and attempts at 'jibbing' on that day. However, from our perspective, drawing as it does upon decades of research into football crowd behaviour and management, from disciplines as varied as anthropology, criminology, sociology, business and management, social psychology, and socio-legal studies, what happened on 'Euro Sunday' was largely predictable and cannot be properly understood in simple terms. Furthermore, the way in which public order degenerated on the day was something that reflected earlier failures and could have been mitigated through established, and well-tested, crowd management and public order policing principals and approaches. We will return to what we think could, and should, have been done differently on that fateful day in Chap. 11, but at this stage we will merely assert that had existing good practice and national guidance been followed, it is highly unlikely that we would have seen anywhere near the levels of disorder, violence, or criminality that Wembley experienced on 11th July 2021.

Remit, Aims, and Original Contribution of This Book

The central theme of this book is the regulation and policing of football crowd disorder and violence in England and Wales, a phenomenon which was commonly, and occasionally still is, referred to as 'football hooliganism'. As we will argue, national responses to the problem of violence, disorder, criminality, and anti-social behaviour at football in this context have typically been made on two fronts, that of changes to law and to policing. This contrasts with many other countries where much more has been expected of football authorities and clubs (Tsoukala et al., 2016). We have both been conducting research in this area since the 1990s and have published extensively in the areas of legal responses to football crowd disorder (e.g. James & Pearson, 2015, 2018; Pearson, 1998, 2021; Pearson & Sale, 2011), English football fan behaviour (Pearson, 2012), understanding football crowd 'riots' (e.g. Stott et al., 2001, 2007, 2008; Stott & Reicher, 1998), and on developing public order policing of football crowds (e.g. Stott et al., 2012; Stott et al., 2019). In this current contribution to the debate, we wish to pull these prior arguments together and underpin them with new evidence to push towards a more integrated and developed analysis, bringing new theoretical arguments and practical recommendations to bear, in four important ways.

First, we will argue that legal and policing responses to football crowd disorder are too often researched, analysed, and understood separately. While we have published together previously (e.g. Stott & Pearson, 2007), largely this has been a cross-disciplinary combination of Pearson's socio-legal and Stott's social psychological approaches. In the current contribution, we have strived for a greater interdisciplinary analysis, and to bring legal and policing debates, challenges, and analysis closer together. We look to identify how the law drives, enables, and can constrain the operational effectiveness of football policing, and, conversely, how policing realities can frustrate the attempts of law in this area. One of the core arguments that we set out is that a focus only on reform of either football policing or the law regulating football crowds, is insufficient to bring about the integrated changes that we believe could drive the management of football crowds forward in a significant and sustainable manner. In the following chapters we will set out the case for why our proposed "New Agenda" to managing football events needs to entail a more joined-up approach to crowd management between legislators, police, and other criminal justice actors. To illustrate this, in Chaps. 3 and 8 we will demonstrate how legislation that was introduced against the advice of the police stored up problems for the public order management of football crowds that has lasted decades.

The second way in which we have sought to move analysis forward has been the focus we provide in this book on the issue of 'risk'. As we will set out in Chaps. 4 and 5, our research suggests the primary focus for all football crowd policing operations in England and Wales, and indeed in some sense internationally, has been on categorising matches and fans in terms of the 'risk' they are judged, by the authorities, to pose to public order and public safety. Over the decades through which our observations have taken place we have noted how the language of 'hooligans', 'prominents', or 'nominals' in policing has been gradually superseded by a systematic and ubiquitous, almost universal, focus on identifying, categorising, controlling, and excluding 'risk supporters'. As we will explain, while such labelling of fans historically provided a breakthrough in football policing in the 1980s, there are multiple problems that arise from this categorisation process, starting with the confusing and inconsistent understanding of what a 'risk supporter' is, the poor quality of intelligence that defines who falls within and out with the category, and, moreover, the mistaken idea that 'risk' in football crowds predominantly comes from those with predispositions towards engagement in violence or disorder, rather than the "perfect storm" factors related to social context and infrastructure so powerfully exemplified on Euro Sunday. In Chap. 8, we introduce new empirical evidence to demonstrate how the current focus on categorising 'risk supporters' can lead not only to ineffective and wasteful policing operations but can also inadvertently create situations where disorder and violence are more likely to occur. Instead, we will argue for the value of understanding risk from the perspective of crowd psychology and therefore as something that ebbs and flows not through the convergence of those with prior disposition but emerges during crowd events through identity-based group and interactional dynamics (cf. Stott & Radburn, 2020).

The third way in which this book drives the debate forward is in its focus upon the value of a human rights approach to football policing. The fact that obligations under Articles 10 and 11 of the European Convention on Human Rights (ECHR) apply to protest is widely acknowledged and understood. However, our argument that it also applies to individuals peacefully assembling in football crowds is only just starting to be acknowledged both in academia and increasingly in football policing operations. In this book, for the first time, we set out in detail the extent to which these human rights apply in a football context and how a rights-based approach to football policing can benefit successful planning and operational outcomes. Our argument here is not just that understanding human rights obligations is important for police forces to avoid potential litigation, but that placing human rights at the forefront of command decision-making can be strategically and tactically beneficial, reducing conflict between fans and police both in the short and long-term, as well improving and protecting police legitimacy.

Finally, this book is the first time in which we holistically apply new empirical evidence from our substantive programme of fieldwork on football policing operations which was the result of two phases of a research and knowledge-exchange project entitled "Enabling an Evidence Based Approach to Policing Football", or "ENABLE" for short. This new data is used in two ways. First, it is used to evidence, develop, and support our arguments about the problems that currently exist with both law and many policing practices in the context of football crowds. Second, it introduces several new developments in football policing that have been piloted, tested, and observed as part of this international research project. From this, we identify various elements of good practice in football policing and distil these to put forward recommendations which, if implemented, we believe will lead to improvements to football policing not just in England and Wales but also internationally.

Methodology

The basis for much of the analysis and theory underpinning the arguments we make in this book arises from decades of research conducted by both authors with football fans and police. Ethnographic fieldwork has been the basis for much of the social scientific research into football fan behaviour since the 1970s (see Chap. 2), and our approach has drawn heavily on this tradition. Our combined research started with Stott's PhD observational fieldwork with England fans at Italia'90 (Stott & Reicher, 1998) and Pearson's study of fans of Blackpool FC for his PhD 1995–1998 (Pearson, 1999). Both authors subsequently went on to independently conduct ethnographic fieldwork among fans at the 1998 World Cup (Stott et al., 2001) and at the 2000 European Championships, before working together when both were early career lecturers at the University of Liverpool primarily on a Home Office-funded project into the policing of English football fans when travelling abroad. This developed into an ongoing collaboration from that point onwards, taking in the UEFA European Championships in 2004 and the 2006 FIFA World Cup, or *Weltmeisterschaft*, in Germany (Stott & Pearson, 2007). Pearson continued with this fan-focused ethnographic work until 2011, publishing his findings a year later (Pearson, 2012) while, as we describe later, Stott developed his ethnography into a form of research designed to drive evidence-based police reforms. This work was ethnographic in the sense that the researchers embedded themselves within the groups in question, primarily using participant observation and interviews to try to uncover and understand the interpretations, understandings, motivations, and behaviour of football fans, as well as of those policing them. This book will therefore draw from this now-extensive body of research on fan, crowd, and police behaviour developed using this qualitative ethnographic approach, as well as upon the findings from the ethnographic work carried out by other social scientists in this field going back to the 1970s.

As our work and collaboration developed, it became increasingly clear that there was a need for, and value in, understanding the problems of football-related disorder from both socio-legal and crowd psychology perspectives. In many ways, it was not merely problems in the domestic leagues but the major riots involving England and English fans when travelling abroad that shaped popular understanding, political discourse, and the legislation responding to the so-called English Disease. In effect, 'hooliganism' as a social and political issue occurred because of conflict that developed during large-scale crowd events at major international matches and tournaments. In other words, it was the media reporting of the rioting at Heysel in 1985, in Germany at Euro'88, during Italia'90, France'98, Euro2000, and WM2006 that drove—indeed arguably constructed—political, policing, and public concerns about, and responses to, the problem of football-related public disorder.

As we shall go on to argue, 'rioting' among English fans is best interpreted through the science of crowd psychology. What that body of evidence and theory tells us is that collective action is made possible through people in a crowd sharing a sense of themselves as a social group. This sense of group membership—or social identity—is a social psychological process that legitimises, enables, and limits specific forms of behaviour. What this helped us to understand was that the so-called 'hooliganism' we were observing was far from 'mindless', but was very meaningful for those involved, developing from shared subjectivities that were being shaped and reshaped by the often-dynamic social contexts within which English fans were regularly finding themselves. In this respect, policing played a fundamentally important role because police actions invariantly constructed the social context through which England fans came to understand their shared identity and their actions towards others around them. What we also began to understand, once we started working alongside them, was that it was the expectation among the police that English fans were 'hooligans' which was shaping how the police were behaving, therefore creating the social conditions for collective violence as a kind of unintended self-fulfilling prophesy.

Our ambition was not just to stand by and pontificate as 'experts' on some of the causal dynamics of these riots, but to use our research to try to change the way the dynamics of conflict were understood by the authorities. Therefore, Stott's work in particular began trying to use the science to reshape police practices, to make their approaches more evidence-based, effective, and less counter-productive. This proved to be a long and ongoing struggle and we will detail the development of this work in more detail in Chap. 6. At this point, it is just important to note that this scientific approach, based empirically on observations and interviews, opened an opportunity to develop theory about the drivers of the conflicts that took place between crowds of football fans and the police in host cities. Over time our work allowed a much fuller picture to emerge of the interactional processes that were at work, which in turn generated opportunities to influence and change the way in which the policing of major football events took place.

After many years, we began to understand that this approach to research, still essentially ethnographic in orientation, was adopting a co-production framework akin to *Participant Action Research* or PAR (McNiff & Whitehead, 2005). What this means is that the scientific work we were driving was becoming less about the dominant positivist scientific tradition of inquiry to discover some sort underlying 'truth'. While this was still an important imperative, the primary goal of the work, and in many ways the key measure of its success, was not merely the 'validity' of theory but the progressive changes in policing practices the knowledge we were producing was bringing about. In other words, the achievement of the science was measured not in terms of a publication in a prestigious journal but by its external impact (Stott, 2020). While we have discussed these methodological aspects of our work elsewhere, it is here that we bring this decades-long programme of ethnographic and action research on fans and policing together and use it to frame analysis of new evidence that we are presenting for the first time.

As discussed above, the new data introduced in this book comes from a series of observations carried out because of two projects analysing the policing of football in England and Wales that we refer to as "ENABLE". The first of these projects, running across the 2017/18 and 2018/19 seasons, was funded by an N8 Policing Research Partnership Innovation and Training grant and involved six observations of matches in the English Premier League, Football Leagues, and the Scottish Premier League. This led to a larger follow-on project that was funded by the English Football League, consisting of 14 medium- to high-risk matches, one in the Premiership and the remainder in the English Football League during the

2019/20 season, until it was forced to conclude because of the closure of football grounds due to the Covid-19 pandemic. All observations were largely qualitative in nature, conducted by a team consisting of a mixture of academics, police (from external forces to the one under observation), and other stakeholders (e.g. the Football Supporter's Association, the English Football League (EFL) and the SGSA). Each observation typically started with pre-event analysis of documentation and interviews with police commanders and attendance at briefings. This was then followed by observations of the policing operation and followed by a post-event debrief. Where feasible, commanders for the observed operation would attend these debriefs both to provide input and gain feedback from the observation team. Our aim, overall, has been to combine data from multiple ENABLE observations to build the evidence-based analysis that we use in this book to underpin several of our far-reaching recommendations for football policing. While many of these recommendations are specific to the context of domestic football in England and Wales, the location of our research within the broader context of football policing and crowd regulation across Europe means that they also have value for those responsible for the management of football crowds more internationally.

Football Crowd Regulation in England and Wales in 2022

At the time of writing, football crowd regulation and management in England and Wales is in a state of flux. For the first time, possibly this century, there are indicators that there may be a nationwide increase in levels of criminality, disorder, and anti-social behaviour in the domestic leagues. Statistics of football-related arrests and 'incidents of disorder' collated by the UK Football Policing Unit (UKFPU)[1] from the 2021/22 season both showed a significant increase from the 2019–2020 season (which was played behind closed doors from March 2020). This reflected the highest number of arrests since the 2015–2016 season (BBC News

[1] The UKFPU is a quango funded by the Home Office responsible for national oversight and coordination of football policing.

Online 21/01/21). As we will set out in the following chapter, arrest statistics are notoriously unreliable as indicators of levels of criminality and usually tell us as much about police priorities and resources as they do crime. Indeed, as we argue later, much of the reduction in arrests at football in the last ten years may be explained in terms of a decade of austerity, falling police numbers, closed custody suites, and the scrapping of arrest 'targets'. It is noticeable that the figures released also indicated, in contrast to the last decade, an increase in police numbers at matches, which we would expect to lead to higher numbers of arrest and reported incidents.

Nevertheless, despite these reservations, we are of the view that the statistics do illustrate at least a temporary uptick in incidents of (mainly low-level) disorder and anti-social behaviour, which is a view shared by many of the police officers, safety officers, and fan representatives that we work with. Indeed, statistics of reported crime indicate a general increase in such offending across society, not just in the context of football. Nonetheless, our suspicion is that this increase is linked to the effect of the Covid-19 control measures where fans were almost entirely unable to attend live matches from March 2020 until July 2021. The return of fans to fixtures may be linked with increased levels of low-level criminality, which in turn may be the result of fans being previously deprived of carnivalesque expressions of identity. It could also be linked to a turnover of 'regular' fans combined with an influx of younger fans and 'irregular' fans who may be less aware of pre-pandemic norms of football spectatorship, who are also less deterred by the threat of CCTV, banning orders, and a loss of a season ticket. It may be that, as a result, fan groups have less-established behavioural norms and peer-regulation capabilities. Ultimately, we simply do not yet know for sure because there is no systematic research evidencing what is happening and generating an evidence-based understanding of potential casual factors.

The so-called Lockdowns will almost certainly also have had a serious impact upon the ability of police and stewards to manage crowds. As we will set out, effective football policing operations rely heavily upon the development of relationships between specialist police officers and the fan groups they are managing. This allows the police to negotiate, establish tolerance limits, and intervene in a proportionate manner. It also provides intelligence about numbers expected to travel to matches and levels of threat posed by individuals. There is, in most cases, a 16-month gap in this vital work which will inevitably hinder forces in the effective management of football crowds. The turnover of public order staff within police forces can be quite rapid and as such, by the time matches restarted, there will have been many who lacked prior experience. Added to this is the staffing crisis caused by a loss of stewarding capability, as many experienced personnel left the profession during lockdown, which closed not only sports events but also gigs, pubs, and nightclubs. Between all these factors, an increase in issues 'post pandemic' was almost inevitable.

Ironically however, during lockdown there was also a review of the national guidance for football policing, which is published by the College of Policing, the organisation within the UK charged with oversight and delivery of police training in England and Wales. This revised official guidance, referred to as Authorised Professional Practice or APP, to which the authors made several contributions, includes a revision of the definition of 'risk supporter' and the changing role of the renamed Operational Football Officers (OFOs, previously known as 'spotters'). We believe the changes, if implemented correctly, are highly progressive and will further embed much of the crowd science from the ENABLE projects into national policing guidance. Given the primary role that good policing plays in successful football crowd management, we are hopeful therefore that the current rise in incidents will be relatively short-lived.

At the same time, 2021 saw the release of four separate reports which all recommended reform to the laws around football. We have already made critical comments about some of the legal proposals in the Casey Review, but in addendum 1 of the Casey Review, Greenberg points out that "Compared to the law of transport safety and security, football disorder law taken as a whole appears to lack policy coherence and strategy" (Casey, 2021, Addendum 1). While we disagree that the way to remedy this is to introduce piecemeal 'fixes' as the result of a single event, we agree about the lack of coherence and strategy in the way that the law regulating football spectators has developed. And the Casey Review was not alone in questioning the effectiveness of the legal framework that year. The Sports Ground Safety Authority's report into "The Management of Persistent Standing at Football Matches" recommended that trials of licensed 'safe standing' areas be carried out, subsequently leading to a change in the law that had been in place since 1994 (SGSA/CFE, 2021; Welford et al., 2022). A few months later, the Department for Culture, Media and Sport (DCMS, 2021) 'Fan-Led Review' recommended that

> The Home Office should review the Sporting Events (Control of Alcohol etc.) Act 1985 to establish whether its measures are still fit for purpose in 2022 and beyond, and that it reflects the football culture of the present day—and to provide robust evidence in its conclusion of such a review,

as well as a trial permitting the consumption of alcohol within sight of the pitch in Leagues 1 and 2. Finally, the Law Commission, while rejecting proposals for extensions to existing laws to prevent 'Hate Crime', noted that

> It may be that in due course the Government will consider that legislation covering offending at, or related to, football needs to be reviewed … Indeed, it may even be questioned whether legislation directed at football specifically rather than sports grounds generally remains appropriate (Law Commission, 2021: para 11.57).

In England and Wales, the combined developments in policing and law, combined with the post-lockdown challenges, mean that this is a perfect time to further develop the academic contribution to the debates around football crowd regulation and management. That is not, however, to suggest that we should only be focusing on this issue when disorder is in the news, or where there are signs that it may be on the rise. Indeed, as we have previously argued, and will become apparent when we move through the sections of this book, you can learn as much from the management of crowds where disorder has not occurred as you can from times where it does. Our key argument is that football crowds should be managed by a combination of evidence-based policing and the application of laws that are suitable, proportionate, and seen as legitimate by those who are being policed with them. This broader point, we believe, is applicable to football crowd management well beyond England and Wales.

The Casey Review was of course correct in describing that ultimately it was behaviour from a minority of fans at the Euro2020 Final that caused the problems. But while policing and law can of course look to limit the number of fans who are known to engage in such behaviour and can look to deter it, we must plan to manage those who do engage in behaviours that are challenging to public order, to reduce the risk that it endangers the safety of other fans or members of the public. But to base an analysis of cause on terminology that does little more than describing what we already know about who was involved and blaming merely them as perpetrators, does not get us very far. As Chaps. 6 and 8 of this book will demonstrate, the evidence shows—perhaps uncomfortably for some—that poor laws and poor policing play an active role in creating environments or opportunities where disorder or violence is more, rather than less, likely to thrive. As we will also contend, our data suggests that those who engage in such behaviour usually have no prior intention towards such disorder and are brought into confrontations because of the context in which they find themselves. This book therefore also seeks to put forward recommendations for both law and policing to help reduce the risks to public order in connection with football matches based on what is currently known about football crowd psychology and behavioural norms.

When we first decided to title this book *A New Agenda for Football Crowd Management*, our intention was to set out a different conceptual framework for approaching policing and regulating football fans to that which tends to dominate. However, our research and knowledge-exchange work with police organisations continued as we wrote, and in the intervening period there have been several significant developments, including the changes to national guidance for football policing and calls for law reform from the different reports set out above. There has also been a whole catalogue of new incidents at the tail end of the 2021/22 season involving pitch invasions, assaults against players, and the woeful treatment of Liverpool fans at the Champions League final in Paris that has made it difficult to keep pace. Effectively, therefore, rather than chasing bad news and simply putting forward recommendations for change, in this book we also detail how crowd science has helped to drive positive reform in the way in which some policing and football organisations manage crowds. There is still a long way to go, as we saw from the near disaster that was the Euro2020 Final, but it is no longer a case of police organisations and academics arguing with each other about the solution, but more a tale of how co-production of research can be beneficial to both parties.

The incidents of disorder seen at Euro2020 and during the 2021/22 season demonstrate once again that the issue of managing football crowd disorder is still pressing. The overall decline in disorder post-1980s (see Chap. 2) is not guaranteed to continue, but neither should we fear that we are returning to the 'dark days of football hooliganism'. Stadium infrastructure and security, and policing methods and organisation, have all developed considerably since the 1970s and 1980s, and we increasingly have the public order policing tools and guidance in place to confront football crowd disorder. However, in this book we intend to demonstrate that, with reform to some of the antiquated laws around football crowds and the continued development of good practice in policing, disorder and violence around matches can become further reduced and major incidents increasingly rare.

References

BBC News Online 16/01/2021 (Updated 17/12/21). *Euro 2020 Final: Small Number of Fans Broke into Wembley Say Police*. bbc.com/news/uk-57799271

BBC News Online 21/01/2022. *Football Arrests 'Highest in Years' & Disorder on the Rise – Police*. https://www.bbc.co.uk/sport/60056492

Casey, L. (2021, December). *An Independent Review of Events Surrounding the UEFA Euro 2020 Final 'Euro Sunday' at Wembley*. https://www.thefa.com/-/media/thefacom-new/files/about-the-fa/2021/independent-review-of-events-surrounding-the-uefa-euro-2020-final-at-wembley-2_december-v5.ashx

DCMS. (2021, November 24). *Independent Report: Fan-Led Review of Football Governance: Securing the game's future*. https://www.gov.uk/government/publications/fan-led-review-of-football-governance-securing-the-games-future/fan-led-review-of-football-governance-securing-the-games-future

James, M., & Pearson, G. (2015). Public Order and the Rebalancing of Football Fans' Rights: Legal Problems with Pre-emptive Policing Strategies and Banning Orders. *Public Law, 3*, 458–475.

James, M., & Pearson, G. (2018). 30 Years of Hurt: The Evolution of Civil Preventative Orders, Hybrid Law, and the Emergence of the Super-Football Banning Order. *Public Law, 1*, 44–61.

Law Commission. (2021, December 6). *Hate Crime Laws: Final Report.* Law Com No 402. https://www.lawcom.gov.uk/project/hate-crime/

Lieberman, D. (1988). Blackstone's Science of Legislation. *Journal of British Studies, 27*(2), 117–149.

McNiff, J., & Whitehead, J. (2005). *All You Need to Know About Action Research*. Sage.

Pearson, G. (1998). The English Disease: Socio-Legal Constructions of Football Hooliganism. *Youth and Policy - The Journal of Critical Analysis, 60*, 1–15.

Pearson, G. (1999). *Legal Responses to Football Related Disorder.* Unpublished PhD Thesis. The University of Lancaster.

Pearson, G. (2012). *An Ethnography of English Football Fans: Cans, Cops and Carnivals*. Manchester University Press.

Pearson, G. (2021). A Beautiful Law for the Beautiful Game? Revisiting the Football (Offences) Act 1991. *The Journal of Criminal Law, 85*(5), 362–374.

Pearson, G., & Sale, A. (2011). On the Lash: Revisiting the Effectiveness of Alcohol Controls at Football Matches. *Policing and Society, 21*(1), 1–17.

Stott, C. (2020). Policing Crowds. In C. Stott, B. Bradford, M. Radburn, & L. Savigar (Eds.), *Making an Impact on Policing and Crime: Psychological Research, Policy and Practice.* Routledge Psychological Impact Series. ISBN 9780815353577.

Stott, C., Adang, O., Livingstone, A., & Schreiber, M. (2007). Variability in the Collective Behaviour of England Fans at Euro 2004: Public Order Policing, Social Identity, Intergroup Dynamics and Social Change. *European Journal of Social Psychology., 37*, 75–100.

Stott, C., Adang, O., Livingstone, A., & Schreiber, M. (2008). Tackling Football Hooliganism: A Quantitative Study of Public Order, Policing and Crowd Psychology. *Psychology Public Policy and Law, 14*(2), 115–114.

Stott, C., Hoggett, J., & Pearson, G. (2012). Keeping the Peace: Social Identity, Procedural Justice and the Policing of Football Crowds. *British Journal of Criminology., 52*(2), 381–399.

Stott, C., Hutchison, P., & Drury, J. (2001). "Hooligans" Abroad? Inter-group Dynamics, Social Identity and Participation in Collective "Disorder" at the 1998 World Cup Finals. *British Journal of Social Psychology., 40*, 359–384.

Stott, C., & Pearson, G. (2007). *Football Hooliganism: Policing and the War on the English Disease*. Pennant.

Stott, C., Pearson, G., & West, O. (2019). Enabling an Evidence-based Approach to Policing Football. *Policing: A Journal of Policy and Practice, 14*, 977. https://doi.org/10.1093/police/pay102

Stott, C., & Radburn, M. (2020). Understanding Crowd Conflict: Social Context, Psychology and Policing. *Current Opinion in Psychology, 35*, 76–80. https://doi.org/10.1016/j.copsyc.2020.03.001

Stott, C., & Reicher, S. (1998). How Conflict Escalates: The Inter-group dynamics of collective football crowd 'violence'. *Sociology, 32*, 353–377.

The Sports Ground Safety Authority/CFE. (2021). *The Management of Persistent Standing at Football Matches.* https://sgsa.org.uk/wp-content/uploads/2021/06/The-management-of-persistent-standing-Final-report.pdf

Tsoukala, A., Pearson, G., & Coenen, P. (2016). *Legal Responses to Football 'Hooliganism' in Europe: A Comparative Human Rights Analysis of Legislation, Policy and Strategies Designed to Regulate Football Crowds.* TMC Asser.

Welford, J., Bowes, L., Stutz, A., & Pearson, G. (2022). *Early Adopters of Licensed Standing Areas in Football Stadia: Report for the SGSA on the Findings from the Independent Evaluation* (CFE/SGSA, July 2022). https://sgsa.org.uk/wp-content/uploads/2022/07/Early-adopters-of-licensed-standing-areas-CFE-Research-evaluation-July-2022.pdf

2

The Historical Development of Policing and the Law at Football Matches in the UK

Introduction

We begin by considering how the legal and policing framework of policing football matches in England and Wales has developed over several decades, and how this relates to changing patterns of fan behaviour over time. One of the central themes in this book will be how fan behaviour, and the way in which football crowds are regulated by the law and managed by police, are fundamentally interlinked. While the evolving legislation and policing strategies surrounding football are, of course, largely driven by fan behaviour, it is also imperative to note that even a cursory glance shows us that football crowd behaviour is in turn driven by those laws and strategies. The most obvious historical example of this is the segregation of home and visiting supporters, which developed as a strategy to reduce conflict between the two sets of fans inside stadiums, but which also almost certainly helped to entrench and develop "us and them" identities (Taylor, 2011, p. 1752) that in turn may have made conflict outside of stadiums, or where segregation broke down, more likely, or more acceptable, within certain fan subcultures.

Nonetheless, to take our argument forward, this chapter sets out first the historical context for our understanding of football crowd behaviour and 'hooliganism' and sets in context contemporary approaches to both

G. Pearson, C. Stott, *A New Agenda For Football Crowd Management*, Palgrave Studies in Risk, Crime and Society, https://doi.org/10.1007/978-3-031-16298-5_2

the legal regulation and police management of football crowd events. We will cover the major incidents that shaped this understanding and the subsequent regulatory framework that evolved in their wake, illustrating how the history of football-related violence from the 1950s onwards set in motion certain policies and approaches designed to tackle the phenomenon of the so-called hooliganism and other safety concerns related to football crowd behaviour. This chapter will also explore how academic research and theory, primarily within sociology, developed in tandem with the policy and practice to inform and shape the debate, functioning to underpin a regulatory approach based upon the concept and control of 'hooligans'.

The Historical Development of Football Crowd Disorder and the Emergence of 'Football Hooliganism'

Socio-historical research of football crowds has long identified the relations between the sport of association football and violence. As Taylor notes, "Football began as a violent pastime of the British peasantry in the thirteenth century" (2011, p. 1752). Violence specifically associated with spectators of football in Britain can also be traced back to the codification of the game in the nineteenth century, although there remains considerable (and probably irreconcilable) disagreement about the levels of violence (ibid, p. 1756–7) and the extent to which apparent fluctuations were actual or simply the result of changing emphasis in the media reporting of match events. In the now classic *Hooligan: A History of Respectable Fears*, Geoffrey Pearson casts scorn on the idea that there was ever a 'golden age' of the sport somehow free of 'disorder', and provides numerous examples of "a well-documented history of pitch invasions, attacks on referees and players, and fighting between rival fans throughout the latter part of the nineteenth century and into the new century" (Pearson, 1983, p. 64). This builds upon, and is supported by, other historical research of football, from 1863 until the start of the First World War, which found numerous reported examples of crowd violence and disorder (Hutchinson, 1975; Mason, 1980) that largely mirrors the different 'types' of football crowd misbehaviour we would recognise today (Vamplew, 1979). The seminal sociological work of Dunning, Murphy, and Williams (a group often referred to as the 'Leicester School', based as it was at that University) also identified a long history of football crowd violence and disorder (1988), concluding that, compared with the 'norms' of newspaper coverage in the 1980s, 'football hooliganism' was probably under-reported (Murphy et al., 1990, p. 50).

Between the wars and up until the late 1950s, incidents of violence and disorder in British football crowds continued (Murphy et al., 1990), albeit possibly at a reduced level to that which occurred before (Taylor, 2011). However, in the period from the late 1950s, instances of violence, disorder, and criminality around football matches started to be reported more regularly. While the late 1960s is often cited as period where 'football hooliganism' became a problem,[1] vandalism on 'football specials'[2] by away fans was being regularly reported in the 1950s, and by 1957 the label 'hooliganism' was being applied to disorder involving football fans and those involved therein referred to as 'hooligans' by the local and national media (Dunning et al., 1988, p. 140–142).[3] Indeed, recorded incidents of vandalism on trains by football fans were significantly higher in 1962 than they were by 1968 (Harrington Report, 1968, p. 44). Inside stadia, the Chester Committee of Enquiry set up by the Football Association reported in 1968 that incidents reported by clubs had nearly doubled from an average of 13 per season in the years 1946–1960 to 25 in the years 1960–1966 (Taylor, 2011, p. 1758).

Although at first it may have been a term used to describe behaviour that would now fall into the category of what we might call 'anti-social behaviour',[4] the label 'football hooliganism' soon developed into a

[1] For example, Dennis Signy's *Pictorial History of Soccer* (1968) refers to the "trend towards hooliganism" from 1967.

[2] The trains chartered to take fans to and from away matches.

[3] The metaphor of 'hooliganism' as a disease was also established by this point. Interestingly, Dunning et al. go on to claim that it was only at the start of the 1966/67 season that the label was being applied by the national media (1988, p. 165).

[4] For fans interviewed by Marsh, for example, the 'hooligan' was more of a jester, who could be contrasted with those more interested fighting rival fans (1978, p. 71–2).

catch-all term that could be used to categorise young male football fans or types of behaviour ranging from criminal damage, running on the pitch, and throwing missiles, through to large-scale public disorder and inter-personal violence, occasionally involving weapons. As the 1968 Harrington Report (titled "Soccer Hooliganism") to the Minister for Sport acknowledged, "soccer hooliganism is a blanket term covering several types of misbehaviour", including "rowdyism", "horseplay", "soccer-mania", and rioting (p. 8–10). 'Hooliganism', therefore, is a term that from the outset was problematic because it encompassed not only specific criminal acts but also a new way of consuming football that, with its potential for disruption and disorder, alarmed both the football authorities and those responsible for public order. By the late 1960s a moral imperative was present in the terminology and football-related 'disorder' was already a national "cause for concern" (Dunning et al., 1986).

The research that underpinned the Harrington Report involved interviews with stakeholders about the levels and severity of the problem, as well as potential solutions. It found police authorities divided as to whether the problem had increased: 26 police authorities reported an increase in 'hooliganism', although only 21 of these thought this increase was significant, 25 authorities reported no increase, and 2 reported a decrease (Harrington Report, 1968, p. 5). This suggests that, in the experience of the police at least, the increase in 'hooliganism' was only occurring in some areas. In contrast to the nuanced national picture presented by the police, the vast majority of managers, players, supporters, and directors of clubs agreed that hooliganism was increasing (Harrington Report, 1968, p. 5–6). The Report concluded that "the majority of our informants viewed the matter of football hooliganism today as an increasing and serious one" (1968, p. 7).

It is difficult to be sure from the historical evidence that either levels or seriousness of the problem had empirically increased throughout the 1960s. As we will see later in this chapter, the influence of the media was likely to have exaggerated the perceived scale, frequency, and intensity of incidents that occurred, particularly as media coverage of football, and football crowds specifically, increased around the 1966 World Cup, and television was itself an emerging phenomenon of news mass-consumption in that decade (Dunning et al., 1986, p. 154).[5] This media influence could well have impacted upon the views of many of those responding to the Harrington survey. Nevertheless, on balance, it looks more likely than not that some form of increase and change in the scale and nature of football crowd disorder did occur during the late 1950s and the 1960s, but was almost certainly exaggerated in nature by the growing importance of mass media reporting and likely to have been experienced in some localities more so than others.

Any changes in football crowd behaviour that took place during this period were likely to have been the result of several inter-related factors. Broadly we should locate them within the general rising crime rates of the 1960s (see Garland, 2001, p. 90–91), which corresponded with the 'baby-boomer' generation reaching their teens and twenties. Youth wages were also rising, and work was plentiful (Dunning et al., 1988, p. 159–60), creating additional disposable income for watching football. With the two-day weekend becoming well-established in the post-Second World War decades, it appears that during the late 1950s and the 1960s, fans started travelling together more to away matches, a practice that became cheaper and easier with the popularity of 'football specials'.[6] It is easy to see with hindsight how confrontations between groups of local fans and the new visitors could occur, particularly as neither the infrastructure of the stadia, mostly designed with only local fans in mind, nor the tactics of the police were prepared for such large influxes of sometimes thousands of visiting supporters. Further, a recommendation following the Burden Park disaster of 1946 that licensing of football grounds (Hughes, 1946) be placed on a statutory footing had been ignored (McArdle, 2000, p. 90). Confusion, congestion, and tension must have been commonplace.

[5] The Harrington Report found that 90% of readers of *The Sun* newspaper who completed a survey felt hooliganism had increased, with only 11% believing its seriousness to be exaggerated (1968, p. 6).

[6] Prior to this, it was common for fans to watch what would become their local rivals on the Saturdays when their first-choice team was playing away. Dunning et al. refer to 1967 as being the year in which Northern football fans first "arrived" *en masse* in London for away matches (1988, p. 166).

The pressing need 'to do something' was made more acute by the emergence of the contemporary 'football ends', which Dunning et al. identify as occurring sometime around, or slightly before, the 1950s (Dunning et al., 1988, p. 164). These 'ends' were increasingly seen by home supporters in them as their 'territory'. The reaction to this perceived increase and seriousness in football-related disorder was an official policy of physically segregating home and away fans in stadia through fencing into different pens (Dunning, 1986, p. 86; Harrington, 1968). In 1967, serious disorder involving travelling Manchester United fans in home sections at West Ham and Chelsea was reported widely in the press, as was the fact that the police lines attempting to separate the fans had been insufficient to prevent the violence (Dunning et al., 1988, p. 166–7). Further, the policy of trying to segregate the fans in stadia did not prevent incidents such as missile throwing or pitch invasions, nor disorder occurring outside stadia. Segregation may have even exacerbated tensions by "sharpening" the "us–them boundaries" and creating hostile collective group-level interactions between home and visiting supporters that spilled out into the streets outside at the end of the match (Taylor, 2011, p. 1759, see also Dunning, 1986, p. 86).[7]

Although there remain uncertainties about the development and extent of the problem, by the end of the 1960s, large numbers of young men in particular were travelling to away matches and doing so with the expectation that disorder and violence would often occur. Home fans, gathered on the terraced 'ends', increasingly began to view 'incursions' into 'their territory' by visiting fans to be illegitimate and therefore provocative. Even for those fans who were not interested in engaging in physical violent confrontation, a new and exciting way to consume football had emerged.

> From the 1960s, football hooliganism emerged as an alternative to other youth subcultures for young males with sufficient means to attend football matches as well as travel to both away matches and international fixtures. More than a decade of moral panic surrounding youth subcultures and

[7] In a similar vein, Vamplew, talking about segregation of fans between popular terraces and (more expensive and exclusive) stands in the late nineteenth century, argues that segregation could have "encouraged disorder" where it led to an increase in crowd density in certain areas (1980, p. 12).

> violence gave the violent hooligan a national attention denied them. Indeed, this young working man was not dominated by antisocial ideas or a violent disposition as a result of any civilising process. Rather, football provided him with a social setting where camaraderie and friendships were sought, and a quest for excitement could be lived, relived and shared as collective memory (Taylor, 2011, p. 1762–3).

The term 'football hooliganism' therefore started to tell us less about specific types of criminal behaviour and more about participation "in the culture of the terrace end" (Melnick, 1986, p. 2). This 'culture' would come to dominate media and political focus when it came to football fandom through to the start of the 1990s. It would lead to developments in crowd management, policing, and the law which would in turn play a role in shaping fan behaviour. Furthermore, it created a label and a stigma, of the lawless football 'hooligan', that would stick with football fans long after the practice of watching live football had changed almost beyond recognition.

'Hooliganism' and State Response: The 1970s and 1980s

The 'hooligan agenda' dominated media reporting of football crowds in Britain during the 1970s and 1980s (Pratt & Salter, 1984), with newspapers in particular engaging in not only sensationalised reporting of incidents (Hall, 1978) but also building an anticipation of future violence (Salter, 1985a). This was assisted by occurrences of disorder involving English football fans abroad, with 'hooliganism' by club fans reported in Paris (1975, Leeds United), St Etienne (1977, Manchester United), Rotterdam (1983, Tottenham Hotspur), and also fans of the England national team, the highest profile incident of which occurred at the 1980 UEFA European Championships in Italy. Perhaps directly because of its salience in the media, by the 1980s 'football hooliganism' had become a significant political issue creating international embarrassment for the UK (Butler, 1991, p. 203). Indeed, by this time it was being referred to by the metaphor of 'the English disease' by both politicians and judges

(Pearson, 1998), with deterrent sentencing now being increasingly used in the higher courts (Salter, 1985b, 1986; Trivizas, 1980, 1981).

In terms of high-profile incidents, the peak was probably the second half of the 1984/85 season. Domestically, a violent mass pitch invasion interrupted a Luton Town v Millwall FA Cup tie as it was shown on live television, and then, on the final day of that season, a fan was killed during serious disorder that occurred both inside and outside the stadium at a Birmingham City v Leeds United fixture which led to 125 arrests and, reportedly, injury to 96 police officers (Giulianotti, 1994, p. 19). That season concluded when 39 Juventus fans trying to escape a terrace 'charge' by Liverpool fans at the 1985 European Cup final at the Heysel Stadium in Brussels were killed by crushing and suffocation when a wall collapsed because of crowd pressure. These incidents, in particular Heysel, precipitated several social control responses. Then Prime Minister Margaret Thatcher was reported as seeing 'hooligans' as part of 'the enemy within' and created a 'war cabinet' to seek solutions.[8] The days of leaving management of football crowds to local police authorities, clubs, and governing bodies were over; the problem was now a national one for which only a governmental response would be sufficient.

In addition to English club sides being banned from European competition for five years by UEFA as result of Heysel, the British Government introduced the Sporting Events (Control of Alcohol, etc.) Act 1985 in an attempt to restrict alcohol consumption at domestic matches. A year later the Popplewell Report made a series of additional recommendations. These included statutory changes to allow "an unfettered right to search" those wishing to enter a football stadium (1986 para 4.38), a new offence of "disorderly conduct in a sports ground" (1986 para 4.74),[9] and the "consideration of some form of membership scheme" for spectators (1986 para 4.128). The subsequent year, Exclusion Orders were

[8] *The Independent*, 19 February 2016 (Harris, D 'Margaret Thatcher's government thought football fans so violent she set up a "war cabinet"'); *New Statesman*, 22 August 2013 (Clavane, A, 'What Thatcher did for Football').

[9] Popplewell noted that this offence "would clearly include throwing a missile, running onto the pitch, seeking to climb over or to pull down a perimeter fence, shining a mirror towards a batsman, throwing bottles or cans onto the field of play", as well as a number of forms of misbehaviour found in other sports (1986, p. 4.74).

introduced by section 30 of the Public Order Act 1986, preventing fans convicted of 'football-related' offences attending matches. These orders, which were to be renamed football banning orders (FBOs), made it a criminal offence for anyone serving an order to attend matches. Between 1988 and 1989, a national police Football Intelligence Unit was developed and established with a brief to gather "hooligan and 'hooligan-related' intelligence" (Armstrong & Hobbs, 1994, p. 218). This was based on the belief that in the 1980s much domestic 'hooliganism' was the result of organised hooligan gangs (or 'firms') conspiring to confront each other (see Redhead, 2010 for further discussion of the 'firms'). Finally, the Football Spectators Act 1989 was introduced, which in Part I aimed to introduce a National Identity Card Scheme for all football fans,[10] and in Part II created 'Restriction Orders' that looked to prevent fans who had been convicted of 'football-related' offences from travelling abroad to attend club and national team matches.[11] Although the National Identity Card Scheme was never implemented, Restriction Orders were, following disorder involving England fans in Stockholm in 1989 (Stott & Pearson, 2007, p. 31–36).

Changing Trends: 1990–2000

The year 1989 also saw the worst disaster to affect football in Britain, the Hillsborough Stadium tragedy in which a crowd crush led to the death of 97 fans. Indeed, it was the Taylor Report into the tragedy that famously ruled the proposed National ID Card scheme to be "a sledgehammer to crack a nut" (Taylor, 1990 para 377), ensuring it would not be implemented.[12] The Taylor Report also had other significant impacts on football spectators, in ruling that it was poor crowd management, in particular by South Yorkshire Police, rather than crowd behaviour that led to the fatalities. This primary conclusion ensured that attention would now also

[10] Sections 2–7.

[11] Sections 15–16.

[12] Although remarkably the scheme actually remained on the statute book until it was scrapped by the Violent Crime Reduction Act 2006.

be given to safety at sports grounds, rather than purely to measures of crowd security. Its recommendation that football stadia should become all-seater also ensured that many crumbling, outdated football grounds, at the top levels of the sport at least, would have to be improved.

The early to mid-1990s saw probably the biggest changes to the practice of attending live matches as had been seen since the 1950s. In effect four different drivers of change had now been introduced in the period 1987–1993: (1) more effective legal provisions including offences of missile throwing, invading the pitch, and racist or offensive chanting football and the new regime for banning orders on conviction (which we will discuss further in Chap. 3), (2) the increased funding for, use, and national coordination of, 'spotters' and 'football intelligence' (which we will discuss further in Chap. 4), (3) post-Taylor stadium re-development, and (4) broadcasting money from satellite television. Serendipity played the biggest role; there was no overall effective grand strategy to reduce football disorder, but each driver of change boosted the impact of the other. Banning orders could be enforced because of the focus on intelligence, and monitoring stadia for banned fans was made possible by modern stands providing better access for police and security, and more effective CCTV systems. A relaxation of physical restrictions, most notably perimeter fencing in new stands and stadia, was considered to be possible thanks partly to the deterrent effect of criminal offences and banning orders supported by football intelligence. The National Football Intelligence Unit was able to do its job because it was enabled by a combination of the new legal provisions and stadium modernisation. And, of course, the stadium modernisations necessary for all of this to work were made possible by broadcasting revenue, which in turn was at least a partial result of the new, 'cleaner', and less violent football 'product'. Perhaps no surprise then that in 1995/96, a survey of supporters found that 82% felt that there had been a decline in 'hooliganism' over the preceding five-year period (Sir Norman Chester Centre for Football Research, 1996).

We will deal with football banning orders (FBOs) in more detail in the following chapter and have in the past been rather critical of the legality of FBOs 'on complaint' (James & Pearson, 2006, 2018; Stott & Pearson, 2006), as well as their ability to prevent disorder abroad (Stott & Pearson, 2007). Nonetheless, we believe that FBOs imposed following the conviction of a 'football-related' offence probably played an important role in the reduction in disorder that was observed in the early 1990s. However, it is difficult to argue this with any conviction given the other factors at play and the lack of direct evidence; despite their assumed success, there has never been a study by the Home Office or the police into how effective FBOs are. Nevertheless, over the course of our research, both fans and police have pointed to the role they believe FBOs played in helping to 'break up' or limit the ability of the football 'firms' to engage in disorder and violence domestically. Such a conclusion seems logical and we have seen no evidence to the contrary to challenge this; it would be useful to analyse data about the extent to which FBOs work (and how they do so), but in the meantime we acknowledge the probable role that FBOs following conviction have had in reducing domestic football-related disorder.

However, while the late 1980s and early 1990s saw a reduction in disorder in and around stadia in England and Wales, and at the 1996 UEFA European Championships in England, the decade saw several further serious incidents of widespread disorder involving English fans abroad. In 1995, violence and missile throwing predominantly by England fans saw the abandonment of an international 'friendly' in Dublin. The year 1997's most serious incidents involved England fans at a World Cup qualifier in Rome and Manchester United fans at a UEFA Champions League match in Porto. Both these incidents were reported, accurately in our view, predominantly in terms of the travelling supporters being the victims of aggressive policing, demonstrating the start of a change of media emphasis in the reporting of English fans abroad. England's next two tournaments saw even more widespread crowd disorder, in Marseille at the 1998 FIFA World Cup, and Brussels and Charleroi in the 2000 UEFA European Championships. The turn of the century also saw disorder in Copenhagen at the UEFA Cup Final between Arsenal and Galatasaray, and collective violence prior to the Germany versus England match in Munich in 2001, which would have been headline news were it not for England's shock 5–1 victory. We have detailed the development and causes of the Marseille and Charleroi 'riots' elsewhere (Stott & Pearson, 2007), but our research at these two, as well as several other events, led us to the conclusion that the disorder was not pre-planned and was instead the result of an escalation of violence in which aggressive and disproportionate intervention by police played a significant, if not a defining, role. It also demonstrated the limitations of FBOs in terms of managing English football crowds abroad, not least of all given that the bulk of those that were arrested had no prior history of involvement in football-related disorder (an issue we will return to in Chap. 6).

Football Violence, Disorder, and Anti-social Behaviour in the Twenty-First Century

The rise and decline of football crowd disorder in England and Wales in the second half of the twentieth century was followed in the twenty-first by a period of relative stability domestically. The annual football-related arrest statistics released by the Home Office demonstrate first, a gradual decline in arrests at and around matches, and secondly, the relative absence of arrests for offences of serious violence or disorder. Further, this reduction occurred at the same time as attendances in England and Wales increased, making the reduction in the proportion of fans arrested, to those attending matches, even more dramatic. In 1984/85, the first year that nationwide arrest statistics were recorded, 16,438,751 attended league matches in England and Wales, with an arrest rate of 43:100,000 spectators. In 2016/17 attendance had nearly doubled to 31,700,000, with the arrest rate falling more than ten times, to 4:100.000. The arrest rate reported in 2018/19, accounting for all matches in England and Wales was only 3:100,000.

The statistics also seem to suggest that arrests as a proportion of attendance reduced the further up the football pyramid you went, and the overall declines have been mirrored in recent years by a gradual reduction in the number of FBOs issued. The table below is drawn from arrest statistics reported by the Home Office and more recently the UK Football Policing Unit (UKFPU), reflecting arrests both overall in England and Wales, and in the Football League and Premier League specifically. The league statistics enable comparison with earlier years, as originally only these statistics were compiled nationally. One must be cautious as there are several discrepancies in the government statistics; where arrests vary across different year's spreadsheets, we have recorded the number that was recorded on the year in question (Fig. 2.1).[13]

How useful are these statistics in enabling us to track levels of disorder? The first thing to note is that these are statistics of arrest, not charge, prosecution, or conviction, and include where the suspect was 'de-arrested' or where there was no further action (although they appear to only record arrests for Schedule 1 FSA1989 offences). They also include non-violent offences, including ticket touting. Moreover, as we have argued, unfortunately arrest statistics are notoriously unreliable, too often illustrating policy decisions, policing priorities, and resources more so they act as a proxy measure of fan behaviours. Put simply, if you deploy

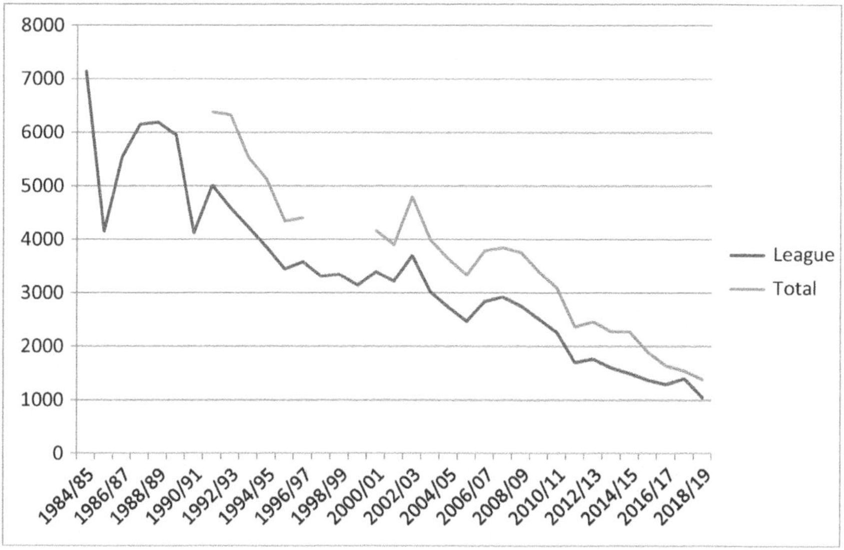

Fig. 2.1 Reductions in arrests for football-related offences

[13] For example, the 2001/02 arrest statistics record a total of 3898 arrests. But in 2002/02 the total arrests for 2001/02 is recorded as 4035. And in 2002/03, 439 arrests for violent disorder were recorded, whereas that 2003/04 statistics record the number of arrests for that offence that year as 447. All this makes comparison of anything other than the general trend very difficult. We cannot account for the spike in 2002/03, which appears to have been driven by increased numbers of arrests for public disorder and pitch invasions.

more police into most locations (e.g. town centre night-time economy), arrests are likely to increase, so arrest figures can be as much about police resourcing as they can be about increasing or decreasing crime.

It should also be noted that the reduction in the number of arrests around football fixtures generally mirrors that in the population overall. In 2007/08, there were 1,475,266 arrests in the UK, dropping to only 671,126 in 2018/19, and the post-2014 reduction occurred at the same time as a sharp *increase* in police-recorded crime.[14] While we find it likely that the dramatic reduction in both number and proportion of football-related arrests seen in the early 1990s is at least in part illustrative of the reduction in violence and disorder at football, it is also likely that some year-on-year reductions (and spikes) were driven by other factors (e.g. the reduction in 2010/11 occurs around the time that police arrest targets across forces were abolished). Reductions in football arrests after this period are as likely to reflect reductions in police officer numbers as a result of government austerity measures (Bradford, 2011), the closure of custody suites, and the general disincentivising of arrest (Pearson & Rowe, 2020, p. 147–150) as much as they are the outcome of a reduction in violence or disorder at football.

Nonetheless, we have drawn our conclusions by comparing these statistics with the views expressed by fans and police in our ongoing research, as well as drawing on other sources. Cleland and Cashmore's survey of fans' views on violence in British football, for example, revealed that "89% of our participants stated how violence no longer exists at a level they had previously experienced" (Cleland & Cashmore, 2016). This certainly reflects the commonly held belief about the reduction of violence in domestic football in England and Wales in the 1990s, but despite the arrest statistics, we have seen little evidence that a decline has continued at any significant rate into the new century. Similarly, we have seen little evidence that we are "returning to the dark days of hooliganism", thanks to a combination of "a grim new breed of hooligan" (*Daily Mail*, 19 October 2018), fuelled by increased cocaine use, and social media.

[14] Home Office, *Arrest Statistics Data Tables: Police Powers and Procedures Year Ending, 31 March 2019*, available at www.gov.uk/government/statistics/police-powers-and-procedures-englandand-wales-year-ending-31-march-2019

Indeed, we found the claim, made in 2018 by the National Police Chief's Council lead for football, that incidents of violence and disorder in and around stadia were "significantly increasing" (*Daily Mail*, 19 October 2018, BBC Sport, 26 February 2018)[15] to be lacking a firm evidence base. This contrasted with more robust evidence of the uptick in disorder following the end of lockdown in the 2021/22 season that we discussed in Chap. 1.

Whatever the nuances, there is consensus that domestic football in England and Wales continues to face challenges in terms of crime and behaviour. Cocaine is increasingly fashionable amongst some fan groups (Treadwell & Ayres, 2014), with one study finding that nearly a third of spectators had witnessed other fans taking cocaine at matches and noting an association between cocaine use and "swearing and shouting at rivals" (Newson, 2021). The increase in cocaine use seems to mirror that in society more generally (ONS, 2020). Pyrotechnic use—particularly the ignition of devices discharging coloured smoke—has also become a common feature in English stadia. Further, as we will see when we consider our research data in Chap. 8, new 'youth firms' can be identified at most clubs and cause significant headaches for the authorities. However, on balance, while the challenges for police at football have changed, we are not sure they have become significantly either harder or easier since the turn of the century. Domestically, disorder and violence at football is highly irregular, and when it occurs it is usually spontaneous and quickly over. The risk of violence and disorder also remains highly localised. It is exceptionally unusual to be able to plot national trends in levels of 'hooliganism', but local forces are all too aware of how for their club, the risk of violence may have increased or decreased over the previous years. New groups emerge, new rivalries develop, but also older risk fans depart, and local derbies can be curtailed by promotion or relegation. However, as we will see in Chap. 8, when we study the policing of these fixtures, what we find empirically is that violence is situationally determined and frequently a self-fulfilling prophesy, arising from the responses of police forces to real or imagined threat.

[15] https://www.bbc.co.uk/sport/football/43140824.

When we consider disorder abroad involving English fans, we can also see a mostly static picture since the European Championships in Portugal, Euro 2004. Since then, the vast majority of matches involving the England national team and English club sides continue to pass off peacefully. However, this is interspersed by the occasional instance of widespread disorder such as that seen during Euro 2004 in Albufeira (England), Rome (Manchester United), Athens (Liverpool) and Seville (Tottenham Hotspur) in 2007, Lille (Everton) in 2014, and Amsterdam and Porto (England) in 2018 and 2019. Most seriously of all were the two days of rioting in Marseille at the 2016 UEFA European Championships, where some England fans engaged in disorder against local gangs, Paris St Germain fans, and the French police, before being violently attacked by Russian ultras. Marseille 2016 saw arguably the most sustained football disorder ever involving England football supporters and reminds us of the ongoing potential for catastrophic crowd disorder, particularly in locations where the police rely upon outdated, ill-informed, and reactionary 'show of force' riot control tactics.

The Development of Academic Understandings of Football Crowd Disorder

The emergence of 'football hooliganism' as a singular, identifiable, phenomenon was followed fairly swiftly by the first academic analysis of the problem. Indeed, from the 1970s until the 1990s, sociological interest in football fandom and identity became almost exclusively focussed on 'hooliganism' (Davis, 2015). The overwhelming focus of the studies in the 1970s and 1980s was on the question of why 'hooliganism' occurred in football. Unsurprisingly, explanations for the phenomenon diverged, often along disciplinary lines. Two of the first explanations from sociology drew upon Marxist theory. Taylor characterised 'hooliganism' as emerging because of the alienation of traditional fans from a game which was being increasingly commercialised (Taylor, 1971), whereas Clarke saw the phenomenon as emerging from a divergence between the professionalisation of football and the desire of working-class young men to remain physically and emotionally part of the spectacle (Clarke, 1978). Both accounts lacked an empirical foundation and come across as largely speculative.

An alternative explanation came from more anthropologically informed approaches, which were more inclined to see 'hooliganism' as a spectacle or ritual (Morris, 1981). One of the earliest empirical studies, led by the social-psychologist and then Director of Oxford United, Peter Marsh, revealed through fan experiences of 'hooliganism' the relative lack of inter-personal violence in these encounters in the tellingly titled *Rules of Disorder* (Marsh et al., 1978, see also Stott, 2020). This gap between the official and media reporting of football violence and the lived reality for those fans that we might consider to be on the 'front-line' was highlighted again 20 years later by Gary Armstrong (1998). When it came to debates about the nature and severity of football violence, a relation between the methodology adopted by the researcher and both tone and conclusion was starting to emerge. Studies focused on survey data or interviews (e.g. Newson, 2017; Spaaij, 2006) have tended to suggest higher levels of, or more serious episodes of, football-related violence, in contrast to observational studies which were more likely to stress a lesser prevalence of serious violence (e.g. Armstrong, 1998; Giulianotti, 1991, 1995; Pearson, 2012; Richards, 2017; Stott & Pearson, 2007). Furthermore, as we will see, particularly in Chap. 8, the gap between official accounts of the problem of football crowd violence and the reality is one that continues to trouble policing responses to the present day.

Other academic investigations into football violence around this time can be seen as falling into what Giulianotti calls the 'continuity thesis' (Giulianotti, 1994, p. 10), arguing that football hooliganism was not an entirely new phenomenon which developed in the 1950s or 1960s. We have addressed this earlier in the chapter and would reiterate the value of the socio-historical analysis of the 'Leicester School', and the comparisons with historical violence connected to sport more widely. This historically informed understanding is essential and leads us to a few important points. First, that the label of 'football hooliganism' that became popular amongst the media, police, and politicians from the mid- to late 1960s was itself a construction (Melnick, 1986) and its usage did not necessarily denote a new phenomenon. As Dunning put it, "the label 'football hooliganism' is not so much a social scientific or social psychological concept as a construct of politicians and the media" (2000, p. 142). Secondly, that the media construction is not merely a neutral or passive *description* of a pre-existing phenomenon but instead is ideological in that it has the power to emphasise certain elements, for example, through the powerful metaphor of 'hooliganism' as a disease (Pearson, 1998), whilst downplaying others. As Stuart Hall explains, "through the selection and presentation processes, the press plays an active and constructive role, not merely a passive and reflecting one" (Hall, 1978, p. 19). One example of this comes from the Popplewell Report, with David Canter noting that often respondents to the research based their views not on their own experience but on what they had read or seen in the media:

> When it comes to actual evidence the picture becomes more hazy. Although 162 of our respondents said they had direct evidence of National Front involvement, closer examination reveals that a number of those based that on media reports. All in all, about 10% of our respondents appear to have first hand knowledge of National Front activities (Pratt & Salter, 1984 5.84).

Thirdly, that the media construction of 'hooliganism' exaggerated the extent, regularity, and severity of the problem of football crowd violence and disorder. In this respect, it can be seen as one of several 'moral panics' that are typically constructed around the behaviours of, usually, working-class young men (Cohen, 2002; Hall, 1978; Pearson, 1983). Football hooliganism is therefore not just a "historical mass media construction" but also a "hysterical" one (Redhead, 1993, p. 3).

Leading from this, we must also consider the extent to which this social construction not only affects media and popular understandings of football violence but can also play into government policy, legislation, judicial judgment, and policing strategy. The law is by no means immune from media frenzy. Legislation is created by governments who try to deliver what they perceive the electorate wants, whether this is for their own legitimacy or with a cynical eye on an upcoming election. The need of those in power to be seen to have been 'doing something' is a driving imperative. After all, one of the key responsibilities of government is to address public disorder and one of the key areas in which successive governments have been challenged in that capacity has been in relation to football. These political imperatives have in our view led to panic legislation, most notably the Sporting Events (Control of Alcohol, etc.) Act 1985 and the Football Disorder Act 2000. Much of this legislation, as we will argue later in this book, has either been ineffective when judged against its aims, or even counter-productive to the effective management of 'public order'. Furthermore, as we shall also contend, these same successive UK governments have had a tendency to react to these moral panics by putting pressure, through the Home Office, on police forces to taker 'tougher' action against perpetrators and to finance them to achieve these aims. This is particularly important where legislation provides police officers with wide discretion to interpret or apply offences. The actions of individual officers when utilising discretion should not be considered in abstract, but within the context of the supervisory and policy framework in which policing takes place. Rhetoric by a Home Secretary or a Chief Constable about the dangers of 'hooliganism', combined with financial incentive to meet specific targets in that regard, has the potential to cascade down through the ranks to officers tasked with managing football crowds, from those making strategic decisions, to those implementing tactical approaches, and the individual operational decisions of officers on the ground.

These kinds of issues have been amplified by the fact that there is no definition of 'football hooliganism' in the law. It is not in itself an offence, nor is there any guidance as to what 'hooliganism' is in terms of sentencing policy. However, historically this has not stopped magistrates and judges from using the label in court as a 'master-stigma' against those who are deemed to fall under it (Salter, 1985b, p. 353). The judiciary, at all levels, has shown itself to be by no means immune from media constructions or moral panics when it comes to football fans. As we will argue in Chap. 3, this has had the effect of both encouraging deterrent sentencing against those considered 'hooligans', and also preventing adequate scrutiny of state powers, most notably football banning orders 'on complaint'.

Much of the social scientific research of the 1970s and 1980s was helpful in contextualising the phenomenon both historically and socially, and by drawing attention to the risks of uncritically assuming sensationalist media constructions. However, the attempts of the academic community to explain why, where, and when specific incidents of large-scale violence and disorder were occurring at football were to us as unconvincing as those of the authorities, and have as a result come in for equally strong criticism. Most powerfully of all, Armstrong and Hobbs criticised what they called the "dangerous liaison between police and academics", arguing that, up to the 1990s at least, "the public cannot rely on the sociological 'experts' to provide a critical eye" (Armstrong & Hobbs, 1994, p. 225). Explanations for disorder at football fell into three broad, disciplinary-driven forms. Influential anthropologist Desmond Morris argued that 'hooliganism' was a small part of the more ritualistic and symbolic display of *The Soccer Tribe*. Partially drawing on Marsh's work, he highlighted that the vast majority of those caught up in 'hooliganism' were not themselves committing serious violent offences, which were largely the territory of a small number of "wild men"—exclude them and the problem would be mitigated (Morris, 1981, p. 268). An alternative explanation was put forward in John Kerr's, *Understanding Soccer Hooliganism* (1994), applying the motivation based 'reversal theory' to football-related violence and suggesting that differing "meta-motivational state dominance" meant that the swing between emotions—such as the fear and exhilaration experienced through violence at football and escaping the attentions of the police—could become addictive at the expense of other activities. Kerr addressed the fact that empirical data showed the majority of 'hooligans' were working class and argued that this could be explained by the lack of educational opportunity leading to a breakdown of movement between certain "meta-motivational states", resulting in "negative learning spirals" and the dominance of an inclination towards 'hooliganism'.

However, by far the most influential theory in the 1980s and early 1990s came from the Sir Norman Chester Centre for Football Research.[16] Drawing upon Norbert Elias's 'civilising process', Eric Dunning, Patrick Murphy and John Williams argued that the cause of 'hooliganism' could be found in "a long-established subculture of aggressive masculinity that is predominantly but by no means solely working class" (Murphy et al.,

[16] Dunning argued that the term 'Leicester School' was misleading due to theoretical differences between the three academics within it (1994).

1990, p. 12–13). *Football on Trial* (Murphy et al., 1990) located the primary source of 'hooliganism' within "rougher", left-behind, working-class communities such as the Kinsley estate in Leicester, where they carried out their empirical work. As with Kerr's thesis, increasing opportunities, particularly in education, for individuals and communities left behind by the process of "incorporation" with the dominant standards in society (Murphy et al., 1990, p. 227) would be the only long-term solution. This did not, however, stop the authors proposing in *Hooligans Abroad*, "A Provisional Scheme for Limiting the Occurrence of Hooligan Behaviour by English Fans at Continental Matches", which focused on restricting the ability of 'maverick' fans from attending matches abroad (Williams et al., 1989, appendix 4). We do not intend to revisit in detail the critiques of the 'Leicester School', most notably by Gary Armstrong (1998, p. 14–20) and Richard Giulianotti (2000, Chap. 3) and which we have discussed previously (Stott & Pearson, 2007, p. 39–52). Instead, we simply note that, despite their nuanced differences, the theoretical explanations of the 'Leicester School', along with Morris and Kerr, effectively created a consensus in that they all ultimately attributed the cause of 'hooliganism' to the *disposition* of football fans, be that caused biologically, psychologically, or sociologically.

These theories for the causes of football 'hooliganism' put forward in the 1970s, 1980s, and early 1990s, from whatever discipline they originated, did not convince the authorities at the time to take particular action. Indeed, Lord Popplewell abruptly and dismissively concluded that "I must have read some thirty or forty reports, studies or books, where an attempt has been made to analyse the problem. I am certainly more knowledgeable on the subject of football hooliganism. Whether I am any wiser I doubt" (1984 para. 5.88). With the benefit of hindsight, having seen the development of football throughout the 1990s and into the new century, we can see no strong arguments to support these early but dominant explanations for why disorder or violence at football occurred. The most useful scholarship from this period remains that which encouraged us to be cynical about the novelty, nature, and seriousness of the phenomenon as painted in particular by the media at the time.

Perhaps most importantly, these explanations based on class or 'motivational states' had limited explanatory power in that they failed to explain why it was that, at most football matches, those fans who were assumed in some way to be socially or psychologically programmed towards engagement in football violence *did not* usually engage in it. They also failed to explain why it was that serious collective disorder or violence was likely to occur more regularly in certain geographical areas than others. In short, they could not explain or predict the specificities of where, and when, incidents would develop or what 'hooligans' would attack when disorder did develop. Why was it, for example, that during the 1990s and early 2000s, violence surrounding England fixtures occurred in some cities but not others (e.g. in Charleroi but not Eindhoven during Euro2000) and that when it did take place that it often primarily involved conflict with local youths of Arab or north African decent (e.g. in Marseilles during France 98).

Theories based on class or educational attainment might point towards a generic explanation for why disorder, at and around stadia, started decreasing as the price of tickets started to increase in the early 1990s. We still hear today claims that hooligans were 'priced out' of football, or their influence was in some way 'watered-down' by new middle-class fans, and increasing numbers of women and children, who started attending matches. But as we will argue as this book progresses, incidents of football crowd violence and disorder still occur in Britain today. And we have heard no explanations for what has happened to the alleged violent tendencies of those fans priced-out of football. Furthermore, when we pay attention to the behaviour of English fans travelling abroad, we can see a litany of incidents of mass anti-social behaviour, disorder, and violence (Stott & Pearson, 2007). We see little, if any, evidence to suggest that potentiality for mass football disorder involving English fans abroad has been limited, given it regularly recurs as it did so catastrophically during Euro2016. Indeed, the evidence is clear that mass disorder involving England and English fans is far more likely to be witnessed in specific foreign countries, relative to others, and more so than it is occurring domestically. The key variables we see associated with these patterns is not fan disposition but infrastructure, legislation, and styles of policing, and this is despite the cost and administrative barriers put up in the way of attending these events to those fans on low incomes or subject to banning orders.

Conclusion

Looking back over 50 years on the development of football crowd disorder, we can draw out several key points that are important for the argument we set out in this book. The first, which is now so well-established it barely needs reiterating, is that 'football hooliganism' as a singular phenomenon is a myth. The media-contrived label which started to dominate discourse in the 1960s was applied to a host of different and often unconnected types of criminality, transgression, deviance, or other behaviour that became ever-more reported during this period. This may have been because they were occurring more regularly, involving more fans, or were simply more apparent in the emerging mass media age. It is clear, however, that many, if not all, these forms of behaviour were occurring to a greater or lesser extent long before the label came into popular usage. As a result, we will not be using the term 'hooligan' or 'hooliganism' in this book unless it is for the purposes of critiquing it or referencing the labelling process, which unfortunately still often plays a role in how football crowd disorder is responded to by media, politicians, and police.

This leads on to a second point, that we need to be careful when trying to identify national trends in football-related 'public disorder'. From the development of the phenomenon in the 1950s and 1960s, it was evident that violence and disorder was localised and connected to structural issues that were more relevant to some clubs or matches than others. In other words, the risk of disorder was not confined to the 'type' of individuals that attended fixtures, but to the environment in which they found themselves. Stadium infrastructures in the 1960s and 1970s were largely in decline and not suited to large crowds of visiting supporters, and police forces and clubs did not possess the necessary knowledge, training, or guidance to be able to understand and mitigate the risks posed. In short, the problem was unlikely to have predominantly been 'hooligans' attending matches with the intention to engage in violence or disorder, but those interactions that resulted from a combination of the peculiarities of geography, crowd movement, and localised history.

Third, we can start to see that football fan behaviour, or 'culture' if you will, is neither passive nor unchanging. It is shaped by external pressures, so reactions to the perceived problem have also changed the landscape. These external pressures include physical changes to stadia, for example, segregating fences, changed access routes, or the development of new stadia that are often out-of-town and far removed from the narrow, confined, and difficult-to-manage urban spaces of their former Victorian-heritage locations. They also include the management of crowds through policing strategies and tactics, and the use of club safety stewards or security personnel. Moreover, we can include laws and regulations. While these external pressures can be beneficial to public order, history has shown that they have too often been ineffective and even counter-productive. From segregation to alcohol restrictions, to banning orders on complaint, regulations and laws have changed football fan behaviour, but not always in the ways intended. As we will see, one potential reason for these failures has been due to a lack of understanding of where the real 'risk' to public order around football events lies. Another is the desire to impose a 'one size fits all' approach to a phenomenon that can be highly localised. And finally, another reason is a repeated failure to engage meaningfully with the targets for such changes, the fans themselves.

References

Armstrong, G. (1998). *Football Hooligans: Knowing the Score*. Berg.

Armstrong, G., & Hobbs, D. (1994). Tackled from Behind. In R. Giulianotti, N. Bonney, & M. Hepworth (Eds.), *Football Violence and Social Identity* (pp. 196–228). Routledge.

Bradford, B. (2011). *Police Numbers and Crime Rates: A Rapid Evidence Review*. https://www.justiceinspectorates.gov.uk/hmicfrs/publications/police-numbers-crimerates-rapid/

Butler, B. (1991). *Official History of the Football Association*. Queen Anne Press.

Clarke, J. (1978). Football and Working Class Fans: Tradition and Change. In R. Ingham (Ed.), *Football Hooliganism: The Wider Context* (pp. 37–60). Inter-Action Inprint.

Cleland, J., & Cashmore, E. (2016). Football Fans' Views of Violence in British Football: Evidence of a Sanitized and Gentrified Culture. *Journal of Sport and Social Issues, 40*(2), 124–142.

Cohen, S. (2002). *Folk Devils and Moral Panics*. Routledge.

Davis, L. (2015). Football Fandom and Authenticity: A Critical Discussion of Historical and Contemporary Perspectives. *Soccer and Society, 16*(2–3), 422–436.

Dunning, E. (1986). Sport as a Male Preserve: Notes on the Social Sources of Masculine Identity and its Transformations. *Theory, Culture and Society, 3(1)*, 79–90.

Dunning, E. (1994). The Social Roots of Football Hooliganism: A Reply to Critics of the 'Leicester School'. In R. Giulianotti, N. Bonney, & M. Hepworth (Eds.), *Football, Violence and Social Identity* (pp. 128–157). Routledge.

Dunning, E. (2000). Towards a Sociological Understanding of Football Hooliganism as a World Phenomenon. *European Journal on Criminal Policy and Research, 8*, 141–162.

Dunning, E., Maguire, J., Murphy, P., & Williams, J. (1986). The Social Roots of Football Hooligan Violence. *Leisure Studies, 1*(2), 139–156.

Dunning, E., Murphy, P., & Williams, J. (1988). *The Roots of Football Hooliganism*. Routledge.

Garland, A. (2001). *The Culture of Control: Crime and Social Order in Contemporary Society*. Oxford University Press.

Giulianotti, R. (1991). Scotland's Tartan Army in Italy: The Case for the Carnivalesque. *Sociological Review, 39*(3), 503–527.

Giulianotti, R. (1994). Social Identity and Public Order: Political and Academic Discourses on Football Violence. In R. Giulianotti, N. Bonney, & M. Hepworth (Eds.), *Football, Violence and Social Identity* (pp. 10–36). Routledge.

Giulianotti, R. (1995). Football and the Politics of Carnival: An Ethnographic Study of Scottish Fans in Sweden. *International Review for the Sociology of Sport, 30*(2), 191–223.

Giulianotti, R. (2000). *Football: A Sociology of the Global Game*. Polity Press.

Hall, S. (1978). The Treatment of "Football Hooliganism" in the Press. In R. Ingham (Ed.), *Football Hooliganism: The Wider Context* (pp. 15–37). Inter-Action Inprint.

Harrington, J. (1968). *Soccer Hooliganism: A Preliminary Report to Mr. Denis Howell, Minister of Sport*. HMSO.

Hughes, M. (1946). *Parliamentary report of the public inquiry into the Burden Park Stadium Disaster*. HMSO.

Hutchinson, J. (1975) 'Some Aspects of Football Crowds before 1914', in, *The Working Class and Leisure, Proceedings of the Conference for the Study of Labour History*, University of Sussex Paper No. 13.

James, M., & Pearson, G. (2006). Football Banning Orders: Analysing their use in Court. *The Journal of Criminal Law, 70*(6), 509–530.

James, M., & Pearson, G. (2018). '30 Years of Hurt: The Evolution of Civil Preventative Orders, Hybrid Law, and the Emergence of the Super-Football Banning Order. *Public Law, 1*, 44–61.

Kerr, J. (1994). *Understanding Soccer Hooliganism.* Open University Press.

Marsh, P. (1978). *Aggro: The Illusion of Violence.* Dent.

Marsh, P., Rosser, E., & Harré, R. (1978). *The Rules of Disorder.* Routledge.

Mason, T. (1980). *Association Football and English Society 1863–1915.* Harvester.

McArdle, D. (2000). *From Boot Money to Bosman: Football, Society and the Law.* Cavendish.

Melnick, M. (1986). The Mythology of Football Hooliganism: A Closer Look at the British Experience. *International Review for the Sociology of Sport, 21*(1), 1–21.

Morris, D. (1981). *The Soccer Tribe.* Jonathan Cape.

Murphy, P., Dunning, E., & Williams, J. (1990). *Football on Trial.* Routledge.

Newson, M. (2017). Football, Fan Violence, and Identity Fusion. *International Review for the Sociology of Sport, 54*(4), 431–444.

Newson, M. (2021). High and Highly Bonded: Fused Football Fans Who Use Cocaine Are Most Likely to be Aggressive Toward Rivals. *International Journal of Drug Policy, 93*, 202107. https://doi.org/10.1016/j.drugpo.2021.103263

Office for National Statistics. (2020). *Drug Misuse in England and Wales: Year Ending March 2020.* https://www.ons.gov.uk/peoplepopulationandcommunity/crimeandjustice/articles/drugmisuseinenglandandwales/yearendingmarch2020

Pearson, G. (1983). *Hooligan: A History of Respectable Fears.* Macmillan.

Pearson, G. (1998). The English Disease: Socio-Legal Constructions of Football Hooliganism. *Youth and Policy - The Journal of Critical Analysis, 60*, 1–15.

Pearson, G. (2012). *An Ethnography of English Football Fans: Cans, Cops, and Carnivals.* Manchester University Press.

Pearson, G., & Rowe, M. (2020). *Police Street Powers and Criminal Justice: Regulation and Discretion in a Time of Change.* Hart.

Popplewell. (1986). *Committee of Inquiry into Crowd Safety and Control at Sports Grounds Final Report* (p. 9710). HMSO Cmnd.

Pratt, J., & Salter, M. (1984). A Fresh Look at Football Hooliganism. *Leisure Studies, 3(2)*, 201–230.

Redhead, S. (1993). *The Passion and the Fashion.* Ashgate/Avebury.

Redhead, S. (2010). Little Hooliganz: The Inside Story of Glamorous Lads, Football Hooligans and Postsubculturalism. *Entertainment and Sports Law Journal, 8*(2), 3. https://www.entsportslawjournal.com/article/id/799/

Richards, J. (2017) *Sports Space: A Conceptual Model of Everton Football Club Match-day Fan Movement.* Unpublished PhD Thesis. University of Sydney.

Salter, M. (1985a). Football Hooliganism: Anticipation and Presence. *Journal of Youth and Policy, 13*, 19–27.

Salter, M. (1985b). The Judges v. The Football Fan: A Sporting Contest? *Northern Ireland Legal Quarterly, 36*(4), 351–357.

Salter, M. (1986). Judicial Responses to Football Hooliganism. *Northern Ireland Legal Quarterly, 37*(3), 280–292.

Signy, D. (1968). *A Pictorial History of Soccer*. Spring.

Sir Norman Chester Centre for Football Research. (1996). *FA Premier League Fan Survey 1995–96*. Sir Norman Chester Centre for Football Research.

Spaaij, R. (2006). *Understanding Football Hooliganism*. Amsterdam University Press.

Stott, C. (2020). Crowd Behaviour and 'hooliganism'. In S. A. Haslam, K. Fransen, & F. Boen (Eds.), *Sports and Exercise Psychology: The Social Identity Approach* (pp. 321–340). Sage.

Stott, C., & Pearson, G. (2006). 'Football Banning Orders, Proportionality and Public Order': *Howard. Journal of Criminal Justice, 45*(3), 241–254.

Stott, C., & Pearson, G. (2007). *Football Hooliganism: Policing and the War on the English Disease*. Pennant.

Taylor, I. (1971). Soccer Consciousness and Soccer Hooliganism. In S. Cohen (Ed.), *Images of Deviance* (pp. 134–164). Harmondsworth.

Taylor, L. J. (1990). *The Hillsborough Stadium Disaster: Final Report*. HMSO.

Taylor, N. A. J. (2011). Football Hooliganism as Collective Violence: Explaining Variance in Britain Through Interpersonal Boundaries. *The International Journal of the History of Sport, 28*(13), 1750–1771.

Treadwell, J., & Ayres, T. (2014). Talking Prada and Powder: Cocaine Use and Supply Among the Football Hooligan Firm. In M. Hopkins & J. Treadwell (Eds.), *Football Hooliganism, Fan Behaviour and Crime: Contemporary Issues* (pp. 49–47). Palgrave.

Trivizas, E. (1980). Offences and Offenders in Football Crowd Disorders. *British Journal of Criminology, 20*(3), 276–288.

Trivizas, E. (1981). Sentencing the Football Hooligan. *British Journal of Criminology, 21*(4), 342–349.

Vamplew, W. (1979). Ungentlemanly Conduct: The Control of Soccer Crowd Behaviour in England, 1888–1914. In T. Smout (Ed.), *The Search for Wealth and Stability* (pp. 139–154). Macmillan.
Vamplew, W. (1980). Sports Crowd Disorder in Britain, 1870–1914: Causes and Controls. *Journal of Sport History, 7*(1), 5–20.
Williams, J., Dunning, E., & Murphy, P. (1989). *Hooligans Abroad* (2nd ed.). Routledge.

3

Legal Measures to Prevent Violence and Disorder at Football

Introduction

This chapter develops our argument by considering the imposition, and in some cases evolution, of legal measures introduced in England and Wales as a response to the problems of football crowd disorder that we discussed in Chap. 2. These fall into several categories. First, what can broadly be seen as licensing legislation and statutory instruments that were designed primarily to improve safety in football stadia, but which also place regulatory restrictions on fans which were perceived to be beneficial to public order. Second, we will consider legislation that was introduced to make certain behaviours criminal offences when they took place in football stadia. Third, we will address 'hybrid' legislation that bridges civil and criminal law through the imposition of what are now called football banning orders (FBOs). Fourth, we will consider the application of powers contained within generic legislation against football supporters. And finally, we will consider how the judiciary have played a role in responding to the issue.

The chapter's purpose is not just to provide an extensive and up-to-date account of the law in this area. We will also consider the legislative intent behind the legislation to raise questions as to the effectiveness of

G. Pearson, C. Stott, *A New Agenda For Football Crowd Management*, Palgrave Studies in Risk, Crime and Society, https://doi.org/10.1007/978-3-031-16298-5_3

the law achieving these aims. The issue of effectiveness, in public order terms, is a particularly important consideration; as we will argue when we address football policing, while legislation can grant useful powers to the police, some of it creates obligations that we contend can be counter-productive because they hamper and restrain police abilities to act operationally in ways that they know will reduce the risk of disorder. Furthermore, where football policing operations feel obliged to enforce laws which may be either irrelevant or counter-productive to public order, this can cause problems in terms of the legitimacy, not just of the law but also of the entire policing operation. If a law is seen as unfair by fans, the risk is that the enforcement of it by officers will also be viewed in this way. One of our overriding arguments in this book is that to improve the management of football fans, it is not just policing strategies or tactics that we need to focus on to ensure they are fair and effective, but also the legitimacy of the laws they are required to enforce.

Stadium Safety Interventions

Prior to the Taylor Report of 1990, football in Britain was marred by a catalogue of stadium disasters that resulted in thousands of reported injuries and the deaths of over 300 spectators (Elliott et al., 1997; James, 2017; McArdle, 2000). The combination of a failure of effective government regulation, licensing by the football authorities, poor policing, over-securitisation, and an "enterprise culture" (Hartley, 2001) culminated in the Hillsborough stadium disaster of 1989. Perhaps the most remarkable feature of the tragedy at Hillsborough, and the Bradford stadium disaster four years before, was that these took place under a regulatory regime that should have prevented both. The Safety at Sports Grounds Act 1975 (SSGA), introduced following the Ibrox disaster of 1971, established a safety regime that still forms the foundations of that which is in place today.

The SSGA requires that in order for spectators to be permitted to attend a designated sports ground, that venue must first be awarded a safety certificate. Originally, this was designed only for outdoor sports grounds with capacity for over 10,000 spectators, but for football, additional designation orders have looked to capture more stadia within the regulatory remit of the legislation. The Department for Culture, Media and Sport (DCMS) have the power (under s.11 Football Spectators Act 1989) to designate any football match for the purpose of imposing safety certificates. The Safety at Sports Grounds (Accommodation of Spectators) Order 1996 extended the regime to cover all football stadia in the Premier League and Football League regardless of size and also all other stadia used for football with capacities of 5000 or more. At the time of writing the Safety of Sports Grounds (Designation) Order 2015 sets out the list of sports stadia falling under the safety certificate regime. Section 26 of the Fire Safety and Safety of Places of Sport Act 1987, which was introduced following the Bradford stadium fire in 1985, also requires that all individual stands with a capacity of 500 or more require a fire safety certificate to admit spectators. Safety certificates are issued by the local authority through a Safety Advisory Group (SAG), which includes council figures, club representatives, and representatives of the police, ambulance, and fire and rescue authorities. SSGA section 3(3) requires all applications for safety certificates to be sent to the Chief Officer of police for consultation about the terms and conditions to be imposed into the certificate and section 2(2A) sets out that "no condition of a safety certificate shall require the provision of the services at the ground of any members of a police force unless the extent of the provision of their services is reserved for the determination of the chief officer of police of the force". In creating a specific role for the local police force in the safety regime, the SSGA was therefore the first piece of legislation to directly empower the police to manage and control football crowds. Although their role in this regime is primarily to ensure safety, the SSGA empowered the police to make demands on structural and organisational changes, such as CCTV, police control rooms, and crowd segregation.

The SSGA is enforced by introducing an offence under section 12 of admitting spectators to a designated ground without a valid safety certificate and providing councils with prohibition notices (s.10) and powers of entry and inspection to ensure the certificate is being followed (s.11). While on paper this scheme was a sensible approach to crowd safety and management at football, in practice, many local authorities did not police the scheme and many clubs did not take the provisions of safety certificates seriously enough. The Popplewell Interim Report (1985) into the 1985 Bradford Fire identified the cause of that disaster to have been a build-up of flammable rubbish under the stand that caught fire, in breach of the club's safety certificate. It also noted that between 1977 and 1983, there had been 86 fires in grandstands, despite the SSGA safety regime. In a similar vein, the safety certificate in place at Hillsborough had failed to prevent that tragedy in 1989; the certificate had not been updated to reflect key structural changes that had taken place in the stadium. Lord Justice Taylor, writing the official report into the Hillsborough disaster, summarised that the existing regulatory framework had "not been strong enough to ensure that basic level of safety" (1990, para 140). He identified not only an "insufficient concern" with spectator safety prior to Hillsborough but also a "preoccupation with measures to control hooliganism" (1990, para 23).

The Taylor Report recommended that the Football Spectators Act 1989, which had been put on hold while the Hillsborough disaster was investigated, could be used to improve safety, rather than to introduce the proposed National Identity Card Scheme (he considered the latter disproportionate and doubted its likely effectiveness). However, the Football Licensing Authority (FLA), which was to manage the scheme, could instead be used to oversee the discharge of the duties of the local authorities, making safety certificates more effective. In addition to following the terms of their safety certificate, football clubs would now also require a "license to admit spectators" that would be issued by the FLA (a duty now taken over by the Sports Grounds Safety Authority [SGSA] when they replaced the FLA in 2011).[1] The licensing authority has the power, again following consultation with the Chief Officer of police and other stakeholders, to impose terms and conditions into the safety certificate (FSA s.13) and to inspect grounds, amend or revoke the licence (FSA s.12), and makes it a criminal offence to admit spectators to unlicensed premises (FSA s. 9). The creation of the licensing system also enabled DCMS, which has overriding authority over the SGSA,[2] to make compliance with the Football Spectators (Seating) Order 1994 a mandatory part

[1] Sports Grounds Safety Authority Act 2011.

[2] ibid s.11.

of the licence, thereby enforcing all-seater stadia for the top two divisions until 2022, when 'safe standing' sections were licensed. The SGSA also possesses an influence in non-football stadium safety through its role in drafting the Guide to Safety at Sports Grounds (the 'Green Guide'), its regional inspectors, and a more general advisory role.

It should, however, be made clear that this complex system of regulating football stadia only gives power to SAGs and the SGSA over the admission of spectators (defined under section 17 of the Act as "any person occupying accommodation provided for spectators at a sports ground"). For example, there is no power in either the SSGA 1975 or the FSA 1989 to allow SAGs or the licensing authority to withhold safety certificates or licences to stop "behind closed doors" matches taking place. Neither does the safety regime extend to non-spectators; maintaining the safety of players, club staff, police officers, and stewards remains with the Health and Safety Executive, operating under the Health and Safety at Work Act 1974 and its numerous regulations. The legislation is, when read alongside the Hansard Commons and Committee Stage debates, unequivocal that the powers of the SAGs and the SGSA arise only in relation to *spectator* safety and can be used only to prevent spectators being allowed access to stadia that do not have a safety certificate. These are powerful limitations to the legislation that do not appear to be widely understood.

The Safety at Sports Ground Bill went through several incarnations through the multiple parliamentary sessions of 1973/74, 1974, 1974/75. It is abundantly clear that politicians feeding into the process considered the focus of both the Wheatley Report (that followed the Ibrox disaster) and SSGA to be the *safety of spectators paying for entry to watch designated football matches*. Viscount Colville of Culross, in moving the Bill onto its second reading at the House of Lords, noted that "The term 'certificate' we have preferred to 'licence' because 'licence' suggests some kind of control over the sporting activity itself; whereas the sole purpose of the Bill is to provide means for spectators' safety to be reasonably assured".[3] Furthermore, a proposal to amend Clause 2 of the Bill to read, "A safety certificate shall contain such terms and conditions as are required in the

[3] Hansard House of Lords, 20 November 1973, Vol. 349, Col. 929–930.

opinion of the local authority to secure reasonable safety for members of the public *and for all other persons* at the stadium when it is in use for an activity or activities specified in the certificate" was rejected at committee stage.

The issue of whether the regime extended beyond spectators in the stadium was queried, first when the SGSA launched a consultation into extending its remit into the safety of non-spectators in 2016. Then, in 2020, the UK Football Policing Unit (UKFPU) indicated that SAGs could be used to prevent 'behind closed doors' matches taking place when there was the risk that fans may gather outside.[4] Indeed, when stadia in England were given the 'go ahead' to host behind closed doors during the Covid-19 pandemic, safety certificates were still being sought, amended, and signed off, even though there was no legal ability for SAGs to stop matches going ahead without spectators. This takes us back to Lord Taylor's claim about the "preoccupation with hooliganism" and the perceived value that became attached to the safety regime in terms of crowd control rather than customer care (McArdle, 2000). The (misplaced) fear that fans would gather *en masse* outside stadia in breach of Public Health Regulations[5] spoke to the misunderstanding about fan behaviour that has categorised many public order responses to match events. It may also speak to the desire of authorities for control over members of the public who, although fans, would ultimately be gathering not as spectators in any sense of the word (they would in fact be choosing not even to watch the relevant match on television). The debates around 'neutral venues' for behind closed doors matches during the 2020 lockdown, at a time when large gatherings were reported in parks, on beaches, at illegal raves, and in protest and counter-protest, show that gatherings of football fans were still seen as inherently *risky.* It seemed to matter little whether this risk was to public order or public health, the need appeared to be for control (we will return to this in Chap. 5).

The Taylor Report 1990 has often been lauded by journalists, fans, and fan organisations across the country. In the social and historical context

[4] See, for example, *The Independent*, 2 June 2020: "Everton hopeful of playing Liverpool at Goodison Park in Merseyside derby".

[5] At the time, the Public Health (Coronavirus) England Regulations 2020/350 were in force.

in which it occurred, it was indeed a remarkable document in which a senior member of the judiciary was able to turn the political tide and halt primary legislation to introduce the Football ID Card Scheme in its tracks. It also successfully prevented blame for the disaster being placed upon the fans who were the victims of it, despite the initial attempts of South Yorkshire Police and the Thatcher Government. Moreover, the safety framework and regime that resulted from it was undoubtedly a driver for the much-needed modernisation of stadiums and a vast improvement on what had come before; at the time of writing, and despite the near miss on 'Euro Sunday', since Hillsborough there has not been another major stadium disaster in this country.

However, its recommendations, and the legislation that followed it, should not be above reproach. At the time of writing, the Taylor Report is over 30 years old. The context in which football is played now is significantly different to that when the report was drafted. In particular, how football is consumed as a product has changed; the Taylor Report was not just pre all-seater stadia, but before subscription TV, social media, YouTube, and British 'ultra' groups. Further, some of the Report's assumptions have proven to be false, most notably the idea that all fans would simply get used to all-seater stadia, and at other times Taylor stepped back from proposing what could have been important and progressive safety measures, for example, by recommending that while "recognised supporters' organisations" should be consulted about safety issues, they should not be "full members" of SAGs (1990 para 152). Finally, although further major disasters have so far been avoided, there are still reported injuries and even the occasional fatality resulting from unsafe stadia or crowd management practices. The number of unreported (usually minor) injuries is incalculable, as it appears that very few of them are officially reported or recorded (Welford et al., 2019; SGSA, 2021).

We will cast a critical eye over the Football (Offences) Act 1991 (FOA) later in this chapter, but for the remainder of this section we will consider the issue of all-seater stadia. Taylor's recommendation that football clubs should replace terracing with all-seater stadia was leapt upon by the government; all-seater stadia had been identified in pre-Hillsborough parliamentary discussions as a potential panacea to the issue of 'hooliganism' in stadia.[6] Subsequently, the Football Spectators (Seating) Order 1994 provided that "only seated accommodation shall be provided for spectators at a designated football match" (Sch 2(1)) and that "spectators shall only be admitted to watch a designated football match from seated accommodation" (Sch 2(2)). This requirement was then included in the licence to admit spectators for all Premier League and Championship clubs by virtue of section 11(1) of the Football Spectators Act 1989 which provides that

> The Secretary of State may, by order, direct the licensing authority to include in any licence to admit spectators to any specified premises a condition imposing requirements as respects the seating of spectators at designated football matches at the premises; and it shall be the duty of the authority to comply with the direction.

The Taylor Report believed that although spectators may initially resist the move to all-seater stadia, they "will become accustomed and educated to sitting" (1990 para 76). However, our research suggests this prediction, and the development of physical infrastructure and crowd management tactics around it has had profound negative impacts upon public order and safety at matches. After what appeared to be initial acceptance of the regulations, by the late 1990s more and more fans started to stand in seated areas, particularly in away sections and the traditional football 'ends'. We regularly observed disputes between fans and stewards tasked to get them to remain seated. Ejections in home sections of some stadia even led to vendettas between fan groups, who resented the interference and treatment of them and their friends, and the club stewards and private security firms tasked with enforcing the all-seater regulations. Disputes between fans wishing to stand and those wishing to sit became common, typically expressed in terms of the difference between being a passive spectator (or "tourist") and an "atmosphere-generating" fan (Pearson, 2012, p. 74–79). At some modernised stadia, fans at the back of stands who stood to see over the fans standing in front of them found themselves still unable to see due to structures holding the roof above

[6] Hansard Commons 19 June 1985 Vol 81 Col 283–5.

their heads which had been designed in the expectation that fans would be seated. Further, as 'persistent standing' became more common, some fans started to take advantage of this situation to stand with friends that may have seats in other areas of the stand. Standing together with friends, which had been a key feature of the old terraces, became an option again. This practice of 'migration' started to become commonplace at some clubs, particularly when their fans travelled away from home.

By the 2010s, the problem of 'persistent standing' in certain stands or blocks at clubs become intractable, forcing safety officers and SAGs to take a more lenient and realistic approach to it, seeing the risk of disorder arising from attempts to force fans to sit as more of a threat to safety than the standing itself. The reality, that in most stands, persistent standing was no more dangerous than jumping up at moments of high excitement, made this relaxation more justifiable. Over time, threats by SAGs to close stands where persistent standing occurred, that had been common in the late 1990s and early 2000s, diminished. This was despite a Joint-Statement in 2013 noting that while "education, persuasion, and positive management of spectators" were preferable, these tactics "may need to be backed up with more robust action" (SGSA, 2013, p. 10–11). The reality was that standing was occurring almost everywhere and enforcement actions were essentially futile, so the focus of stewards and safety officers switched instead to protecting against the more direct concerns to spectator safety, such as keeping radial stairways clear. Some clubs, such as Cardiff City FC, even began to operate a model of localised risk assessment which effectively allowed them to develop semi-formalised standing sections in areas where it was judged to be safe because of the low-rake angles in the lower tiers of their new stadium. Nevertheless, while standing itself is not dangerous, migration that becomes possible only with persistent standing, does cause safety problems. Fans clustered together are more likely to fall over seats in front of them, sparking what is known as 'progressive crowd collapse', where fans falling create a domino effect, pushing down those in front. While we have yet to see a major crowd incident, minor injuries are commonplace, and it appeared only a matter of time before a fan was seriously injured or killed in a crowd collapse connected to migration (SGSA, 2021; Still, 2021).

Then, in arguably the most progressive reform to football crowd regulation since the Taylor Report, DCMS and the SGSA started to address the growing safety concerns about standing in seated areas. A rapid evidence review published in 2019 identified the scale of the persistent standing in England and Wales, along with the concomitant problems of migration, congestion, and the risk of progressive crowd collapse and injury (Welford et al., 2019). This led to the establishment of an SGSA-funded research project into the way in which different clubs were managing the issue. The final project, led by CFE Research and advised by Pearson and Professor Keith Still, concluded that the introduction of rails into each row where persistent standing occurred (known as 'safe standing') would help to mitigate the risks of crowd collapse and injury (SGSA, 2021). Following this finding, the Football Spectators (Seating) Order 2021 was introduced, which opted five "early adopter" clubs[7] out of the previous all-seater requirements and permitted the admission of spectators into 'safe standing' areas. In July 2022, the review into the operation of the "early adopter" sections reported significant improvements in crowd safety and no concurrent increase in disorder or problematic fan behaviour (Welford et al., 2022). Subsequently, the Football Spectators (Seating) Order 2022 permitted accommodation for, and the admission of spectators into areas, "where there are seats incorporating a barrier or seats with an independent barrier" (Sch. 1).

The Sporting Events (Control of Alcohol, etc.) Act 1985

The Sporting Events (Control of Alcohol, etc.) Act (hereafter SECAA) was introduced shortly before the Parliamentary recess of 1985 and as a reaction to the Heysel disaster and several incidents of violence and disorder at domestic football matches in the second half of the 1984/85 season. Its purpose was to reduce alcohol consumption before and at football matches, and in doing so to hopefully also reduce 'hooliganism'. The Bill was based on the Criminal Justice (Scotland) Act 1980 which

[7] Cardiff City, Chelsea, Manchester City, Manchester United, and Tottenham Hotspur.

prohibited completely the consumption of alcohol in football grounds[8] and on football 'specials', following the McElhone report of 1977 which had asserted there was a strong link between football violence and alcohol intake. Early on, the 1980 Act was credited for a reduction in disorder at Scottish grounds (Stoddart, 1983), but an attempt to introduce the ban south of the border in 1981 had been blocked by the then Conservative Government. The Bill was first read only 20 days after the Heysel disaster, and MPs complained about "the problems caused by the haste in which the Bill had been drafted".[9] The Bill did not receive the scrutiny of a standing committee and representatives of both Houses referred to the "unseemly haste" with which the Bill passed through the Commons, in a single rather bad-tempered debate, and onto the Lords.[10] SECAA was brought in despite the findings of the Report of the Official Working Group on Football Spectator Violence only a year earlier, which had recommended that alcohol legislation was unnecessary because the police had reported to them that alcohol was *not* a major factor for football violence in England and Wales, in contrast to the situation in Scotland pre-1980.[11] There is no doubt that alcohol (particularly beer) consumption, and visits to pubs, is an important feature of many fans' matchday experience (Brown, 1993; Dixon, 2014; Gibbons, 2019; Millward, 2006; Pearson, 2012; Richards, 2017; Rookwood, 2009; Stone, 2002; Sugden, 2002; Williams et al., 1989), but the widespread presumption that this consumption leads to increased violence at and around matches is not unproblematic (Pearson & Sale, 2011), and research from elsewhere in the world has also questioned the effectiveness of alcohol prohibitions on sale of alcohol in stadia (Nepomuceno et al., 2017).[12]

The statutory foundation for the attempt to reduce alcohol-related disorder at football matches is the offence created by section 2(2), which

[8] Section 18 Criminal Law (Consolidation) (Scotland) Act 1995 allows sporting events to be designated for the purpose of alcohol controls. In addition to football matches, senior men's international rugby union matches played at Murrayfield and Hampden are also designated.

[9] Hansard Commons 03 July 1985 Vol 82 Col 426.

[10] Hansard Commons 03 July 1985 Vol 82 Col 427; Hansard Lords 11 July 1985 Vol 466 Col 325.

[11] Paragraph 5.

[12] The courts, however, had previously been happy to support this purported link (*R v Doncaster Justices ex parte Langfield* QBD 149 JP 26, 22 Oct, 1984).

prohibits being "drunk" inside a designated sports ground or trying to enter the sports ground while drunk. To date, only football grounds have been "designated" for the purposes of the legislation.[13] The number of arrests or convictions under section 2(2) is not published by the Home Office, but the number of arrests for "alcohol offences" (which include all SECAA arrests and also the arrests for drunk and disorderly behaviour) have dropped ten-fold, from 1041 in 2010/11 to 153 in 2018/19. Given the long-established importance that alcohol has for the match-going behaviour of many fans in England and Wales, particularly those who travel away from home, the low number of arrests per season may be surprising. However, this merely illustrates what we have observed in our studies of fans and fan policing in England and Wales.

The observations carried out for this book supported previous findings, that generally, a wide amount of discretion is used by police officers and stewards when it comes to levels of intoxication; very drunk fans are allowed into football grounds in England and Wales as a matter of routine. It was usually the case that only when fans were so obviously drunk that they were literally unable to walk straight that they ran the obvious risk of being denied access to stadia, and even then, an arrest for the offence was unlikely. Sometimes fans would be advised to go away for a coffee and come back when they appear less drunk, but more often, they would not be given a second chance. On occasion, s.2(2) might be used to prevent access to a fan who smelled of alcohol and was acting in a disorderly manner, but other powers or conditions of entry could have been used to achieve the same result. It should also be noted at this point that we also observed several incidents where the police gave fans coercive escorts to public houses (i.e. gave them no option other than to be located within a public house that had been designated by the police as the 'away' pub), or contained fans in pubs for hours before kick-off, threatening with them with arrest if they left. This then raised very serious questions

[13] The Sports Grounds and Sporting Events (Designation) Order 2005 Schedule 1 covers, "football matches in which one or both of the participating teams represents a club which is for the time being a member (…) of the Football League, the Football Association Premier League, the Football Conference National Division, the Scottish Football League or Welsh Premier League, or represents a country or territory." It also covers matches in the FA Cup beyond the qualifying and preliminary rounds.

of the legitimacy of then subsequently arresting some of these very same fans for being drunk at turnstiles when they had previously been allowed to proceed, or even forcefully escorted, to the stadium for the match.

We are not criticising police officers or stewards for the discretion they show here to allow drunk fans into stadia. Drinking alcohol prior to watching a football match is normative for hundreds of thousands of match-going fans in Britain, and, as such, the numbers are simply too great to enforce this section rigorously without creating conflict, congestion, and potentially disorder, often at a time when crowds are starting to congregate around turnstiles shortly prior to kick-off. Arresting fans for section 2(2) would either create an impossible situation of mass arrest that would overwhelm officers and custody suites, or look unfairly arbitrary. Any arrest at such points would take officers away from their duties of crowd management during and after the game. At pre-match briefings we have attended, it was common for the Silver Commander to acknowledge that fans 'like a drink', but that officers should use their discretion not to arrest drunken fans unless there was no choice because they were so drunk they were a danger to themselves and others (usually because they could hardly walk, never mind fight). And often, as we will detail further in Chap. 8, enabling pre-match drinking provided a key strategic and tactical benefit for police operations. Put simply, facilitating access to alcohol is an important means through which police can reduce the threat of disorder. Furthermore, even denying access, rather than arresting, creates problems. Where the drunken supporter is an away fan, a refusal to allow them entry means they are left hanging around outside the stadium waiting for the match to finish or trying to locate a pub to watch the game. At almost all matches we observed for the purposes of this book, where such police action occurred, there would often be a handful of fans sat forlornly outside waiting for the match to finish and for them to be allowed back on the supporters coach or for their friends, with whom they would be travelling home. Some of these people were also left vulnerable to either attack from opposition fans or injury for other reasons such as a traffic accident or robbery.

This lack of enforcement undermines the potential power of section 2(2), because it means that fans can, and do, generally pay little attention to this provision and are often unaware that it is a criminal offence (as opposed to a breach of a condition of entry) to attempt to enter a football stadium while drunk (Pearson, 2012, p. 141). Furthermore, when combined with the other provisions of the SECAA, the failure to rigorously enforce section 2(2) not only undermines the legislation but also makes it counter-productive. We have criticised SECAA previously (Pearson, 2000; Pearson & Sale, 2011; Stott et al., 2012),[14] and the new observations that make up the empirical aspect of this book, particularly in Chap. 8, have done nothing but to support our scepticism. We can only conclude that SECAA offers no solutions to the problem of football-related violence, disorder, or anti-social behaviour, and that it has failed in its attempt to reduce alcohol consumption around matches. Moreover, it throws up several additional and exacerbating problems and as such it is our contention that SECAA is not an effective piece of legislation.

At the time the Bill flew through Parliament, the most contentious provision of SECAA was section 2(1), which makes it a criminal offence to be in possession of alcohol or (section 2(3)) any non-reusable (such as a flask) container for holding "any drink" which is capable of causing injury if thrown:

> (a) at any time during the period of a designated sporting event when [the spectator] is in any area of a designated sports ground from which the event may be directly viewed, or (b) while entering or trying to enter a designated sports ground at any time during the period of a designated sporting event at that ground.

Section 2(1) was introduced against widespread criticism about its public order utility and the damage it might cause to the income streams of clubs. It was also introduced despite the fact that there was already a ban on alcohol at the three matches that SECAA was a direct response to,[15] and despite the fact that the Association of Chief Police Officers did not want a ban and instead took the view that "strictly controlled drinking inside grounds is easier to police than increased and more dispersed

---

[14] See also the criticisms of Hall (2018).

[15] Hansard Commons 03 July 1985 Vol 82 Col 445.

drinking in pubs and in the streets away from the ground".[16] Several Lords and MPs noted that the problem of alcohol consumption at football was predominantly one that occurred outside stadia, and Lord Dean of Beswick argued that

> I have yet to see what the Minister or the Bill are trying to imply—people quaffing beer from cans in the stands at Maine Road or Elland Road. It just does not happen. I have never seen people sitting down in the stands swigging pints of beer at the football grounds to which I go. A lot of this is based on a completely false premise.[17]

The effect of the ban on alcohol consumption within sight of the match is difficult to measure due to a few variables that have altered over time. New generations of supporters have replaced those attending matches in the 1970s and 1980s, local pubs and bars around grounds have closed and new ones opened, attitudes to alcohol consumption have changed, and there has been widespread re-development of stadia and facilities in concourses. It is difficult to disentangle what impact SECAA s.2(1) has had in this wider context of change. What is clear is that many fans prefer to drink in pubs outside the stadium rather than arriving early and drinking in concourses, so one outcome of s.2 is that more fans may consume more alcohol in town or city centres prior to entering the stadium. 'Binge drinking', 'pre loading', or getting 'tanked up' before a match is a phenomenon many police officers talked about during our observations and which we observed routinely. This had the potential to create public order problems because, rather than consuming alcohol in a strongly regulated and segregated environment, fans would be more likely to drink in unsegregated pubs, usually out of sight of the police and we will detail examples of this in Chap. 8. Further, but perhaps most importantly in terms of public safety, the practice of getting 'tanked up' pre-match, rather than being able to consume alcohol while the match was taking place, also meant that some fans would arrive later at the

[16] Hansard Lords 11 July 1985 Vol 466 Col 325.

[17] Hansard Lords 11 July 1985 Vol 466 Col 333.

stadium, creating congestion at turnstiles, at vomitories, and on radial stairways (Pearson & Sale, 2011; Pearson, 2012; SGSA, 2021).

The efficacy of s.2(1) was revisited in the Taylor Report, which concluded that given that alcohol "aggravates problems of crowd control" (1990, p. 43), the ban should remain. The inquiry did not consider whether the legislation increased the likelihood of fans arriving later at stadia (which had been a concern expressed by the Football Association), but noted that there was little evidence that fans would be encouraged to arrive earlier if the ban was relaxed, due to the poor quality of service and beer. Taylor concluded that

> I hope, in halcyon days ahead, a better atmosphere at football grounds may justify bans being relaxed. I do not, however, think the present time is ripe for such relaxation… it would be a retrograde or at least premature step at this time to restore a blanket license to sell alcohol at designated sports events (1990 Para 256 and Para 258).

But it is our view that s.2(1) has had an additional negative impact upon crowd safety, which was not considered in the Taylor Report. With concourses typically the only place where alcohol can be consumed, these areas regularly become congested with fans queuing at bars and drinking alcohol. With limited space, and few entrances or exits, these can be areas that police enter only with trepidation, particularly if they are needed to defuse disorder (Pearson & Sale, 2011). Over the decades of our more general observations, we have directly observed two major disturbances that have occurred inside stadiums as a direct result of alcohol restrictions being imposed. In one case, bar staff mistakenly opened bars in the concourse at half-time only to close them a short time later, after realising their error. This in turn led to minor confrontations with fans becoming aggressive because the bar had been open but then had been closed. The police then responded to by sending officers in full 'riot gear' into the crowded concourse. The subsequent interactions between police and fans then escalated the tensions and the situation developed into widespread collective violence that continued outside the stadium after the fixture had concluded. According to our observations, had the bar simply remained open the violence simply would not have developed. One relatively recent notable development in the norms of fan behaviour, particularly amongst travelling fans, has been the emergence of 'concourse parties', whereby fans gather at half-time, or sometimes pre-match, to sing, chant, and throw beer into the air in collective revelry. This practice has developed to be very common amongst a number of clubs' travelling support, usually despite resistance and complaints from other fans. In these ways section 2(1) therefore continues to play a potentially negative role when it comes to fan experience and safety.

Section 1 of SECAA attempted to confront the problem of fans becoming drunk on transport to matches, thereby posing a threat when they arrived at the match venue. The section applies only to "public service vehicles" and trains that are used for the "principal purpose" of carrying passengers to a match. Section 1A[18] extends this to other vehicles capable of carrying more than eight passengers. Sections 1 and 1A make it an offence to knowingly cause or permit alcohol to be consumed in the vehicle or for passengers to be drunk or have alcohol in their possession on the journey. Section 1 appears to have its roots in the problems historically caused on 'football specials' which we detailed in Chap. 2. However, by the time the Sporting Events Bill passed through Parliament, there was concern that the methods used by many fans to travel to matches had changed, with greater use of scheduled train services and private vehicles[19] that would not be covered by Section 1. As Denis Howell MP noted in the Commons during the brief passage of the Bill, "In my experience there is a much greater problem on ordinary passenger trains than on trains likely to be covered by the designation procedure. That will be extremely important in five or 10 years' time, when most people have forgotten these debates."[20] It was also noted that football

[18] Added by the Public Order Act 1986 s.40(1).

[19] Interestingly, the government took the position that the ban should not be extended to private vehicles because it would be too difficult for police to prove their primary purpose was to attend matches despite the courts (in what was presumably a reference to *Moss v MacLachlan* [1985] IRLR 76) recently supporting the policing doing exactly this in regard to flying pickets during the Miners' Strike. (Hansard Commons 03 July 1985 Vol 82 Col 428, Douglas Hogg MP).

[20] ibid.

'specials' had not been a factor in the Millwall v Luton riot, as the travelling fans had instead used scheduled train services.[21]

As with section 2, our argument is that section 1 of SECAA has, at best, had a modest impact upon spectator behaviour and consumption of alcohol. While it is safe to say that the restrictions have reduced (although not eliminated) alcohol consumption on chartered transport (particularly 'official' club coaches), it has also had the impact of pushing some fans away from official travel and towards independent travel. Research has also noted how fans wanting to drink on long journeys to matches at away or neutral venues would look to mitigate the impact of alcohol restrictions by travelling earlier or smuggling alcohol on board (Pearson & Sale, 2011; Pearson, 2012). This can have an adverse effect on supporter behaviour but also the ability of police to manage visiting fans, with many supporters arriving early, unexpectedly drunk, or at different and unexpected locations. A case study of Cardiff City's troublesome visiting support in the early 2000s (to which we will return in Chap. 9) noted how the legislation appeared to be encouraging fans from chartered coach services, which could be more easily monitored, onto scheduled train services where the risk of confrontation with rival supporters was more likely. Attempts to work around the legislation by turning a blind eye to alcohol consumption on the coaches had a dramatic impact on reducing disorder involving visiting Cardiff supporters, but inevitably came up against blockages from some police commanders and forces who were not willing to support the policy of flexible enforcement (Stott, Hoggett and Pearson, 2012). The number of police hours put into working around or mitigating SECAA, a statute they never asked for, with deficiencies that were made abundantly clear at the time, remains remarkable. Large numbers of fans on scheduled services can also cause problems in terms of behaviour and over-crowding for other travellers, who may feel intimated by large groups of raucous (usually) men. In 2018 this led to the creation of a cross-sector 'Transforming Football-Related Travel' working group to consider how best to mitigate the problem, but time and time again SECAA proved a blockage to progressive proposals.

---

[21] ibid Col. 435.

Aside from the practical problems related to the enforcement of SECAA and its unintended consequences, there is another issue that needs to be raised before we move on: its perceived (il)legitimacy. The first issue here is that both sections 1 and 2 of SECAA rely on a subjective definition of "drunk". It is not only in SECAA that the subjective definition of drunkenness appears in English law, without any attempt at defining the term, the Licensing Act 1872 is still in force and makes it an offence to be drunk in a public place. However, offences where the crime can be made out by virtue of the subjective opinion of a police officer, do raise questions of legitimacy where this opinion is disputed by the arrestee or onlookers. Furthermore, the offences of being drunk in a stadium or on regulated transport, or of carrying alcohol or other drink containers are strict liability offences. Despite concerns expressed about such 'absolute offences',[22] there is no requirement for the prosecution to demonstrate *mens rea*, that is, that the defendant has possessed recklessness or criminal intent; accidentally getting drunk, carrying alcohol, or consumption within sight of the pitch is still a criminal offence.[23] Finally, many fans consider that the application of these alcohol regulations to football, and not to other sports, leisure events, or crowd gatherings, is inherently unfair. These concerns are important, particularly when we consider whether 'procedurally just' policing can assist in reducing the risk of crowd disorder.

Sporting Events Act (Fireworks)

Section 40(2) of the Public Order Act 1986 introduced a new section 2A into SECAA, making it an offence to be in possession of "any article or substance whose main purpose is the emission of a flare for purposes of illuminating or signalling (as opposed to igniting or heating) or the

[22] Described by one MP in the Commons debate on SECAA as "obnoxious" (Hansard Commons 03 July 1985 Vol 82 Col. 443).

[23] While this is not a common problem, it is possible for fans to innocently carry alcohol into areas of concourses where the pitch is in view, to forget about miniature bottles of liquor that they had intended to consume earlier, or to carry alcohol into the stand because they are ignorant it is an offence.

emission of smoke or a visible gas" within sight of the pitch at, or while attempting to enter, a designated sporting event. Once again, although the title of the statute refers to 'Sporting Events', this only applies to football matches. Although setting off flares or smoke bombs at designated football matches has been an offence since 1987, numbers of smoke bombs that have been released have increased dramatically as the twenty-first century progressed. In the research conducted by the authors during this time in England and Wales, smoke bombs were by no means ever present, but it was not unusual for us to observe one or two to be ignited, particularly in away sections, following important goals. This is in contrast with many ultra groups elsewhere in the world, who use pyro extensively, particularly in pre-planned 'Tifo' displays (e.g. Brechbühl et al., 2017; Stott et al., 2018).

Citing the potential risk to the health and safety of spectators by the ignition of pyrotechnic devices, there have been a number of attempts by governing bodies and safety authorities to warn spectators against their use. A 2016 UEFA Report (Smith, 2016) set out the potential health dangers in terms of burns and smoke inhalation, but was rather limited in scope to a chemical analysis of different forms of device and failed to engage with crowd or medical science in its conclusions. Its failures to consider safer alternatives led to *Football Spectators in Europe*, who were credited as a partner to the report, openly criticising it. In contrast, messaging from the Football Supporters Association focused less on the danger of the device and more on the danger of being caught with a pyrotechnic and being subject to criminal proceedings. Arguably, such risks are much more observable and realistic to fans using smoke bombs in England and Wales and were reinforced by pyro 'amnesty bins' and the use of 'sniffer dogs' by police and stadium security staff. As a result, in contrast to some of the other laws discussed in this chapter, and many approaches to pyro elsewhere in Europe, s.2A can be seen not only as a proportionate law to reduce a genuine risk but also as a law that has largely been applied sensibly, working with supporters. Pre-'Lockdown', this was potentially reflected in the arrest statistics for football-related offences in England and Wales; while pyro arrests increased from 8 in 2010/11 to a peak of 188 in 2013/14, there followed a steady decline, with 82 arrests made in 2018/19.

The Football (Offences) Act 1991 and the Criminal Justice and Public Order Act 1994

The Taylor Report famously recommended that perimeter fences around football matches should be removed, or lowered and/or have spikes detached, to help prevent the kind of crush that occurred at Hillsborough. However, given the perceived threat of 'hooliganism' at the time, and the relatively high number of reported 'football-related' arrests, it was felt that removing fences could only be done safely with some mitigation of the risk of fans invading the pitch. This led to Football (Offences) Act 1991 and s.166 of the Criminal Justice and Public Order Act 1994, which criminalised pitch invasions and a number of other activities that were considered likely to provoke disorder and pitch invasions, indecent and racist chanting, missile throwing, and ticket touting. The suggestion of criminalising more activities at football was not a new one, and the Popplewell Report recommended in 1986 that "running onto the pitch without good reason and missile throwing should constitute offences" (Popplewell, 1986: 4.47). Throwing missiles and indecent or racist chanting could be prosecuted under existing legislation, particularly the relatively new section 5 Public Order Act 1986 offence of Causing Harassment Alarm or Distress, which could also capture aggressive pitch invasions themselves. However, Taylor considered that the offences were not just needed to punish but deter, (1990, para 299), and many clubs took the opportunity to advertise the new crimes on the reverse of advertising hoardings, although whether this had any effect is less clear (Pearson, 2000).

The Football (Offences) Act applies to designated football matches only,[24] and section 2 of the statute makes a criminal offence "to throw anything at or towards", the playing area, the area between the stands and the pitch, and any area where fans may be present. The section contains

[24] Section 1. s.(2), The Football (Offences) (Designation of Football Matches) Order 2004 defines a designated match for the purposes of the legislation as being "an association football match in which one or both of the participating teams represents a club which is for the time being a member (…) of the Football League, the Football Association Premier League, the Football Conference or the League of Wales, or represents a country or territory". The Football (Offences) (Designation of Football Matches) (Amendment) Order 2022 adds elite women's football to this list.

a defence of lawful authority or excuse, contained in a reverse burden of proof which means the defendant would need to demonstrate to the court it was more likely than not that they had this authority or excuse. The defence of lawful excuse would presumably cover a situation where a fan picked up an already-lit flare or smoke bomb to throw onto the pitch to protect them or other fans from burning or smoke inhalation. How lawful authority would operate as a defence is less clear, but presumably, this may capture fans being given balloons or ticker-tape to throw by the home club. As the legislation does not limit itself to spectators, lawful authority or excuse would presumably also cover players taking throw-ins! Section 2 had been largely unproblematic and sensibly enforced—fans are likely to be charged for throwing missiles (usually coins, lighters, bottles, or mobile phones) at players, but there has been a relative absence of contentious cases relating to balloons, ticker-tape, or inflatables. However, arrests for missile throwing bucked the pre-Covid-19 lockdown trend, rising from 64 in 2010/11 to 113 in 2018/19, possibly as improving CCTV technology made identification and prosecution of perpetrators more possible.

Section 3 of the Football Offence Act 1991 introduced a specific criminal offence to "engage or take part in chanting of an indecent or racialist nature at a designated football match". Although, at the time of the Taylor Report, chanting which could cause harassment, alarm, or distress was already an offence under s.5 of the Public Order Act (POA) 1986, it was felt that creating a specific offence of indecent or racialist chanting would make prosecutions easier, as there was no requirement for the prosecution to prove the likelihood of the effect of the chanting. It is important here to remember the context of this legislation, which was proposed alongside the removal of perimeter fences; the legislative concern was not the chanting itself, but the risk that the chanting might provoke a response from opposition supporters who, without fences, might invade the pitch to confront their rivals. Originally the legislation only criminalised engaging in, "the repeated uttering of any words or sounds in concert with one or more others",[25] meaning that individual chanting would not be captured (but could be an offence under s.5 POA

[25] Original FOA 1991, s.3(2)(a).

1986). As the under-secretary of state for the Home Office explained at the time,

> it would be a mistake to criminalise a single racialist or indecent remark that might not be widely audible in the ground; to do so would set the threshold for criminal behaviour too low. We wish to prevent group chanting, which is repeated and loud and may spark trouble, and if it occurs, to prosecute and punish the offenders.[26]

What was 'indecent' was not defined, although it was suggested rather obscurely during the Bill's progress through Parliament that it meant words or phrases that would be "unprintable in Hansard".[27] If we apply *R v Stamford*[28] (a case relating to indecent photographs), it was held that it would be up for the Tribunal of Fact to determine whether particular words or phrases were indecent. 'Racialist' chanting would also include chanting that referred to nationality.[29]

Since the enactment of the Football (Offences) Act, there has been significant legislative creep of the provision relating to indecent or racialist chanting. Section 9 of the Football (Offences and Disorder) Act 1999 removed the requirement that the chanting needed to be carried out "in concert with one or more others" and extended the prohibition to individual chanting. This therefore deviated from the initial intention of LJ Taylor and Parliament. Increasingly s. 3 FOA became a regulatory offence, cut adrift from its rationale in terms of reducing violence in stadiums. It has been used extensively to charge and prosecute individuals engaged in homophobic chanting, regardless of whether the words in the chant could be deemed indecent, or whether the provocation of violence was likely. A further legislative extension, the Football (Offences) Amendment Bill 2017, would have further extended the offence, replace 'racialist' with 'racist', include gestures as well as words, and cover sexual

[26] Hansard Commons 19 April 1991 Vol 189, Col 733.

[27] Hansard Lords 09 May 1991 Vol. 528 Col 1268.

[28] (1972) 2 QB 391.

[29] Hansard Lords *09 May 1991 Vol 528 Col 1273*. In *Director of Public Prosecutions v Stoke on Trent Magistrates' Court and Another* [2003] EWHC 1593 Admin, which remains the only reported case on the FOA 1991, it was confirmed that "paki" was a "racialist" term for the purposes of s.3 (see also Parpworth, 2003).

orientation, gender reassignment, and any protected characteristics under s.4 of the Equality Act 2010. In 2019 it failed to complete its passage through Parliament, and proposals to extend the law in this direction were rejected by the Law Commission in 2021 (Law Commission, 2021).

Despite improvements in CCTV, and systems at many clubs allowing fans to anonymously report fans for indecent racist chanting, section 3 has proven difficult to enforce.[30] Between 2010/11 and 2018/19, the UKFPU reported an average of just 24 arrests. In recent years, most of these reported arrests have been for either racist or, increasingly, homophobic chanting. The widespread indecent chanting that accompanies almost all professional football matches in England and Wales appears to have been unaffected, and while clubs will occasionally eject or ban fans for indecent language, arrests are almost unheard of for this under section 3. The overt racist chanting of the 1970s and 1980s has died out, and while chants with racial undertones do from time to time appear, in recent years these have tended to die out, or at least be pushed away from the stadia, by a combination of club messaging and self-regulation amongst fans (Pearson, 2012, p. 162–7).[31] However, the low numbers of arrests under s. 3 do not reflect the number of "football-related racist incidents" recorded by UKFPU which increased to 152 in the 2018/19 season. This tracked, at a slightly lower level, incidents of racist abuse reported to the 'Kick it Out' campaign.[32] However, this does not necessarily mean that instances of racial abuse in and around stadia, or even involving match-going football fans, are increasing, with many of the incidents reported taking place on social media platforms.

Section 4 of the Football (Offences) Act makes it a criminal offence to "go onto the playing area, or any area adjacent to the playing area to which spectators are not generally admitted, without lawful authority or lawful excuse". The introduction of an offence of invading the pitch was recommended by LJ Taylor who concluded that "running on the pitch

---

[30] Greenfield and Osborn (1996b) argued that this was partially due to the fact that it was stewards rather than police who were more likely to observe the offence.

[31] It appears that similar progress is being made to reduce the mass homophobic chanting such as "Chelsea Rent Boys".

[32] House of Lords 'Racism in Football' Library Briefing *researchbriefings. files. parliament.uk*

often provokes and is a prelude to disorder",[33] although it had been suggested as an amendment to SECAA back in 1985.[34] Interestingly, Taylor hinted that the police should "exercise sensible discretion and judgment" not to use the new offence against traditional pitch invasions, "when the game is over simply from *joie de vivre* or to pat players on the back".[35] Arrests for a breach of s. 4, in contrast to s. 3, are much easier to make, with pitch invaders usually caught by security and handed immediately to police officers in the stadium. In 2018/19 there were 158 arrests, slightly down on the nine-year average of 186 per season.

Section 4 is, by criminal law standards, an exceptionally brief statutory offence, which is widely drafted to incorporate any incursion into any area beyond that which spectators are "generally admitted". At the time the section was drafted, most stands were directly adjacent to the pitch, usually separated by no more than waist-high advertising hoardings and a narrow 'cinder track'. Therefore, leaving the stand would almost inevitably lead to encroachment onto the pitch and interference with the game. However, post-Taylor Report, stand and stadium reconstructions saw this area between stand and pitch increase. In particular, space started to increase between the stand and the advertising hoardings. At the elite level, these old wooden hoardings were replaced by larger, wider LED boards, their increased size dictated by the regulations of the elite tournaments. Leaving the stand at most grounds therefore no longer means encroaching onto the pitch, with its potential provocative effect. Nevertheless, presence in these areas remains covered by the offence, meaning that a larger area is off-limits than when the legislation was drafted. Further, when LJ Taylor initially recommended the offence, his assumption was that fans in seated areas would be sat down; he did not foresee the dynamic that we currently see when football is viewed from popular seating areas, with standing, migration, and clustering of supporters, and blockages of radial stairways.

[33] Para 289.

[34] Hansard House of Lords 11 July 1985 Vol 46 (Lord Harris of Greenwich moved Amendment No. 14: after Clause 2).

[35] Para 301.

The defence of 'lawful authority' would include a situation where a police officer or club official invited the fan to enter this area and lawful excuse would include a fan needing to enter this area 'when there is a hazard or an emergency',[36] which would include crowd disorder or crowd crushing.[37] It would also include being a member of staff working at the event (not least a football player!). Lawful excuse might arise from being pushed over the perimeter divide by another fan, or escaping over the divide to avoid injury, for example in a crowd crush. However, once again the statutory defence places the burden of proof upon the defendant. While it is easy enough for a defendant to demonstrate that they had lawful authority to be in the prohibited area, demonstrating they were there because they had been pushed or needed to escape raises problems, particularly when access to CCTV footage may be key to proving the defence. In short, the s.4 offence criminalises a greater amount of non-harmful fan activity, while simultaneously making it difficult for fans to avail themselves of any defence. The legality of these reverse burdens of proof has not yet been tested in the courts, but following the leading case of *Sheldrake*,[38] they could be considered an unlawful infringement of Article 6(2) European Convention on Human Rights (ECHR), which establishes the presumption of innocence. Following the Supreme Court decision in *Director of Public Prosecutions v Ziegler and others*,[39] the 'lawful excuse' defence also raises the possibility of defendants being able to successfully contest s. 4 prosecutions on the grounds of the freedom of assembly and expression under ECHR Articles 10 and 11, particularly where fans invade the pitch to protest. We will return to the human rights issues in Chap. 7, and to reform of the Football (Offences) Act 1991 in Chap. 10. However, at this stage it will suffice to say that, once again, we have a legislative provision that has the potential to be applied in ways that fans would not see as legitimate for its stated purpose of preventing crowd violence and disorder, and which is outdated in terms of both the development of football fandom and the law.

---

[36] Football (Offences) Bill, Standing Committee C, 27 March 1991.

[37] The Standing Committee specifically referred to Heysel.

[38] *Sheldrake v The Director of Public Prosecutions* [2004] UKHL 43.

[39] [2021] UKSC 23.

The final offence proposed by the Taylor Report took a little longer to reach the statute book. Section 166 of the Criminal Justice and Public Order Act 1994 introduced an offence for an unauthorised person to sell, offer, or expose for sale a ticket for a designated football match in a public place or, while acting in the course of a trade or business, anywhere. This offence was subsequently extended[40] to cover service providers in the UK advertising and selling tickets to customers based in other European Economic Area countries or on the internet. Despite the prevalence of unauthorised sale of football tickets on websites and social media, and what should be a fairly easy trail of inculpatory evidence, in 2018/19 there were a mere 17 arrests for the offence, although it is possible that online touts in particular are being charged following voluntary attendance at a police station. The purpose of the new offence was to prevent ticket 'touts' undermining segregation policies, but in reality the professional touts were able to continue largely unhindered, while the legislation too often caught fans selling on tickets of friends or family members at face value to supporters of the same team. Touting tickets for other sports, entertainment, and music events is not a criminal offence (although it will be unlawful under civil law), and purchasing a football ticket off a tout is also not an offence.

There are several key points to draw out of the analysis of the offences recommended by the Taylor Report. First is the fact that despite a number of attempts to provide piecemeal updates to them, they have failed to keep pace with either changes to football fan practices, developments in stadia infrastructure, development of human rights protections, or societal developments relating to equality and discrimination. Increasingly, they look like regulatory offences rather than ones needed to prevent public disorder, as was their initial aim. Secondly, the way that the offences are designed, seemingly to make conviction for the behaviour easier, again creates law which looks unfairly balanced against fans, without justification. Once more, this reflects our earlier arguments about the desire for *control* over fan behaviour and raises questions of the legitimacy of the law in the eyes of the fans, as well as the legitimacy of police action trying to enforce it.

[40] Section 53 of the Violent Crime Reduction Act 2006 introduced s.166A.

Other Relevant Legislative Provisions

While the imposition of new offences in football was unusual for its specificity, there was a wider political context in which this criminalisation and regulation regime took place. The 1980s and 1990s Conservative Governments introduced a number of broader criminal offences which, although primarily brought in with other public order targets in mind, such as picketing miners, illegal 'ravers', or hunt saboteurs, were also used extensively against football fans. We will not consider these in detail here, but the use of the core Public Order Act 1986 offences was evidenced in our observations. In particular, section 4 "threatening behaviour" and section 5 "behaviour likely to cause harassment, alarm or distress" are widely used offences, with sections 3 (affray) and 2 (violent disorder) typically reserved for mass incidents of violence away from stadia. Despite a suggestion that section 14 powers allowing the police to place restrictions on assemblies could be used to impose restrictions on football matches,[41] we are not aware of any such use of this power in football.

In addition to the Public Order Act, the offence of drunk and disorderly behaviour, and common law powers the police possess to detain to prevent a breach of the peace, there are several other powers that have been utilised against football fans in a more controversial manner. Often it appeared to us that football 'risk supporters' were guinea pigs for the police testing of new powers. For example, section 60 of the Criminal Justice and Public Order Act 1994 permits stop and search for weapons or other prohibited items where a s.60 order is put in place by an officer of the rank of Inspector or above. We observed first-hand, and heard accounts in the courts, of s.60 being used extensively against football fans, although there was a reduction in its use following the introduction of the *Best Use of Stop and Search* scheme in 2014 by the Home Office and College of Policing. It often seemed that these stops were less about searching fans for weapons (the use of which are relatively rare in violent encounters between the 'firms') and more an opportunity for gathering

[41] For example, Margaret Thatcher's statement to Parliament following Heysel (Hansard Commons 3 June 1985 Vol 82 Col 21). See also Williams (1987, p. 174).

intelligence about the names and addresses of groups of suspected 'risk fans' (see also Greenfield & Osborn, 1996a, 1996b).

The now repealed section 27 of the Violent Crime Reduction Act 2006, which provided the police with the power to direct an individual engaging in alcohol-related disorder or anti-social behaviour away from a locality, was also briefly used against groups of football supporters in a manner which was not anticipated in the drafting of the legislation. This led to several successful compensation claims by groups of football fans against whom the power had been unlawfully used (James & Pearson, 2015). Finally, our observations revealed the unlawful use of Anti-Social Behaviour Dispersal Orders under section 35 of the Anti-Social Behaviour, Crime and Policing Act 2014. As with section 27, while these powers could be lawfully used against individuals, in football contexts some forces used them more broadly against groups, in absence of the individual assessment of risk that is required. Indeed, on one occasion while carrying out fieldwork, Pearson was corralled by police and was in the process of being issued a s.35 dispersal order as part of the group he was observing. Once again, we can see both the potential misuse of police powers and also the likelihood that fans will *perceive* the illegitimate use of powers against them. Indeed, on the occasion in question, the local newspaper ran a story the following day, questioning the legitimacy of the policing operation (see Chap. 8, case study 3). This perception, which may also result from vicarious reports in newspapers of successful legal challenges by other fans, or incidents that happen directly to them, or are recalled by close friends or even family, can also have the effect of making fans believe that powers are being used illegitimately by police in the context of a football match even when, legally, they are not.

Football Banning Orders

Football banning orders (FBOs) are perhaps one of the most controversial legal tools used against football fans. FBOs are civil orders that were designed to prevent those who are known to pose a risk of violence or disorder in connection with football matches from attending matches, or other locations, on matchdays where disorder may occur, and from leaving the UK when the fan's club or national team is playing abroad. The idea of a 'prohibition order' was first discussed in the Commons debate over SECAA, specifically to prevent fans who had breached the proposed alcohol restrictions from entering a sports ground, but was not included in the legislation as it was felt there was no adequate means of enforcement.[42] Hopes at that time seemed instead focused on the proposed, but ultimately abandoned, Fan ID Card Scheme. However, the first iteration of the FBO, the Exclusion Order, arrived on the statute book by virtue of section 30 of the Public Order Act 1986, focusing on banning fans convicted of 'football-related' offences (as defined in the statute) from domestic matches. This was followed by the introduction of Restriction Orders by the Football Spectators Act 1989, which required fans convicted of football-related offences to report to their local police station when their club or national team was playing abroad, thereby preventing them from travelling. Following underuse of Restriction Orders, and major disorder involving England fans in Marseille 1998 and Brussels and Charleroi 2000 (see Stott & Pearson, 2007), the Football (Disorder) Act 2000 amalgamated these powers into a single 'Football Banning Order'. This can be imposed in one of three ways.

First, following conviction of a relevant offence under the amended section 14A of the Football Spectators Act 1989. Relevant offences for section 14A are set out in Schedule 1, which lists both specific football-related offences and also a wider array of offence if they occur at or on a journey to or from a match, "where the court makes a declaration that the offence related to that match or to that match and any other football match which took place during that period". The Police, Crime, Sentencing and Courts Act 2022 added to this any offences aggravated by hostility on the grounds of race, religion, disability, sexual orientation, or transgender identity,[43] where "the court makes a declaration that the offence related to a football match, to a football organisation or to a person whom the accused knew or believed to have a prescribed connection

[42] Hansard Commons 3 July 1985 Vol 82 Col 461-2.

[43] Protected characteristics currently set out in s.66(1) of the Sentencing Act 2020.

with a football organisation".[44] The inclusion of these new offences was a response to online racial abuse directed at players, particularly following the Euro2020 final, and indicates a departure from the previous aim of the power to confront disorder at football matches. At the time of writing there are also proposals for sale or possession of cocaine to be added to Schedule 1.[45] Previously, under s.14A(2), a court would then be expected to issue a FBO if "satisfied that there are reasonable grounds to believe that making a banning order would help to prevent violence or disorder at or in connection with any regulated football matches", but following the Police, Crime, Sentencing and Courts Act 2022, this requirement has been removed with an instruction instead that "the court must make a banning order in respect of the offender unless the court considers that there are particular circumstances relating to the offence or to the offender which would make it unjust in all the circumstances to do so". This will almost certainly make 14A FBOs easier to secure. Combined with the addition of online offences, the changes also increasingly give 14A FBOs the characteristics of punishments, rather than the preventative measures that they were originally intended to be.[46]

Second, in addition to offences proven in British courts, section 22 also provides that a FBO can be imposed upon conviction of a corresponding offence outside the UK. And third, in a significant extension of the FBO following the disorder at the 2000 European Championships, they can be imposed following an application ('on Complaint') by the Chief Officer of police under section 14B. Here, once it has been proved to the court that the respondent "has at any time caused or contributed to any violence or disorder in the United Kingdom or elsewhere"[47] and the court is "satisfied that there are reasonable grounds to believe that making a banning order would help to prevent violence or disorder at or in connection with any regulated football matches",[48] an FBO should

[44] Section 190. The Football Spectators (Prescription) Order 2022 defines, widely, the definition of regulated matches, organisations, and potential victims connected to organisations.

[45] *The Guardian*, 19/05/22. https://www.theguardian.com/football/2022/may/19/five-year-ban-fans-cocaine-football-matches?CMP=share_btn_tw.

[46] This potentially raises questions of double jeopardy under domestic law.

[47] Section 14B(2).

[48] Section 14B(4)(b).

also be imposed. Section 14B therefore does not require proof that the fan has committed any criminal offence.

Breach of an FBO is a criminal offence, even though imposition of one under s.14B does not require a conviction, meaning that FBOs are often referred to as 'hybrid' law (i.e. a mix of criminal and civil law) (Gardiner et al., 1998; Ashworth, 2004) or "two step provisions" (Von Hirsch & Simester, 2006). Football fans were once again guinea pigs for the development of novel legal instruments to attempt to manage social problems. The original FBOs pre-dated civil preventative orders such as Anti-Social Behaviour Order, Criminal Anti-Social Behaviour Orders, and Sexual Offences Prevention Orders. Reflecting our arguments above about fans being a testing ground, their structure and tests have also informed newer civil preventative orders such as Criminal Behaviour Orders and the proposed Serious Disruption Prevent Orders (aka 'Protest Banning Orders'). Furthermore, the threshold of 'helpfulness' that needs to be passed in order to justify imposition of a s.14B FBO is significantly lower than the 'necessity' threshold that operates for most other civil preventative orders.[49]

A significant amount has been written about the legality of football banning orders and this is ground that we do not intend to re-tread in detail here. Concerns were first expressed when the proposal for FBOs 'on complaint' was made about the extent to which this would disproportionately restrict the civil liberties of fans (Pearson, 1999) and their rights under EU law (Stott & Pearson, 2006). Following the key case of *Gough and Smith v Chief Constable of Derbyshire*,[50] the legality of the s14B FBO appeared to be confirmed by the Court of Appeal, albeit with the proviso from Lord Phillips that magistrates needed to be sure to a standard of proof approaching the criminal standard that the (unconvicted) defendant had been engaged in the previous football-related violence and disorder as alleged in the application. Whether this standard was being applied in practice was questioned following a study of s14B cases in the Magistrates and Crown Courts (James & Pearson, 2006). This study also

[49] Although the helpfulness test has been adopted in the Criminal Behaviour Order (Anti-social Behaviour, Crime and Policing Act 2014 s.22(4)).

[50] [2002] EWCA Civ 351.

cast doubt as to the justification for applying for a number of s.14B FBOs in observed cases; some appeared based on flimsy evidence of little more than guilt by association, whereas others had such strong evidence of violent criminality that questions needed to be asked why criminal prosecutions had not been brought instead. The study also reported the high costs that were awarded to the police for unsuccessfully contested applications and questioned whether this could be incentivising FBO applications. Hopkins further developed this, arguing that a number of forces used s.14B FBOs in order to fund football policing units (Hopkins, 2014), an argument largely supported by the more recent findings of Hester (2021) and our own observations. We know of one force that was even using the money generated in this way to fund other areas of policing not connected to football.

Further, whether the contemporary FBO is still compliant with ECHR Articles 6 and 7[51] is highly questionable. There has been significant and sustained legislative creep in the restrictive power of both s.14A and 14B FBOs, with bans lasting for longer periods and entailing more restrictive conditions (e.g. confiscation of passports during 'controlled periods' around matches abroad, and 24-hour exclusion zones around stadia, train stations, and town centres) that are typically applied to all FBOs, regardless of the reason for their application. This has, in effect, transformed the FBO into a "super-FBO" (James & Pearson, 2018). These developments have taken place concurrent with the increased use of FBOs not only against those who organise and engage in serious football-related violence, who were the original targets of the s.14B FBOs, but increasingly against low-level disorder and anti-social behaviour (James & Pearson, 2018). Taking all factors into account, the comparison of the contemporary super-FBO with a civil injunction, which was one of the arguments used to uphold the legality of s.14B FBOs in *Gough*, no longer holds water.

Even if we accept the Court of Appeal's ruling in *Gough* that s.14B FBOs were compliant with Arts.6 and 7 ECHR, FBOs have developed

[51] Article 6—Right to a Fair Trial; Article 7—No one shall be held guilty of any criminal offence on account of any act or omission which did not constitute a criminal offence under national or international law at the time when it was committed.

> considerably since then, both through legislative amendment and through the range of conditions that have been imposed by the courts. *Gough* is quite simply no longer applicable to the current super-FBO regime (…) The use of generic conditions and durations of bans that do not reflect the supposedly preventive nature of FBOs, combined with questionable application of the higher standard of proof, leaves FBOs unlawful under Arts.6 and 7 ECHR. Thirty years of adaptation and abuse have seen the first CPO develop into an intrinsically punitive state sanction that is imposed unrestricted by the rigours of criminal evidence and procedure (James & Pearson, 2018: 61).

The unclear drafting of section 14 of the Football Spectators Act 1989 has received considerable criticism and attempts at clarification from the Court of Appeal (see below). Despite considerable effort by that Court to clarify the law relating to FBOs, it is difficult to disagree with Mark James's contention that another major appeal case or a statutory amendment is "inevitable" (James, 2017, p. 321).

We will return to the issue of possible legal reform of FBOs in Chap. 10, but for our current purposes we need to ask once again how effective the law has been in reducing football violence and disorder, how legitimate current laws relating to FBOs are seen by match-going fans, and what potential effect their pursuit by football policing units has upon groups of supporters. The problem here is that despite FBOs having been in place in various forms for over three decades, there has yet to be any research into their effectiveness in reducing football-related violence or disorder, either domestically or abroad. While the increase in FBO powers has corresponded with a decline in arrest figures at football, this does not tell us much given the unreliability of arrest statistics as indicators of crime (as discussed in Chap. 2). Even when we consider recidivism figures, which can be measured, the picture is confused, with claims of recidivism of only 8% nationally contrasting with local figures that suggest a rate as high as 70% (Hamilton-Smith et al., 2011, p. 44).

This means that in our assessment of the effectiveness of FBOs, we have to rely on conversations with fans and police officers about their perceptions of the impact of the powers. Both our observations, and those of a team of Scottish academics evaluating FBOs in England and

Wales, suggest FBOs are popular amongst officers and perceived to be effective in reducing the risk of violence; "we love the legislation," explained a participant in the Scottish study (Hamilton-Smith et al., 2011, p. 43). As we stated in Chap. 2, we think it is safe to conclude that s.14A FBOs have had a positive impact on reducing disorder. Banning fans who have been convicted of football-related offences of violence and disorder, not only from stadia but also from other areas where disorder can occur, is likely to mean that at least some of the fans will not reoffend for the duration that the order is in place. There is also the likelihood that the restrictions attached to FBOs mean that they will deter some fans from engaging in disorder. Again, this is the view of most football officers we have spoken with, and some of the fans we have carried out research with, going back to the 1990s. Whether FBOs have any impact upon disorder *abroad* involving English fans is less certain, with much evidence pointing to the fact that those who engage in mass disorder abroad, such as in Marseille (1998 and 2016), Albufeira (2004), and Charleroi (2000), are usually unknown to the police (Stott & Pearson, 2007).

When we specifically consider s.14B FBOs, once again there is little evidence that such orders have any significant impact on the likelihood of whether disorder abroad will occur or not. But unlike s.14As, there are also questions about the effectiveness of s.14Bs in reducing disorder domestically. First, there is the doubt that has been cast over the extent to which s.14B FBOs are being used against fans who are engaged in football-related violence (James & Pearson, 2006, 2018). Second, we need to consider the impact of s.14Bs upon the relationships between police and fans. As we will detail in this book, positive interaction and dialogue are shown to be fundamental to the effectiveness of football policing operations, and yet such dialogue relies on police legitimacy in the eyes of the fans. FBOs following the conviction for violence and disorder appear to be seen as legitimate by most fans, even those who would consider themselves as 'risk'; there is often the understanding expressed that it is 'a fair cop'. However, the perception of s.14B FBOs is different, and the traditional role of spotters in gathering intelligence to build profiles enabling s.14Bs to be applied for is well-known in match-going fan circles. We have heard fans expressing the belief, rightly or wrongly, that some spotters have looked to 'fit up' innocent fans, and that staying out of the way of spotters was the best way to avoid having a FBO imposed upon you. Here, it is not necessarily important whether this is true; the outcome is that relationships between fan groups and football policing units at some clubs have at times completely broken down, with even 'non-risk' fans refusing to engage with spotters (Pearson, 2012, p. 116–7). This consequently reduces the ability of these officers to pick up useful intelligence or to be able to build relationships that could be useful in preventing or defusing disorder at a later date. We will discuss how this dynamic has played out when spotters are tasking with engaging in formal liaison duties later in the book.

Judicial Responses

We conclude this chapter with a brief discussion of judicial responses, through which of course the offences we have detailed above are interpreted and enforced through the courts. Early legal and socio-legal analysis of football crowd disorder, with no football-specific legislation to evaluate, focused on judicial responses to those charged with football-related offences. Reflecting our discussion in the previous chapter of the 'moral panic' that developed over 'football hooliganism' in the 1960s, 1970s, and 1980s, there has been some debate about the extent to which the judiciary bought into this panic, and whether this has been reflected in decisions on sentencing in these cases. It has been suggested that those against whom the 'hooligan' label was attached during the height of the moral panic about hooliganism in the late 1970s, were likely to receive higher sentences upon conviction than for those accused of the same offence but in different circumstances (Trivizas, 1981).[52] An analysis of reported sentencing appeal cases around this period appears to support this argument, with appeal court judges upholding high custodial sentences where "football hooliganism is established",[53] although there is some debate about the extent to which this sentencing policy was applied

[52] Trivizas argued that even when adjusted to take into account the demographics of those convicted, fines imposed for threatening behaviour in a football crowd context were 35–50% higher than for equivalent offences in non-crowd or political crowd contexts (1981, p. 344).

[53] *Mail v McDowell* [1980] 6 WLUK 302, per Kilner Browne, J.

at this time in the lower courts (Salter, 1985, 1986). At its extremes, judicial application of the 'hooligan' label could sound little different from the most sensational tabloid reporting:

> By the conduct of these defendants and others engaged in that riot the reputation of this country and of every person in it has been brought into contempt, certainly in Europe if not in the rest of the world. I know of my own knowledge that the foreign press call this particular form of mindless violence 'the English sickness'. It is a sickness and a scourge that threatens to destroy civilised life in our country and only sentences of the utmost severity in my view are adequate to demonstrate to all football hooligans everywhere what will happen to them if they take part in such violence and they are prosecuted to conviction (*R v Rogers-Hinks* 1989).[54]

Moreover, such participation by the judges in the construction of the phenomenon could have a very serious impact upon the trial outcome for the defendant (Pearson, 1998), as indeed it did in *Rogers-Hinks*.

The second way in which we saw the impact of judicial 'buy-in' to the social construction of football crowd disorder was in the failure of the courts to rigorously apply the principle of proportionality to the impact of FBOs on Complaint. When the case of *Gough and Smith v Chief Constable of Derbyshire* reached the High Court,[55] it was tasked to apply the test of proportionality,[56] to balance the restrictions of the ability of citizens to leave their EU member state against the suitability and necessity of FBOs. Such an assessment never took place with any rigour. Instead, once again, a sensationalised construction of 'hooliganism' was applied. Laws LJ painted a picture of a "rising spectre"[57] of 'hooliganism', that was "evil",[58] "a shame and a menace",[59] and a "sickening ill".[60] This was not based upon empirical evidence beyond statements made by the

[54] *R v Rogers-Hinks* (1989) 11 Cr App R (S) 234 at 237.

[55] *Gough and Smith v Chief Constable of Derbyshire* [2001] EWHC Admin 554.

[56] Drawn from *de Freitas v Permanent Secretary of Ministry of Agriculture* [1999] 1 AC 69.

[57] *Gough and another v. Chief Constable of Derbyshire* [2001] EWHC Admin 554, at heading 3.

[58] ibid, para 42.

[59] ibid, para 1.

[60] ibid, para 81.

Home Office. While Lord Phillips in the Court of Appeal did attempt to place restraints on the standard of proof required when s.14B FBOs were applied for, the hopelessly unbalanced assessment of the proportionality of the powers under EU law was not revisited.

The problem with evaluating judicial responses to football crowd violence and disorder is that most of this takes place out of view. While the UKFPU collate and publish the number of arrests and FBOs annually, they do not do the same for charges, prosecutions, or convictions (or indeed, acquittals). The football-specific offences detailed above are all triable at the Magistrates Court only and rarely lead to appeals that are recorded in the official law reports. Observations of s.14B FBO cases in the Magistrates Courts tended to suggest that magistrates and District Judges appeared to favour evidence presented by the applicant rather than the defendant and failed completely to scrutinise the proportionality of conditions. This supports long-established criticisms of criminal justice in the Magistrates Courts which point to high conviction rates, a system weighted in favour of the police, and a lack of critical attention (Carlen, 1976; McBarnet, 1981). Much of what McBarnet found in the late 1970s and early 1980s in terms of the "dressing down" of defendants by magistrates was observed in FBO cases. Considering the complexity of the FBO legislation, the fact that the Magistrates Court is still "a theatre without an audience" (McBarnet, 1981, p. 195) should be a matter of concern. However, despite these concerns, observations of FBO cases indicated little evidence of the reproduction of a moral panic about 'hooliganism' that we saw from the higher courts in the 1970s and 1980s. Some magistrates or District Judges even made a point of noting that they were match-going fans themselves.

Notwithstanding this, it is clear that there is a wide discrepancy in terms of success rate for FBO applications depending on the force applying for them (Hamilton-Smith et al., 2011, p. 45–56). Furthermore, the UKFPU funds available to apply for FBOs have reduced from £908,766 in 2010/11 to £385,833 in 2012/13 (Hester, 2021), driven by austerity in the Home Office. This decline in available funds correlates with a fall in FBOs during the same period, from 960 new orders to 471 (Hester, 2021). By August 2019, the number of FBOs in total had dropped to only 1771, from a peak of 3174 in 2011.[61] This reflected, pre-pandemic, an apparent move away from, the target-driven FBO industry, and a focus by some forces on alternative approaches (Hester, 2021).

Although it has to date not been engaged in the football-specific offences, the Court of Appeal has been forced to undertake a significant interpretative role in terms of FBOs, to the point that it has indicated its own displeasure at the legislative drafting. In *R v Doyle*, Lord Justice Hughes noted that "not for the first time, the complexity of legislation enacted in pursuit of an entirely necessary objective has caused no little trouble".[62] Characterising the Court of Appeal's role in its interpretation of FSA 1989 s.14 is difficult. On the one hand, it has held that "an isolated first incident" of violence or disorder can be sufficient for an FBO to be applied,[63] and that there is no need "for either repetition or propensity" of the behaviour,[64] which seems to go against the legislative intention of the section which was to confront those with the disposition towards organising or engaging in violence or disorder in the context of football matches. Furthermore, in *R v Thorpe*, the Court of Appeal held that a court had no discretion to impose an FBO that only banned the defendant from regulated matches involving particular clubs.[65] This was particularly disappointing given that blanket conditions make FBOs less likely to comply with ECHR Articles 6 and 7 (James & Pearson, 2018), an argument that was not considered by the Court despite the requirement in the Human Rights Act for it to do so.

On the other hand, the Court of Appeal's interventions have also had the effect of restricting some of the more draconian effects of both s.14A and 14B FBOs. In *Gough*, Lord Phillips was so concerned about the "serious restraints" on freedoms imposed by FBOs that he raised the standard of proof imposed upon the application to prove previous misbehaviour from a balance of probabilities to "a standard of proof that will, in

[61] Numbers have fallen further since, but due to the number of matches played behind closed doors due to Covid-19, it is impossible to read anything into this.

[62] *R v Doyle (Ciaran) and Others* [2012] EWCA Crim. 995, para 25.

[63] *R v Curtis* [2009] EWCA Crim 1225.

[64] *R* v *Hughes* [2005] EWCA Crim 2537, para 13. See also *R (White)* v *Blackfriars Crown Court* [2008] EWHC 510 (Admin).

[65] *Commissioner of Police of the Metropolis v Thorpe* [2015] EWHC 3339 (Admin).

practice, be hard to distinguish from the criminal standard".[66] In *R v Boggild*, the Court made it clear that an FBO should not inevitably follow from a conviction for a football-related offence,[67] and the Court of Appeal also ruled that s.14A FBOs should not be imposed following criminal behaviour, on journeys to and from matches, that was incidental to the match itself.[68] In *R v Elliott*,[69] the Court ruled that there had to be some 'nexus' between the offences committed and the match. This was further clarified in *R v Doyle*,[70] when Hughes LJ ruled that the first leg of the s.14A FBO test was only passed where the offence was "related to football matches", which was not proven by virtue of the fact that the offence took place on a journey to or from a match, but instead required the judge to make a "conscious conclusion that it was the football and its tribal excitement which had led to the unpleasant behaviour".[71] Following *Doyle*, and the more recent case of *Jelf*[72], "tribal chanting" at or around the time of the offence can play a pivotal evidential role in demonstrating a relation to a match,[73] which takes us round in a neat circle to the original anthropological explanations for football violence, when the phenomenon first entered the public perception (see Chap. 2). We will need to wait to see whether the changes to s.14A FBOs introduced by the Policing, Crime, Sentencing and Courts Act 2022 will limit the impact of these latter cases and make it harder for courts to reject the imposition of s.14A FBOs following conviction of a Schedule 1 offence.

---

[66] Para 90.

[67] *R v Boggild and Others* [2011] EWCA Crim 1928.

[68] *R v Smith* [2003] EWCA Crim 2480; *R v Mabee* [2007] EWCA Crim 3230; *R v Arbery* [2008] EWCA Crim 702.

[69] *R v Elliott* [2007] EWCA Crim 1002.

[70] *R v Doyle (Ciaran) and Others* [2012] EWCA Crim. 995.

[71] Para 25.

[72] *R v Jelf* [2020] EWCA Crim 631.

[73] Although in *Jelf*, the match itself was an England World Cup match being watched on television, when the offences actually arose from a local club rivalry.

Conclusions

Several inter-related arguments have been raised in this chapter that are important for our wider discussion of football regulation and management. First, we have detailed the way in which football fan behaviour has been regulated or criminalised, creating the increased potential for tension between fan groups and those tasked with policing them. Second, much of this legislation has been either poorly drafted, causing problems for the courts or raising questions about legality under the ECHR, or rushed through without consideration of the likely consequences (both in terms of enforcement and unintended consequences that in some cases can increase, rather than reduce, the risk of disorder). Third, research has shown that many of the legislative powers are seen by fans as being illegitimate. Offences are imposed on football fans rather than those of other sports and are often proven by way of strict liability or require a reverse burden of proof for a defence to come into play. And yet the penalties for even minor offences can be significant, with the imposition of a football banning order. Fans may be forgiven for feeling that the law is out to get them, and this in turn raises serious problems when it comes to the legitimacy of the police enforcing these laws. Finally, there has been a failure by successive governments to revisit and reform legislation that was introduced in a different era and a different context of both physical infrastructure and fan behavioural norms. Much of it was drafted for a different age of football fandom and has evolved into sometimes petty regulatory offences rather than those that genuinely confront public disorder. We will put forward our own recommendations for reforming the deficiencies we have identified, once we have discussed them in their empirical context, in Chap. 10.

References

Ashworth, A. (2004). Social Control and "Anti-social Behaviour": The Subversion of Human Rights? *Law Quarterly Review, 120*, 263–291.

Brechbühl, A., Schumacher-Dimech, A., & Seiler, R. (2017). Policing Football Fans in Switzerland—A Case Study Involving Fans, Stadium Security

Employees, and Police Officers. *Policing: A Journal of Policy and Practice, 14*(4), 865–882.

Brown, A. (1993). Ratfink reds: Montpellier and Rotterdam in 1991. In S. Redhead (Ed.), *The Passion and the Fashion: Football Fandom in New Europe* (pp. 33–44). Averbury.

Carlen, P. (1976). *Magistrates Justice*. Law. in Society.

Dixon, K. (2014). The Football Fan and the Pub: An Enduring Relationship. *International Review for the Sociology of Sport, 49*(2–3), 382–399.

Elliott, D., Frosdick, S., & Smith, D. (1997). The Failure of "Legislation by Crisis". In S. Frosdick & L. Walley (Eds.), *Sport and Safety Management*. Butterworths.

Gardiner, J., et al. (1998). Clause I – The Hybrid Law from Hell? *Criminal Justice Matters, 31*, 25–27.

Gibbons, T. (2019). *English National Identity and Football Fan Culture: Who Are Ya?* Routledge.

Greenfield, S., & Osborn, G. (1996a). When the Whites Go Marching In? Racism and Resistances in English Football. *Marquette Sports Law Review, 6*(*2*), 315–335.

Greenfield, S., & Osborn, G. (1996b). After the Act: the (Re)Construction and Regulation of Football Fandom. *Journal of Civil Liberties, 1*(*1*), 7–28.

Hall, M. (2018). Alcohol and Football Spectators: Time for a choice. *Criminal Law and Justice Weekly, 187*, 62–64.

Hamilton-Smith, N., Bradford, B., Hopkins, M., Kurland, J., Lightowler, C., McArdle, D., & Tilley, N. (2011). *An Evaluation of Football Banning Orders in Scotland*. Scottish Government Social Research.

Hartley, H. (2001). *Exploring Sport and Leisure Disasters: A Socio-Legal Perspective*. Cavendish.

Hester, R. (2021). Assessing the UK Football Policing Unit Funding of Football Banning Orders in Times of Austerity. *Policing: A Journal of Policy and Practice, 15*(*2*), 1188–1201.

Home Office/College of Policing. (2014). *Best Use of Stop and Search Scheme*. Home Office. https://assets.publishing.service.gov.uk/government/uploads/system/uploads/attachment_data/file/346922/Best_Use_of_Stop_and_Search_Scheme_v3.0_v2.pdf

Hopkins, M. (2014). Ten Seasons of the Football Banning Order: Police Officer Narratives on the Operation of Banning Orders and the Impact on the Behaviour of "Risk Supporters". *Policing and Society, 24*(*3*), 285–301.

James, M. (2017). *Sports Law*. MacMillan Law Masters.

James, M., & Pearson, G. (2006). Football Banning Orders: Analysing their use in Court. *Journal of Criminal Law, 70*(6), 509–530.

James, M., & Pearson, G. (2015). Public Order and the Rebalancing of Football Fans' Rights: Legal Problems with Pre-emptive Policing Strategies and Banning Orders. *Public Law, 3*, 458–475.

James, M., & Pearson, G. (2018). 30 Years of Hurt: The Evolution of Civil Preventative Orders, Hybrid Law, and the Emergence of the Super-Football Banning Order. *Public Law, 1*, 44–61.

Law Commission. (2021). *Hate Crime Laws: Final Report*. HC942 Law Com No 402

McArdle, D. (2000). *From Boot Money to Bosman: Football, Society and the Law*. Cavendish.

McBarnet, D. (1981). Magistrates Courts and the Ideology Justice. *British Journal of Law and Society, 8*, 181–197.

Millward, P. (2006). We've All Got the Bug for Euro Aways. *International Review for the Sociology of Sport, 41*(3), 357–375.

Nepomuceno, T. C. C., de Moura, J. A., Silva, L. C., & Cabral Seixas Costa, A. P. (2017). Alcohol and Violent Behavior Among Football Spectators: An Empirical Assessment of Brazilian's Criminalization. *International Journal of Law, Crime and Justice, 51*, 34–44.

Parpworth, N. (2003). The Offence of Racialist Chanting at a Football Match. *The Justice of the Peace, 167*(31), 586–588.

Pearson, G. (1998). The English Disease: Socio-Legal Constructions of Football Hooliganism. *Youth and Policy - The Journal of Critical Analysis, 60*, 1–15.

Pearson, G. (1999). Legitimate Targets? The Civil Liberties of Football Fans. *Journal of Civil Liberties, 4*(1), 28–47.

Pearson, G. (2000). Legislating for the Football Hooligan: A Case for Reform. In S. Greenfield & G. Osborn (Eds.), *Law and Sport in Contemporary Society* (pp. 182–200). Frank Cass.

Pearson, G. (2012). *An Ethnography of English Football Fans: Cans, Cops, and Carnivals*. Manchester University Press.

Pearson, G., & Sale, A. (2011). On the Lash: Revisiting the Effectiveness of Alcohol Controls at Football Matches. *Policing and Society, 21*(1), 1–17.

Popplewell Committee of Inquiry into Crowd Safety and Control at Sports Grounds. Interim Report, July 1985. London: HMSO Cmnd 9585.

Popplewell Committee of Inquiry into Crowd Safety and Control at Sports Grounds Final Report. 1986. London: HMSO Cmnd 9710.

Richards, J. (2017). *Sports Space: A Conceptual Model of Everton Football Club Match-day Fan Movement*. Unpublished PhD Thesis. University of Sydney.
Rookwood, J. (2009). *Fan Perspectives of Football Hooliganism: Defining, Analysing and Responding to the British Phenomenon*. VDM Verlag.
Salter, M. (1985). The Judges v. The Football Fan: A Sporting Contest? *Northern Ireland Legal Quarterly, 36*(4), 351–357.
Salter, M. (1986). Judicial Responses to Football Hooliganism. *Northern Ireland Legal Quarterly, 37*(3), 280–292.
Smith, T. (2016). *Pyrotechnics in Stadia: The Health and Safety Issues Relating to the Use of Pyrotechnics in Football Stadia*. UEFA. https://www.uefa.com/MultimediaFiles/Download/uefaorg/Stadium&Security/02/48/11/68/2481168_DOWNLOAD.pdf
Sports Grounds Safety Authority, et al. (2013). *Standing in Seated Areas at Football Grounds*. https://sgsa.org.uk/wp-content/uploads/2020/11/Standing-in-seated-areas.pdf
Still, K. (2021). *Applied Crowd Science*. Taylor Francis.
Stoddart, C. (1983). Criminal Justice (Scotland) Act 1980 - Its Early Years. *The Journal of Criminal Law, 47*, 209.
Stone, C. (2002). The Role of Football in Everyday Life. *Soccer and Society, 8*(2–3), 169–184. Signy.
Stott, C., Hoggett, J., & Pearson, G. (2012). Keeping the Peace: Social Identity, Procedural Justice and the Policing of Football Crowds. *British Journal of Criminology, 52*(2), 381–399.
Stott, C., Khan, S., Madsen, E., & Havelund, J. (2018). The value of Supporter Liaison Officers (SLOs) in Fan Dialogue, Conflict, Governance and Football Crowd Management in Sweden. *Soccer and Society, 2*(2), 196–208.
Stott, C. and Pearson, G. (2006). Football Banning Orders, Proportionality, and Public Order Policing. *Howard Journal of Criminal Justice, 45*(3), 241–254.
Stott, C., & Pearson, G. (2007). *Football Hooliganism: Policing and the War on the English Disease*. Pennant.
Sugden, J. (2002). *Scum Airways: Inside Football's Underground Economy*. Mainstream.
Taylor, L. J. (1990). *The Hillsborough Stadium Disaster: Final Report*. HMSO.
The Sports Ground Safety Authority/CFE. (2021). *The Management of Persistent Standing at Football Matches*. https://sgsa.org.uk/wp-content/uploads/2021/06/The-management-of-persistent-standing-Final-report.pdf
Trivizas, E. (1981). Sentencing the Football Hooligan. *British Journal of Criminology, 21*(4), 342–349.

Von Hirsch, A., & Simester, A. (2006). Regulating Offensive Conduct through Two-Step Prohibitions. In A. Von Hirsch & A. Simester (Eds.), *Incivilities: Regulating Offensive Behaviour*. Hart.

Welford, J., Beard, A., Corley, A., Birkin, G., Francis, N., & Lamb, H. (2019). *Standing at Football: A Rapid Evidence Assessment*. DCMS. https://www.gov.uk/government/publications/standing-at-football-evidence-review-report

Welford, J., Bowes, L. Stutz, A., & Pearson, G. (2022, July). *Early Adopters of Licensed Standing Areas in Football Stadia: Report for the SGSA on the Findings from the Independent Evaluation*. CFE/SGSA. https://sgsa.org.uk/wp-content/uploads/2022/07/Early-adopters-of-licensed-standing-areas-CFE-Research-evaluation-July-2022.pdf

Williams, D. (1987). Processions, Assemblies and the Freedom of the Individual. *Criminal Law Review*, 167–179.

Williams, J., Dunning, E., & Murphy, P. (1989). *Hooligans Abroad* (2nd ed.). Routledge.

4

Policing a Football Match in the Early Twenty-First Century

The Local Structures of Policing

To adequately understand football policing, it is necessary to recognise the significant levels of localised direction and control of the police that operate with in England and Wales. There is not, and never has been, a singular national police force in either nation, so the way football policing is delivered varies considerably from one location to another. Depending on how one defines them, the UK has around 45 police forces. Each is essentially run as an independent organisation and usually governed through a partnership between a locally elected official, either the Police and Crime Commissioner, Police Crime Fire and Rescue Service Commissioner, or Mayor, and the most senior officer within the relevant police force. This local relationship is overseen, but not governed, by central government via the Home Office, and regulated via the crown authority of Her Majesties Inspectorate of the Constabulary and Fire and Rescue Services (HMICFRS). As a result of this localised control, it is generally the Chief Constables who are ultimately operationally responsible for the nature of policing in their force areas, although this is always devolved, usually to an Assistant Chief Constable (ACC). For territorial forces in England and Wales, jurisdictions are defined largely by county

G. Pearson, C. Stott, *A New Agenda For Football Crowd Management*, Palgrave Studies in Risk, Crime and Society, https://doi.org/10.1007/978-3-031-16298-5_4

(e.g. Staffordshire) or by metropolitan district (e.g. West Yorkshire). There are also several special police forces; the most relevant in terms of football policing is British Transport Police (BTP), whose jurisdiction oversees the rail transport infrastructures which football fans regularly use to cut across national, county, and city boundaries. While BTP is run by a Chief Constable, it is overseen by the Department of Transport rather than the Home Office. In Greater London the situation is different yet again, as the Metropolitan Police Service (MPS) is headed by a Commissioner and led in partnership with the Mayor's Office.

This devolved and complex nature of police governance and leadership across England and Wales has meant that national coordination between police forces has never been a given, and instead has been a historically emerging process. The development of the first professional police forces began in London in 1829 and others soon followed, each established with complete autonomy from one another. As policing became more established, there was a growing requirement to address the issue of coordination because crime itself increasingly transgressed the narrow borders of local jurisdiction. To address this, Chief Officers formed a series of regional informal collaborative bodies that took national shape as the *Association of Chief Police Officers* (ACPO) in 1948 immediately after the Second World War. The subsequent year, separate railway forces were amalgamated into a single British Transport Police and over the next 50 years multiple town and city forces began to merge into the structure we have today. For example, on 1 April 1974, Birmingham City Police, Dudley, Walsall, and Wolverhampton Borough Police, along with areas formerly parts of Staffordshire, Warwickshire, Coventry, and West Mercia Constabularies, amalgamated to form what is currently referred to as West Midlands Police (WMP). Over time, ACPO became ever more involved in facilitating the national coordination and cooperation of police forces, as well as becoming the primary body for Chief Constables to influence policing policy at a governmental level. As we shall see, ACPO, along with other organisations, has played a key role in superseding local variations and helping to shape a more nationally coordinated approach to football policing across England and Wales (see Emsley, 1996 for a detailed historical overview).

The Emergence of a Standardised Approach to Policing Public Order

Football policing is to all intents and purposes a sub-division of the same kinds of policing that are applied to protests and industrial action. In policing parlance, this is referred to formally as public order and public safety policing, or POPS. As we have discussed in earlier chapters, the 1970s and 1980s were decades within which there were a series of pivotal football-related 'public order' events, but these took place alongside other social conflicts such as the so-called race riots of 1980 and 1981 and the miners' strike of 1984–1985. Together, these challenges to public order were increasingly seen by government, the media, the police, and indeed large sections of the public, as posing a significant national security threat to British society. A growing sense of crisis was developing across these decades (e.g. Hall et al., 1978), in part because public disorder, both inside and outside of football, increasingly exposed the ineffectiveness of a localised and decentralised policing approach to public order. In this sense, football 'hooliganism' was a key part of this emerging sense of national crisis and was used consistently by the media to pose powerful challenges directly to government ministers about their capacity to provide security for the nation.

This sequence of incidents of widescale public disorder arguably began with the international disturbances in 1968, which included a riot in Grosvenor Square in London. These events were part of an international revolutionary movement that led to a perception of threat within the British state being posed by left-wing political militancy. A few years later in 1972, Birmingham City Police failed to prevent striking coal miners from closing the Saltley coke depot, which at that time was one of the last capable of supplying this vital fuel to British heavy industry. Saltley was a key factor in securing victory for the miners in their dispute with the government, and a powerful example of how disorderly crowds have formidable political ramifications. Then, in 1974, issues surrounding the policing of crowds came to a head with the death of Kevin Gately during violent clashes between National Front, anti-Nazi demonstrators, and police in central London. Gatley's death led to a formal inquiry into the policing of the protest chaired by Lord Justice Scarman in 1975, and while this found the police not to have been at fault for Gatley's death, the conclusions from it were significant because they led directly to the foundations of a nationally coordinated approach to public order policing led by ACPO.

These foundations were arguably based on two central developments for localised public order policing in England and Wales. The first was the creation of an increasingly standardised tactical approach referred to as Police Support Units (PSUs), which are now the key police formation for all public order policing in England and Wales, including football. These PSUs are squads of 25 police constables (PCs) organised into three groups typically called serials. Each serial is constituted by six PCs, a sergeant, and a driver. A PSU is usually commanded by an inspector. The officers are specially trained, accredited, and issued with protective equipment such as riot (or NATO) helmets, protective padding, fireproof overalls, boots, shields, and batons. Each of the three serials has their own carrier vehicle and as such a PSU can move rapidly from one location to another allowing dynamic tactical deployments.

The second development was a system for coordinating these units across and beyond local force jurisdiction via a framework called 'Mutual Aid'. This system was developed to enable PSUs in any local police force to be mobilised together and deployed at very short notice from their own jurisdiction to support the public order operations of another.[1] These developments in turn meant that England and Wales did not move towards a paramilitary approach with a dedicated standing army of 'riot police', as, for example, exists in countries such as France or Italy. Instead, officers who perform other duties for most of the time are specially trained and mobilised into PSUs to provide a capacity for public order policing only when necessary.

Not long after their development in the late 1970s, these two key advances in public order policing were powerfully tested when, in 1980, rioting developed in the St Paul's district of Bristol. As we shall argue in Chap. 6, this riot was pivotal for several reasons, but not least of all

[1] At time of national crisis—for example during the 2011 August riots in England—this Mutual Aid would be coordinated by National Police Coordination Centre (NPoCC).

because it was the first in a sequence of so-called race riots, that in the summer of 1981 spread to Brixton in London, the 'L8' or 'Toxteth' area of Liverpool, Handsworth in Birmingham, Chapeltown in Leeds, and Moss Side in Manchester, as well as other locations. During these riots, the embryonic nature of national coordination was exposed and meant that police Mutual Aid was slow to mobilise. When officers arrived, they often struggled to work together because they had different tactics, training, and equipment. But the riots were also important because, in their wake, another Scarman-led inquiry (Scarman, 1981) led ACPO to publish the first national guidance document for public order policing in England and Wales.[2] However, given the local governance of policing, ACPO had no mandate to instruct Chief Officers, which hampered further development of national police coordination, a problem aggravated by the fact that the different forces still delivered public order training 'in-house'. Thus, alongside the new national guidance, the 1980s saw the emergence of a national framework for police education and training in public order policing. By 1993 this had evolved into national police training (NPT), a formal organisation which, for the first time, amalgamated previously separate police training establishments into a single national entity.

Over the following decades, POPS has become ever-more nationally coordinated. The Criminal Justice and Police Act 2001 brought further change to the landscape because it led to the creation of the Central Police Training and Development Authority (CPTDA or Centrex), which took over the responsibility for national police training from NPT. Centrex, a limited company, played a key role in advancing the national agenda but was itself replaced after just a few years in 2007 by the National Policing Improvement Agency (NPIA). Finally, in 2013 the NPIA was superseded by the College of Policing. In 2015, ACPO itself was disbanded and its responsibilities were taken over by the National Police Chiefs Council (NPCC) and the College. Specifically, the new College dovetailed into the declining role of ACPO and the rising power of 'evidence-based policing' to take over primary responsibility for setting

[2] Referred to as the 'Public Order Manual of Tactical Operations and Related Matters' https://archiveshub.jisc.ac.uk/search/archives/bb7bdd1c-a97d-3843-92d3-d8e4f22f98a2

statutory national guidance, which it began publishing as Authorised Professional Practice (APP) in 2016. This framework of emerging national leadership, guidance, and training has been a key factor in creating a nationally coordinated approach to the policing of public order and therefore to the policing of football.

At time of writing, the Public Order Public Safety Unit, a team within the College of Policing, is responsible for developing and maintaining the National Public Order Training Curriculum, as well as for designing and overseeing the delivery of command training for police commanders and their tactical advisors. They are linked to several of the NPCC public order policing committees such as the Public Order Training, Tactical, Training & Equipment Working Group, whose role is to ensure that each force's public order capability, capacity, and contribution meet the regional and national requirements of what is referred to as the Strategic Policing Requirement (SPR)—the minimum level of capacity that all forces must always maintain. The College oversees the delivery of its curriculum via a national programme of courses delivered through regional training centres. These training centres are important in delivering a nationally coordinated approach because they are invariantly run by large territorial police forces, generally servicing the training needs of the surrounding, smaller, county forces. These courses all share the national curriculum, delivering to recognised national minimal standards that are developed, accredited, and overseen by the POPS team at the College.

From Policing Public Order to 'Football Hooliganism'

As we established in Chap. 2, by the 1980s violent or disorderly behaviour at football matches in the domestic leagues of England, Scotland, and Wales had become a ubiquitous feature of newspaper headlines and television news. Nonetheless, football-related public order policing remained a niche and relatively insignificant area of ACPO's growing portfolio. In this sense, it had not yet become an opportunity for aspirational Chief Officers to make a career for themselves on the national policing stage. As we touched upon, this changed in 1985 in the wake of the rioting at the FA cup sixth-round tie between Luton Town and Millwall in March, the Birmingham v Leeds United fixture later that season, and then the Heysel stadium disaster in May. As we discussed in Chap. 2, this series of football-related riots was addressed by the subsequent Popplewell Inquiry which drove changes not only in the law but also in the significance of football-related public order policing within ACPO.

Layton and Endeacott (2015) argue that around this time West Midlands Police had already begun to initiate embryonic football policing operations using Divisional Observations Teams (DOTs). These DOTs were surveillance units staffed by detectives from their Criminal Investigations Department, drawn into football operations at the local level to gather evidence on what were the increasingly high-profile criminal activities of organised 'hooligan' groups. These ad hoc initiatives ultimately led WMP to develop "Operation Red Card" in 1987, designed to use undercover police to infiltrate and then convict several participants of the "Zulu Warriors", the notorious hooligan group affiliated to Birmingham City FC. At much the same time, the MPS public order unit, then called TO20, initiated "Operation Own Goal", the ironically named highly flawed undercover police operation designed to confront football violence in London.[3] West Yorkshire Police (WYP) had evidently also begun similar covert operations, again using detectives, to gather intelligence and evidence on 'hooligan groups' affiliated to Leeds United and Bradford City football clubs. However, it was in the wake of the Hillsborough stadium disaster in 1989 that these sporadic innovations began to coalesce into a far more nationally coordinated response.

When Lord Justice Taylor's report into Hillsborough was published in late 1989, ACPO's Public Order Sub-Committee was chaired by the controversial, reactionary, and outspoken Chief Constable of Greater Manchester Police (GMP) James Anderton. Because of the disaster, the sub-committee, along with the Home Office, began to construct

[3] The convictions resulting from the covert operation were quashed by the Court of Appeal. For a critique of Operation Own Goal and other undercover operations in the 1980s, see Armstrong and Hobbs (1994).

platforms for national cooperation surrounding these previously ad hoc football policing operations and did so by creating and jointly governing the National Football Intelligence Unit (NFIU). The NFIU was developed in 1988 following disorder at the UEFA European Championships in Germany but was not formally launched until November 1989. Led initially by Superintendent Adrian Appleby, the NFIU was accountable to ACPO through ACC Malcolm George. Both Appleby and George were, like Anderton, senior commanders from GMP, indicating the significant influence of the force's senior management team in national developments in football policing at this critically important time. It appears that George therefore effectively became the first formal ACPO 'National Football Lead', sitting within, and reporting to, the Public Order Sub-Committee, an organisation that itself evolved to deal with national security threats posed by riots, strikes, and political agitation. This positioning of 'football hooliganism' alongside other national security threats is something we believe has left a problematic legacy in how police in England and Wales still orient towards the issue today.

Cost Recovery and 'Special Police Services'

Over the subsequent decades, successive ACPO leads for football began to develop national guidance documents specifically for football, to supplement the public order manual of guidance published initially by the NPIA and currently as APP by the College.[4] These ACPO and NPCC Football Leads have been centrally important because each has played a key role in driving national policy and coordination. For example, during the 2000s, under the ACPO leadership of the late Ron Hogg, the strategic agenda for football policing became heavily focused on the issue of cost recovery. As the strikes and riots of the 1980s ebbed away, disorder in football retained its place as an ever-more salient social and political issue into the 1990s and 2000s. But, perhaps more importantly, the

[4] The successive leads include Tim Hollis, (South Yorkshire), David Swift (Staffordshire), Ron Hogg (Durham), Steve Thomas (GMP/BTP), Andy Holt (SYP), and, at time of writing, the Chief Constable of Cheshire, Mark Roberts.

management of football crowds was costing police forces across England and Wales millions of pounds every year. Correspondingly, the emerging national public order policing infrastructure in the UK was developing a sophisticated, well-funded, and coordinated football-related component. While this security arm of the state was initiated within ACPO to tackle the political and serious urban disorders on the 1970s and 1980s, by the turn of the century it was not protest so much as the year-on-year costs of football policing that was creating the biggest public order headache for Chief Officers, particularly those outside London.

Exact figures are impossible to calculate, Hansard records the estimated cost of policing professional football matches in England and Wales in 2019 at over £48 million a year, of which police were able to claim back through the Special Police Services (SPS) only around £5.5 million.[5] As another example, Steve Thomas, while he was National Football Lead, estimated to us that his, the second largest police force in England and Wales, spent around 80% of their entire public order budget on policing football. Whatever the exact expenditure, football policing costs the UK taxpayer millions of pounds every year. Consequently, during Hogg's tenure as ACPO lead for football, police forces in England and Wales developed shared protocols using section 25 of the Police Act 1996[6] to try to ensure football clubs made significant financial contributions to the costs of the policing operations surrounding their clubs. Correspondingly, under his leadership the ACPO manual of guidance for football was redrafted and read much like a manifesto for cost recovery.

Paying significant contributions towards policing was not, and is not, an issue for the bigger and more financially successful Premier League clubs. However, for smaller clubs in the lower tiers, any contribution can be financially catastrophic. Consequently, cost recovery came to head in various inter-related court rulings. It has been long-established that clubs have to pay for 'Special Police Services' (SPS) in the stadium and other land they own or control,[7] and that in effect the police can force a club to 'invite' it onto its premises, or risk having its safety certificate under the

---

[5] Hansard Commons 4 June 2019 Vol 661 Col 55.

[6] Formerly s. 15(1) Police Act 1964

[7] *Harris v Sheffield United Football Club Ltd* [1988] 1 QB 77.

SSGA 1975 blocked (see Chap. 2). However, there have subsequently been two attempts to essentially stretch the meaning of SPS. In the first of these, GMP brought an action against Wigan Athletic FC in an attempt to recover its policing costs on land controlled by the club. The club's appeal against the High Court's ruling in favour of GMP was successful; in *Greater Manchester Police v Wigan Athletic FC*,[8] the Court of Appeal ruled that as the club had not requested the higher level of SPS, the force could not claim the costs back. In 2013, there was an even more audacious attempt, albeit with the same outcome. In *Leeds United Football Club v West Yorkshire Police*,[9] the Court of Appeal unanimously dismissed WYP's appeal against the High Court's decision that it could not reclaim policing costs for the football policing operation outside of the land that was owned or controlled by the football club. These expensive, and ultimately fruitless, cases for the forces were ultimately very important for football policing in England and Wales because they began to clearly delineate where, and when, clubs were required to pay for football policing.

The current situation is therefore that clubs are only required to pay for police who they invite to enter the so-called operational footprint of their stadium. Correspondingly, club safety officers and stewards have become increasingly qualified and responsible for 'policing' the behaviour of fans within, and immediately around, stadiums. Consequently, each force now exists in a sometimes rather perilous relationship with their respective clubs and seeks to establish memorandums of understanding and agree a season-wide cost structure based upon shared pre-season risk assessments. As we shall see below, given these risk assessments are developed at a very early stage, they are often based on historical assumptions but then tie the clubs and police into a set of agreements, with financial implications, that can be difficult to change. As we have observed during our research, sometimes these SPS relationships can become so fractious they break down entirely, with clubs refusing to invite any SPS at all.

[8] [2008] EWCA Civ 1449.

[9] [2013] EWCA Civ 115.

Specialist Operations

Today, football policing in England and Wales has become, first and foremost, what can be understood as an intelligence-led POPS operation. Importantly, at an organisational level, POPS as a portfolio is generally organisationally distinct from, and additional to, the delivery and leadership of 'everyday' local policing. While still ultimately accountable to their Chief Constable and local governance structures, they are what is referred to as 'specialist operations'. As such, they utilise a nationally coordinated public order leadership command and control structure and are expected to adhere to the public order and football guidance now issued by the College. They also draw upon officers accredited and specially trained via the national curriculum. For the most part, training for POPS is delivered through regional centres, and forces use similar specialist equipment and wear comparable protective uniforms, all of which have been nationally standardised to enable effective Mutual Aid. While POPS operations sit under the portfolio of the forces' relevant ACC, it has become increasingly difficult, if not impossible, for any local force to deviate away from the national doctrine. Indeed, to do so would expose that local force, the relevant ACC, and the command team of that operation to serious problems if things were to go wrong 'on their watch', as they did so powerfully for Chief Superintendent Duckenfield who was the senior tactical commander at Hillsborough on that ill-fated day in 1989. Thus, this centralised and standardised way of approaching football policing has also meant that it is now very difficult to drive change at a local level, unless these developments come from, or are endorsed by, external national bodies such as the NPCC, the College, or the United Kingdom Football Policing Unit (UKFPU).

When a football policing operation is judged to be required, the relevant force's operational planning department is invariably faced with a major and very complex logistical exercise, mobilising sometimes hundreds of staff into the associated POPS operation. The planners need to identify officers across the sub-divisions of the force who have the required levels of training and accreditation to participate within the PSUs or other required roles. They then need to ensure these individuals are already in, or placed into, shift patterns that allow them to be abstracted from their normal duty or 'day job' to be available on the day of the event. For example, if the officer is working on a 'late shift' as a response officer, they will need to be rested the day before, and the day after, the POPS operation. Furthermore, when a large operation is required, the force often needs to cancel the planned rest days of officers. In other words, where an officer was scheduled to take a day off to relax and spend time with their family, this must be rearranged. Where the staffing availability within the police force is insufficient, the planning team may also need to use the Mutual Aid framework to request and obtain resources from another force. This is normally a neighbouring force, but we have often observed football policing operations that have had to draw Mutual Aid staff from hundreds of miles away. As we will argue later in this book, not only are such mobilisations incredibly expensive, particularly where they are reliant on overtime payments and Mutual Aid, but they also have a 'hidden cost' of a dramatic negative impact on the force's overall capacity. In other words, changing shift patterns and drawing officers from their 'day job' seriously undermines police capacity to deliver its 'business as usual', undermining its abilities to respond to, prevent, and investigate a whole range of non-football-related crimes.

Given this underlying complexity, and for many forces also the regularity of policing the same stadium multiple times a season, operational planning departments often rely heavily on formulaically recreating historical procedures, tactical plans, and agreed costing arrangements. In other words, rather than constantly reinventing a plan for a policed fixture at a specific stadium, planning departments tend to agree a template and set level of resourcing for each category of risk, and use these operational plans (or 'op orders') repeatedly. This formulaic approach has at least two negative consequences. First, any changes to resourcing can often create disputes with the clubs over the costs of policing, which are confrontations that many police forces would simply rather avoid. Consequently, the plans, and their associated financial agreements, get 'locked in' by the pre-season agreements with clubs over SPS. In effect, where agreement has been reached with the club that a high level of police resourcing is required, the police will sometimes stick with this level, even where it is subsequently understood that it is not actually necessary.

Second, as we have argued, operational orders relating to stadiums in the Football Leagues have usually evolved over decades and, as a result, are often deeply entrenched. This creates an 'off the shelf' approach where the mobilisation plan from one fixture is 'copy and pasted' into the next. Reflecting this, we have observed several pre-match briefings where the title slide covering that day's Op Order had not been updated from the earlier fixture. In short, while this 'formulaic' approach makes the complex mobilisations, and its array of decisions, more efficient, it also creates further internal difficulties for anyone within the organisation seeking to remedy ongoing problems related to resourcing or deployment, bring innovation, or drive change to the policing of football.

Command and Control

To enter the specialist world of public order operations, and therefore to police football, any commanding officer of a POPS operation will have to progress through one or several courses and is required to retake them on a regular basis to retain their accreditation (colloquially referred to as their 'ticket'). Where a football POPS operation is judged necessary, this is formally marked by the appointment of a Gold Commander, who is always at a senior level and often a Chief Officer for the respective force. As with any POPS operation, Gold is responsible for setting the strategic parameters of that operation and will appoint a Silver Commander who is responsible for establishing the tactics for achieving these strategic goals. Silver then appoints several Bronze Commanders, who are in turn responsible for developing the specific plans that relate to the operational delivery of Silver's tactical plan and Gold's strategic objectives. For football policing operations, Gold Commanders are generally 'on call' rather than present on the day of a fixture.[10]

How each force then implements this command structure varies. For example, at time of writing, West Mercia Police has jurisdiction in the

[10] For the larger forces such as the MPS and WMP, it is common to have several fixtures on the same day as well as other public order operations relating to non-sporting events. On these occasions a Gold Commander may be 'on duty', but in our experience only very rarely would they be physically present in control rooms, etc.

English counties of Herefordshire, Shropshire, and Worcestershire. Despite the large geographical area, they have only a few football clubs and even fewer policed football fixtures each year, most of which are connected to the largest club in the region, Shrewsbury Town FC. In contrast, WMP, as a larger adjacent metropolitan force, has six, mostly larger, clubs within its jurisdiction. As a result, WMP has dozens of policed fixtures annually and can sometimes have two or three policed fixtures on the same day. Given football matches in these larger metropolitan forces attract multiple public order operations across a season, the Gold Commander generally sets the strategy for football operations, across a whole season, rather than merely for each event, whereas in smaller county forces like West Mercia, Gold may set a separate strategy for each match.

In line with national guidance, several forces also have a 'football lead', who takes overall responsibility for coordinating the force-wide approach. Some forces will also develop a cadre of senior commanders who are trained and accredited to be Silver Commanders. This 'cadre' approach can be valuable because it creates greater consistency given the Silver Commanders' overall impact on how a football policing operation is shaped and delivered. However, being a POPS Silver is part-and-parcel of gaining promotion, so many forces end up with dozens of accredited Silvers, many of whom will only ever police a few matches. This latter approach can create a whole raft of problems, where inexperienced Silver Commanders take over the policing of a fixture and deliver an operation that can have an entirely different quality to the policing surrounding preceding and subsequent fixtures at the same stadium, commanded by other Silvers.

The Silver Commander for every POPS operation is therefore ultimately responsible for designing a tactical plan to achieve Gold's strategic objectives and parameters. Silvers vary in rank but are almost always at a senior level within their respective organisation, usually at least of Chief Inspector rank but often, for larger stadiums, Superintendents or Chief Superintendents. In effect, Silver Commanders are responsible for analysing the nature of the threats and risks of the situation they believe they will be confronting and proposing the policing resources that they judge will be required, even though these are ultimately 'signed off' by Gold. The Silver (or tactical) plan will examine the intelligence and the nature of the geographical location for the event and then, with the assistance of their Bronze Commanders, set out the required resources, including how, where, and when these will be deployed to manage the perceived risks. With respect to football policing operations, the tactical plans are generally developed several weeks before the fixture, unless of course these are cup ties which often require a much quicker turn around. As we shall see below, these plans will always be underpinned by an intelligence report submitted by the Dedicated Football Officer for that club (DFO), usually informed by input from the DFO from the visiting force.

In this respect, being a Silver Commander carries a great deal of responsibility, because it is with them that the respective accountability for the 'success' or 'failure' of that public order operation often ultimately resides. As Tank Waddington and others have pointed out, such responsibilities often have a profound impact on decision-making within POPS operations (Cronin & Reicher, 2006; Stott, 2016; Waddington, 1994). In short, the 'risk' that Silver Commanders, and others, are managing is not just a threat to what Waddington referred to as "on the job trouble", in this case 'public disorder'. It is also that such "on the job trouble" creates "in the job trouble" for those commanders who are left having to explain to their superiors how and why things went wrong 'on their watch' (Waddington, 1994). Such accountability pressures are very dangerous for a Silver Commander and can even be career threatening, if colleagues judge that problems developed because they had failed to adequately 'grip' the situation, either by under-resourcing it in the planning phase, being reticent to allow the use of force when their operational subordinates judged it necessary, or being too 'heavy handed', attracting subsequent complaints, negative newspaper headlines, or provoking formal inquiries (Hoggett & Stott, 2010, 2012; Stott et al., 2008). As we will discuss in Chap. 9, such accountability pressures mean it is difficult for Silver Commanders to innovate and act outside the orthodoxy, because doing so leaves them exposed. In this sense, moving outside the hegemonic doctrines that guide national POPS doctrine and training is an incredibly dangerous thing for any senior commander to do and, as

Leach (2021) argues, this stifles innovation. As we shall see in Chap. 8, it can lead commanders to surround themselves wherever possible with unnecessary and costly resources as a 'comfort blanket' just in case unexpected incidents of conflict develop.

Resourcing

The bulk of the police staff mobilised onto a football policing operation will be used to populate the respective PSUs. As discussed above, PSUs were first developed in the late 1970s and are the way police forces across the UK enable the rapid and dynamic deployment of 'riot trained' officers (see also Northam, 1988). While the terminology used in POPS is constantly evolving, according to the HMICFRS in 2009, each force in England and Wales maintained three different levels of training and readiness for PSU deployment. Level 3 is the minimal required and is delivered to all officers as part of their basic training. While Level 3 resources are used in football, this is only in relationship to specific functions where conflict is not expected to take place, such as providing cordons or managing queues at turnstiles. A Level 2 officer would have been a PC for at least two years and will be trained in additional 'high-end' public order tactics (e.g. baton charges) at least twice a year. They will have access to, and depending on the situation be equipped with, specialist gear (i.e. helmets, shields, baton, protective fireproof uniforms, and padding). Finally, Level 1 officers have the highest and most regular amounts of public order training. These officers would be trained and equipped to Level 2, but in addition receive regular refresher training, usually once a month. It is predominantly Level 2, but occasionally Level 1, resources that are used for most football policing functions, such as forming cordons, clearing public houses, containing, and escorting fans to and from stadiums, as well as using force to disperse and separate, and make arrests where conflict arises.

Although contemporary figures are treated with some secrecy and are in constant flux, to give some idea of the level of resourcing that underpins the UK public order policing, in 2009, 19 of the forces in England and Wales maintained Level 1 staff and nationally there were approximately 22,500 officers that were trained to at least Level 2 standard. Level

1 officers will also usually be a specialist and full-time unit. Such Level 1 teams, maintained predominantly by the larger territorial forces, are the closest that the UK gets to 'riot police'. But even here while these units specialise in public order, they also provide other dedicated functions such as providing the force with searching capability. These Level 1 units vary in size and name, referred to in GMP as the Tactical Aid Unit (TAU), in West Yorkshire and West Midlands Police as the Operational Support Unit (OSU), or in London as the Territorial Support Group (TSG). In addition, several other specialist football and POPS roles will be deployed into football such as DFOs, Operational Football Officers (OFOs, previously known as 'spotters'), mounted police, dog units, Evidence Gathering Teams (EGTs), as well as custody officers to manage anyone arrested, detectives to investigate any crimes that took place, and traffic officers to implement road closures and escort vehicles, such as the team and organised fan coaches.[11]

The primary decisions about the required level of mobilisation for a football policing operation relate primarily to its risk categorisation. While these are nationally standardised, what they ultimately mean in terms of resourcing will vary from stadium to stadium and from force to force. In general terms, what in historical terminology was categorised as a Category A or 'low risk' event, would attract only a minimal level of resourcing, often merely one or two serials of Level 2 or 3 trained officers. For some clubs, this negligible level of resourcing might even be part of a season-wide SPS agreement. We have observed at least two clubs where such a relationship exists, and in both cases, these SPS agreements grew from the clubs moving into new stadiums with large 'operational footprints'. As a result, the clubs knew they would be required to pay for an SPS and, rather than dispute this, both the respective forces and clubs agreed a more functional and constructive relationship. By inviting a significant SPS for each policed fixture, the respective forces were able to offer its staff a role on these operations on an overtime basis. In other words, staff could volunteer for the role on one of their scheduled days off, and as such to be paid overtime rates for it, in addition to their salary. This meant that a dedicated cadre of staff began to emerge who became skilled at taking the club's 'customer service' approach forward and was

[11] Our ENABLE observations also saw early use of drones.

made possible given the fact there were no perceived underlying threats to public order for most of their deployments, a very different situation from their 'public order' colleagues who were often only present at higher-risk fixtures precisely because there was an acknowledged threat of violence.

Category B (Medium), C (High), and C-IR (Increased Risk) fixtures would invariantly attract a far larger policing response.[12] As always, there is considerable variability between different stadiums and forces, so there is not a set formulaic national approach to the levels of resourcing that apply. Such decisions lie firmly in the hands of Gold and Silver Commanders with each respective force. However, as a rule of thumb, for fixtures at average size stadiums, one might expect one or two PSUs on a Category B fixture, and upwards of five or six for a Cat C-IR, usually supplemented with several mounted police, dog units, and other resources. However, we are aware of some Cat C-IR football POPS operations that have ultimately attracted several hundred police officers. For example, at a Stoke City v Cardiff City fixture in 2001, 27 PSUs were ultimately deployed, which alone amounts to 675 officers. Consequently, for fixtures that are likely to present problems, the level of resourcing is always something that is considered as far in advance as is possible, precisely because of its scale, complexity, and impact. Not least of all, the force will need to consider how it can minimise the cost by minimising the number of officers on rest days and overtime.

As we have discussed, in the larger metropolitan areas it would not be unusual to have two or even three higher-risk football policing operations on the same weekend, so staffing them adequately is always a challenge. These fixtures therefore need to be identified in the initial pre-season risk assessment, so the heavy demand can be anticipated and planned for well in advance. This means that when Silver Commanders are appointed, usually just a few weeks prior to the event, there is already an expectation within their respective organisations that significant public order resources will be required, and the plan for mobilising these resources is also usually already well underway. As we will illustrate in Chap. 8 in particular, according to our observations this means at least two things. First, the

[12] At time of writing UK guidance for the classification of fixtures has changed from these historical categorisations. They are currently 1. Police free; 2. Operational Football Officers Only; 3. Low; 4. Medium; 5. High.

initial planning is always based almost entirely on historical, rather than contemporary, intelligence and information. Consequently, as we shall argue below, large football policing operations are often set up to police the size and reputation of the fixture, rather than on concrete contemporary intelligence. As a result, subsequent 'intelligence' is often used to legitimise resourcing decisions that have already been made, rather than as the basis of critiquing and 'rolling back' on them. Second, given that they have already been budgeted for, legitimised, and planned, it would often be illogical for the Silver Commander to reject these human resources given the negative accountability that they would suffer if things did go wrong and there were not sufficient resources in place (Leach, 2021). In other words, the planning cycles, historical reputations, and logic of accountability have a way of organisationally cementing-in police resources to football POPS operations, when they might not actually be required.

'Football Intelligence' Units

It is our contention that football policing in England and Wales is built on two foundational pillars. The first, as already discussed, is the national coordination of the football POPS capability of territorial forces, harmonised nationally via the emerging leadership of ACPO and the NPCC, and underpinned by frameworks of guidance, training, and accreditation that are cascaded out via the College of Policing. The second is a nationally coordinated network of police officers involved in surveillance, criminal intelligence coordination, evidence gathering, and prosecutions, all predominantly oriented towards securing FBOs against fans who have already been involved in violent criminality in the context of football or are suspected as being *predisposed* towards being so in the future. As we will discuss in more detail in Chap. 5, in modern football policing parlance, such individuals are no longer referred to as 'hooligans', but as 'risk fans'. In Chap. 5 we will also place the development of football intelligence within the historical context of the more general move towards the management of risk in policing and the 'culture of control' (Garland, 2001).

As we have discussed, the embryonic approaches to football policing became more formalised in the wake of 1989 Hillsborough disaster.

ACPO and the NFIU stepped in to generate the guidance, agreements, protocols, and legislation, and lobby for the government funding necessary to develop coordinated football units within every force that hosted a football club playing in the first four tiers of the English and Welsh leagues. Given England hosted the UEFA European Championships in 1996, the coordination of the policing response for the host cities of London, Manchester, Liverpool, Birmingham, Leeds, Sheffield, Newcastle, and Nottingham was led by the NFIU and overseen by the ACPO football lead. With an almost trouble-free tournament,[13] further investments were made by the Home Office, and it was this funding that created the UKFPU. This, in turn, cemented the increasingly embedded and nationally coordinated, intelligence-led policing response, focused on securing FBOs, that was understood by both government and police as necessary to fight the so-called English disease both at home and abroad.

The criminal detective origins of the DOTs that evolved into the intelligence-led frameworks of the NFIU and then UKFPU, further underpinned by the post-2000 FBO legislation, fed the development of what is now a well-established national network of uniformed police officers specifically dedicated to the policing of football. From the early 1990s, these officers were employed by, and remained accountable to, their own local force but used in standardised roles that began life as Football Intelligence Officers (FIOs), Football Liaison Officers (FLOs), and Spotters. When first developed, the primary, though not exclusive, responsibility of FLOs was to support liaison between the host force and the football clubs. Their remit was not to liaise with football fans, so much as it was to oversee the planning of the public order aspects of the policing operation, negotiate the SPS, and maintain a close working relationship with the club, usually through its in-house safety officer. In contrast, the FIO's primary responsibilities were to oversee the criminal intelligence aspects of football policing. They would work alongside, and lead, teams of 'spotters', whose part-time function was to attend fixtures home and way to monitor football fans, gather intelligence, support the host police force POPS operation, capture evidence, pursue prosecutions,

[13] There were several disturbances following England defeat in the semi-final against Germany including a major incident in Trafalgar Square in London. In another incident, police dispersed a crowd of around 1000 England fans who had queued through the night attempting to buy semi-final tickets at the Wembley box office.

and secure FBOs. The FIO would coordinate this activity and intelligence and feed it into the NFUI and UKFPU. The roles have evolved under guidance from the UKFPU issued in 2020 and have been formally replaced by Dedicated Football Officers (DFOs) and Operational Football Officers (OFOs), but at present their overall remits remain broadly the same, with DFOs replacing FIOs and FLOs, and OFOs replacing spotters.

As they evolved, the levels of staffing attached to these locally embedded roles varied from force to force. For example, in Merseyside and Manchester the respective forces invested heavily in several staff involved in full-time football units, primarily because these forces hosted large successful clubs, whose fans travelled regularly in great numbers both home and abroad. The units in Merseyside and GMP, for example, were historically embedded within the local policing divisions within which the stadiums were located. For example, M Division in the west of Manchester was the home of the policing operation connected to Old Trafford and Manchester United, whereas the policing operation for Manchester City resided in a different division in the east. Historically jobs in, or connected to, these larger metropolitan football units were, and remain, highly attractive, given they are far removed from the mundane reality of routine 'day-to-day' policing. The office walls of DFOs and OFOs are invariantly adorned with flags, scarves, and police mementoes signalling the multiple trips working in football policing affords. Visits to Rome, Paris, Madrid, Munich, Amsterdam, and other continental cities became a regular feature of working life for the units attached to the most successful clubs in England.

Correspondingly, the bigger units began to develop highly experienced officers who would work within them, often for many years. In several cases, our observations record how this led to some rather nepotistic relationships, in that ambitious senior police officers approaching their retirement would target roles in these Divisions where they would by default become the senior Silver Commander overseeing the football operations in some of England's largest stadiums. Power struggles emerged when their colleagues saw the obvious need to centralise football operations while those, often very senior colleagues embedded within the respective Division, would resist changes to the status quo. Perhaps unsurprisingly, when these commanders then retired, some went on to be employed by clubs as Safety Officers, or in some cases by UEFA as well-paid and high-powered security delegates at Champions and Europa League fixtures across Europe. In stark contrast, smaller clubs in the lower leagues would tend to see little investment and would merely have officers, and sometimes even civilian staff, deployed in football roles, sometimes only on a part-time basis.

As we have discussed above, a key component of the growth of the nationally coordinated football policing response has been the development of a detective-led criminal intelligence framework that led into the role of the 'spotter', the name itself reflecting the idea that their primary role is to identify so-called hooligans. In 1992, shortly after its creation under ACPO, the NFIU was subsumed within the broader National Criminal Intelligence Service (NCIS), where it developed across the next four years under the leadership of NCIS Deputy Director and ex MPS officer, Bryan Drew. Then in 1996, in line with agreements secured internationally and in the wake of the European Championships in England, the United Kingdom Football Policing Unit (UKFPU) was established. The UKFPU was headed initially by Drew who was already a key architect of the new national approach to football policing, alongside Deputy Director Tony Conniford and David Bohannon, a civil servant who at that time headed the Public Order unit in the Home Office. Bohannon and Drew both played key roles in shaping the new national and international agreements and frameworks for football policing that had been evolving since the Heysel stadium disaster.[14]

The powerful collaboration between Drew, Bohannon, and Conniford, support by the ACPO lead and Home Office, meant the UKFPU was able to both drive and mesh with the emerging football legislation. Accordingly, it developed exponentially across the next few years to assert itself as the primary coordinating and oversight body for football policing across England and Wales. The UKFPU also incorporated, and currently manages, the Football Banning Orders Authority (FBOA) and delivers the accredited training for DFOs and spotters (now OFOs), coordinating

[14] The UKFPU is no longer a part of NCIS but a standalone quango that is funded by the Home Office and accountable to the NPCC Football Lead.

and disseminating intelligence, and furthering the securing of FBOs. Since its formation, it has controversially offered grants to police forces based upon target numbers of s.14B FBOs that a force estimates it is likely to achieve across a season, thereby providing the financial incentives for police forces to achieve these estimates.[15] The financial incentive to secure s.14B bans compounds the concerns about the absence of the normal criminal justice safeguards we set out in Chap. 3. UKFPU also evaluate and provide reports on what they judge to be the effectiveness of football policing operations and provide funding for high-profile post-match police investigations such as MPS Operation Ternhill which was set up by the Metropolitan Police to identify those responsible for the serious disturbances which occurred surrounding a Chelsea v Cardiff City 5th Round FA Cup match in February 2010. Many of the 96 people charged with affray and violent disorder were convicted, with some receiving prison sentences and six-year FBOs. Its Senior Investigating Officer in the MPS was quoted as saying,

> the public perception is that football disorder involves young men fighting in the street, but I must stress this is not the case. A large number of the men, who have now pleaded guilty or been convicted of charges in relation to this incident, are career football hooligans who have been involved in serious acts of violence over a number of years.[16]

We will deal with the critiques of NFIU and the role of spotters, particularly in the early years of intelligence units, in Chap. 5.

Intelligence-Led Policing?

Through the growth of this national football policing infrastructure, the 'intelligence reports' created by spotters and DFOs have become one of the key factors determining whether a football event is judged to require

[15] See James and Pearson (2006), Hopkins (2014), and Hester (2021) for critiques of the s.14B FBO regime relating, specifically regarding this funding model.

[16] https://fsoa.org.uk/wp-content/uploads/2012/01/UKFPU-UK-NFIP-Role-Responsibilities--FSOA-Oct-11.pdf

a policing operation. Almost as soon as the domestic fixture list is created in the early summer, police forces across England and Wales assess each fixture for what might be required. Central to this assessment will be an intelligence feed coordinated through the UKFPU database on the history of the fixture and of the fan groups involved. According to our observations, almost invariably, if a fixture has experienced serious disorder in the preceding season or the visiting fan group had a track record, this was flagged up by the host force as a fixture posing risk. For example, fans of Millwall have a notorious reputation and regular history of being involved in incidents across several decades. Given this general history, such visiting clubs can attract a relatively high-risk categorisation from the outset, particularly at clubs where there have been specific issues with conflict historically. As we will go on to demonstrate in Chap. 8, this can even be when such conflict took place decades ago. Nonetheless, in making these assessments, host forces also draw upon UKFPU formulas, databases, and computer systems to categorise the fixture, labelling it in terms of the assessed levels of threats and risks to public order it is judged to pose. We have discussed these categories above, but from the 1990s onwards, this revolved around the four increasing levels of risk A, B, C, and Cat C-IR. If there was not judged to be any underlying risk, and no policing operation required beyond the almost ever-present spotters, this would be classified as a Club Security Only (CSO) fixture.

In this sense, all football policing operations in England and Wales will claim to be 'intelligence-led' as they will receive several intelligence reports, or 'feeds', into their operational planning processes from the visiting club's DFOs. The first of these generally arrives around four to six weeks before the fixture itself. There will then be other intelligence feeds in the weeks and days leading up to the event. Each of these will have various levels of rating, to assess the underlying confidence in the validity of the information they contain. Given their sensitivity, we were only occasionally given access to the precise feeds, although their sanitised content always finds its way into the documentation surrounding policing operations, the most important of which is as discussed above: the summary of the policing set-up referred to as the 'Op Order'. However, we do know from the intelligence we have examined that the underlying confidence of the information was evaluated along two key dimensions, largely in line with national standards.[17] The first was the 'source evaluation' (S), assessed in terms of level of their reliability ranging from (A) always, (B) mostly, (C) sometimes, to (D) unreliable and (E) untested. There is also an 'intelligence evaluation' (I) ranging from (1) known to be true without reservation, (2) known personally to source but not to an officer, (3) not known personally to the source, but is corroborated, (4) cannot be judged, to (5) suspected to be false. Finally, there are a set of handling codes, denoted again by numbers 1 through to 5 signifying the extent to which the intelligence can or cannot be shared with other organisations with 1 indicating it, "may be disseminated to other law enforcement and prosecuting agencies, including law enforcement within the EEA and EU compatible". Thus, intelligence that can be shared with other organisations which had a high level of confidence would be coded as A11, whereas that with a much lower level of confidence could be tagged E41.

These intelligence feeds in the weeks leading up to a POPS operation are very important and we have observed several policing operations that have been downgraded in their pre-season classification because of them. In the main, however, our observations concluded that they often contained very little useful information, and generally what they did provide, appeared to be used somewhat uncritically to confirm that the initial risk categorisation was largely correct. As we argue later in the book, the main issue that our research highlights in relationship to football intelligence is that the information these reports provided almost always bore little, if any, relationship to what materialised behaviourally during events and in this sense several opportunities to predict or prevent disorder are being missed (Hoggett & Stott, 2010; Stott et al., 2019).

Almost invariantly, the intelligence we have observed provides information about the historical behaviour of the fan groups, usually across the last few seasons at other locations, and about whether so-called risk fans that affiliate to the clubs will be attending the respective fixture. In Chap. 5 we will detail the rather convoluted and unhelpful definition of 'risk' and 'non risk' fans that informed such categorisation until very

[17] See College of Policing https://www.college.police.uk/app/intelligence-management/intelligence-report

recently. At this stage, it suffices to say that defining someone by virtue of whether or not they pose "a possible risk to public order or antisocial behaviour" (College of Policing, 2019) is such a loose definition it runs the danger of potentially including many otherwise peaceful fans within the 'risk' category at some point. Many spotters and DFOs have equally expressed to us how difficult they found using these definitions, to the point that they simply gave up and developed their own idiomatic ways of categorising fans to communicate perceived threats to public order (e.g. "their main lads", "scarfers", "anti-socials", "youth risk", etc.). Nonetheless, it is self-evidently the case that the largest single factor determining the scale of a POPS operation within any police force that we have observed are these intelligence reports, particularly when they suggest that significant numbers of risk fans from the visiting club are intending to travel to a fixture. Where a report indicated that such fans would attend in number, then the host force would invariantly classify the fixture as at least a Category B or higher, and as a result a significant policing operation would be mobilised.

Those intelligence reports that we have observed in the course of our research varied considerably in terms of underlying detail, and we focus on two here as a comparative case study for how we contend 'intelligence' often operates. The first example relates to a local derby fixture that we discuss in more detail in Chap. 8 (Case Study 6). The intelligence for the fixture was collated into an extensive 'pre-match' assessment document that was over ten pages of A4. The fixture was rare in that it had been downgraded from its pre-season category C status to a category B fixture. Nonetheless, it was still one of the largest football policing operations that force would mount that season and drew in upwards of 150 police officers from across the county. The report was produced by the DFO of the host club and was unusually detailed, providing in-depth descriptive accounts of the 'disorderly' behaviour of both home and away fans at 13 different fixtures, stretching back over three years. Yet, within the document, there was little information that related meaningfully to fans' intentions or likely behaviour relating to the fixture in question. The report began by laying out a broad and rather vacuous description of the visiting club's fan base. In line with intelligence reports we saw in other operations, it set out the general idea that the level of threat among the away supporters can be measured to some considerable extent by their levels of compliance with instruction. As it states, the "vast majority of the [visiting club's] supporters are well behaved and are compliant to directions given by both police and stewards". However, having inferred this generally positive demeanour, it then also went on to imply that even these 'non-risk' fans posed a level of threat, due to circumstances that often develop in the context of football. It stated, as "with most groups of supporters on occasion their behaviour is influenced by events on the field and can lead to spontaneous poor behaviour". Yet in contrast to this implied generalised threat, the report concluded by pointing out that the "behaviour of the [visiting] supporters away from home last season was overall very good with just one drug related arrest". How or why the latter arrest is meaningful is not made clear, other than its implication that several visiting fans may well be in possession of illegal drugs and therefore have criminal intent. In this way it was clear to us that the report created a general implication that disorder could be expected, but the evidence it presented could equally have supported a more positively focused slant. The very same report could have been used to support the conclusion that across the preceding season this fan group had been largely well-behaved, that only one fan affiliated to the club had been arrested, and that was for an offence ostensibly unrelated to violence or disorder.

The report went on to provide detailed information of the visiting club's 'risk supporters'. It noted that the club has an "established risk group that can number 100+ for high profile matches", which of course this local derby was, and that they "will range from 15–55 years of age", a depiction we imagine captures around 90% of any travelling fan base. In terms of underlying criminality, they "are known to use cocaine" and that "if travelling for disorder [they] will attempt to arrive early and evade police". The report went on to claim that they "have been active at high profile home fixtures over the last 12 months", but then in contrast that they "have not been active at away fixtures since May 2017, although a group of 100 travelled to [another regionally located town]". In any case, it reports that despite the presence of this large group of risk fans, there had "been no major issues". It then goes on to detail six preceding fixtures earlier that season, and the two corresponding derby clashes in 2016 and

2017, where various numbers of the visiting 'risk' fans had attended and fluctuating levels of 'anti-social' behaviour, smoke grenades, gesturing and 'verbals' had taken place. It concluded with a detailed description of the last reverse derby fixture involving the teams, two years previously, during which serious pre- and post-match disorder developed. It is evident that police commanders appraising this ten-page catalogue would, unless they were critical readers, get a sense of a turbulent history, where both clubs had risk groups who had extensive track records of involvement in various types of criminality, anti-social behaviour, drug use, and violent football-related disorder, especially when the two clubs played each other. Moreover, it was equally evident that the primary driver for the risk assessment of this local derby was not contemporary intelligence relating to the current fixture, but historical data of the corresponding fixture two years earlier.

Interestingly, what is only mentioned briefly in the "intel/information update" section towards the end of the report is information that one of the spotters attached to the visiting club had described to us in detail. In an interview before the fixture, he explained how he was present at the preceding regional fixture noted above where over 100 of the 'risk fans' from the visiting club had unusually and unexpectedly travelled. Although there had been no disorder at that fixture, through interaction with some of the 'risk fans', the spotter described how several had made it clear to him and his colleagues that they were collectively *not* planning to attend the subsequent derby fixture. It seems surprising this contemporary, relatively high-grade, information does not feature more saliently within the intelligence report. Instead, buried deep on the penultimate page of the ten-page report, there are two sentences that the visiting club's "older risk state they are not coming without tickets, and they know they believe they will be sent back if they turned up. This intel has come from many different sources." It was classified as "reliable-known directly to the source" (i.e. B2). Yet this was immediately followed by a more recent update that the home club's "risk are arranging a disorder at [a local] train station with [the visiting club] in a pub on [a specific town centre] street for 09.00 on the day of the game". This information was classified as untested-not known (i.e. E4) and was never mentioned to us by the spotter we interviewed. As we will see in Chap. 8, in line with the higher-grade intelligence, it was the case that very few of the visiting club's 'risk fans' attended and there was, perhaps unsurprisingly, no significant 'disorder' on the day of the fixture.

Our assessment of this report is, like many others we have seen, that it is very difficult to see how, or in what way, the extensive and detailed historical information provided in it was relevant or meaningful in terms of accurately assessing and predicting the challenges for the current fixture. Rather, while the policing operation claimed to be 'intelligence-led', this information did little more than act as a catalogue of prior incidents, that taken together circumstantially began to imply an inevitability of disorder at the derby fixture. This in turn functioned to justify and legitimise the large-scale policing operation that had already been mobilised some weeks beforehand, 'just in case' history was to repeat itself. The report offered little to no contemporary information about the legitimate intentions of the over 1000, largely compliant 'non-risk' visiting fans that would, and did, attend. Indeed, it merely reported that 1150 visiting fans could be expected and that only around 200 of them would travel directly to the stadium in three coaches and two minibuses. The remaining 950 fans were almost totally ignored in the report. There was little mention they would presumably therefore be travelling by train, or in their own cars, and that many would inevitably congregate in a town centre pub and need to walk some considerable distance to the ground. There was no mention that, as a result, one of the key 'risks' would not be the demeanour or predisposition of the visiting fans, but the fact that home fans might seek to confront them simply for having the temerity to travel to the host city. Perhaps the most significant piece of high-grade information, that coincidentally might have functioned to downgrade the classification of the fixture, was most notable by its superficial position at the tail end of an otherwise extensively detailed but largely superfluous account of prior disorder.

Our second example is another fixture that we also discuss in more detail in Chap. 8 (case study 3). In contrast to the above example, the first intelligence feed amounted to nine lines of text from the visiting DFO outlining C21 information (i.e. from a sometimes-reliable second-hand source not known to the police) delivered six weeks before the fixture, that a notorious 'risk group' affiliated to the visiting club may be intending to travel to the fixture to celebrate the anniversary of their formation some four decades ago. This intelligence meshed neatly with the host force operation, which had already classified the fixture as Category C in its pre-season assessment. This first intel feed was followed by a second a few weeks later (again C21) which confirmed that upwards of 400 risk fans from the visiting club would be attending. The Silver Commander had been appointed and was understandably clear in his commitment to retain the fixture's high-risk classification. As we shall see in Chap. 8, these two feeds were later superseded by a third, much firmer, level of intelligence several days before the fixture. This new B21 intelligence contradicted the former reports by clearly stating that the risk groups *would not* be attending as had previously been anticipated. In short, the intelligence supporting the initial Category C classification was entirely removed, which should have led to a complete reassessment of the policing requirement. However, by then the mobilisation was already in place and the policing operation went ahead with its initial categorisation.

Our two examples capture what was for us a general pattern of so-called intelligence led football policing operations. That is, in the main, the intelligence that drives them focuses heavily on descriptive catalogues of historical disorder or relatively weak contemporary intelligence about the expected movement of so-called risk fans, at least until much closer to the event itself. In this way, the emphasis in this intelligence is almost entirely on the likely demeanour of risk fans and the numbers likely to be present within the visiting fan contingent. This focus is at the expense of any analysis of the circumstances that are likely to lead to disorder (other than bland assumptions that any contact between risk fans will inevitably involve confrontation), or information about what it is that the visiting fan base are legitimately likely to be seeking to do or achieve (or cultural or identity-based sensitivities that the host police should be aware of). There is also an overwhelming emphasis on the visiting fans and a respective under-emphasis on the likelihood that home fans may launch unprovoked attacks, which according to our observations was by far the most likely scenario. In short, these intelligence feeds often lack information about the underlying identity of the fans and how this feeds specific behaviours, motivations, and intentions, particularly among those fans who have no intention of behaving criminally but who might get drawn into disorder as a function of circumstances. In this sense it is difficult to sustain the idea these are genuinely intelligence-led operations, an issue we will return to in Chap. 9. Taken together, the systems and practices for identifying, analysing, overseeing, and utilising most football intelligence fall far short of what would normally be expected of intelligence-led policing operations (see Walsh, 2006).

Conclusions

Since it was first developed by ACPO, national guidance for public order policing has flowed down through an array of emerging police committees and organisations to create a progressively coordinated, national infrastructure and approach to policing crowds that is applied in the context of football. That organisational network of governance, training, and accreditation has delivered a relatively standardised approach to strategy, tactics, equipment, training, and operational deployment. It is this nationwide infrastructure that creates what is in effect a relatively rigid, centralised national doctrine that underpins the policing deployments week-in week-out at football fixtures across England and Wales. Thus, while there is still a good deal of local autonomy and variation, the power and authority of local forces to deviate from the national guidance has been ever-more constrained. As we have argued, what began as relatively localised issues of hooliganism soon took on a national level of significance. Thus, as the local autonomy of the police to deal with local football-related public order issues has ebbed, an increasingly powerful framework of national guidance, intelligence, governance, oversight, and accreditation has flowed. This centralised response has gradually evolved over decades, in parallel with legislation, to build a nationally coordinated surveillance infrastructure, designed to identify, monitor, and where possible ban so-called risk fans. The approach has made significant progress, and disorder has seen a significant decline, but continues as an intractable problem that costs policing millions of pounds annually, as well as impacting significantly on their effectiveness in other areas. Our extensive research on these football operations has identified a set of more complex factors that need to be addressed if further progress is to be made. As we shall argue in more detail in later chapters, we need to reform the nature of intelligence and the orthodoxy of the public order-focused policing approach. These approaches were initially designed and developed to deal with major security threats to the state, and as such, are usually unsuitable to the policing of what are, in reality, merely sporting events where the overwhelming majority of people that attend have no prior intention of engaging in disorder.

References

Armstrong, G., & Hobbs, D. (1994). Tackled from Behind. In R. Giulianotti, N. Bonney, & M. Hepworth (Eds.), *Football Violence and Social Identity* (pp. 196–228). Routledge.

Cronin, P., & Reicher, S. (2006). A Study of the Factors that Influence How Senior Police Officers Police Crowd Events: On SIDE Outside the Laboratory. *British Journal of Social Psychology, 45*, 175–196.

Emsley, C. (1996). *The English Police: A Political and Social History* (2nd ed.). Longman.

Garland, A. (2001). *The Culture of Control: Crime and Social Order in Contemporary Society*. Oxford University Press.

Hall, S., Roberts, B., Clarke, J., Jefferson, T., & Critcher, C. (1978). *Policing the Crisis: Mugging, the State, and Law and Order*. Macmillan.

Hester, R. (2021). Assessing the UK Football Policing Unit Funding of Football Banning Orders in Times of Austerity. *Policing: A Journal of Policy and Practice, 15*(2), 1188–1201.

Hoggett, J., & Stott, C. (2010). Crowd Psychology, Public Order Police Training and the Policing Of Football Crowds. *Policing: An International Journal of Police Strategies & Management, 33*(2), 218–235.

Hoggett, J., & Stott, C. (2012). Post G20: 'The Challenge of Change, Implementing Evidence Based Public Order Policing'. *Journal of Investigative Psychology and Offender Profiling, 9*, 174. https://doi.org/10.1002/jip.1360

Hopkins, M. (2014). Ten Seasons of the Football Banning Order: Police Officer Narratives on the Operation of Banning Orders and the Impact on the Behaviour of "Risk Supporters". *Policing and Society, 24*(3), 285–301.

James, M., & Pearson, G. (2006). Football Banning Orders: Analysing their use in Court. *Journal of Criminal Law, 70*(6), 509–530.

Layton, M., & Endeacott, R. (2015). *Hunting the Hooligans*. Milo Books.

Leach, I. (2021). 'It's on my head': Risk and Accountability in Public Order Policing. *The Police Journal: Theory, Practice and Principles*. https://doi.org/10.1177/0032258X211041021

Northam, G. (1988). *Shooting in the Dark: Riot Police in Britain*. Faber & Faber.

Scarman, L. (1981). *The Brixton Disorders 10–12 April 1981: Report of an Inquiry*. HMSO. Cmnd 8427.

Stott, C. (2016). Revisiting the Classics: Policing Coercion and Liberty: A Review of P.A.J. Waddington's Liberty and Order (1994) and Policing Citizens (1999). *Policing and Society, 26*(1), 114–119. https://doi.org/10.1080/10439463.2015.1107297

Stott, C., Livingstone, A., & Hoggett, J. (2008). Policing Football Crowds in England and Wales: A Model of "Good Practice"? *Policing and Society, 18*, 258–281.

Stott, C., Pearson, G., & West, O. (2019). Enabling an Evidence-based Approach to Policing Football. *Policing: A Journal of Policy and Practice, 14*, 977. https://doi.org/10.1093/police/pay102

Waddington, P. A. J. (1994). *Liberty and Order: Public Order Policing in a Capital City*. UCL Press.

Walsh, P. (2006). Managing Intelligence: Innovations and Implications for Management. In M. Mitchell & J. Casey (Eds.), *Police Leadership and Management* (pp. 61–74). Federation Press.

5

Risk Supporters? Understanding the Behavioural Norms of Football Fans

Introduction

In this chapter we turn our attention to the central focus of policing and legal responses to football crowd disorder: the behaviour of the football fan. This chapter seeks to engage with several issues. First, it looks to conceptualise the idea of football fandom by setting out the authors' understanding of football fan behaviour and 'culture'. Second, it critiques the dominant model of the 'risk supporter', as this is used in football policing, and considers to what extent this category maps onto the reality of football fan behavioural norms in the twenty-first century. Finally, this chapter considers the extent to which organised fan groups in England and Wales play, or should play, a role in the policing strategies and tactics used to manage them. Once again, the arguments put forward in this chapter are based on ethnographic research with, and on, groups of football fans conducted by both authors going back to the 1990 World Cup in Italy. In the intervening 30 years, the authors have conducted extensive embedded research with fans of the England national team, and English club sides including Arsenal, Blackpool, Cardiff City, Leeds United, Liverpool, and Manchester United. In addition to this, through the 'ENABLE' projects, both authors have made observations of many other fan groups of clubs in the Premier League and Football League as well as

G. Pearson, C. Stott, *A New Agenda For Football Crowd Management*, Palgrave Studies in Risk, Crime and Society, https://doi.org/10.1007/978-3-031-16298-5_5

internationally in Denmark, Sweden, and Switzerland. The authors' arguments in this chapter also take into account some other excellent embedded ethnographic studies of football fan groups, including Armstrong (1998, Sheffield United), Giulianotti (1991, 1995, the Scottish national team), King (2000, 2002, Manchester United), Richards (2017, Everton), and Rookwood (2009, Liverpool and Cardiff City). Ethnographic research is invariably microscopic in nature (Geertz, 1973, p. 21), and we need to be careful when extrapolating findings from an in-depth study with one group of fans to another. However, the patchwork of ethnographic studies in this area has identified remarkably similar norms, and we can be fairly confident that while there are always differences in behaviours between and within different clubs, the picture we set out in this chapter is replicated broadly across most of England and Wales.

Football Fan 'Culture'

In 1981, *The Soccer Tribe* by Desmond Morris was published. In the hefty coffee-table book featuring "580 photographs, nearly 500 of them in colour", Morris argued that human interest in the game of 'soccer' would prove a puzzle to an outsider, and that the easiest way to understand it was to engage in anthropological study of "tribes" that attend matches to watch their team. Revisiting this book now, we are struck by both the patronising tone and the assumptions about the everyday working life of the football fan.

> Who are these devout followers and where do they come from, the millions who flock to the soccer matches every week throughout the long season? The vast majority are city-dwellers, the offspring of the industrial revolution. Their typical week is spent in the factories and offices, the shops and streets of the busy urban world of the twentieth century. Their work lacks any sharp climax and is often monotonously repetitive, so that when the match-day arrives they eagerly anticipate the peaks of high tension and emotional drama that the game will bring, breaking their steady routine with surging moments of almost unbearable excitement (Morris, 1981: 234).

Morris split each 'tribe' into the old supporters (who typically watched from the seats) and the young ones (preferring the terraces), and discussed the rituals of attending matches and supporting the team. Understanding football fan behaviour in this way was an attractive proposition, and the idea of fandom as ritual, and 'hooliganism' as ritual aggression, was shared by Peter Marsh and colleagues in their early analysis (Marsh et al., 1978, see also Stott, 2020). In a similar vein, but with a different emphasis, other researchers have attempted to explain away the passion of football fandom through the lens of ritual and religion (Bromberger et al., 1993; Martyn & Taylor, 1997). As we saw in Chap. 2, anthropological understandings of football fans played an important role in challenging the moral panic around 'hooliganism' in the 1970s in particular, and King developed this approach in the 1990s, to shift the focus from 'hooliganism' onto the "ecstatic ritualistic celebrations" (King, 1997, p. 332) of the 'lads', applying Durkheim's (1964) theoretical framework from *The Elementary Forms of Religious Life.*[1] Other sociologists researching fandom have been more inclined to use Bourdieu's (1977) developed concept of *habitus* (Armstrong, 1998; Gibbons, 2019; Millward, 2006).

Throughout all of this, the mainstay of anthropology, ethnographic research, has proven the most popular, and indeed fruitful, approach to understand fan behavioural norms. However, the idea that there is some underlying football fan 'culture' guiding fan behaviour that can be uncovered through this research is also dangerous. First, we need to consider what we mean when we talk about 'culture'. Colonial anthropologists typically viewed 'culture' as being an entity that existed to be discovered. 'Culture' was conceptualised as an amalgamation of language, customs, ceremonies, artefacts, and beliefs that seemed to bind communities together, but which were alien to the anthropologist (Agar, 2006; Clifford & Marcus, 1986; Marcus, 1998). This version of culture has been roundly critiqued for failing to account sufficiently for the variances *within* 'cultures', made particularly evident by differences in gender, religion, and place of origin (Agar, 2006; Gupta & Ferguson, 1992), and in

[1] There has been a recent resurgence in the use of anthropological explanations for football fan behaviour in the work of Newson and others (e.g. Knijnik and **Newson** (2021); Newson (2017)).

anthropology at least, the idea of culture as an observable singular entity has been largely discounted (Agar, 2006; Brightman, 1985). Instead, it is more useful to see 'culture' as an ethnographic *product*, a translation of those 'rich points' of difference (Agar, 2006) between the community that the ethnographer observes and their own, which may be helpful to describe interpretations and behaviours within any particular community. So, while it may be helpful to use the concept of a fan culture to help explain why fans behave in the way that they do to outsiders, it is not the case that a fan base's match-going 'culture' will *drive* the behaviour of fans within it. To try and 'explain away' how a particular fan (or for that matter a police officer) behaves by reference to an overarching 'culture' that in some way guides their action is to obscure the varieties and variations within communities and organisation. Match-going fans have many shared experiences, interpretations, and behaviours, but the more they are observed the more the sub-group and individual differences between them become apparent.

The danger of getting this translation of interpretational and behavioural norms wrong is not only that the wrong types of understanding or behaviour may be attributed to fan groups (which is less likely with embedded ethnographic research than 'outsider' research based on 'white-room' interviews or statistical analysis) but also that similarities within a team's match-going support will be exaggerated. While there are differences *between* how match-going fans of different teams consume football and express their identity, the idea of a monolithic 'culture' has the unwelcome effect of downplaying differences *within* a club's support. When the idea of a guiding fan 'culture', which may be illustrated by stereotypes of fan group behaviour (e.g. "Newcastle fans like a drink"), is used to inform crowd management practice, this can result in the practical problem of police or stewards either misinterpreting behaviour in line with the idea of 'culture' that they have been briefed on or imposing this idea upon all individuals within a match-going support. As we shall argue, understanding what fans want, and what they consider to be legitimate, is fundamental to reducing the risk of conflict between fans and police, but those managing crowds need to be mindful of the complexities at play, not only between the accepted behavioural norms of different clubs but also within a club's support, and how the unique structural or situational factors of the match event affect this. A static and universal version of what a club's match-going 'culture' is, has the potential to do more harm than good; if one then bases crowd management approaches on such broad assumptions about collective behavioural interpretations and norms, we run the risk of these leading to tactics that will not be understood as legitimate by many of their targets. Basing a match policing plan around a cultural explanation or stereotype of how a group of fans is likely to behave is, of course, preferable to the idea that all fans are inherently dangerous and must be policed according to this apparent threat, but however much effort goes into the account, it cannot replace the value of a dynamic risk assessment on the day that is reached following ongoing engagement with the supporters.

Fan Subcultures and 'Carnival Fans'

The idea of fans of a particular club as belonging to a tribe has had its day, if indeed it was ever anything more than a slightly tongue-in-cheek way of popularising a particular academic perspective that was dominant in psychology at that time (Marsh, 1978). Generally, as social scientific research into fandom has developed, increasing attention has been paid to complexities within it. For example, Gibbons highlights the many different aspects of fandom in relation to the England national team, identifying variations in the understandings and priorities among English football fans and the way this illustrates the complex and varying nature of the relationship between fan 'culture' and English national identity (Gibbons, 2019, p. 160). However, if empirical research points to as many differences as similarities, and to the importance of change as to that of tradition, is there any value in 'culture', in terms of overarching 'football fan culture' or that belonging to a particular team, as an explanatory concept at all? The label neither adequately explains what is observed, nor enables us to predict how football fans will, as a group, interpret and behave in different situations.

One way in which social scientists studying football fan behaviour have responded has been to move away from the concept of a unified culture and onto the idea that a club's support instead contains different subcultures (Richards, 2017; Richards & Parry, 2019). It may be overstating the point to talk of a 'subcultural shift' in academic scholarship on football fandom, but undoubtedly there is increased attention on different minority groups, often researched by ethnographic 'outsiders' (Pearson, 2016), which has not only teased out the differences between match-going supporters of the same club but also, in doing so, identified the similarities that can be found between groups supporting different clubs. Predominant amongst these groups has been the long-overdue academic attention on the experiences and understandings of women football fans (e.g. Jones, 2008; Pope, 2013). Falling out of fashion for research in the UK at least has been the focus on what we might call the 'hooligan' subculture, which, a number of researchers have argued, has faded from view, to be replaced by the development and significance of the hooligan memoire genre (Redhead, 1997, 2010, 2015), the voyeuristic identification and fetishisation of "hooligan nostalgia" (Spaaij, 2006, p. 399), and what Poulton calls, "deviance by proxy" (Poulton, 2008, 2013). Increasingly, even amongst those who might consider themselves to engage in occasional disorder or violence, the label and identity of 'hooligan' is broadly used only in jest (Pearson, 2012, p. 90; Hodges, 2016, p. 412).

For the purposes of this book, we pay particular attention to what we refer to as the subculture of the "carnival fan". The idea of football fandom as an expression of the carnivalesque can be traced back to Richard Giulianotti's work with Scottish fans in the early to mid-1990s (Giulianotti, 1991, 1995). However, in 2012, Pearson looked to develop the concept of the "carnival fan" in *An Ethnography of English Football Fans*, following 16 years' fieldwork with fans of Blackpool, Manchester United, and the England national team. The concept draws on the Bakhtinian ideal of the 'carnivalesque' (Bakhtin, 1984) derived from studies of the feasts and festivals of early modern Europe (Burke, 2002). Indeed, Bakhtin has retained popularity for writers talking about crowds in leisure contexts more generally (Webb, 2005, p. 121).

An Ethnography's core argument is that rather than trying to understand the interpretations and behaviours of a single unified 'supporter culture', the population of match-going fans of any particular club is divided up into various subcultures, each of which possess very different behavioural norms and understandings of the purpose and value of attending a live match. Importantly, these subcultures are fluid, in that a fan may not only change their 'membership' of the subculture during the course of their time attending matches,[2] but that they might opt in or out depending on the type of match attended and the opportunities available to 'join' another subculture. In short, the assertion is that while subcultural norms of interpretation and behaviour may influence the behaviour of the carnival fan, this was only insofar as that fan chose to be part of, or identified with, that specific subculture. In other words, individual behaviour remained context-specific; a fan's actions were not predetermined by their disposition but mediated through the decision to engage in the carnivalesque, which may in turn be influenced by practicalities such as time of kick-off, availability of public transport, or access to tickets. In this sense we can see carnival fan behaviour as being, to a certain extent, performative. Reflecting the arguments of Agar and Brightman set out in the preceding section, it is not therefore the case that 'membership' of a particular (sub)culture will drive a fan to act in a particular way or provide them with a predisposition towards certain behaviours.

In *An Ethnography* it is argued that while the 'carnival fan' subculture represented only a minority of fans at home matches, it tended to dominate away followings, and that carnival fans from different clubs typically shared several understandings and behavioural norms. The primary objective of attending matches, for fans that formed part of this subculture, was to engage in a carnivalesque transgression from the norms of everyday life. This transgression typically involved gathering in large groups, heavy consumption of alcohol and/or drugs, humour and tomfoolery, and the collective expression of identity, both in and outside stadia, through fashion, colour, and the chanting of football songs.

> For a large number of football fans who travel home and away with their team, fandom is analogous to carnival. For the fans observed during the period of this research, a key motivation, if not the *primary* motivation for travelling to matches was to experience and take an active role in the carnivalesque. For these 'carnival fans', gathering in large groups, singing, drink-

[2] Which would reflect Marsh et al. (1978) idea of a 'career' of football fandom.

> ing and being rowdy was at least as important than what was actually happening on the pitch… while only forming a small part of the club's overall support, this subculture were disproportionately influential on creating 'atmosphere' at matches, and without their networks and activities football grounds would be much quieter and less passionate environments (Pearson, 2012, p. 184).

Among this subculture, these gatherings, rather than merely the match itself, were anticipated for days, and sometimes weeks, in advance, and reminisced about both at subsequent assemblies and on social media in between match events. This 'type' of fan has been identified by a number of researchers under different labels. The understandings and behavioural norms are comparable to King's 'lads' (see above),[3] and this description from *The Changing Face of Football* highlights some of the other key identifiers of the subculture when the authors argue that being seen as a 'real football fan' involved not only attending matches but also an "assimilation of masculinist/class inflected argot of consumption (involvement in the spheres of football fandom: pre-match drinking, familiarity with networks of rumour, gossip and football folklore)" (Back et al., 2001, p. 95). It is important to note here that while what might be seen as 'traditional' masculine and working-class norms and understandings dominate the discourse and behaviour of the carnival fan, the vast majority appeared to be from secure middle-class (usually white-collar) backgrounds, and that although the vast majority were men, there were also a significant minority of women (Pearson, 2012).

Describing these groups as carnival fans draws attention to one particular element of this 'laddish' subculture: transgression. In Early Modern Europe, the time of carnival was described as one of a transgression from the norms and drudgery of everyday working life, when the world was turned "upside-down" (Curtuis, 1953, p. 94–8; Burke, 2002, p. 185) or "inside out" (Bakhtin, 1984, p. 11). Carnival was governed by its own laws (Bakhtin, 1984, p. 7) and informal codes of conduct in which the normal rules of authority and rank were suspended and challenged

[3] With regard to the carnival fans observed at Manchester United, it is not beyond the bounds of possibility that some of the participants from King's earlier work appear in *An Ethnography* under different pseudonyms.

(Bakhtin, 1984, p. 10; Stam, 1988, p. 134; Burke, 2002, p. 187).[4] Therefore, while playing or watching football can be mimetic in providing an opportunity for excitement (Elias & Dunning, 1986), but in a regulated and relatively safe environment, the carnival fan transgresses from the expected norms of the twenty-first-century football consumer, and in terms of courting the risks of injury and the wrath of the criminal justice system, fits more with Bakhtinian versions of the carnivalesque (Morrissey, 2008). In this sense, the carnivalesque metaphor is an alternative way of looking at what many criminologists might refer to as crime (and sub-criminal transgression) as risky but pleasurable or thrilling behaviour (e.g. O'Malley, 2010).

Those sympathetic to the ideals of carnival point to its potential cathartic function; acting as a "safety-valve" to allow participants to "let off steam" and defer the risk of more serious and less contained disorder and violence (Burke, 2002, p. 202; Presdee, 2002, p. 33), effectively making the population easier to police in the longer term (Sales, 1983, p. 169). Indeed, it has long been argued that there is a link between boredom and crime (Ferrell, 2004; Steinmetz et al., 2016). Nevertheless, even *if* the carnivalesque performs a cathartic function (and the hypothesis lacks robust empirical evidence), carnival contains all the elements that would make most police officers very nervous. According to the normal rules of behaviour at other times, carnival by nature requires 'anti-social behaviour' verging on 'disorder', and the carnivals of Early Modern Europe were frequently associated with instances of violence (Burke, 2002, p. 188). Managing the carnivalesque therefore poses particular challenges to those in authority; the expectation for transgression on behalf of carnival fans simply does not fit with police expectations of normal public behaviour.

Revisiting the account of the carnival fan subculture in *An Ethnography* nearly ten years on, it can be criticised for an uncritical and undeveloped use of the term 'subculture' to describe the different understandings and norms of behaviour associated with the different type of groups who attend matches. The anthropological critiques of culture as a concept are

[4] It should be noted that the Bakhtinian view of carnival has been criticised as "nostalgic and over-optimistic" (Stallybrass & White, 1986, p. 18).

powerful, and while there are echoes of these in *An Ethnography*'s arguments relating to the disparate nature of a club's support, there was a failure to engage with debates around the meaning of 'culture' in the context of football fans more generally. Nevertheless, as a mode of ethnographic translation (Agar, 2006), we believe that using 'subcultures' is helpful in describing to those charged with policing matches how to conceptualise the differences in psychology and behaviour among fans, so long as sufficient attention is paid (a) to the fluidity between these subcultures, and (b) the differences between different groups of carnival fans, both within a club's support and across different clubs. Without such nuance, subcultural approaches to understanding football crowds highlight only similarities and tradition, and not difference and change. The pigeon-holing of fans into different subcultures should not be seen a panacea to understanding what policing approaches different fans will view as legitimate, and cannot replace the dialogue that is necessary to uncover the ongoing contextual complexity that drives fan understandings and behaviours at a particular match event.

Nevertheless, the concept of the carnival fan is a valuable starting point for those managing football crowds and those travelling away from home in particular. It provides a basis for understanding supporter identity and why some groups of fans may choose to act in ways that may be otherwise incomprehensible to officers approaching the policing of match events through a lens purely contrasting 'risk supporters' with 'non risk'. The carnival fan explanation helps to account for why the same fan may act very differently in different contexts. It can account for the way fans dress, why they choose to travel to matches in particular ways, or drink in certain places. It can explain why they may attend matches without tickets, and why they might miss kick-off, remain in the concourse after the restart, or leave a match early. Understanding these behaviours is important for those policing matches, not least because an alternative assumption might be that these behavioural decisions are motivated by a desire to violently confront rival supporters.

Contemporary Developments in Match-Going Fan Behaviour

Match-going behaviours have changed radically since the days of the football specials detailed in Chap. 2. Changes in both the composition of match-goers and their behaviour have been driven by several external and inter-related factors, including, as we argued in Chap. 3, the law. The outlawing of the traditional terraces has both directly and indirectly changed spectator behaviour. With the bulk of fans of professional clubs now having designated seats (or safe-standing places), rather than needing to find their own location on the terrace, there is less incentive to arrive early at the stadium. Whereas on the old Anfield Kop or Stretford End terraces, fans would need to be in the queue for the turnstile around two hours prior to kick-off in order to get a preferable position to watch the match, now the rush at the turnstiles in those stands tends to be in the 15 minutes prior to kick-off. This gives fans considerably more leisure and socialising time that the police need to be take into account. The Sporting Events (Control of Alcohol, etc.) Act 1985 (SECAA) further discouraged those fans who wanted to consume alcohol from using chartered buses and trains, although many fans had started to use scheduled train services more prior to the legislation being enacted. Similarly, although the later arrival of fans at matches is primarily related to the outlawing of the traditional terraces, SECAA (combined with the poor quality of most concourse bars) is likely to have also had the effect of discouraging early arrival by some supporters.

An indirect effect of the move to all-seater stadia was that, in comparison to the entry fee for a space on a terrace, the ticket for a seat in the equivalent stand was significantly more expensive. The end of the terraces and the new facilities led to a huge churn in spectators; some fans were excluded by the increased ticket prices, while at the same time new fans were enticed to attend matches, or attend more regularly. In particular, more women started to attend and a Premier League report found that by 2013, on average 23% of spectators were women.[5] Although women

[5] In addition, 11% of spectators at Premier League watches were from ethnic minorities (*The Telegraph* 10 January 2013).

remain in the minority when it came to the gender composition of carnival fan groups, those who are part of the groups sometimes play central and active roles, albeit often by assuming traditional masculine outlooks and modes of expression (Pearson, 2012). The price of tickets in the new seated stands also had the effect of pushing up the average age of fans, particularly of Premier League clubs, although there is some suggestion that this trend may be reversing as stadium capacities increase.[6] The days of train loads of teenage fans of the away team descending on stadiums, that posed so many crowd management challenges in the 1950s, 1960s, and 1970s, are behind us, despite current concerns about groups of 'youth risk'.

From our observations, combined with discussions with police, stadium safety and security personnel, and security representatives from various governing bodies, the challenges to safety and public order in and around stadia are quite different from the typical match-going norms that led to the legislation of the 1970s, 1980s, and early 1990s, and the creation of the National Football Intelligence Unit (NFIU). The groups of fans attending matches with any predisposition to engage in violence with opposition supporters appear to have diminished in size and significance. These have been replaced by more disparate groups of what, as we saw in Chap. 4, are often referred to as 'risk supporters', a term which we will consider further in the following section. Violent incidents do still take place, but these appear to be much rarer, and are mostly quite different in nature to the typical clashes of the 1960s–1980s, with fewer fans involved and incidents typically taking place further from stadiums. Our research, which we will detail in Chap. 8 and elsewhere, suggests they are also almost always spontaneous events arising from a combination of a sequence of interactions combined with structural factors. At the time of writing, most forces have concerns about groups of what they term 'youth risk'. These groups are typically made up of teenage boys (although girls were also occasionally present) dressed in football casual clothing, but who were often too young to get into licenced premises unaccompanied,

[6] The 2013 Premier League survey found the average age of a fan was 41, down from 44 in the previous survey of the 2004/05 season. Although there is no direct comparison, a survey by Manchester United in the 1970s found the average age of fans in the Stretford End to be only 17 (*The Telegraph*, 10 January 2013).

and therefore hung around in the streets pre-match. On several occasions during our observations for this book, these groups posed not only a risk to public order but also a risk to themselves should they come into confrontation with groups of older risk supporters from the opposing team. As such, they gave rise to considerable safeguarding issues for the forces responsible for them.

Another change to the norms of supporter behaviour has come from the development of what might be called a British 'Ultra' supporter culture. This development has come from groups looking to imitate the Ultra culture that is particularly prevalent in southern Europe. The self-styled Ultra groups in England and Wales, of which Crystal Palace's Holmesdale Fanatics are currently probably the most prominent, mimic typically non-violent ultra-style behaviour, primarily concerned with creating atmosphere in the stadium through chanting, banners, flags, and occasionally pyrotechnics. The Ultra groups (whether named as such or not) are

> a reaction against the corporate dulling-down of matchdays: against the big clubs' prawn-sandwich faction; against snatches of music being piped down the stadium PA system to 'celebrate' a goal for the home side; against the swathes of all-seated silent support, distant physically and emotionally. Rejecting these aspects of football today becomes an all-encompassing denial of modernity in the Italian ultras' motto '*No al calcio moderno*' (No to modern football) (…U)ltras in the UK concern themselves mostly with making matchdays a visual and aural carnival, festooning the stands with flags, banners, cards and streamers (the choreographed *tifo* display), and making an almighty racket (Green, 2007).

This reaction to the perceived over-regulation and 'bourgeoisification' of football fandom can also partly explain the failure of the all-seater stadium project and the problems caused by migration discussed in Chap. 3. The growth in the use of pyrotechnics in British stadia, initially handheld distress flares, but more recently usually coloured smoke 'grenades', has been one of the marked changes in the traditional methods of creating atmosphere at matches in Britain, and due to their illegality, and potential health risks, they cause considerable problems for both police and matchday security staff. Indeed, the use of pyrotechnics at football in the UK is far more prevalent now than it was when the Public Order Act 1986 extended SECAA 1985 to include fireworks.

Finally, and connected with the growth of 'Ultra' modes of expression, is the influence of online social media (Woods & Ludvigsen, 2021). From the first online football message-boards of the 1990s, through to current use of platforms such as *TikTok*, *Twitter*, or *YouTube*, and encrypted chat facilities such as *Telegram* or *Whatsapp*, social media has impacted on fan behaviour in a number of ways. It has allowed fans to form virtual communities alongside their match-going ones, to relive and anticipate important gatherings, further embedding carnivalesque forms of identity (Pearson, 2012 ch. 8). It has also allowed fan groups to experience alternative modes of expression from other fans, particularly from abroad. In this respect there has been a cross-fertilisation of ideas and development of the concept of what 'authentic' fandom means. The prevalence on social media platforms of videos of pyrotechnic use and *tifos* by fans abroad, for example, may have influenced fans in England and Wales to engage in similar expressions of identity. And the potential financial rewards from 'viral' posts are likely to be encouraging some individual fans to engage in risky behaviours, such as invading the pitch to get 'selfies' with star players. At the time of writing, however, while encrypted chat functions provide a clear opportunity for groups who wish to engage in violence to confront each other away from the gaze of the police, in England and Wales at least, this potentiality appears to be only very rarely realised.

Lost in Translation? The 'Risk Supporter'

In Chaps. 2 and 4, we argued that the creation of the NFIU in the late 1980s was one of the three core factors that led to a reduction in disorder and violence in and around stadia. The development of football intelligence units, combined with the ability to ban those convicted of violence at football, and improvements in stadium infrastructure and CCTV, almost certainly assisted in the reduction of violence and disorder following from the late 1980s onwards. The original purpose of the NFIU, now the UK Football Policing Unit (UKFPU), was to collate information and intelligence about 'known hooligans', which could be shared amongst domestic forces and, as the protocols developed, with foreign police forces when British teams played abroad. They also worked with foreign forces to try and ensure that anyone arrested abroad would be identified and, where appropriate, served with a football banning order (FBO). To enable this, the NFIU created a database which by the 1990s had around 6500 names of so-called Category C hooligans on it (Garland & Rowe, 1999).

At this stage we need to acknowledge the criticisms that have been made of the shift towards intelligence-led policing of football and the role of the NFIU. There has been criticism of the way in which this database was collated and used (Armstrong & Hobbs, 1994; Garland & Rowe, 1999), in particular, that many of those on it were not necessarily 'hooligans', and many may have been caught up in the type of mass indiscriminate arrest that took place during the 1990 World Cup in Italy (Armstrong & Hobbs, 1994) and the 2000 European Championships in Belgium (Stott & Pearson, 2007). In *Tackled from Behind*, Armstrong and Hobbs cast a critical eye over what they saw as the 'normalisation' (Armstrong & Hobbs, 1994, p. 224) of police tactics of surveillance upon football fans. They also asked questions about the legitimacy of police interventions, deportations, and the recording and retention of personal data that occurred during the 1990 World Cup (Armstrong & Hobbs, 1994, p. 221–2). Nevertheless, categorisation of a fan as 'risk' soon also started to determine when, and where, football intelligence officers were deployed on matchdays (i.e. to monitor those fans categorised as risk). Furthermore, this categorisation became even more significant following the introduction of FBOs 'on complaint' in 2000 (see Chap. 3); now gathering evidence of 'risky' behaviour even in the absence of a criminal offence could be sufficient to secure an FBO, which, if sufficient thresholds were met, would in turn could help secure Football Banning Orders Authority (FBOA) funding for the unit.

The traditional police 'spotter' played an increasingly central role in this process and their actions at and around football matches started to be viewed by suspicion by many fans. Stories of spotters 'fitting up' fans with FBOs circulated among fan groups and many match-going regulars started to shun engaging with spotting teams (Pearson, 2012, p. 116–117), and relationships between some fan groups and individual spotters became irreparably damaged. An analysis of the operation of s.14B FBOs in the courts revealed this suspicion was not without foundation, illustrating the flimsiness of some of the evidence that was being presented, particularly that which was little more than guilt by association with other fans categorised as 'risk' (James & Pearson, 2006). Effectively then, in some forces, an unhealthy combination of FBOs without conviction, the NFIU/UKFPU funding regime (see above Chap. 4), and the criminal surveillance approach and attitude of some spotters severely curtailed the ability of football policing units to create dialogue-based policing approaches. As we will argue as this book develops, this lack of dialogue in turn can hamper attempts to accurately ascertain levels of risk and develop more effective, and less costly, football policing tactics.

As we introduced in Chap. 4, the way in which the NFIU, working with domestic intelligence units, aimed to create this database was to categorise fans. In England and Wales, fans were labelled Category A if they were seen to pose no risk of disorder or violence, Category B, if while they would not initiate disorder they might become involved if it occurred around them, particularly if they were drunk, and Category C if the individual "was prepared to initiate and organize acts of disorder in the context of football" (Stott et al., 2001, p. 366). From this point onwards, categorisation of fans as either posing a risk of disorder or not became central to the policing of football crowds. This was, as we have already acknowledged, an important step forward, as tactics started to move from mass reactionary public order policing to differentiation, segregation, and intelligence gathering. Without this sea-change in approach, the effectiveness of FBOs on conviction would have been limited, and the value of the infrastructural changes that took place in football post-Hillsborough may not have been realised.

Nevertheless, categorisation of fans has a relatively limited utility. Data relating to those English fans arrested in France during the 1998 World Cup began to reveal significant limitations to the operation of a purely criminal intelligence-led policing model. For example, prior to the 1998 World Cup in France, the NFIU informed the media that around 100 'Cat C hooligans' were attending, along with around 1000 'Cat Bs' (Stott et al., 2001, p. 367). However, when mass disorder occurred in Marseille, it became clear that those engaged in it were typically *not known* to the British police spotters in attendance (Garland & Rowe, 1999; Stott & Pearson, 2007). Of the total number of arrests at 'France 98', only 12% of those arrested were already considered by the NFIU as 'Category C supporters', only 6% were 'Category B', but that correspondingly 82% of those arrested were unknown to the British authorities prior to the tournament (Garland & Rowe, 1999). There was a similar gap between NFIU categorisation and actual engagement in 'hooliganism' during the disorder at the European Championships in Brussels and Charleroi in 2000 (Stott & Pearson, 2007). It is not entirely clear what the explanation for this disparity in NFIU intelligence was, other than that a range of other factors were drawing fans with no prior history into disorder. Further, the mass arrests enacted against fans at that tournament will have meant that large numbers of fans were swept up by indiscriminate police tactics. It was clear that the early categorisation system was not adequate to understand the complex social psychological dynamics of these sometimes-major disturbances. However, more fundamentally, the static categorisation of fans in this way often offers very little predictive power to indicate whether fans will engage in disorder or not. We will return to this in more detail in Chap. 6.

By the early 2000s, many local police football intelligence units were increasingly using the term 'prominent', rather than 'Cat C', to refer to those who were seen to be instrumental in football violence between rival 'firms'. Although the term prominent is still used in football policing (and is sometimes used interchangeably with the terms 'risk' or 'nominal'), generally the language of football intelligence has moved away from the idea of 'prominents' towards the more all-encompassing term of 'risk supporter' (James & Pearson, 2006; Stott et al., 2018). The definition of risk supporter that operated in the context of policing football across the first two decades on the twenty-first century comes primarily from the UKFPU's role in establishing a common definition across the European Union, while the UK was still a member.[7] The definition was binary, clumsy, grammatically confusing, and, as we raised in Chap. 4, far too

[7] EU Council Resolution 2006 OJC/322.

wide to be of much assistance to those looking to rely on it in making strategic or tactical decisions in relation to policing football. The exact wording was as follows:

> **Risk Supporter** – a person, known or not, who can be regarded as posing a possible risk to public order or antisocial behaviour [sic], whether planned or spontaneous, at or in connection with a football event.
>
> **Non-risk Supporter** – a person, known or not, who can be regarded as posing no risk to the cause of or contribution to violence or disorder, whether planned or spontaneous, at or in connection with a football event.

If we assume that those that drafted the definitions intended that those posing a risk *of* anti-social behaviour (rather than "posing a possible risk to it") should be included, then this involves a wide range of behaviours that go well beyond both premeditated and spontaneous football violence and disorder. In other words, the definition included not only those associated with football violence but also anyone that the police believed posed a *possible* risk of *anti-social behaviour.* Depending on your definition of anti-social behaviour, this could include heavy drinking, swearing in conversation, or the chanting of even inoffensive football songs away from the immediate environs of the stadium. A literal application of the definition would extend to all members (or potential members) of Ultra or carnival fan groups, as well as what the police often colloquially describe as 'drinkers' and therefore likely to transgress the normal boundaries of behaviour acceptable to the police. The definition is therefore as absurd in terms of its applicability to sensible and achievable football policing as it is impenetrably written.

Bryan Drew, who led the drafting of these definitions, had the intention of using them to try to force police to consider surrounding circumstances, to develop a more nuanced understanding of the factors driving risk at the time the fans were categorised. Thus, in an attempt to clarify and possibly rein-in, this label, the College of Policing notes in its 2022 version of Authorised Professional Practice (APP) that

> It is essential that the risk in relation to individuals and groups is quantifiable and dynamically assessed. ***The description of a group or individual***

as 'risk' is not sufficient on its own, there must be a specific reference to the actual risk posed by individuals or groups.

Unfortunately, we would assert such laudable intentions were never properly or fully realised, and policing has generally fallen back on a rather blunt and simplistic interpretation of the categorisations that rarely, if ever, refers to broader situational drivers. The 'Risk Supporter Checklist'[8] that was subsequently provided by the UKFPU, confused the matter even further. It included several behaviours that, if displayed, would suggest the individuals in question were 'risk'. Given the definition above, it is odd that the list does not include 'anti-social behaviour'. It does, however, include behaviours or conditions that fall short of disorder or anti-social behaviour, including "away supporters in home sections", "travelling supporters without tickets", "political tension/use of banners", "alcohol related problems", and, possibly most bizarrely of all, "knowledge of police tactics". If the checklist was followed, then we could add to the label of 'risk supporter', parents and their children sitting together supporting different teams, alcoholics, flag-wavers, and any police officer or policing academic who happens to watch their local team on a day off. On the other extreme, the list also includes "terrorism", despite terrorists being dealt with by an entirely different set of laws, preventative orders, and specialised policing units. In short, the problem with the checklist, as with the basic EU-wide definition, is that neither provides qualitative or quantitative clarity to help anyone to accurately determine who is, or is not, a 'risk supporter' at the time when such judgements are made.

Moreover, the EU-wide definition is logically flawed in that it does not explain *what risk is*. This means the category is at best clumsy, with the potential of being counter-productive, when it comes to assisting the police to understand when, and how, risks to public order can develop. Instead, it functions to reify risk as if inherent within specific individuals and groups, such that when these categories are applied by police, the targeted fans become fixed into the category within and across different events. When, as often happens, a constable radios through to command

[8] http://library.college.police.uk/docs/APPref/Risk-Supporter-Checklist.pdf

that there "are a group of risk supporters in a pub", this could—if following the definition and checklist—technically mean just about anything and involve just about anyone. It could infer that the group do not possess tickets, or are singing an inoffensive chant, or are drunk, none of which are offences, or which necessarily require or demand police intervention. Accordingly, although such situations have never arisen, it could equally imply a group posing a risk of terrorism in connection with a fixture which, in contrast, would require very specialist police intervention. Perhaps as a result, our observations indicated that on occasion some police commanders would try to critically assess such assessments. Accordingly, our observations also show that Dedicated Football Officers (DFOs) and spotters (now Operational Football Officers [OFOs]) typically use a much narrower, nuanced, and colloquial definition, of fans who they judge pose a risk of engagement in football-related violence or criminal disorder, which *should* mean that only those fans will find themselves on a police database of risk supporters.

Contextualising Football Intelligence: The Risk Society and the Culture of Control

The fact that those responsible for the policing of football events are so focused on controlling and managing 'risk supporters' will come as no surprise to academics who have studied the modern criminal justice system. The concept of the 'Risk Society', a central concept within security studies more generally, was developed by, amongst others, Ulrich Beck (1992) and Anthony Giddens (1990, 1999). The basic argument is that in contrast to humans living before modernity, hazards or dangers in contemporary society are no longer likely to be seen as *force majeure* (Giddens, 1999) and are instead conceptualised as risks that need to be managed, essentially a desire to achieve the "taming of chance" (Hacking, 1990). Although Beck (1992) argues that all of us are now in the position where we are negotiating these risks, the management of risks by the police has attracted particular interest, most famously by Ericson and Haggerty's *Policing the Risk Society* (1997). Douglas argues that authorities prefer to use the term "risk", to "danger", because it places discretionary power in their hands (1992, p. 44), and thinking about managing, and mitigating, risk in policing is "not only pervasive but also routinised", meaning that "criminal justice is charged with managing the risk of crime" (Hudson, 2003, p. 43). Ericson and Haggerty (1997, p. 6) go further, arguing that "collective fear and foreboding underpin the value system of an unsafe society, perpetuate insecurity, and feed incessant demands for more knowledge of risk", so risk and safety, security, and control become fundamentally inter-related (see also Giddens, 1999). Such theoretical perspectives certainly help us to understand the surge in statutory provisions designed to regulate the conduct of football fans that we considered in Chap. 3, as part of what Garland calls a culture of control, based on strategies of preventative partnership and punitive segregation (Garland, 2001). We can contextualise the parallel growth in legal powers designed to confront 'football hooliganism' and the development of football policing operations as examples of both the development of the 'risk society' and the emerging 'culture of control' it subsequently generated.

Haggerty and Ericson correspondingly argue that police work is both organised and driven by classifications of risk that are supported by technologies which gather "risk knowledge". As they assert, the "yearning for security drives the insatiable quest for more and better knowledge" (Ericson & Haggerty, 1997, p. 85). However, at the same time, such risk-based approaches enable proactive action not merely in response to knowledge of risk but to uncertainty and the unknown (Zedner, 2009). The police therefore have a "growing orientation towards information gathering, anticipatory engagement, proactive intervention, systematic surveillance and rational calculation of results" (Johnson, 2000, p. 57). This is also potentially a cost-effective way of approaching criminal justice, aligning it with the neo-liberal political approach (O'Malley, 2010). But, as Zedner summarises, "risk relies not upon the legal designation of the individual, but upon administrative techniques" (Zedner, 2009, p. 39). This prioritisation of pre-emptive administrative processes in turn drives the deployment of resources. Risk classifications create the impression not only of reliability and certainty but also of legitimacy, allowing them to be accepted, "as normative obligations and therefore as scripts for action" (Ericson & Haggerty, 1997, p. 6). All these structures and processes are at work in football policing. We have already discussed in Chap. 4 how 'football intelligence' drives resourcing, shapes deployments, and sets the overall 'tone' of policing at individual football events. We also established how early pre-season categorisation of a match as high risk would not only influence deployments but could also affect the function, and reduce the influence, of later more accurate intelligence reports.

Furthermore, risk categorisations also impact upon individual rights. As Tsoukala sets out, risk-management policies tend to prioritise "group-based profiling" which emphasise pre-emptive control, "the marginalization of evidence and the subsequent growth of suspicion links", which is particularly of concern where the "legal upgrading of the control of deviance" has a punitive effect based on suspicion rather than proof of previous criminal activity (Tsoukala, 2013 p.141). Others contend that risk considerations and assessments tend to trump the rights of suspects, particularly through a process of bureaucracy designed to justify risk-management actions (Bullock & Johnson, 2012), which in turn makes it difficult to protect or balance competing rights (ibid; see also Zedner, 2006). This is a process we would assert is most clearly observable in the regulation of football through the creation and imposition of FBOs on 'complaint' rather than merely following conviction.

Categorising an individual as a risk to public order also deemphasises what Ericson and Haggerty describe as an individual's "moral culpability or responsibility for a particular act or wrongdoing" (Ericson & Haggerty, 1997, p. 42), as well the importance of other influences such as decision-making and action, including by the police themselves. "Categorical suspicion" is therefore also a means through which individuals come to be regarded as a threat, not as a result of their observed behaviour but because of the groups that they affiliate with (Marx, 1988; Hudson, 2003, p. 45). Unidentified individuals in risk groups often pose a challenge for OFOs; does their presence and association with others already classified as 'risk' indicate that they also pose a risk? Certainly, the content of spotter profiles in observed s.14B FBO cases suggested that some officers considered association with 'known risk' supporters to be evidence to this effect (James & Pearson, 2006). Further, observations in Magistrates Court identified the standardised definition of 'risk supporter' was regularly used by magistrates and District Judges in FBO cases to determine whether or not a ban should be imposed (James & Pearson, 2006) and by the Criminal Prosecution Service to determine whether conditional cautions are appropriate (CPS, 2022). The association with other risk supporters could be key evidence for imposing a s.14B FBO, and that this "guilt by association" could be cumulative (James & Pearson, 2006). In many ways, the "risk supporter" label causes the same legal problems as "football hooligan" once did (see Pearson, 1998). The label permeates the criminal justice system's response to football-related violence and disorder and can have a direct and serious impact upon criminal justice outcomes for supporters. But, as we have seen, there is an inherent problem in how the term is interpreted by these criminal justice actors and a potentially dangerous breakdown in translation between them.

As attention shifts from what individuals do, to what company they keep or category they belong to, so the line between criminality and sub-criminal transgressive behaviour becomes blurred (Hudson, 2003, p. 69). This process of categorisation differentiates, along stark and often immovable lines, the 'risk' and the 'normal' fans, again something which is an acknowledged feature of policing the risk society (Hacking, 1990; Ericson & Haggerty, 1997, p. 87). However, the fans themselves, whether 'risk' or not, are kept away from this process of differentiation, although they may be best placed to make these decisions and are significant stakeholders in the outcomes of such labelling. It is our argument then that too little attention is paid to "consensus making" between police and fans (Douglas, 1992, p. 12). Instead, policing in the risk society is understood to require expert information-gatherers and collators (Ericson & Haggerty, 1997; Garland, 2001, p. 171); in this context it is DFOs and OFOs who, as anointed experts, impose categorisations as if objective truth. As we will see in the forthcoming chapters, if a 'risk supporter' label is applied by a DFO or OFO, that fan can remain classified as 'risk' at future events, even if there is nothing to suggest they are intending to engage in violence and disorder. Conversely, fans outside of this category do not always or automatically become 'risk' merely by virtue of them engaging in spontaneous violence or disorder (although they may be categorised as such later). Interestingly, during our observations, categorisations of fans as 'risk' by other, 'non-expert', officers (e.g. British Transport

Police [BTP] constables) did not operate in this way and were often challenged until ratified by DFOs or OFOs.

Categorisation of the ordinary and the other in this way enables those charged with keeping order at football matches not only to assess risk but also to determine resources, and direct deployments, so lead directly to the policing of different groups in different ways. While 'non-risk' fans will be treated as ordinary citizens enjoying their leisure time, seen as deserving of rights and policed proportionately, those categorised as risk would typically become the focus of a more 'robust' policing operation. 'Risk supporters' were more likely to be subject to restrictions on movement, contained, 'escorted', and 'heldback', and the ongoing surveillance that characterises the policing of risk. This raises the question of rights. As Hudson points out, "risk control strategies throw into sharp relief the perennial questions of whose rights matter" (Hudson, 2003, p. 76). As we will see in Chap. 7, 'risk supporters' should enjoy comparable human rights of free expression (ECHR art. 10), peaceful assembly and association (art. 11), and should not have their liberty curtailed (art. 5) or their privacy infringed (art. 8). However, these are qualified rights, and the existence of risk profiles can provide a legal justification for the state to take action that may restrict these rights because the categorisation itself may be seen as rendering such action necessary and proportionate to prevent violence, disorder, criminality, or the infringement of others' rights. In particular, suspects' rights are eroded "in favour of surveillance system rights to obtain knowledge of suspects" (Ericson & Haggerty, 1997, p. 66). While surveillance is focused on the 'risk supporters', when these are in the wider football crowd, it is all fans who need to accept surveillance by CCTV and Evidence-Gathering Teams (EGTs), OFOs coming into their pubs, (usually covertly) surveillance of social media conversations online, and even the payment by police to 'risk' fans who then act as a Covert Human Intelligence Source (CHIS). It is, as the logic goes, all 'necessary' for their safety and security. Preventative legal measures such as the FBO also "provide an appealing offer" (Hebenton & Seddon, 2009, p. 343) for the state in response to the prevailing risk discourse in criminal justice. Civil liberties decline in the culture of control and the management of risk, and protection *from* the state is replaced by protection *by* the state (Garland, 2001).

It is clear that changes which have taken place in football crowd management in terms of both law and policing reflect these wider theoretical debates about the development of the pre-emptive turn in criminal justice, the increased focus on risk management, and the development of the 'culture of control'. But, more than this, we would argue that from the 1980s onwards, the management and control of football fans has been at the forefront of a change in approach, which has subsequently affected other areas of the 'risk society'. Furthermore, when it comes to preemptive law, what football did yesterday is still influencing what may happen in other areas of society tomorrow.[9] The development of the type of risk-management frameworks, processes, and procedures detailed in this section are clearly at play in the arena of football crowd policing, but super-charged. The identification, categorisation, and management of risk, both of individuals and events, have become the dominant focus for football policing operations in England and Wales, locked in at an early stage by planning and funding considerations. An entire nationally coordinated branch of policing has been set aside to prescribe how risk should be measured, how risk categorisations are established, and how these identified risks should then be managed. This is supported by oversight and funding from the UK Home Office, and its quango, the UKFPU, to encourage compliance with this approach among otherwise autonomous police forces and bolstered by a legislative regime of "super Football Banning Orders" (James & Pearson, 2018) that have blazed a trail for the development of further civil preventative orders in other areas of society. The risk-focused framework in football both encourages categorisation and surveillance, and discourages other legal and criminal justice tools used in other areas of society and which, in individual cases, may actually prove to be more effective. We will return to this argument in Chaps. 10 and 11.

[9] For example, the recently proposed Serious Disruption Prevention Orders, aka 'Protest Banning Orders'.

Redefining Dispositional Risk

Despite all of this, we do contend that the 'risk supporter' category is, in one way at least, an improvement on the static labels of A, B, and C, as it acknowledged that whether or not an individual engages in disorder on any particular occasion is not a given by virtue of their predisposition towards violence. It acknowledges that a 'risk supporter' will not always engage in violence, and implicitly suggests that the situation, and therefore policing approaches, can influence outcomes. However, as we have explained and will illustrate more fully in Chap. 8, the label is, and will remain, problematic for football policing. First, while policing resources are inevitably focused on those labelled 'risk supporters', often (but not always) this is without an assessment of their intentions on that day. Secondly, and linked to this, once labelled a 'risk supporter', our observations suggest that it is very difficult to lose this stigmatised identity. Years of avoiding any violence or disorder were usually insufficient, and despite arguments about the apparent effectiveness of FBOs in terms of reducing recidivism (Hamilton-Smith et al., 2011), having been served an FBO often cemented a life-long risk label. Thirdly, the label can encourage the police to pay insufficient attention to those who are not pre-classified in this category, ignoring the fact that certain interactions involving 'non-risk' fans can, and often do, pose a risk of disorder.

Finally, our observations suggested that the label 'risk supporter' is used in different ways by different forces, or even within forces, with DFOs/OFOs more likely to apply a narrower, more nuanced, context-dependent definition. While any group of men drinking heavily in casual clothing on their way to the football could be declared to be 'risk' (particularly as we will see when gathering on trains and at stations), the DFOs and OFOs we have observed instead tended to use the term more sparingly and discriminately, to refer to those that would have previously been considered 'Cat Bs or Cs' or 'prominents'. Indeed, we have observed DFOs and OFOs deliberately holding back information about the movement of 'risk fans' because they judged such information would be misinterpreted by commanders and therefore attract unnecessary police attention towards them. In short, depending on who was using the term, those categorised as a 'risk supporter' could range from what used to be called a 'Cat C', a 'Cat B', or even someone who was unknown to the police but simply looked the part. We believe this ambiguity and ubiquitous applicability has the potential to lead to both disproportionate policing of individuals and groups, and the misdirection and waste of increasingly scarce police resources.

In 2020, the UKFPU led on revising Football Policing APP for the College of Policing and, during this revision, consulted with the authors. As a result, we developed a paper that recommended a revised individual risk categorisation, which focused less on historical behaviours or association-based suspicion, and more on current intelligence, context, and behavioural outcomes. Our proposed definitions also sought to define the different 'risks' that might be posed by individuals during a football match event. Our recommendations were subsequently accepted and have been incorporated into the new APP, a preliminary version of which was circulated to all forces for the 2021/22 season. The new risk categorisations were as follows:

- **NON-risk Supporter:** There is no current intelligence or information that the supporter intends, or is likely, to engage in disorderly, anti-social, or criminal behaviours.
- **LOW-Risk Supporter:** There is current intelligence or information that the supporter may engage in anti-social behaviours or under specific circumstances commit low-level disorder or other criminal offences (e.g. because of heavy alcohol consumption or use of controlled drugs).
- **MEDIUM-Risk Supporter:** There is current intelligence or information that the supporter is likely to engage in anti-social and disorderly behaviours that may under specific circumstances involve violence or other more serious criminal offences (e.g. if confronted or provoked by opposition supporters).
- **HIGH-Risk Supporter:** There is current intelligence or information that the supporter intends to actively seek out and initiate violent confrontations and/or commit other significant criminal offences or aims to influence others around them to do so.

We believe this is an important step which helps clarify both what 'risk' means and tries to focus the attention of those developing intelligence assessments upon the specific event in question, rather than historical behaviours. However, the extent to which these new definitions will change the approach of policing operations, has yet to be understood.

Moreover, the new categorisations still rely to a great extent on the idea that disorder is primarily the result of the predisposition of individuals. So long as that focus remains, football operations will always struggle to predict and respond effectively to crowd management challenges. As we have argued, understanding the role, and contentiousness, of the risk-profiling of individuals is fundamental to understanding the limitations of the current model of football policing. In the previous chapter, we detailed the role that DFOs and OFOs play in driving football policing operations, but this process only works if the risk categorisations are accurate. Our argument, which will be illustrated in the following chapters, is that labelling individuals as 'risk' or 'non risk', even following the new, refined definition in APP, fails to adequately consider the contextual complexities or interactional dynamics of a football crowd event and is therefore often not helpful in predicting when, where, or why conflicts will occur. And yet, the existence of this information drives many strategic, operational, and tactical decisions. As we saw in Chap. 4, officers come to rely on it not only out of habit but also because of a fear of what might happen to their own careers if they fail to act on intelligence that proves to be accurate. Furthermore, as we will demonstrate, the focus on dispositional risk is not only unhelpful in predicting when, and how, disorder will occur, but too often becomes the focus of the police operation itself; categorising and then applying the category can become the primary function of the operation, which is set up to identify and tactically orient itself towards this understanding of risk. In this sense, it is the language and systems of control that we identified earlier that have become not only the means by which football policing operations take place but also their very ends.

The Role of Organised Fan Groups

The concept of 'risk' and 'non risk' supporters is, to reiterate, in our view an improvement in that the new definition is significantly refined and more precise. However, as we have stressed, there are underlying problems with the labels and categorisations, the ways in which fans can find themselves labelled, and the way in which risk assessments based on these labels can lead to inappropriate match categorisations, and subsequent deployment and tactics. Nonetheless, the creation of the 'non-risk' supporter should provide the opportunity for police to feel comfortable in reaching out to, and engaging with, these fans, to assist in devising their policing plans. There has undoubtedly been an improvement in communication between police and fan groups, partially as a result of both parties now sharing social media platforms, particularly *Twitter*. Some police forces have approached the leadership of organised fan groups to invite them for pre-match or pre-season meetings, or post-match debriefs, and there are examples of police tactics or advice being changed as a direct consequence of these meetings. Across several years, for example, meetings were held involving Merseyside and Greater Manchester Police (GMP) and representatives from the organised fan groups of Liverpool and Manchester United, which, we would argue, played an important role in helping to reduce the levels of confrontation surrounding one of the highest-risk fixtures in the country.

This is just one example of how the ability of the police to engage with fans has been improved by the creation of organised independent fan groups, be they independent supporters' groups concerned with match-going supporter welfare, Supporter Trusts, other pressure groups formed in response to management or ownership concerns, or groups concerned with the creation or improvement of 'atmosphere' at matches. There has been a rise not only in the number of such organised fan groups but also in the number of clubs in England and Wales looking to engage with these groups and encourage them, to varying degrees, to become involved in decision-making processes (Cleland, 2010). During the course of our research, we came across, and developed relationships with, a number of representatives of independent club fan groups or Supporters' Trusts, or

Supporter Liaison Officers (SLOs)[10] embedded within the football clubs themselves. From this, we were able to gain an understanding of the extent to which fan groups were involved in football event policing decisions.

Once again, there are geographical differences between supporters' group involvement in these processes; some have developed strong working relationships with their local force, while others have found their force to be less receptive to meaningful dialogue. However, it seems clear from our conversations with police and fan group representatives that there are several identifiable positive developments across the country. First, police forces are generally now more receptive to the principle of engagement and dialogue with fan groups than they were in the past (although relationships may sometimes falter with the changing of police or fan group personnel). Second, that most, if not all, police forces in England and Wales are keen to involve supporters as part of their outgoing communication strategy with fans, to assist in what is sometimes called a 'no surprises' approach to football policing. Third, most police forces are willing to involve supporter groups in debriefs after critical incidents, although the extent to which this results in change varies widely. "Supporters always have the opportunity to air grievances," noted one SLO.[11]

Most of the supporter representatives we spoke to explained that they had a very good relationship with their local DFO or OFOs. Where these relationships were allowed to develop over time, representatives felt able to speak openly to the DFO, who would make a point of saying hello when paths crossed at matches and who would invite the representative to planning meetings. The one problem identified, was that this dialogue was often dependent on an individual DFO being in post over a long period of time, whereas many DFOs would move to different roles in the police. Where DFOs changed regularly, it became difficult to establish

[10] SLOs are mandatory for all clubs under UEFA regulations, but while on the continent these are often roles filled by supporters who sit outside the club, in the UK they are more likely to be club employees, and often, the role is part of a wider public relations or marketing position. As such, SLOs in England and Wales typically play a more peripheral role when it comes to fan/police negotiation than their counterparts abroad.

[11] Supporter Representative 2, Interview, September 2020.

meaningful relationships and trust between parties. One representative noted that while the outgoing DFO would pass on information about the representative to the incoming one, typically the representative would have no information about the incoming DFO. "Gains have been made", one representative noted, "but the relationship should be better."[12] Another believed that there had recently been less contact between the fan organisation and the local force, "because we'd addressed most of the problems and the policing approach had changed … a lot of the things we had been working on had been taken on board".[13] The supporter representatives were broadly of a view that the DFOs in particular trusted the supporter representatives, and that this had improved over time: "we know we can have conversations in confidence."[14] At planning meetings, forces were willing to share information (although usually not sensitive intelligence on individuals or groups) and, at critical incident debriefs, police video footage. However, one representative suggested there was occasional tension when they felt there was an expectation that they would "tip off" the police about individuals or expected incidents. The representative's view was that this would undermine their legitimacy with their supporter-base and potentially put them at risk.[15] Nevertheless, it is clear that there has been considerable progress.

Although relationships of trust between fan representatives and DFOs were generally perceived to be good, most representatives identified a wider distrust of fans, including the representatives, amongst the wider policing operation. As one put it, "there's a natural distrust in the police of football fans … Football fans are [seen as] trouble." Meetings tended to take place on "police territory", with a pressure towards the informal, and often the police were seen as "quite defensive".[16] This was supported by another representative, who noted that while a number of officers heavily involved in football policing in his area were seen to be "committed to fan dialogue", this was not a view shared by all officers, many of

[12] Supporter Representative 3, Interview, September 2020.
[13] Supporter Representative 4, Interview, September 2020.
[14] Supporter Representative 3, Interview, September 2020.
[15] ibid.
[16] Supporter Representative 4, Interview, September 2020.

whom (including senior officers) still saw "football fans as a group to be dealt with".[17] "There has been a shift in their approach and their attitude … But they revert to type very quickly."[18]

Fan representatives generally suggested that they had limited impact upon policing tactics, but with some notable successes. Again, responses diverged across the country. Some forces, particularly serving smaller lower-league teams, were seen as being less responsive. Many representatives expressed frustration that meetings were too often focused on "passing on information to us rather than consulting … [Meetings] became a confirmation of previous procedures that had been put in place …"[19] While representatives agreed that it was useful to know what the police were planning, and saw a value in passing this information on to supporters, sometimes they were uncomfortable with its content and resented not being brought into the decision-making process earlier. One representative noted that pre-match meetings two to three days before the event were too late to influence key decisions,[20] while another stated that there were too many instances of the meeting being used simply by the force to inform fans of what would happen, "rather than it being a collaboration".[21] One example provided of this was when a supporter representative was invited to a pre-match meeting to be informed that the usual entrance and exit routes for visiting supporters were being changed. The representative explained that fans would resent the change and that it could lead to disorder. However, the decision had already been made, and as predicted by the representative, the change led to "chaos and violence".[22]

Nevertheless, all the club supporter representatives were able to point to examples where they felt they had achieved a positive impact on policing attitudes or tactics either generally or in relation to a particular fixture. One representative pointed to the relaxing of some of the most

[17] Supporter Representative 3, Interview, September 2020.
[18] Supporter Representative 1, Interview, September 2020.
[19] Supporter Representative 4, Interview, September 2020.
[20] Supporter Representative 3, Interview, September 2020.
[21] Supporter Representative 1, Interview, September 2020.
[22] Ibid.

stringent restrictions attached to a local derby,[23] while another believed they had helped to press their local force into using Liaison Officers to improve communication between police and fans at a high-risk fixture that had frequently seen disorder in the past, although they had a "feeling the police were going in that direction anyway".[24] The difficulty in measuring what impact the supporter groups have achieved on changing police approaches was something raised by a number of representatives, with some believing that their force were often unwilling to admit that the change had been the supporters' idea. One area in which more than one fan representative felt progress had been made as a result of fan pressure, was in officer dress. A combination of regular complaints about heavy-handed tactics and pressure, both locally and nationally from fan organisations, had been seen to influence the downgrading from 'riot gear' or hybrid uniforms to standard uniforms. However, the greatest impact upon police tactics from supporter group pressure was seen as coming from a reduction of "behavioural messaging".[25] A number of interviewees noted that their fan groups had complained to forces about them releasing statements, either on social media or through local media, warning fans to behave themselves at upcoming matches. After a while, pressure on this front had resulted in these messages reducing, and there were also several examples of behavioural messaging statements that were released without consultation with fan groups being deleted from online sources immediately after a complaint.

It is evident from both our observations of football policing operations and the views of supporter group representatives that, while levels of dialogue vary widely, police forces in England and Wales are typically paying more than just lip-service to the idea of engagement with fan groups. Instead, fan groups are increasingly being seen not only as conduits for communication, in line with the 'no surprises' approach to policing crowds, but as stakeholders in the development of effective and proportionate policing strategies and tactics. But at present this only goes so far. As we saw in the previous chapter, the key determinant of police

[23] Supporter Representative 2, Interview, September 2020.

[24] Supporter Representative 1, Interview, September 2020.

[25] Supporter Representative 3, Interview, September 2020.

resourcing of match events is its risk categorisation. Given the wealth of knowledge that regular match-going supporters have of the physical risks posed by attending certain fixtures, and the impact of such categorisations *upon* them, it might be expected that they are engaged in discussions about how matches should be categorised. However, none of the representatives we spoke to felt they had any input into this key decision. "It is something we talk about but they won't let us influence," explained one representative.[26] Other representatives agreed that match categorisation was something that was communicated to them, usually only shortly before a match, as if it was an objectively determined fact rather than a decision they could or should influence. In most cases, the representatives felt the police categorisation was fair, but a couple noted that there had been disagreements between the fans and police as to a categorisation, although that this had never resulted in the decision being changed.[27] "I don't sense that the police want to concede any control over match categorisation," concluded another, noting that in the event of disagreement the police would resort to claiming "we have intelligence" of risk of which the fans were unaware, in line with our arguments above. There was a fair amount of scepticism, particularly from the independent representatives, about these claims, details of which were often not shared.

Perhaps less surprisingly, given the ethical and data protection implications, fan representatives were also not consulted about categorisations of supporters. While, of course, many of the representatives will have knowledge about the involvement or otherwise of supporters involved in criminality, disorder, or violence, no representatives interviewed as part of this project suggested a desire to be involved in this process. This was not to say that they were all comfortable with how the risk supporter categorisation operated, but they did not consider it to be their job to 'tip off' intelligence officers about individuals or anticipated criminality. Moreover, they recognised that if they were involved in such decisions, this may damage their legitimacy and reputation as representatives of their fan base.

[26] Supporter Representative 2, Interview, September 2020.

[27] Supporter Representative 4, Interview, September 2020.

Conclusions

In this chapter, we have made several key arguments. First, that the accepted norms and behaviour of match-going fans has, for varying reasons, changed dramatically since the legislative changes of the 1970s and 1980s. The legislation was introduced to confront a very different situation than exists currently. Second, we contend that there is no uniform or overarching supporter 'culture' that can be used to police and plan match events. While there are differing norms of accepted behaviour between supporters of different clubs, the differences between fan groups following the same team are as pronounced as the similarities. A 'one size fits all' approach to policing fans of a particular team is therefore set up to fail. Third, we have contended that police knowledge of the behavioural drivers of different fan groups is vital for making assessments about the risks posed. Most importantly, that transgressive and carnivalesque behaviour, while needing careful management, should not be mistaken for a desire to engage in violence or serious disorder. Fourth, we drew attention to the problems and tensions inherent in the use of the 'risk supporter' label in differentiating those who supposedly pose a risk of violence and disorder from 'ordinary' supporters and consider how policing and the criminal justice system's responses to football disorder should be seen at the forefront of the wider move to the management of risk, pre-emptive justice, and the 'culture of control'. Finally, we saw how organised supporter groups were starting to play a role in the development of policing approaches to football, albeit at a limited and embryonic level.

Realistic, dynamic, and up-to-date knowledge of a club's support is absolutely vital for those charged with policing football. But forces also need to acknowledge that the supporters themselves possess vital knowledge that can be tapped into. Fans should not merely be seen as the targets of policing operations, but as a vital resource for those operations. On moral grounds alone, fans should have input into key strategic and tactical decisions, because they are the most important stakeholders in these decisions; as we have seen from tragedies such as Heysel and Hillsborough, it is the fan's life that is typically on the line if poor decisions are made. But there is an equally strong argument on practical grounds for why fans should be involved; put simply, fan knowledge can help to direct effective and proportionate decisions on strategy, deployment, tone, and tactics, and ultimately increase the legitimacy of police approaches and their chances of success.

The progress that has been made in dialogue between fan groups and the police should be applauded, but limitations should also be recognised. Fans at many clubs are now having a regular and important impact in decisions over styles of dress and tone of communications, but they also need to be more heavily involved in key tactical decisions. If fans are to be genuine trusted stakeholders in football policing decisions, they should also be consulted about the risk categorisations of matches. Currently, the language of risk is used to exclude fans from the strategic decisions that affect their own safety, once again demonstrating that risk is seen as personalised not as contextual, and predominantly a matter of control over supporters. The 'risk supporter' categorisation stigmatises some individuals and groups, but conversely those fans categorised as 'non-risk' do not seem to achieve elevated status when it comes to intelligence-sharing, or consultation over strategic or tactical decisions. The fact that "Knowledge of Police Tactics" was a risk determiner on the College of Policing's 'risk supporter' checklist shows that despite the progress in engagement, and the obsession with individual risk categorisation, there remains very much an 'us and them' attitude shown by too many officers engaged in football policing.

References

Agar, M. (2006). Culture: Can You Take it Anywhere? *International Journal of Qualitative Methods, 5*(2), 1–12.

Armstrong, G. (1998). *Hooligans: Knowing the Score*. Berg.

Armstrong, G., & Hobbs, D. (1994). Tackled from Behind. In R. Giulianotti, N. Bonney, & M. Hepworth (Eds.), *Football Violence and Social Identity* (pp. 196–228). Routledge.

Back, L., Crabbe, T., & Solomos, J. (2001). *The Changing Face of Football: Racism, Identity and Multiculture in the English Game*. Berg.

Bakhtin, M. (1984). *Rabelais and His World.* Midland Books, Indiana University Press.
Beck, U. (1992). *Risk Society: Towards a New Modernism.* Sage.
Bourdieu, P. (1977). *Outline of a Theory of Practice.* Cambridge University Press.
Brightman, R. (1985). Forget Culture: Replacement, Transcendence, Relexification. *Cultural Anthropology, 10*(4), 509–546.
Bromberger, C., Hayot, A., & Mariottini, J. (1993). Allez L'OM, forza Juve: The passion for football in Marseille and Turin. In S. Redhead (Ed.), *The Passion and the Fashion: Football Fandom in New Europe* (pp. 103–151). Avebury.
Bullock, K., & Johnson, P. (2012). The Impact of the Human Rights Act 1998 on Policing in England and Wales. *British Journal of Criminology, 52*(3), 630–650.
Burke, P. (2002). *Popular Culture in Early Modern Europe.* Ashgate.
Cleland, J. (2010). From passive to active: the changing relationship between supporters and football clubs. *Soccer & Society, 11*(5), 537–552.
Clifford, J., & Marcus, G. (1986). *Writing Culture: The Poetics and Politics of Ethnography.* University of California Press.
CPS. (2022). Football Related Offences and Football Banning Orders: Legal Guidance. Updated May 5, 2022. https://www.cps.gov.uk/legal-guidance/football-related-offences-and-football-banning-orders
Curtuis, E. R. (1953). *European Literature and the Latin Middle Ages.* Pantheon.
Douglas, M. (1992). *Risk and Blame: Essays in Cultural Theory.* Routledge.
Durkheim, E. (1964). *The Elementary Forms of Religious Life.* Allen and Unwin.
Elias, N., & Dunning, E. (1986). *Quest for Excitement: Sport and Leisure in the Civilising Process.* UCD Press.
Ericson, R., & Haggerty, K. (1997). *Policing the Risk Society.* Clarendon.
Ferrell, J. (2004). Boredom, Crime and Criminology. *Theoretical Criminology, 8*(3), 287–302.
Garland, D. (2001). *The Culture of Control: crime and social order in contemporary society.* Oxford University Press.
Garland, J., & Rowe, M. (1999). The 'English Disease'—Cured or in Remission? An Analysis of Police Responses to Football Hooliganism in the 1990s. *Crime Prevention and Community Safety: An International Journal, 1*, 35–47.
Geertz, C. (1973). *The Interpretation of Cultures.* Hutchinson.
Gibbons, T. (2019). *English National Identity and Football Fan Culture: Who Are Ya?* Routledge.
Giddens, A. (1990). *The Consequences of Modernity.* Polity Press.
Giddens, A. (1999). Risk and Responsibility. *Modern Law Review, 62*(1), 1–10.

Giulianotti, R. (1991). Scotland's Tartan Army in Italy: the Case for the Carnivalesque. *Sociological Review, 39*(3), 503–527.

Giulianotti, R. (1995). Football and the Politics of Carnival: An Ethnographic Study of Scottish Fans in Sweden. *International Review for the Sociology of Sport, 30*(2), 191–223.

Green, P. (2007). Ultra Sensitive. *When Saturday Comes 242.*

Gupta, A., & Ferguson, J. (1992). Beyond "Culture": Space, Identity, and the Politics of Difference. *Cultural Anthropology, 7*(1), 6–23.

Hacking, I. (1990). *The Taming of Chance.* Cambridge University Press.

Hamilton-Smith, N., Bradford, B., Hopkins, M., Kurland, J., Lightowler, C., McArdle, D., & Tilley, N. (2011). *An Evaluation of Football Banning Orders in Scotland.* Scottish Government Social Research.

Hebenton, B., & Seddon, T. (2009). From Dangerousness to Precaution: Managing Sexual and Violent Offenders in an Insecure and Uncertain Age. *British Journal of Criminology, 49*, 343–362.

Hodges, A. (2016). The Hooligan as the "Internal" Other? Football fans, ultras culture and nesting intra-orientalisms. *International Review for the Sociology of Sport, 51*(4), 410–427.

Hudson, B. (2003). *Justice in the Risk Society.* Sage.

James, M., & Pearson, G. (2006). Football Banning Orders: Analysing their use in Court. *The Journal of Criminal Law, 70*(6), 509–530.

Johnson, L. (2000). *Policing Britain: Risk, Security and Governance.* Longman.

James, M., & Pearson G. (2018). '30 Years of Hurt: The Evolution of Civil Preventative Orders. *Hybrid Law, and the Emergence of the Super-Football Banning Order Public Law, 1*, 44–61.

Jones, K. (2008). Female Fandom: Identity, Sexism, and Men's Professional Football in England. *Sociology of Sport Journal, 25*(4), 516–537.

King, A. (1997). The Lads Masculinity and the New Consumption of Football. *Sociology, 31*(2), 329–346.

King, A. (2002). *The End of the Terraces: The Transformation of English Football in the 1990s.* Leicester University Press.

Knijnik, J., & Newson, M. (2021). '"Tribalism", Identity Fusion and Football Fandom in Australia: The Case of Western Sydney. *Soccer and Society, 22*(3), 248–265.

Marcus, G. (1998). *Ethnography through Thick and Thin.* Princeton University Press.

Marsh, P. (1978). *Aggro: The Illusion of Violence with a Foreword by Desmond Morris.* Dent & Sons.

Marsh, P., Rosser, E., & Harré, R. (1978). *The Rules of Disorder.* Routledge.

Martyn, P., & Taylor, R. (1997). Something for the weekend, sir? Leisure, ecstasy and identity in football and contemporary religion. *Leisure Studies, 16*(1), 37–49.

Marx, G. (1988). *Undercover: Police Surveillance in America*. University of California Press.

Millward, P. (2006). We've All Got The Bug For Euro-Aways': What Fans Say about European Football Club Competition. *International review for the Sociology of Sport, 41*(3–4), 375–393.

Morris, D. (1981). *The Soccer Tribe*. Jonathan Cape.

Morrissey, S. (2008). Performing risks: catharsis, carnival and capital in the risk society. *Journal of Youth Studies, 11*(4), 413–427.

Newson, M. (2017). Football, Fan Violence, and Identity Fusion. *International Review for the Sociology of Sport, 54*(4), 431–444.

O'Malley, P. (2010). *Crime and Risk*. Sage.

Pearson, G. (1998). The English Disease: Socio-Legal Constructions of Football Hooliganism. *Youth and Policy - The Journal of Critical Analysis, 60*, 1–15.

Pearson, G. (2012). *An Ethnography of English Football Fans: Cans, Cops and Carnivals*. Manchester University Press.

Pearson, G. (2016). Ethnography and the Study of Football Fan Cultures. In M. Buchowski, G. Kowalska, A. Schwell, & N. Szogs (Eds.), *New Ethnographic Perspectives on Football in Europe*. Macmillan.

Pope, S. (2013). The "Love of My Life": The Meaning and Importance of Sport for Female Fans. *Journal of Sport and Social Issues, 37*(2), 176–195.

Poulton, E. (2008). Towards a Cultural Sociology of "Fantasy Football Hooliganism". *Sociology of Sport Journal, 25(3)*, 331–349.

Poulton, E. (2013). The culture of production behind the (re)production of football hooligan culture, or "Fantasy football hooliganism". *Continuum, 28*(4), 770–784.

Presdee, M. (2002). *Cultural Criminology and the Carnival of Crime*. Routledge.

Redhead, S. (1997). *Post-Fandom and the Millennial Blues: The Transformation of Soccer Culture*. Routledge.

Redhead, S. (2010). Little Hooliganz: The Inside Story of Glamorous Lads, Football Hooligans and Postsubculturalism. *Entertainment and Sports Law Journal, 8*(2) Online https://www.entsportslawjournal.com/article/id/799/

Redhead, S. (2015). Terrace Banter: Researching Football Hooligan Memoirs. *Sport in Society, 18*(3), 313–328.

Richards, J. (2017). *Sports Space: A Conceptual Model of Everton Football Club Match-day Fan Movement*. Unpublished PhD Thesis:. University of Sydney.

Richards, J., & Parry, K. (2019). Beers and blurred boundaries: The spatial and gendered organisation of pre-match venues for English football fans. *International Journal for the Sociology of Sport, 55*(6), 647–663.
Rookwood, J. (2009). *Fan Perspectives on Football Hooliganism: Defining, Analysing and Responding to the British Phenomenon*. VDM Verlag.
Sales, R. (1983). *English Literature in History 1780–1830: Pastoral and Politics*. Hutchinson.
Spaaij, R. (2006). *Understanding Football Hooliganism*. Amsterdam University Press.
Stallybrass, P., & White, A. (1986). *The Politics and Poetics of Transgression*. Methuen.
Stam, R. (1988). Mikhail Bakhtin and left cultural critique. In E. Kaplan (Ed.), *Post-modernism and Its Discontents* (pp. 116–145). Verso.
Steinmetz, K., Schaefer, B., & Green, E. (2016). Anything but boring: A cultural criminological exploration of boredom. *Theoretical Criminology, 21*(*3*), 342–360.
Stott, C. (2020). Crowd Behaviour and 'hooliganism'. In S. A. Haslam, K. Fransen, & F. Boen (Eds.), *Sports and Exercise Psychology: The Social Identity Approach* (pp. 321–340). Sage.
Stott, C., Hutchison, P., & Drury, J. (2001). "Hooligans" abroad? Inter-group dynamics, social identity and participation in collective "disorder" at the 1998 World Cup Finals. *British Journal of Social Psychology, 40*, 359–384.
Stott, C., & Pearson, G. (2007). *Football Hooliganism: Policing and the War on the English Disease*. Pennant.
Stott, C., West, O., & Radburn, M. (2018). Policing football "risk"? A participant action research case study of a liaison-based approach to "public order". *Policing and Society, 28*(1), 1–16.
Tsoukala, A. (2013). Controlling football-related violence in France: law and order versus the rule of law. *Sport in Society, 16*(2), 140–150.
Webb, D. (2005). Bakhtin at the Seaside: Utopia, Modernity and the Carnivalesque. *Theory, Culture and Society, 22*(3), 121–138.
Woods, J., & Ludvigsen, J. (2021). The changing faces of fandom? Exploring emerging "online" and "offline" fandom spaces in the English Premier League. *Sport in Society, 1*. https://doi.org/10.1080/17430437.2021.1904902
Zedner, L. (2006). Neither Safe nor Sound? The Perils and Possibilities of Risk. *Canadian Journal of Criminology and Criminal Justice, 48*(3), 424–434.
Zedner, L. (2009). Fixing the future: the pre-emptive turn in criminal justice. In B. M. McSherry, A. Norrie, & S. Bronitt (Eds.), *Regulating Deviance* (pp. 35–58). Hart.

6

Understanding the Psychology of Football Crowds

Introduction

As we have already argued in Chap. 2, football hooliganism became a high-profile social and political issue in the latter part of the twentieth century in part because several major incidents challenged the police and brought embarrassment to the UK Government. There can be no more powerful example of this than the Heysel Stadium disaster in 1985 and the subsequent banning of English club sides from UEFA competitions for five years. Indeed, it is arguably the case that from the mid-1980s onwards, it was predominately the behaviour of England fans at *international* football competitions that drove both media and political attention towards the issue of *domestic* 'hooliganism'. As we saw in Chap. 4, the 1980s were essentially a 'decade of disorder'; high-profile incidents such as the summer riots of 1980 and 1981 and the 'Battle of Orgreave' during the 1984 Miners' Strike, along with continuing problems at football, resulted in ongoing concerns about police and government capacity to control public order. In short, the perceived failures to control 'football hooliganism' were a key element of a broader and ongoing sense of crisis (cf. Hall et al., 1978).

G. Pearson, C. Stott, *A New Agenda For Football Crowd Management*, Palgrave Studies in Risk, Crime and Society, https://doi.org/10.1007/978-3-031-16298-5_6

With England fans involved in three days of serious disturbances in Dusseldorf during the 1988 UEFA European Championships, there were ever-increasing political pressures to act to address the so-called English Disease. Yet, while the term 'hooliganism' was, and still is, readily applied to the kinds of incidents witnessed at Heysel and in West Germany, another term is equally if not more relevant: 'riot'. As one article describing events in 1988 noted:

> the violence spread quickly across Dusseldorf, 35 miles north of Bonn, with rioters using beer bottles, fists, chairs and tables as weapons. The fans wrecked 20 automobiles, broke rows of shop windows and demolished furniture in sidewalk cafes, causing damage estimated at hundreds of thousands of dollars, police said.[1]

This shift in terminology, from hooliganism to rioting, may seem a relatively moot point, but in this chapter, we will argue that it is both fundamental and valuable because it allows us to look at the same issues from a different theoretical perspective, that of crowd psychology.

As we have already established, the term 'hooliganism' is at best deeply problematic, not least of all because it tends to be applied as both a description of events and an implicit theory of cause. For example, Heysel is still widely described and understood as one of the worst examples of English football 'hooliganism' in the history of modern football and it is often assumed, as it was by many at the time, that the disaster was caused by the convergence of 'hooligans' who followed Liverpool FC. However, in international policing circles, Heysel's underlying causal dynamics have long been understood to have been far more complex, with multiple contributing factors, not least of all a failure of international police cooperation. Consequently, to address such failures, in the wake of the disaster the Belgian police and their English counterparts led on establishing the first framework for international football police cooperation through the Council of Europe in Strasbourg. So, for the authorities at least, Heysel needed to be understood and managed not merely in terms of

[1] https://www.upi.com/Archives/1988/06/15/Hundreds-of-British-and-West-German-soccer-fans-clashed/1440582350400/

'hooliganism', but as a crowd event. Thus, as we will argue in this chapter, while there is a value in rejecting the notion of 'hooliganism' as a descriptive and analytical concept altogether, it is equally important to understand the issues of football-related collective conflict in terms of social identity-based crowd psychology. We will argue that when we do so, it is possible to draw upon and develop knowledge that not only helps to advance academic understanding but also to facilitate solutions that might not otherwise have been possible.

Classical Theory of Crowds

Like the concept of football 'hooliganism', crowd psychology has a long and often troubled history which has clouded popular understandings, so it is important we begin by clarifying the terminology and background science. The problem is that 'common sense' perspectives on the behaviour and psychology of crowds are everywhere in contemporary popular, political, and media discourse. These common-sense assumptions are extremely problematic and have their origins in the 'science' of crowd psychology that emerged during the latter part of the nineteenth century. At that time, the industrial revolution had been underway for over 100 years and had brought about unprecedented changes to society, most notably in the form of urbanisation and with it the birth of mass society (Barrows, 1981). As people flooded away from the old agrarian social arrangements of the countryside, the 'peasantry' took up low-paid work in the unsafe, unregulated, working conditions of the newly emerging factories of the industrial capitalist economy. These new 'working classes', or as Marx called them the *proletariat*, were forced to live and work in appalling conditions within rapidly expanding cities (see Engels, 2009). Correspondingly, without access to wealth or land, these workers had no political franchise to improve their lives and situations.

The birth of 'mass society' also gave delivery to new political theories, most notably those authored by Karl Marx and Fredrick Engels that began to call for socialist revolution to overturn this new capitalist social order (Wheen, 2010). In this sense, the nineteenth century was marked not only by an industrial revolution but also by an economic, social, and political one. Correspondingly, the social sciences, which emerged through the mid to late nineteenth century, have their origins, at least in part, in trying to understand how to manage the problems of criminality and disorder that this new form of mass urban society had created. As events at Peterloo in Manchester in 1819 had already demonstrated, the crowd, and its revolutionary potential, began to pose a growing threat to the increasingly rich and powerful industrial capitalists and their aristocratic allies. Therefore, central to the intellectual project of the new social sciences was crowd or mass psychology, a discipline that evolved towards the end of the century, arguably as an attempt to develop a technology of social control. For example, foundational to this new science was a debate between two criminological perspectives trying to grapple with the thorny issue of how to prosecute people who had been arrested for their involvement in riots (McClelland, 1989; Stott & Drury, 2016).

The first of these perspectives was led by Schipio Schegle, an Italian sociologist and Lombrosian criminologist who studied law at the University of Rome and taught at the Free University of Brussels from 1892 to 1902. Put very simply, Schegle drew upon the ideas of Enrico Ferri and the phrenologist Cesare Lombroso, who assumed that there are sub-classes of humanity who are physiologically inclined towards crime. This perspective asserted that criminality in crowds occurs because of the convergence of people who are predisposed towards criminality, hence crowd psychologists call this the 'convergence perspective'. The second, contrasting, theoretical and philosophical standpoint was led by Gabriel Tarde, who worked as a magistrate and investigating judge in France between 1869 and 1894. Reflecting his intellectual status towards the end of his career, Tarde was appointed a Professor in Modern Philosophy at the Collège de France in 1900. Tarde was critical of the Lombrosian idea of the atavistic criminal, arguing instead that even 'ordinary' people could be drawn into criminality in crowds through processes of imitation. It was Tarde who developed the concept of the 'group mind' that was later popularised by the most infamous nineteenth-century crowd theorist, Gustave Le Bon (1895). The central idea put forward by both Tarde and Le Bon is that the crowd is a place where people become anonymous and, as a result, their consciousness or 'rationality' is inhibited, and their behaviour is temporarily driven by an inherently violent and anti-social 'mob-psychology'.

Both perspectives seem somewhat simplistic and fanciful from a twenty-first-century perspective; indeed, subsequent research has demonstrated that they are. The key problem with both the 'mad mob' and 'convergence' versions of these classical perspectives is that neither can adequately account for how crowds behave or predict where crowd violence will happen. Remarkably, however, these two contrasting perspectives still find their way into contemporary 'common sense' understandings and media coverage of crowd violence.

We will consider the 'mob-psychology' perspective first. The basic proposition here is that when people enter crowds, they lose the rational control of their own behaviour (e.g. Zimbardo, 1969). The normal constraints of guilt and shame are assumed to disappear and an underlying universal tendency to act in anti-social and criminal ways comes to the fore. This is presumed to occur because, from this perspective, people in crowds are anonymous, an assumption that itself is problematic, because people in crowds are not necessarily indistinguishable to each other or indeed anyone else. In any case, the argument is that because of gathering, people in crowds have a natural—indeed unavoidable—tendency to become violent and randomly destructive. The logic of this is that, empirically, all crowds, or at least most of them, should be violent and destructive most of the time, which is quite obviously absurd. One does not need to look far to observe that most crowd events pass off entirely peacefully and therefore even at face value the 'mob-psychology' account is quite clearly flawed. In this sense, the mob psychology approach retains its popularity not because it is valid but because it serves useful ideological functions in attributing blame to crowd participants and legitimatising repressive policing (see Stott & Drury, 2016 for a fuller explanation).

However, it tends to be the convergence perspective (i.e. that crowd violence is the product of the coming together of those predisposed towards crime) that finds stronger resonance in popular accounts of crowd conflict in the context of football. After all, 'hooligans' are, by definition, assumed to be predisposed towards violent criminality or 'hooliganism' and it is their convergence that is widely understood to be one of the primary factors determining whether disorder may occur. But, once again, the convergence 'explanation' suffers key explanatory weaknesses. If we are to accept, as seems reasonable, that some people are more inclined towards violence than others (e.g. the people who self-identify as, or who are labelled, 'hooligans'), we would still need to accept such people are not violent all the time and therefore there remains the need to explain the specific social conditions that translate the assumed disposition into behaviour. In short, the dispositional argument, while initially attractive, explains little and predicts even less. It is empirically demonstrable that so-called hooligans, or 'risk fans', regularly populate football crowds where collective violence does not occur, and are often not present when it does. As we pointed out earlier and will show again, one of the key features of the rioting involving English fans attending international tournaments is that the majority of those arrested have little to no history of violence-related offending. This makes it very difficult to sustain the idea that such people are somehow predisposed towards violence. The label 'hooligan' or 'risk' therefore often offers little more than a circular, *post hoc*, description of their behaviours (i.e. we assume their involvement is because they are hooligans but only know they are hooligans because they are already involved). In effect, the core empirical problem is how to explain the involvement of thousands of fans in major football-related riots who have displayed no prior evidence of violent predisposition. Put slightly differently, the challenge we have is not how do we explain the involvement of hooligans but how is it that so many 'non-hooligan' fans get involved in collective violence, particularly at major international tournaments?

New Perspectives on Crowd Psychology

As we have already discussed, in the summers of 1980 and 1981 the news was filled with stories about the wave of so-called race riots that swept across England. The first of these occurred in April 1980, in the St Paul's district of the city of Bristol. At that time, a group of social psychologists had begun to establish themselves in the Department of Psychology at Bristol University and were busy developing radically new ways of understanding how groups and group psychology operate. The team was initially led by a French emigree called Henri Tajfel, who unfortunately died later that year (Brown, 2019). However, working alongside him was his former but equally influential PhD student, John Turner, who at that time was supervising a postgraduate student, Steve Reicher, whose specific interest was the study of the crowd. It was fortuitous for him and for us that the first of these summer riots took place just down the road from the University.

Reicher's research on the St Paul's riot challenged classical crowd theory (in both its mob psychology and convergence forms) and laid the foundation of a new social identity perspective on crowd psychology (Reicher, 1982). Key to this innovative approach was rejecting the idea that crowds are places where people lose the rational or meaningful control of their behaviour. Instead, from the social identity perspective, crowds are places where people reorient away from a sense of themselves as unique individuals, towards an awareness of their shared participation in a social category or group. So, for example, when people are standing in a crowd on the Kop at Anfield singing "You'll never walk alone", they will have a sense of their shared solidarity, a focus on the things that bind them together and make them similar. They will also have a strong sense of collective history in terms of how they relate to others and how others have related to them. In other words, psychologically speaking, crowds are places where people can shift from thinking about themselves as *I* and *me*, to thinking about themselves as *we*, *us*, and *them*.

In more technical terms, in crowds there can be a qualitative shift in the psychological system referred to as 'the self', where people move away from seeing themselves and acting in terms of their personal idiosyncratic identities (e.g. Geoff or Cliff), towards defining themselves and acting in terms of their social- or group-level identities (e.g. academics protesting whilst on strike). When analysing the St Paul's riot using this theoretical perspective, Reicher was able to explain, and make sense of, the patterns of behaviour he observed empirically within it. By analysing what people in the riot did behaviourally, he was able to demonstrate that their collective behaviours were far from random (as mob psychology would predict). Instead, people spontaneously collectively attacked some targets, like the police, but actively ignored, or even defended, others (e.g. shops owned by locals). By interviewing people involved, he was able to determine that these behaviours all related meaningfully to a sense of identity defined in terms of locally manifested structural-racism and what it meant to be black in Britain at that time. In other words, collective behaviour during the riot was not a product of a loss of identity, but a refocusing among participants on themselves as members of a social group. In this way, this ground-breaking study was able to add to the growing body of work in other disciplines (such as social history) that was already seeking to reject the classical crowd perspectives of the nineteenth century by showing that rioting was far from a random explosion of irrational destruction (e.g. Rudé, 1964). In short, the study demonstrated that it was far better to understand the behaviour of the crowd in terms of a historically—and contextually determined—social identity than it was to assume a loss of identity brought about by anonymity and mob psychology. In the case of St Paul's, an identity defined in terms of what it meant to be British and black in a structurally racist society (Reicher, 1984, 1987).

While it remains, a major theoretical breakthrough, this social identity approach (SIA) to crowd behaviour was very much focused on explaining what people in the crowds did after a riot had already begun. As such, empirical and theoretical questions still remained about how riots develop in the first place and it was around this issue that Stott began his PhD research under Reicher's supervision in the Department of Psychology at Exeter University in late 1989. The first element of that PhD was an ethnographic and interview-based study of the 1990 'poll tax riot', which began as one of the largest peaceful demonstrations witnessed in central London during the latter part of the twentieth century. The demonstration took place on 31st March, the day before a new taxation system referred to as 'the Community Charge' was due to be implemented by the Conservative Government under Margaret Thatcher. Dubbed the 'poll tax', resistance to the new levy was popular and widespread, and culminated in around a quarter of a million people gathering to protest. The demonstration began with a rally in Kennington Park on the south side of the river Thames, snaked its way over Lambeth Bridge, past the Houses of Parliament, along Whitehall, and into Trafalgar Square, where a second rally was scheduled to take place.

The demonstration was so large that by the time the front of the march had reached Trafalgar Square, people were still leaving Kennington Park some two-and-a-half miles away. As a result, while events were entirely peaceful, during the early stages the route became very congested and a sit-down protest in Whitehall took place adjacent to Downing Street. Based on his research, Stott was able to conclude that this congestion and the sit-down ignited a series of police/crowd interactions that fundamentally changed the nature of the identity, driving and enabling collective action in the crowd. His research suggested that initially, protesters had defined themselves in terms of an identity that limited crowd behaviour to peaceful, collective, protest about what was perceived to be an unjust taxation system and the government that introduced it. As a result, crowd participants saw themselves and others as acting legitimately and posing no threats to public order. In contrast, the police, particularly the senior commander in Whitehall, viewed the situation surrounding the sit-down protests very differently. Drawing upon a 'mob psychology' perspective, he interpreted the behaviour in that location as the first signs that the crowd was beginning to manifest its natural tendency towards disorder. Consequently, he ordered police to intervene in large numbers who began forcefully dispersing everyone from the area (Stott & Reicher, 1998a).

The police intervention was, by its very, nature indiscriminate in its use of force, affecting everybody in the location in the same way, regardless of prior intentions and behaviour. Stott and Drury (2000) argue it was this changing social context, brought about through police intervention, that altered the form and content of crowd participants' social identity along two key dimensions. First, given protesters saw themselves as acting legitimately, people in the crowd interpreted the police intervention as illegitimate, unwarranted, and dangerous, not least of all because it was creating crushing due to the crowd density in that area. In this new intergroup situation, people in the crowd came to see conflict against the police as a legitimate reassertion of their rights and even a form of self-defence. Second, the indiscriminate nature of the police intervention meant hundreds, if not thousands, of people were affected. This created a shared sense of fate among people in the crowd that in turn created a psychological unity among them, defined through a common relationship to the perceived illegitimacy of the police. This sense of psychological unity then led many in the crowd to feel empowered enough to actively resist police actions. The emergence of collective conflict then confirmed police assumptions of the hostile crowd, so they deployed more resources, drawing more people into the increasing cycle of escalation, culminating in one of the largest riots relating to a political demonstration ever witnessed in London (see also Reicher, 1996). In this way, collective confrontation against the police was not an inherent feature of the crowd, or a result of the predispositions of those within it. Instead, it emerged as a function of the situation because of a group-level interaction between crowd participants and police.

Policing Football Crowds: Violence as a Self-fulfilling Prophesy

These early social identity studies of riots began to help advance crowd psychology well beyond the classical perspectives, and just two months after the poll tax riot, England fans began arriving on the Italian island of Sardinia, where the national team were drawn to play Egypt, the Netherlands, and Ireland in the group stages of the 1990 FIFA World Cup Finals. The tournament provided the first opportunity to explore the problems of 'football hooliganism' from a social identity-based crowd psychology perspective. With English club sides still banned from Europe, the collective behaviour of England fans was again high on the media and political agenda. Indeed, amid the controversy, the British Government were reported to have been in dialogue with the Italian authorities to curb the so-called hooligan menace through 'tough action'. The Italian media too were busy at work, reporting on the potential invasion of English 'hooligans'. Reflecting the perceived threat, around 7000 Italian police and Carabinieri were deployed to the island and there were indeed several incidents of 'disorder' involving England fans in the two weeks they were on the island. The largest, and most significant of these, was a riot between England fans and the police just prior to England's second fixture of the tournament against the Netherlands. The British Government and media were quick to attribute that collective violence to 'hooliganism' and praise the Italian police for their "swift, tough and decisive action" (Colin Moynihan the then UK Government's Minister for Sport, cited in Stott & Reicher, 1998b).

A study of this riot formed another component of Stott's PhD research, which suggested it was an outcome of similar interactional dynamics and social identity processes to those that had been observed in the poll tax riot. Stott and Reicher (1998b) argued that the Italian authorities had developed an expectation that England fans converging onto the island posed a universal and unavoidable threat to public order. Yet, in contrast, the research suggested that almost all the England fans arriving on Sardinia had no intention of committing offences and were there merely to peacefully gather, drink and celebrate their identity, enjoy themselves boisterously, and watch the football. Nevertheless, presumably based on their pre-tournament expectations, across the first week the police had begun to treat all England fans as if they were uniformly dangerous, at times aggressively dispersing various forms of otherwise peaceful collective self-assertion (e.g. gathering to sing and chant outside bars), which they incorrectly assumed were manifestations of 'hooliganism'. For example, after England's opening match against Ireland, thousands of England fans had to walk from the stadium to Caligari city centre railway station, as no buses had been laid on to transport them from the stadium, which was located on the outskirts of the city. It was late evening, so by the time fans arrived, the last scheduled trains to the surrounding resort towns, where many were staying, had already departed, leaving thousands of England fans stranded. Following a minor altercation provoked by some locals, the police then baton-charged the large crowd of several thousand England fans, leading to multiple arrests and injuries. As a result of this and other incidents, England fans all across the island experienced policing as the arbitrary and illegitimate denial of their rights. Consequently, for many, what it meant to be England fans in that context (i.e. their identity) changed and they increasingly came to define themselves in oppositional terms to an unjust police force and to see confrontation against the police as legitimate social action. When these forms of crowd/police interaction occurred in the context of a march towards the stadium involving of upward of 6000 England fans, just prior to the fixture against the Netherlands, there was an opportunity for many to feel empowered enough to confront the intervening police, and as such, collective violence developed and escalated (see Stott & Pearson, 2007 pp. 59–82).

Put simply, this research began to empirically demonstrate, for the first time, the importance and value of understanding and analysing these incidents of 'hooliganism' from the theoretical perspective of crowd psychology. What the study and its related theory exposed, is that the same interactional social and psychological processes underpinning the emergence of violence in the poll tax riots also appeared to be at work during this incident of so-called hooliganism. Indeed, the analysis suggested that attributing cause to the dispositional aspects of the England fan base was flawed because it was equally police expectations and practices that were central to understanding the interactional dynamics of these kinds of high-profile football-related riots. In this case, the Italian police assumptions that England fans were inherently and uniformly violent, apparently led to practices that ironically seemed to have created the social and psychological conditions for collective violence to emerge.

It is important to stress, at this early stage, that such analysis is not seeking to blame the police or somehow legitimise the violence of fans; rather, it is to recognise the need to move beyond attributing cause to a single parties (police or fans) and recognise the central role played by the interactional dynamics between them. Nonetheless, as Stott and Reicher argued, the importance of these insights is not just theoretical but also practical because for the police:

> [A] one-sided focus on the danger of so called 'hooligans' is liable to become a self-fulfilling prophesy. To the extent that police and authorities focus entirely on the other they fail to address their own actions. To the extent that they approach football crowds in terms of danger, their actions may serve to create a common category out of an initially heterogenous crowd. In the end, the irony is that a fear of hooligans may produce the very conditions where they gain influence over those who hitherto eschewed them. (Stott & Reicher, 1998b p. 374)

The 1998 World Cup Finals

The explanatory value of a social identity crowd psychology perspective in helping to move beyond hooligan convergence theory gained further support from studies of fan behaviour at the FIFA World Cup Finals held in France in 1998.[2] Once again, there was serious rioting involving England fans, most notably in the southern port city of Marseille across consecutive days prior to, and during, England's opening fixture against Tunisia. On arriving into the ethnically diverse city, England fans began to gather in the 'Old Port' area. In the evening two days before the fixture, a series of interactions developed between groups of England fans and local youths of north African heritage, who were predominantly supporting Tunisia. Many of the emerging antagonisms were driven by the decision (subsequently declared unlawful by the European Commission) to sell 70% of tickets to French citizens, which meant that most of the English travellers would need to buy tickets at inflated prices from the locals. That evening saw a number of increasingly violent altercations between English fans and locals, and, whatever the cause, many English fans started to share a fear that they were being targeted by local gangs, through pick-pocketing, street robberies, violent assaults, and simply being 'ripped off' by touts. During these episodes the police were largely notable by their absence.[3]

The following afternoon, large numbers of French riot police were deployed ahead of a march through the Old Port by a mixture of travelling and local Tunisia fans. The exact spark for the riot that followed is not completely clear but was likely to have been the throwing of a bottle by an England fan. This led to a brief exchange of missile throwing between the Tunisia fans and a small group of England fans. This was followed by the firing of teargas and a baton-charge by riot police, which dispersed not only the two-dozen or so England fans who had approached the march, but also the thousands of England fans peacefully drinking

[2] For more detail on this, see Stott and Pearson (2007).

[3] The development of the riot in Marseille in 1998 was mirrored almost to the exact location and time by the first skirmishes of a bigger riot that occurred when England played Russia in Marseille at the UEFA European Championships in 2016.

outside bars at the other end of the Old Port. These patterns of interaction, involving provocation from local youths, an initial lack of police intervention to prevent the attacks, the violent reaction of a minority of England fans, followed by police reaction using force indiscriminately, continued across the next two days, culminating in a major riot. Violent to-and-fro confrontation between ever-growing numbers of England fans and riot police occurred for the duration of that day, as police used teargas and baton-charges to clear bars where fans were committing no offences. The day of the match saw further altercations, most notably when local youths threw bottles at England fans watching the match on a big screen on the beach as they celebrated the first goal. This led to a violent response by some England fans, arguably in self-defence, and to more indiscriminate teargassing and baton-charging.

As usual, the media were quick to morally condemn and attribute the violence to the pathology of English hooligans, and the government and police were challenged about why they had not prevented these from travelling to France. Yet, our research suggested the overwhelming bulk of England fans had come to Marseille and its surrounding resorts with no intention of creating confrontation. Indeed, once again the vast bulk of those arrested, around 82%, had no history of football-related criminality (Stott et al., 2001). The research suggested that over time, the combination of local provocation and indiscriminate and violent policing led to changes in how many England fans defined their identity, and related to others around them, most notably the police and local protagonists. Many of the thousands of England fans arriving into the city came to either hear about, or directly experience, the hostility of these local youths and police. It appears that as a result, many came to understand the surrounding intergroup relationships as illegitimate and that conflict against these outgroups was not only legitimate but sometimes necessary as their only form of collective self-defence. Equally, far from eschewing those fans prepared to confront the local youths as 'hooligans', many came to see those becoming involved in violence as heroic England fans, as common ingroup participants who, in the absence of protection from the police, were prepared to put themselves at risk to defend themselves and others around them from these illegitimate attacks.

In this sense, the research at France'98 moved beyond the work at Italia'90 by highlighting the complexity of the interactional dynamics that can surround fan groups. This was not simply a matter of police crowd interaction but dynamics between multiple groups. Within such complexity, the research emphasised how a lack of police intervention, in this case to manage these dynamics earlier in the cycle, can also lead to circumstances where confrontation escalates. It was evident that this 'slow to react' approach was, and at the time of writing remains,[4] typical for French police, but had they intervened earlier, and in a more targeted manner, the hostilities may not have escalated in the same manner. Furthermore, the pre-dispositional, or pathological, explanation for the Marseille riot and explanations based on levels of alcohol consumption (which were equally popular with the media) were quickly shown to be lacking in credibility. For the second match of the tournament, England travelled to Toulouse for the first competitive match against Argentina since the infamous 1986 'Hand of God'. It was largely the same fans as had been present in Marseille who travelled, although there was some suggestion that more 'hooligans' would be present; "Our message to the French is that there are more [hooligans] coming', warned one senior commander from the UK police delegation to the World Cup."[5] Furthermore, we would argue roughly the same amount of beer was drunk (in fact, the second match was an evening rather than an afternoon kick-off). Yet, in the absence of the provocations by local gangs and the lack of coercive dispersal techniques by the local police, the match event passed off with no major incidents.

During the same tournament, Scotland played three fixtures, all of which were essentially 'trouble free'. Indeed, in contrast to the sometimes-murderous sectarian hostilities of the Scottish domestic league,[6] Scotland fans cemented their positive reputation for boisterous but peaceful carnivalesque behaviour at international tournaments (Giulianotti, 1991). The research suggested their pre-tournament reputation had a big impact

[4] The drafting of this manuscript coincided with major policing problems at the 2022 Champions League Final between Liverpool and Real Madrid, held in Paris.

[5] 'Violence to Worsen—Police' (*The Guardian* 17/06/1998).

[6] https://www.theguardian.com/football/1999/sep/18/newsstory.sport15

precisely because it shaped the intergroup interactions that the fans experienced. First and foremost, the research suggested that the absence of collective violence was not simply because no so-called hooligans follow Scotland. Rather, because of their positive reputation and culture, Scotland fans did not find themselves involved in the same interactions with local youths or police, in contrast to their English contemporaries. Indeed, there were several circumstances where the boisterous and drunken behaviour of Scotland fans was indistinguishable from their English counterparts and as such posed considerable challenges, such as when a large and drunken crowd sat outside a pub, blocking a major roadway and causing severe congestion in Bordeaux city centre. While a few heated altercations between local aggravated drivers and fans took place, the police did not intervene.

In the absence of the hostile interactions and policing that surrounded the English, the data suggested that Scotland fans perceived their intergroup relationships as facilitatory and legitimate. Correspondingly, in this social context a strong culture of self-regulation was evident so that when other Scotland fans behaved in ways that were violent or provocative, they could expect to be admonished, even violently so, by their compatriots. Indeed, the study suggested that this culture of 'self-regulation' was driven consciously to actively differentiate themselves from the English, so as not to attract the same kind of hostility. As one Scotland fan put it when describing his experiences of the local population, "once they realize we are not English, they are alright" (Stott et al., 2001, p. 374). Equally, the study also explored several circumstances where minor incidents of confrontation—or 'hooliganism'—did develop among Scotland fans. It showed that in each case interactional dynamics revolving around the perceived legitimacy of behaviour were once again central (ibid).

From Theory to Practice: Understanding and Managing Risk at Football Events

Following France'98, it was becoming increasingly evident that a crowd psychology approach provided a much more powerful theoretical framework for explaining, understanding, and even predicting whether major incidents involving football fans would occur. From this theoretical perspective, the evidence was also increasingly clear that police attitudes and behaviours were quite fundamental. The next major tournament that England were due to participate in was UEFA Euro2000 and once again the issue of 'hooliganism' was always going to be a news story on a par with the football. Euro2000 was co-hosted by Belgium and the Netherlands, and given that both countries were easily accessible, it was expected that thousands of England fans, the majority without match tickets, would flood into the host cities and that confrontation was therefore almost inevitable. Indeed, in the months prior to the tournament, news outlets were claiming that serious disorder was being planned. For example, on Sunday, 2nd April, *The Observer* published an article based on 'investigation' by two of its journalists. Its headline pronounced that "Hooligans link up on the Net to plot mayhem at Euro 2000". The article went on to claim that

> Gangs of football hooligans throughout Europe are plotting to turn this summer's European Championships into an orgy of violence and mayhem. Thugs who follow England plan to join forces with local troublemakers to confront the police, stage pitched battles against rival fans and wreck city centres, railway stations and seaside resorts. The hooligans believe Belgium and Holland, where the tournament will be held in June, will prove an easy touch, because of 'soft' policing, open borders and access to drugs and alcohol. Violent followers of Millwall and Chelsea, two London clubs notorious for misbehaviour by their fans, boasted last week that the Low Countries would be a 'hooligans' paradise.[7]

---

[7] https://www.theguardian.com/football/2000/apr/02/newsstory.sport7

At the heart of this so-called soft policing approach were the Dutch Police and an influential academic Otto Adang, who was employed at the Dutch Police Academy to help deliver their public order training. Adang and his colleagues were keen to learn the lessons from previous tournaments and saw value in the emerging science of crowd psychology. Central to this Dutch-led model was a so-called low profile approach. Put simply, instead of deploying a vast array of visually prominent police resources, such as highly visible squads of riot police and vehicles to act as a deterrent (sometimes called 'show of force' policing), the Dutch would begin their tactical interventions by using pairs of officers in standard uniform. Their job would be to patrol among the fans and proactively interact and communicate, encouraging them to behave appropriately, facilitating (e.g. providing information about travel arrangements to the stadiums) and, where necessary, intervening in a low-key manner if a situation was becoming tense (e.g. a local dispute had emerged, or a fan was behaving inappropriately). There was nothing 'soft' about this approach; these resources could always be quickly reinforced or replaced by a much firmer response using greater numbers of well-equipped officers (i.e. riot police) if the situation required it. It was merely that the policing approach was designed to be less confrontational so these additional police resources would be kept well out of sight unless they were needed. In other words, regardless of the prior assumptions, while the situation remained calm behaviourally, the proportion of police to crowd participants would appear 'low', hence the term 'low-profile'. Another way to describe this model is proportionate and information-led proactive public order management.

As we shall see below, while this model was adopted for the tournament, structured observational research suggested that it was only successfully applied in the Flemish-speaking cities that hosted matches during the tournament, four out of five of which were in the Netherlands (Adang & Cuvelier, 2001). One of these was the Dutch city of Eindhoven, which hosted over 15,000 England fans who had travelled to the venue for the team's opening fixture against Portugal. England lost the match and both Dutch and UK police acknowledged that there were over 100 English 'known hooligans' present in the city. Yet, there was no disorder and only a handful of arrests, all of which were for minor non-violence-related offences (e.g. ticket touting). This was quite a remarkable outcome given prior expectations. Several news outlets placed their causal explanation for the absence of violence on the ready availability of cannabis, the low-alcohol tournament beer, and the fact that hooligans were 'holding themselves back' for England's next fixture against Germany in Charleroi, Belgium. Yet the Dutch police proudly argued that their 'low profile model' played a central role. Indeed, the *Guardian* newspaper reporting on events at the time claimed that

> England's disappointment on the field has been offset by temporary joy off it following one of the most peaceful matches involving its fans for over a decade, winning them rare praise from the police and city officials for good behaviour. Johann Beelan, Eindhoven police spokesman, yesterday revealed the tactics that helped ensure peace in the city.[8]

The article goes on to describe how the early police proactive verbal engagement with the 'risk fans', made possible through the low-profile approach, helped keep fan behaviours in check without recourse to the use of force.

A few days later, tens of thousands of England and Germany fans flowed into the French-speaking city, Charleroi. The Belgian police had long been preparing for confrontations between these rival fan groups. As a result, the city centre had essentially been divided in half, with German fans on one side and England fans on the other, police cordons preventing significant movement across the divide. Not being a tourist destination, accommodation in Charleroi was limited, so many England fans were staying in nearby Brussels and Lille, where there had already been significant incidents of disorder the night before. On matchday, the media gaze centred on the Place Charles II, a largely pedestrianised hub in Charleroi city centre in the heart of the England zone, around the perimeter of which there were several bars and cafés. On the day of the fixture, England fans began gathering in the Place from the early morning onwards, and soon the entire area was filled with large crowds of fans drinking and celebrating. Despite the tournament-wide model of

[8] https://www.theguardian.com/uk/2000/jun/14/football.footballviolence

policing, it was apparent from our observations that the 'low-profile' policing approach of the Flemish-speaking cities had disappeared. It had been replaced by a different approach, reliant on large squads of riot police who, instead of interacting with fans, stood apart from the crowd, watching and waiting. After a short time, and before any problems had developed, two watercannon drove into position and were parked in a highly visible location. This was 'deterrence' policing, clearly designed to demonstrate to the fans that the police were ready to react with overwhelming force. What the police operation clearly lacked was a desire to interact with fans beforehand.

Given the Place was given over exclusively to England fans, the atmosphere was initially largely celebratory. The subsequent escalation of disorder is detailed in our first book, *Football Hooliganism*:

> As the afternoon progressed, a small but significant fight broke out apparently between some English and German fans on the north side of the square, during which some plastic chairs were thrown. There was a rapid surge of people moving up toward the fighting, and almost immediately the police drove a water-cannon into the square and began to fire it at the entire crowd in a wide arc (it was the first reported incident of a water-cannon used against English football supporters). In response, a large number of England fans began to throw plastic chairs, plastic glasses and bottles at the cannon, but those who did not get out of its way were knocked over by the force of the water … Television footage of the incident shows incontrovertibly that the conflict rapidly escalated *after* the initial water-cannon burst; there was a dramatic increase in the number of missiles (mostly plastic chairs) thrown at the cannon itself (Stott & Pearson, 2007, pp. 152–3).

Mounted police then charged into the Place as hundreds of England fans began picking up and throwing the chairs and other missiles towards the police. Then, hundreds of riot police responded by using baton-charges and cordons to disperse everyone from the vicinity, eventually clearing the Place entirely. There were no further significant incidents in Charleroi, but after the match several hundred England fans travelling back to Brussels were involved in further confrontations. The train they were on had terminated early, forcing the fans to walk back to the city centre, and as they did so, several violent interactions developed with locals. Ultimately, over 965 England fans were arrested and deported back to the UK from Belgium (in contrast to just six in the Netherlands).[9] A spokesman for the then Prime Minister, Tony Blair, was quoted as saying that "[Blair] is determined that anybody who seems hellbent on going abroad and causing destruction should be condemned by everyone. The Belgian police have our full support for cracking down on hooligans as hard as they need to."[10] Yet, a spokesman from the National Criminal Intelligence Service (NCIS) was quoted as saying the violence was not the result of an organised hooligan conspiracy but that "probably just fairly normal lads who have [got] on a ferry with their mates, drank too much and then let themselves get caught up in the trouble".[11]

A key question arising from Euro2000 is therefore how was the contrast between Eindhoven and events in Belgium possible? What was it about the two situations that meant when upwards of 15,000 England fans, including known 'hooligans', travelled into the Netherlands, events there passed off entirely peacefully? In stark contrast, when similar numbers travelled into Belgium how, and why, was it that there was widespread and serious disorder, once again involving fans who were not previously known to police? While the scientific research is quite limited, the data behind the hyperbolic news headlines paints a more nuanced picture. One of the key studies was funded by the European Commission and conducted by Adang and his teams of university and police academy students, supported by international police commanders. These accredited research teams were deployed to the tournament's match cities to conduct systematic structured observations in the city centres and streets surround the venues. On almost every matchday in every host city, a team of observers would set out for several hours the evening before and the day of the fixture to find places where fans of the visiting teams were gathering in number. They would stand in those locations and take a series of measurements every 15 minutes. They gathered observational data along various dimensions including the numbers of fans and police

[9] Only 1 of these 965 fans was ever charged with a criminal offence.

[10] https://www.theguardian.com/uk/2000/jun/18/footballviolence.football

[11] https://www.independent.co.uk/news/world/europe/rioting-fans-shame-england-5370547.html

that were present, the nature of their behaviour, the styles of police uniform, and the nature of fan/police interactions.

Their data was then collated and painted quite a revealing picture of the overall policing of the tournament. There were statistically significant differences between what were termed 'high-profile' and 'low-profile' match cities. As we have discussed above, it was the three French-speaking cities in Belgium, including Charleroi and Brussels, that adopted the 'high-profile' approach. Their analysis then broke the data down to compare the styles of policing between those fixtures classified by the authorities as 'increased' and 'normal' risk. In each scenario, high-profile cities had far greater numbers of ordinary police officers, riot police, and riot vehicles visibly deployed on the streets, the differences greater in high-risk scenarios with nearly three times the level of visible police deployment compared to low-profile cities. Yet in both normal- and increased-risk scenarios, the levels of observed proactive contact between officers and fans were not significantly different. This suggested that police in low-profile cities may have been less visible but were far more proactive in terms of their verbal engagement with fans. The research team also qualitatively assessed the nature of these interactions and scored them on a set of scales. Accordingly, they judged that police in low-profile cities were more approachable, showed greater levels of respect, contributed to the festivity of the event, were more likely to treat visitors as guests, act in just ways, and were quicker to recognise violence-prone situations. In other words, low-profile policing was not just more proactive, it was of a distinctly different quality. The study was also able to identify that, somewhat counterintuitively, across the tournament the highest levels of disorder had been observed in normal-risk scenarios but where high-profile police had been deployed. Moreover, they were also able to determine that in increased-risk scenarios, there were no significant differences in observed levels of disorder (Adang & Cuvelier, 2001).

These were very meaningful and powerful findings because they demonstrated some key issues that stood in stark contrast to the media and political storm that flowed out from the tournament in the UK. First, the research showed that the way the police authorities assessed risk was problematic, because the greatest level of observed disorder was occurring in scenarios where it had been assumed it was unlikely to occur. This was perhaps not surprising, given that police risk assessments appear to have been so heavily skewed by the idea that disorder is a consequence of the convergence of so-called hooligans, who it was assumed tend to follow specific national teams (Stott, 2003). Second, the research also added support to the argument that policing was related to increased levels of observed disorder. In this specific case, where policing was disproportionate to the assumed levels of risk, it corresponded with the highest overall levels of observed conflicts. Beyond this, the data also indicated that high-profile policing was at best ineffective because in high-risk scenarios, despite deploying nearly three times as many police, riot police, and riot vehicles, this made no measurable impacts on the observed levels of disorder. In other words, in each scenario there was a statistically and theoretically meaningful relationship between the styles of policing and the levels of conflict. Put simply, according to this data, high-profile policing in this context was at best ineffective and at worst counterproductive (Adang & Cuvelier, 2001).

Participant Action Research and Influencing Police Policy

Nonetheless, despite the science, the political embarrassment of the disorder at Euro2000 for the UK Government was intense and as such they established a Working Group led by the then policing Minister, Lord Steve Bassam. Given our expertise and working relationships, we were invited to participate and contribute evidence to the Group. As a result, our work came to the attention of David Bohannon and his team in the Home Office. Bohannon had already begun to recognise that the overwhelming focus on identifying and controlling so-called hooligans was not providing solutions and there was a need for a new, more comprehensive, approach. Bohannon and his team had been present in the Netherlands and Belgium, which helped them to recognise that the underlying causes of the problems involving England fans were highly complex and to a large extent related to the situations that surrounded them. As a result, they were receptive to the arguments our work was putting forward, shifting the then-dominant academic focus on the sociology of the 'hooligan' towards a conceptual approach based on crowd psychology. The Home Office recognised the value of the research on Italia'90 and France'98, showing that football crowd psychology was identity-based and revolved around interactional dynamics of intergroup legitimacy and power. They also valued the arguments about how proactive low-profile, or reactive high-profile, policing styles could, contrastingly and respectively, empower cultures of self-regulation or initiate and escalate disorder.

A key motivation for the UK Home Office was to affect change in the preparations for the European Championships to be held in Portugal, Euro2004. This was the next tournament where fan behaviour would come under the spotlight and would, in the event of serious disorder, once again bring powerful questions to bear on government. In preparation for Euro2004, the Home Office agreed to fund a programme of participant observational work examining the policing of English fans travelling into continental Europe. Our remit was to help develop a research-based model of good practice that could be fed forward to try to influence the Portuguese policing of the tournament. In this context, protocol is extremely important and the fact that the Dutch had hosted Euro2000 meant that they had developed a sophisticated network of international police partnerships that could be drawn upon to take our work forward. Working closely alongside the Dutch Police Academy, we were able to facilitate working relationships with clubs like Manchester United, Liverpool, Arsenal, Leeds, and Newcastle, all of whom were participating in UEFA competitions at that time, as well as with the Football Association. Through these partnerships we were able to access tickets that enabled us to travel to their away fixtures and undertake over 35 observations in 9 different European countries across the next two years. We detail the data and analysis from this research elsewhere (see Stott & Pearson, 2007), but focus below on the core principles and model of policing good practice that was derived from them.

Although we did not realise it at the time, we were in effect deploying was a form of Particiapnt Action Research (PAR) where our enquiry was being co-produced alongside other stakeholders, including fans, and as a result, the knowledge we produced was successful in driving important changes in policy and practice. More specifically, due to our partnerships, during several observations we were able to gain access to the local police operations, the visiting UK police delegations, and the fans. This access not only improved the depth and quality of the data; it also began to open occasions to influence change. Fortunately, during this pre-Euro2004 work, the Portuguese club side of Boavista F.C. drew Manchester United in the Champions League. This provided an opportunity for us and the Dutch Police Academy to formally request the support of the Portuguese authorities for our observations.

Portugal has three separate police forces: the *Polícia de Segurança Pública* (or Public Security Police, PSP) which is the national civil police force of Portugal and has jurisdiction for urban areas; the National Republican Guard (GNR), a gendarmerie force, typically responsible for smaller towns, rural areas, and the road network; and the Judicial Police, who are responsible for investigating major crimes. It was the PSP that were responsible for policing at the Boavista fixture, as well as the majority of the seven venues being developed for the tournament, and Stott and Adang were able to secure support for research collaboration with them. Several of the PSP commanders had been present in an observational capacity during Euro2000 and had seen the effectiveness of, and understood the rationale for, the Dutch 'low-profile' approach, something they wanted to recreate for Euro2004, but something that some of their Portuguese colleagues, particularly their more senior commanders, were less convinced about. It was clear that this would be a collaborative partnership, utilising our data and expertise to help the PSP commanders drive the preparations for the tournament in a direction they already knew they wanted to travel. In this sense, this was less about us as 'experts' informing them as 'practitioners' and more about a knowledge co-production partnership where scientists and forward-thinking police officers were working together to affect progressive change.

A Model of Good Practice

This research programme allowed us to develop a theory-led model of police good practice. In part this was based on, but also informed, a set of principles derived from the social identity approach, that were first published in 2004 (Reicher et al., 2004; see also Reicher et al., 2007). These principles drew heavily upon our Home Office-funded ethnographic research on the policing of English fans and set out a form of guidance for police forces in how to best approach the management of the social psychological interactional dynamics of football crowd events. First, we suggested that police should address their strategic perspective, which is usually overwhelmingly focused on the control of negative or criminal behaviour. Instead, we recommended that policing should also place a strong strategic focus on understanding and facilitating what it is that people in crowds legitimately and positively want to do (e.g. gather, drink, celebrate, and watch football). With this broader strategic focus, our research and theory suggested that police would be far more likely to build and maintain perceptions of police legitimacy among crowd participants, and therefore prevent disorder, through promoting behavioural self-regulation.

We also argued that the intelligence that the police generated and operated around needed to change. In addition to any information about fans travelling with criminal intent, police would also need information to provide an understanding of what fans legitimately wanted to achieve. Once these strategic and information-based changes were in place, the police then needed the capacity to communicate with fans about their role in facilitating them. Finally, if all of this failed to prevent problems from developing, and police needed to intervene further, then they should do their upmost to avoid the undifferentiated use of force, which our studies suggested was a primary causal factor in escalations. Reicher et al. (2004) then summarised these principles as Educate, Facilitate, Communicate, and Differentiate (ECFD). These principles have subsequently been taken up by the College of Policing, as guidance provided for police public order commanders in the UK via APP, and the principals also underpin crowd policing in Sweden.

Beyond this, our research also suggested a radical reform was necessary in the way police went about making risk assessments. Then, as is broadly still the case, the police operated with relatively fixed categorisations of risk surrounding specific fixtures. In general terms these would vary from low- to high-risk scenarios *as if* the event presented a uniform level of threat and risk to public order. While it is a useful way of predicting demand and mobilising resources, as we have argued, this is far too rigid a means of understanding the nature of risk, as it ebbs and flows through the differing patterns of interaction that take place during the event. Indeed, put simply, you could have a high-risk fixture where at no point were there any interactions that posed significant moments of increased risk, so in fact the 'high-risk' event would remain 'low-risk' throughout. Equally, one could have a low-risk fixture where patterns of interaction occurred such that significant disorder did materialise, so this 'low-risk' event could become 'high-risk' under specific circumstances. It was therefore important for the police to conceptualise that, for any crowd event, risk was not static but exists on a continuum that varies from high to low, and that movement up and down this scale could occur at any time but would do so as a function of specific and predictable types of interaction. Correspondingly, we recommended that the police should therefore develop an approach based around developing a capacity for ongoing dynamic risk assessment, to identify these emerging interactions and shape them in ways that helped de-escalate the situation.

It was already evident that a low-profile approach was far more successful in achieving such outcomes. According to our observations, and underpinned by the background research and theory, it was apparent that one of the key factors affecting movement up and down this continuum was what we called the 'balance' between the observed nature of emerging risk and the styles of policing. Where we were making observations in what we judged were low-risk scenarios (i.e. where there was no observed immediate threat to public order) and police deployed in a low-profile manner, we noted that fans would tend to perceive the way they were being policed as legitimate. Correspondingly, we would also observe an increased likelihood of what we have already called self-regulation among the fans, where confrontational or provocative behaviours would be seen by most fans as illegitimate and any fellow fans indulging in such activity would be marginalised, censured, or actively controlled by others around them. Such self-regulation was often empowered by low-level early police intervention against minor acts of anti-social behaviour, defining to fans in the vicinity the limits of police tolerance. This 'balance' between the observed risk and police deployment would then correspond with a situation that we judged would be inconducive to generalised conflict and we never observed disorder escalate under such circumstances. However, where a similar *low-risk* scenario was met with *high-profile* policing, this tended to correspond with perceptions among fans of police *illegitimacy*. Correspondingly, this increased the likelihood we would observe support for anti-social and aggressive activity among fans, a decline in self-regulation, and the emergence of conditions conducive to generalised conflict. While we did not always observe conflict develop or escalate, when we did, it was often, if not always, under these conditions.

This was not to say that high-profile policing was intrinsically problematic. In some circumstances where we judged risk was increasing, or violence had already developed, we observed police use of force and heavy police resourcing that was equally perceived by fans as legitimate, but this was very dependent upon how such policing interacted with the specific situation. Where police dynamic risk assessment was accurate, we observed it flowed into policing targeted correctly against the source of the problem (e.g. it differentiated between those fans provoking the conflict and bystanders). Where such differentiation occurred, we observed there was an increased likelihood that police use of force would be interpreted as proportionate and acceptable by many of the fans in that immediate situation. Correspondingly, we also observed that there would be an increase in the likelihood of fans retaining their prior self-regulatory attitudes and behaviours and the situation would tend not to escalate. In contrast, if police use of force was indiscriminate, this tended to again correspond with perceptions of police illegitimacy, the loss of self-regulation, and the emergence of the conditions for, and on several occasion the escalation of, collective conflict. Thus, taken together, these concepts of 'dynamic risk assessment' and 'balanced tactical profile' were taken forward by the PSP as key organisational principles for the policing of the tournament. Indeed, following the tournament these principles were developed into a diagram and adopted by the EU and UEFA as core policy guidance for police in approaching football matches with an international dimension (see Fig. 6.1).[12]

The recommendations derived from the research were then distilled by the PSP into a policing model of what we now refer to as 'graded tactical deployment'. This would begin with a Dutch-like low-profile approach, involving officers working in pairs in normal uniform, spread across areas where fans would gather. Their role would be to monitor their environment, interact with the fans, facilitate them (e.g. by providing information and addressing questions), and where necessary communicate the boundaries of acceptable behaviour (i.e. tolerance limit setting). If problems were identified, and further resources required, it would be important to continue interacting and seeking to de-escalate the situation, not least of all by explaining the nature of police concerns. By going through these stages, police would then be better informed about the exact nature

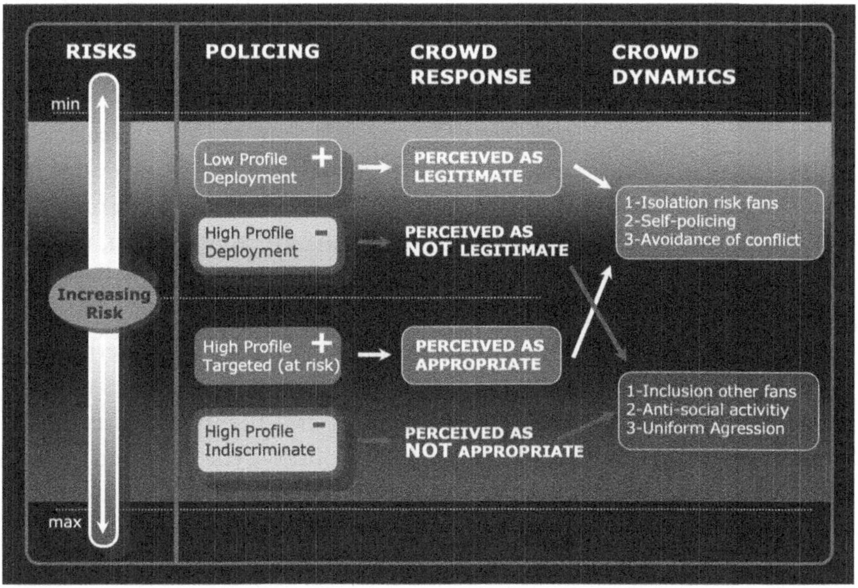

Fig. 6.1 The diagram adopted by the EU Manual of Guidance representing the processes described above

[12] https://eur-lex.europa.eu/legal-content/EN/TXT/?uri=celex%3A32016G1129%2801%29

of the problem and what was causing it. Thus, if units were deployed to exercise use of force, provided there was good information flow, it would be more likely that the intervention would be accurately targeted and capable of avoiding undifferentiated and disproportionate use of force. Having dealt with the situation and removed the problem, it would then be important for the police to de-escalate and withdraw to return to their original low profile. In this way, through our collaboration with the PSP, our research was able to support them in developing a strategic and tactical approach based on this body of recommendations.

Policing Euro 2004

The next stage was to evaluate the effectiveness of the PSP's Euro2004 policing policy, which was achieved through an Economic and Social Research Council-funded research team made up of academics and police practitioners from across Europe. Our collaborative research position now provided a comprehensive overview of the security policy in Portugal, as well as intimate knowledge of the background international relations in the run up to the tournament. The research team made observations at 14 matches, utilising a combination of structured and flexible observations. Stott also gathered data using a pre- and post-tournament survey questionnaire distributed among England fans. In combination, the data demonstrated that the PSP successfully implemented their theory-based strategic and tactical approach. In match cities they applied a facilitation approach and deployed their resources initially at what they referred to as 'level one'. As had been recommended, these were police officers working in standard uniform, wearing baseball caps, and highly visibility florescent tabards. These officers were briefed to observe the situation around them and, where possible, assist fans by providing them with information and support. The officers were supported by teams of police in plain clothes, who moved around the city monitoring fans and looking out for any emerging problems. As, and where, problems were identified that could not be resolved at level one, the PSP moved to a 'level two' deployment involving larger squads of officers who, while still in standard uniform, carried helmets and other protective equipment. Their role would be to intervene and initially try to resolve the situation through dialogue and low-level use of force (e.g. pushing). If that failed, these officers could then put on their helmets and draw their batons and use higher-level force which constituted a 'level three' deployment. If the situation then escalated further, specially dedicated teams of riot police would intervene. These elite PSP units, the *Corpo de Intervençao*, had access to full protective equipment including batons, fireproof overalls, padding, helmets, and shields as well being supported by watercannon. These 'level four' units were kept deliberately out of sight unless needed.

The data from the structured observations confirmed that across all the tournament venues, uniformed officers were visibly present in just over 50% of the 1896 samples taken. However, while officers were visible, these remained in very low numbers proportionate to the amount of fans gathered in these locations, and these officers were also dressed in standard uniform as opposed to 'riot gear'. Most importantly, the structured observations also detected very low levels of disorder across the tournament, amounting to less than 1% of the samples, compared to 10% observed at Euro2000. Indeed, Euro2004 still remains one of the most peaceful international football tournaments ever held in Europe during the modern era (Stott et al., 2008). The quantitative structured observational data also corresponded with the qualitative ethnographic evidence; riot police were only deployed on occasion and then, according to commanders, in a preventative and symbolic manner during the final to prevent a pitch incursion. Across all the venues and match cities controlled by the PSP, their low-profile facilitative approach corresponded with the almost total absence of serious conflict, even though police intelligence, and our observations, indicated hundreds of so-called hooligans from various countries were present at the tournament. As we had predicted, the data correspondingly suggested that a widely held perception of the legitimacy of policing and strong norms of self-regulation grew up in that policing context. By way of contrast, during the tournament thousands of fans stayed in the resort area of the Algarve, predominantly in the small town of Albufeira which is under the jurisdiction of Portugal's second police force the GNR. The GNR did not adopt the crowd psychology-led model adopted by the PSP, but instead chose to rely on policing akin to the high-profile approach witnessed in Belgium during Euro2000. In the absence of early proactive intervention, the town experienced two consecutive nights of escalating rioting, which corresponded with what appears to have been the relatively indiscriminate police use of force. Observational and other data suggest that police/crowd interactions in the town were experienced as illegitimate and events escalated in precisely the manner our theoretical approach predicted (Stott et al., 2007; Schreiber & Stott, 2015).

Conclusions

There can be little doubt that the policing of Euro2004 was a major success and a breakthrough for the crowd psychology approach. The capacity of the theory to understand the dynamics of escalation within football crowds was valuable in and of itself. By understanding the issues from a social identity and crowd psychology perspective, it was possible not just to explain and understand the conditions under which these very serious, dangerous, and highly politically damaging events were occurring. But, drawing on a well-worn cliché, we have also shown how there is nothing more practical than good theory. The knowledge and understanding generated by crowd psychology acted as a tool kit for helping to shape policing approaches that were measurably effective at managing these social psychological dynamics in such a way that disorder could be almost completely avoided, regardless of whether fans who saw themselves, or were classified by police, as hooligans were present or not. Some might assert that the reason violence was largely avoided at Euro2004 was because new legislation meant that thousands of English fans had been banned from attending, but this misses the problems of such an explanation. Our research observations show very clearly that disorder involving England fans *did* take place in Portugal and so-called hooligans *were* present in significant numbers. We would contend it is impossible to have it both ways, to assert a 'hooligan'-based account for both the presence and the absence of violence. If hooligans were present, why did the disorder they provoked only occur in one location and not others? If hooligans had been kept away, why was it that rioting occurred across two consecutive nights in Albufeira? If 'hooligans' were then the cause of that violence, why were they subsequently unable or unwilling to provoke disorder in any of the match cities where we know they were also present and had ample opportunity to do so?

Indeed, as our research at subsequent tournaments such as the 2006 World Cup in Germany has shown, fans who self-identify as 'hooligans' are still ever-present among the England fan base and will continue to pose challenges to those tasked with policing them (Stott & Pearson, 2007, Ch. 13). However, the extent to which disorder then materialises in our view shows a clear and consistent relationship to the patterns of intergroup interaction that surround them. In this sense, if there is one consistent lesson to be drawn from the background research on the policing of football matches with an international dimension, it is that risk to public order in the context of football is better understood as interactional, more so than it is dispositional. Pre-event risk categorisations, however nuanced and developed, are rarely able to predict whether, when, and to what extent serious disorder occurs. It is therefore the capacity of the policing operations to understand and manage these interactional social psychological dynamics, that is the hallmark of its success. In those terms, the evidence from international football is already clear: a low-profile, graded, and dialogue-led model of policing, based upon facilitation and dynamic risk assessment, is by far the best approach.

It is also clear that it is in the relationship between police and fans, that is key to developing a proportionate and effective football policing operation, whether it be in Lisbon or Liverpool. Fundamental to this is the ability of police to understand the motivations and expectations of fans; the PSP were only able to achieve what they did because they made a clear effort to understand these legitimate expectations and then to try and facilitate them. We concluded Chap. 5 with a discussion of the steps that have been taken to this end in England and Wales, and the distance that many forces still must go. And, as we move on to Chap. 7, we continue to think about the importance of legitimate fan expectations of what they want from a football event and how they expect to be treated by those policing them. Only now, we will consider these legitimate expectations in terms of human rights, and in particular the rights under the European Convention on Human Rights of Freedom of Assembly and Expression.

References

Adang, O., & Cuvelier, C. (2001). *Policing Euro2000: International Police Co-operation, Information Management and Police Deployment.* Ubbergen.

Barrows, S. (1981). *Visions of the Crowd in Late Nineteenth Century France.* Yale University Press.

Brown, R. (2019). *Henri Tajfel: Explorer of Identity and Difference.* Routledge. ISBN 9781138589810.

Engels, F. (2009). *The Condition of the Working Class in England.* Oxford University Press.

Giulianotti, R. (1991). Scotland's Tartan Army in Italy: The Case for the Carnivalesque. *The Sociological Review, 39*(3), 503–527.

Hall, S., Critcher, C., Jefferson, T., Clarke, J., & Roberts, B. (1978). *Policing the Crisis: Mugging, the State and Law and Order.* Basingstoke.

Le Bon, G. (1895). *The Crowd: A Study of the Popular Mind.* Ernest Benn.

McClelland, J. (1989). *The Crowd and the Mob: From Plato to Canetti.* Unwin Hyman.

Reicher, S. (1982). The Determination of Collective Behaviour. In H. Tajfel (Ed.), *Social Identity and Intergroup Relations* (pp. 41–84). Cambridge University Press and Paris: Maison des Sciences de l'Homme.

Reicher, S. (1984). The St. Pauls Riot: An Explanation of the Limits of Crowd Action in Terms of a Social Identity Model. *European Journal of Social Psychology, 14*, 1–21.

Reicher, S. (1987). Crowd Behaviour as Social Action. In J. Turner, M. Hogg, P. Oakes, S. Reicher, & M. Wetherell (Eds.), *Rediscovering the Social Group: A Self-Categorization Theory.* Blackwell.

Reicher, S. (1996). "The Battle of Westminster": Developing the Social Identity Model of Crowd Behaviour in Order to Explain the Initiation and Development of Collective Conflict. *European Journal of Social Psychology, 26*, 115–134.

Reicher, S., Stott, C., Cronin, P., & Adang, O. (2004). An Integrated Approach to Crowd Psychology and Public Order Policing. *Policing: An International Journal of Police Strategies and Management, 27*, 558–572.

Reicher, S., Stott, C., Drury, J., Adang, O., Cronin, P., & Livingstone, A. (2007). Knowledge Based Public Order Policing: Principles and Practice. *Policing: A Journal of Policy and Practice, 1*, 403–415.

Rudé, G. (1964). *The Crowd in History. A Study of Popular Disturbances in France and England,* 1730–1848. Wiley. New edition Serif, 2005, ISBN 978-1897959473.

Schreiber, M., & Stott, C. (2015). Policing International Football Tournaments and the Cross-Cultural Relevance of the Social Identity Approach to Crowd Behavior. In J. Albrecht, M. Dow, D. Plecas, & D. Das (Eds.), *Policing Major Events: Perspectives from Around the World.* Florida.

Stott, C. (2003). Police Expectations and the Control of English Soccer Fans at "Euro2000". *Policing: An International Journal of Police Strategies and Management, 26,* 640–655.

Stott, C. J., & Drury, J. (2000). Crowds, Context and Identity: Dynamic Categorization Processes in the Poll Tax Riot. *Human Relations, 53,* 247–273.

Stott, C., & Drury, J. (2016). Contemporary Understanding of Riots: Classical Crowd Psychology, Ideology and the Social Identity Approach. *Public Understanding of Science.* https://doi.org/10.1177/0963662516639872

Stott, C., & Pearson, G. (2007). *Football Hooliganism, Policing and the War on the English Disease.* Pennant Books.

Stott, C., & Reicher, S. (1998a). How Conflict Escalates: The Inter-Group Dynamics of Collective Football Crowd Violence. *Sociology, 32,* 353–377.

Stott, C., & Reicher, S. (1998b). Crowd Action as Inter-Group Process: Introducing the Police Perspective. *European Journal of Social Psychology, 26,* 509–529.

Stott, C., Hutchison, P., & Drury, J. (2001). Hooligans Abroad? Inter-Group Dynamics, Social Identity and Participation in Collective Disorder at the 1998 World Cup Finals. *British Journal of Social Psychology, 40,* 359–384.

Stott, C., Adang, O., Livingstone, A., & Schreiber, M. (2007). Variability in the Collective Behaviour of England Fans at Euro2004: Hooliganism, Public Order Policing and Social Change. *European Journal of Social Psychology, 37,* 75–100.

Stott, C., Adang, O., Livingstone, A., & Schreiber, M. (2008). Tackling Football Hooliganism: A Quantitative Study of Public Order, Policing and Crowd Psychology. *Psychology Public Policy and Law, 14*(2), 115–114.

Wheen, F. (2010). *Karl Marx.* Fourth Estate.

Zimbardo, P. G. (1969). The Human Choice: Individuation, Reason and Order Versus De-individuation, Impulse and Chaos. In W. J. Arnold & D. Levine (Eds.), *Nebraska symposium on motivation* (Vol. 17). University of Nebraska Press.

7

Human Rights and Football Policing

The European Convention on Human Rights and the Human Rights Act

Probably the most significant legal development in crowd and public order policing in the UK in the twenty-first century has arisen through the impact of the European Convention on Human Rights (ECHR). Although Britain played a predominant role in the drafting of the Convention and ratified it as far back as 1953, it was only with the introduction of the Human Rights Act 1998 (HRA, which commenced in 2000) that a direct duty was placed upon police not to act in a way that infringed the rights granted to individuals under the ECHR. Section 6(1) of the HRA 1998 provides that "It is unlawful for a public authority to act in a way which is incompatible with a Convention right". Prior to this, the actions of the police had on occasion led to the UK being found in breach of the ECHR, but the HRA for the first time placed a domestic legal obligation upon police forces. The HRA changed residual freedoms to rights (Mead, 2010, p. 204) and marked "a new beginning and a fundamental shift to a rights-based system of law" in the UK (Starmer, 1999, p. 1). The HRA 1998 places direct obligations on police forces (this is known as the "vertical effect" of the HRA) not to act in a way that is incompatible with the ECHR, although it does not place the same

G. Pearson, C. Stott, *A New Agenda For Football Crowd Management*, Palgrave Studies in Risk, Crime and Society, https://doi.org/10.1007/978-3-031-16298-5_7

obligations on private individuals or organisations (e.g. clubs or stewards).[1] Section 8 of the HRA provides that a court finding a public authority is acting, or proposing to act, in a manner that is contrary to ECHR "may grant such relief or remedy, or make such an order, within its powers as it considers just and appropriate". This may include the quashing of police force's decision, an order for it to cease a particular tactic, or an award of damages to those adversely affected by the breach. In short, acting in a manner contrary to ECHR has the potential to cause significant reputational and financial damage to a police force. Arguably, the HRA 1998 was the most important development in policing in England and Wales in modern times (Dixon, 2007, p. 32), and in relation to expression and assembly presented "a potentially climactic break with the traditional UK constitutional position" (Fenwick, 2009, p. 661).

To date, the HRA's influence on football policing has been under-recognised by those tasked with football crowd management. For the first time, in this chapter we will provide a systematic analysis of the nature and scope of the human rights protections that apply in the context of football events, and the extent of the negative and positive obligations placed upon related policing operations. Moreover, we will argue that not only do the police have obligations under the HRA which are often overlooked, thereby potentially raising legal liabilities for forces, but that a human rights-based approach to football policing can provide officers making key decisions with a legal toolkit to enhance the effectiveness of their decision-making in terms of legitimacy amongst football fans which, as we argued in Chap. 6, is fundamental to a successful football policing operation. This is significant, particularly as that at the time of writing, there are proposals to replace the HRA with a "British Bill of Rights", which would be likely to diminish, at a domestic level at least, the human

[1] However, where legal disputes arise relating to ECHR, s.2 of the HRA requires domestic courts to "take into account" Strasbourg jurisprudence when considering a human rights question, although it does not require courts to mirror ECtHR decisions (Fenwick & Masterman, 2017), s.3 requires that domestic courts interpret domestic legislation in a manner that is "compatible with convention rights" (known as 'reading down' a statutory provision), and s.4 allows a court to declare primary legislation "incompatible" with ECHR. Although a literal reading of s.3 does not limit its scope to the courts, the White Paper that accompanied the Human Rights Bill appears to clarify this (Home Department, 1997). We have, however, come across examples of police documentation erroneously suggesting that s.3 has a direct effect on the police.

rights obligations of police forces. Exactly what form the Bill of Rights will take, assuming it is enacted, is at this point unclear. However, the draft bill looks to retain the obligations on the police not to infringe ECHR, but to potentially significantly reduce the positive obligations to facilitate ECHR rights (particularly for our purposes Arts. 2, 10, and 11).

Proportionality and Articles 2, 3, 5, and 8 ECHR

Several ECHR rights are significant to the application of criminal law and police powers to football crowds. However, while there have been several football crowd human rights cases elsewhere in Europe, some of which have even reached the European Court of Human Rights (ECtHR) in Strasbourg,[2] in the UK there have been none, and instead we must draw guidance from a plethora of cases mainly arising from the policing of protest (James & Pearson, 2015) all of which have clear implications for policing football. At the most basic level, ECHR Article 3 provides an unqualified prohibition on torture and inhumane treatment. This means that HRA 1998 s.6 requires that police forces should not utilise tactics that treat match-going fans in this manner. As an unqualified right, all breaches of Article 3 will be unlawful whatever their supposed justification.

However, the bulk of human rights are qualified rights, meaning that restrictions may be placed on them under certain circumstances without breaching the ECHR itself. When determining whether restrictions on an individual's qualified human rights are lawful or not under the HRA 1998 and the ECHR, the courts should apply an assessment of proportionality which "inevitably involves a value judgment at the stage at which a balance has to be struck between the importance of the objective pursued and the value of the right intruded upon".[3] A test of proportionality is therefore something that officers making decisions that may restrict the human rights of fans should always take into account.

[2] For example, *Ostendorf v Germany* (2013) App 15598/08; *S.V. and A. v Denmark* (2018) App 35553/12.

[3] *Bank Mellat v HM Treasury* [2013] UKSC 39 para 71.

However, as has been noted more generally, conducting these kinds of human rights assessments is often not straightforward (Bullock & Johnson, 2012; Neyroud & Beckley, 2001; Pearson et al., 2018; Pearson & Rowe, 2020), and police officers are often inclined to only balance the rights of the suspect with the wider community, rather than also considering the *necessity* of the restriction and whether there are least restrictive *alternatives* available. In 2013, the UK Supreme Court approved Lord Reid's four-stage proportionality test, which shall be the basis for our use of the test in this book:

1. whether the objective of the measure is sufficiently important to justify the limitation of a protected right,
2. whether the measure is rationally connected to the objective,
3. whether a less intrusive measure could have been used without unacceptably compromising the achievement of the objective, and
4. whether, balancing the severity of the measure's effects on the rights of the persons to whom it applies against the importance of the objective, to the extent that the measure will contribute to its achievement, the former outweighs the latter [...] In essence, the question at step four is whether the impact of the rights infringement is disproportionate to the likely benefit of the impugned measure.[4]

It should be noted that "the facts relevant to the different requirements may merge into one another" and that in certain circumstances the third leg of the test (often referred to as the 'least onerous means' test) may overlap with the fourth, meaning that it may be "an element to be considered rather than an essential requirement to be satisfied", provided that the interference with the right is proportionate overall.[5] Importantly, in the event of a police force being challenged in court under s.6 HRA, the burden of proving that an action which has restricted an ECHR right is proportionate falls on the state: "the onus is on the police to show that what was done was no more than was necessary."[6]

[4] *Bank Mellat* para 74.

[5] *PWR v DPP; Akdogan and another v DPP* [2022] UKSC 2 Para 70.

[6] *R (Laporte) v Chief Constable of Gloucestershire* [2006] UKHL 55, para. 85 (Lord Rodgers).

There are three other 'negative' human rights obligations that the police must take into account when managing football crowds; Article 2 provides the Right to Life, Article 5 provides the Right to Liberty, and Article 8 the Right to Privacy and Respect for Family Life. As these are qualified rights, the ECHR provides circumstances in which they can be restricted in a proportionate manner. For example, state actors may not deprive an individual of their life except as a result of use of force that is 'absolutely necessary' in personal defence, to effect an arrest, or to 'quell a riot', and the liberty of individuals can be restricted following lawful arrest or detention (e.g. for suspects remanded in custody or serving a custodial sentence). Our observations showed that the Right to Life is often placed front and centre of crowd policing strategies; if crowds become disorderly as a result of police failings and individuals subsequently die, the fear is that the police will be found to have breached Article 2.[7]

The police must also comply with the negative obligation under Article 8, for the state to provide a Right to Privacy. As we noted in Chap. 4, the surveillance of fans through means such as CCTV and hand-held video cameras (and increasingly, like the rest of the public, Body-Worn Video) has been a key feature of football policing since the late 1980s. This has also corresponded with the collation and storage of data (both in the form of video footage, but also intelligence 'profiles' put together by DFOs/OFOs, and personal data) on those suspected of engagement in football-related violence, disorder, or other criminality. Article 8 is also qualified, meaning an interference with the right can be justified if it is lawful, and necessary "for the prevention of violence or disorder" (Article 8(2)). The video recording of individuals, even when they are in public places and without retention of data, can engage Article 8 and as a result needs to be both legally regulated and proportionate.[8] This is a relatively low bar though, and supporters whose images are captured by police-controlled devices will not have a human rights remedy provided that the

[7] See *Osman v United Kingdom* (2000) 29 EHRR 245.

[8] *R. (on the application of Bridges) v Chief Constable of South Wales* [2020] EWCA Civ 1058, considering the use of Automatic Facial Recognition Technology. On private land, such as a football stadium, recording by the club (i.e. not a public authority) will not engage Article 8, and usually one of the standard terms and conditions of entering a football stadium is that you agree that you may be recorded and that your image could be used in the club's marketing.

police are recording images in compliance with legal guidance and to prevent or investigate criminality.

However, Article 8 claims are more likely to be successful where they relate to the continued storage of this data by the police without good reason. In *Wood*,[9] the Court of Appeal held that police retention of photographs of an individual connected with a group opposed to the arms trade was an interference with Article 8, as the police had failed to justify why they retained it for more than a few days, after which there was no reasonable basis for fearing that the claimant would commit an offence at an arms trade fair. Further, in the ECtHR case of *Catt*,[10] the retention of records of a complainant's participation in peaceful demonstrations also breached Article 8. While the Court agreed the collection of the personal data was justified because the complainant had aligned himself with a violent protest group, the police had not demonstrated a 'pressing need' to retain the data and there were no effective safeguards for this data to be deleted. We can therefore conclude that the creation of intelligence profiles containing personal data of those suspected of engagement in football-related offences is a proportionate interference with Article 8, particularly where this data may be used to support a prosecution. However, where such data is kept beyond the period of suspicion, especially when the data relates only to suspected low-level offending or anti-social behaviour, Article 8 may be infringed.

We now move on to the Article 5 Right to Liberty.[11] While this is significant in policing generally, particularly whenever a decision to arrest an individual occurs, the extent to which it restricts the ability of officers on football policing operations to use the wide and highly ambiguous (Stone, 2001; Glover, 2018) common law power of arrest to prevent a breach of the peace, or to utilise other coercive powers such as 'kettles' (when a group are corralled by police into a certain location and not allowed to leave) or stadium 'hold backs' has been somewhat watered down by decisions of the Supreme Court and the ECtHR. The only precedent in the

---

[9] *Wood* v *Commissioner of Police for the Metropolis* [2009] EWCA Civ 414.

[10] *Catt v United Kingdom* App 43514/15.

[11] In England and Wales there is no human right of free movement, as the UK has not ratified Article 2, Protocol 4.

courts of England and Wales relating to 'kettles' comes from a number of protest cases, culminating in *Austin.*[12] Following these cases, it is clear that the use of compulsory police 'escorts', 'kettling', and the 'hold-back' of fans in pubs or stadia would be viewed by the courts to be only a *temporary restriction on*, rather than a *deprivation of* liberty, meaning that Article 5 is not engaged. Article 5 would only be engaged in these situations if the decision to restrict liberty was an arbitrary one (i.e. applied indiscriminately or based on no fear of imminent disorder or violence), and in this situation the fact that supporters had acquiesced to the restrictions would not necessarily protect police from successful legal action (Mead, 2009, p. 390; James & Pearson, 2015). Furthermore, the ability of the police to make arrests to prevent a breach of the peace has recently been extended by two ECtHR cases[13] which controversially extended the ability of the state to detain individuals under Article 5(1)(c) "for the purpose of bringing him before the competent legal authority … when it is reasonably considered necessary to prevent his committing an offence", in effect permitting preventative arrest so long as it was non-arbitrary, related to specific individuals and a specific threat, and lasted no longer than was necessary.[14] Such arrests are relatively common in football policing elsewhere in Europe, such as Germany, but have to date not been a tactic for football policing in England and Wales.

Free Expression and Assembly and Positive Obligations

While the danger of a half-competent football policing operation coming unstuck against an Article 5 challenge is therefore unlikely, this does not give the police *carte blanche* when it comes to placing coercive restrictions

[12] *Austin v UK* (2012) 55 E.H.R.R. 14.

[13] *S.V. and A. v Denmark* (2018), relating to anticipated violence before a Denmark v Sweden fixture, and *Eiseman Renyard and Others v United Kingdom* App 57884/17 (relating to arrests to prevent a breach of the peace by protesters on the day of a Royal Wedding).

[14] *Eiseman Renyard* paras 42–45. This decision relied heavily on the minority decision in *Ostendorf* (2013), which related to pre-emptive arrest of a suspected 'hooligan' who had refused to follow a police direction by hiding in a toilet cubicle.

on fan gatherings. Football policing operations need also to be mindful that they do not infringe Article 10 (Freedom of Expression) and Article 11 (Freedom of Association and Assembly). Article 10 covers, but also goes beyond, free speech, to include other forms of expression, such as dress and *tifo* displays. It applies to forms of expression that may be shocking, disturbing, or offensive,[15] "unacceptable ... to the authorities", and "ideas which challenge the existing order".[16]

Article 11 applies to both static gatherings and marches or processions, but only to peaceful assemblies. An assembly which is violent by nature or intent will not gain protection from Article 11, and, as a result, police interventions do not have to be proportionate under 11(2) (although other rights may of course still apply). However, individuals do not lose their Article 11 rights as a result of "sporadic" violence, "if the individual in question remains peaceful in his or her own intentions or behaviour" (ibid para 26)[17] and "an assembly tarnished with isolated acts of violence is not automatically considered non-peaceful so as to forfeit the protection of Article 11" (CoE, 2021, para 28). Further, in situations where there is a significant risk that the assembly may result in disorder "as a result of developments outside the control of those organising it", Article 11 protections will still remain and any restriction to avoid the disorder must be proportionate in line with Article 11(2).[18]

Articles 10 and 11 have been described as "companion" articles (e.g. Fenwick et al., 2017, p. 295) and Strasbourg has ruled that in most cases, "Article 11 must also be considered in the light of Article 10. The protection of opinions and the freedom to express them is one of the objectives of freedom of assembly and association enshrined in Article 11."[19] This is important when we consider the extent of the human rights protections that apply to football fans. While media commentators, some academics, and even the College of Policing (2013) refer to the right or freedom 'to protest', the Convention itself draws no distinction between protest and

[15] *Muller and Others v Switzerland* [1988] ECHR 5; *Perinçek v Switzerland* (2016) 63 EHRR 6.

[16] *Kuznetsov v. Russia*, App 10877/04, para 45.

[17] *Ziliberberg v. Moldova*, App 61821/00.

[18] See *Schwabe and MG v Germany* Apsp. 8080/08 and 8577/08.

[19] *Öllinger v. Austria* App 76900/01, para 38.

other forms of expression and assembly. This unfortunate and erroneous narrow interpretation of Articles 10 and 11 (we deal with this in more detail below) has proven problematic for the policing of football. Moving on to consider Article 9, as appealing as it has been for some social scientists to theorise football fandom as akin to religion (see Chap. 5), it is unlikely that Article 9 Freedom of Thought, Religion, and Belief would extend to support of a particular football team. The test here is whether the support of a team would reach a "certain level of cogency, seriousness, cohesion and importance" (CoE, 2020, para 5) and could be considered comparable to a belief in pacificism[20] or veganism.[21] We would contend that notwithstanding some of the arguments raised in Chap. 5, it is unlikely that a higher court in the UK would reach such a conclusion.

Articles 10(2) and 11(2) establish that both these freedoms may be restricted by measures that are both "prescribed by law" and "are necessary in a democratic society", for a limited number of reasons including *inter alia*, national security, public safety, the prevention of disorder or crime, the protection of health or morals, or for the protection of the rights and freedoms of others. It has further been held that, "necessary", "implies the existence of a pressing social need", albeit with a margin of appreciation for different states.[22] Any restriction will need to be proportionate following the test of proportionality set out above. In *R (Laporte) v Chief Constable of Gloucestershire*, one of the most significant early cases concerning Expression and Assembly under the HRA, a police decision to stop three coachloads of protesters attending a protest at RAF Fairford and return them to London was held by the House of Lords to be a disproportionate breach of Articles 10 and 11; the fact that there was evidence that some individuals on the coaches were intent on engaging in criminality could not justify such a premature and indiscriminate tactic.[23] However, the domestic courts have been equally critical of failures

---

[20] *Arrowsmith v UK* App. 7050/75 (Report of the European Commission of Human Rights, 1978).

[21] *W v United Kingdom* App. 18187/91 (European Commission of Human Rights [Second Chamber] 1993).

[22] *Perinçek v Switzerland* (2016) 63 EHRR 6, para 196. The term "margin of appreciation" refers to the room to manoeuvre that the ECtHR (and other supra-national legal organisations) allows different national authorities to fulfil their obligations.

[23] *R (Laporte) v Chief Constable of Gloucestershire* [2006] UKHL 55.

to restrict assemblies where established notification rules have not been followed and which have resulted in disorder or the interference with the Article 8 rights of others.[24] Operational guidance and treatment of complaints which undermine rights under Article 10 can also be challenged under the HRA and any interference must be demonstrated to be proportionate.[25]

These closely linked freedoms not only prevent public authorities from disproportionate or arbitrary restrictions on citizens' ability to express themselves and gather together, but also provide "positive obligations to secure the effective enjoyment of these rights",[26] and protect them from interference by others. The principle of a positive obligation is not directly contained in the text of the Convention rights, but instead arises from how the ECtHR has interpreted the Freedoms of Articles 9–11, and the wording of Article 1 which requires that rights under the Convention should be "secured" by contracting states. Positive obligations in relation to these rights are required to elevate them from being merely "theoretical and illusory" and guarantee their practical and effective realisation,[27] through the use of "positive measures"[28] where necessary against non-state actors. In practical terms, this places an obligation on police forces to protect individuals looking to exercise their rights (OSCE, 2016), and in determining the extent of the positive obligation placed upon them, consideration should be given to striking a fair balance between the general interest of the community and that of the individual seeking to exercise their right.[29] There is a particular obligation on states to ensure the effective enjoyment of Article 11 for individuals participating in assemblies, "with unpopular views or belonging to minorities, because they were more vulnerable to victimisation".[30] In *Berkman*, for example, the

[24] *DB v Chief Constable Police Service of Northern Ireland* [2017] UKSC 7.

[25] *Miller v College of Policing* [2020] EWHC 225 (Admin).

[26] *Wilson and the National Union of Journalists and Others v. the United Kingdom*, Apps. 30668/96, 30671/96 and 30678/96, ECHR 2002-V Para 41.

[27] Ibid; *Airey v Ireland*, 11 September 1979; *Artico v Italy* [1980] ECHR 4; *Kudrevičius and Others v. Lithuania* App. 37553/05.

[28] *Plattform "Ärzte für das Leben" v Austria* (1988) 13 EHRR 204.

[29] *Özgür Gündem v. Turkey [2000]* ECHR 104; *Kharaahmed v Bulgaria* App 20587/13, paras 110–111.

[30] *Bączkowski and Others v. Poland* App. 1543/06.

ECtHR was critical of the Russian police adopting a purely public order role rather than one looking to facilitate a pro-LGBTI assembly in the face of aggressive counter-protest that they did little to confront.[31] However, a positive obligation "must be interpreted in a way which does not impose an impossible or disproportionate burden on the authorities",[32] and Dyke notes how case law has tended to favour the authorities where this is disputed (Dyke, 2009, p. 189).

The Extension of Articles 10 and 11 Rights to Football Fans

Freedom of Expression is usually associated with the expression of political opinion, and it is established that "Freedom of political speech is a freedom of the very highest importance in any country which lays claim to being a democracy".[33] "Political views, unlike 'vapid tittle-tattle' are particularly worthy of protection,"[34] and when determining the extent to which expression should be protected or facilitated, whether the expression relates to "very important issues" and whether the views being expressed were such that "many would see as being of considerable breadth, depth and relevance" can both be taken into account, along with the extent to which the complainants, "believed in the views they were expressing".[35] Fenwick et al. note that in political expression ECtHR cases, the margin of appreciation granted to individual states has been "narrowed almost to vanishing point" (Fenwick et al., 2017, p. 294). However, Freedom of Expression is not limited merely to forms of

[31] *Berkman v Russia* App. 46712/15, paras 50–58. They were also critical of the domestic courts for a similar narrow interpretation of ECHR obligations (para 53).

[32] *Osman v United Kingdom*, para 116, in relation to Article 2.

[33] *R (Prolife Alliance) v British Broadcasting Corporation* [2003] UKHL 23, para 6 (Lord Nicholls).

[34] *DPP v Ziegler and others* [2021] UKSC 23, para 86.

[35] *City of London Corpn v Samede* [2012] EWCA Civ 160, paras 40–41.

political expression,[36] and other forms of expression also engage Article 10, as expressed by Lord Neuberger:

> it can be appropriate to take into account the general character of the views whose expression the Convention is being invoked to protect. For instance, political and economic views are at the top end of the scale, and pornography and vapid tittle-tattle is towards the bottom … However, it cannot be a factor which trumps all others, and indeed it is unlikely to be a particularly weighty factor: otherwise judges would find themselves according greater protection to views which they think important, or with which they agree.[37]

From this, we can conclude that while not receiving the highest protection, and presumably permitting the state a generous margin of appreciation when interpreting whether restrictions upon it are necessary, Article 10 ECHR applies to expression by football fans. Chants, flags, and other displays of fandom speak to identity, history, and locality that are essential aspects of fans' everyday lives and, as we saw in Chap. 5, the importance of football fandom to supporters has been constructed by various researchers as being tribal (e.g. Morris, 1981), religious (Bromberger et al., 1993; Martyn & Taylor, 1997), and a love affair (King, 2003, p. 152). But even without going this far, it is well-established that for many fans, actively supporting their team is a serious endeavour that speaks to their very identity and purpose (Pearson, 2012, especially p. 56–59). Football fandom evidently goes beyond 'tittle-tattle', is more significant to individuals than commercial expression, and should not be unduly downplayed in significance by the state.

It is therefore clear, from the application of domestic and ECtHR jurisprudence to decades of social scientific analysis of football fans, that Article 10 applies to expressions of football fandom in a not-insignificant way and would be engaged by any attempt to arbitrarily or disproportionately restrict what chants fans engaged in, what banners they flew, or

[36] *X and Church of Scientology v Sweden* (1979) App. 7805/77; *McCartan Turkington Breen v Times Newspapers Ltd* [2001] 2 AC 277; *Miranda v Secretary of State for the Home Department and Ors* [2014] EWHC 255, 44–45.

[37] *Samede* [2012], para 41.

what clothes they wore to express their identity.[38] This does not, however, prevent powers, such as those included in s.3 of the Football (Offences) Act (FOA), or more generally ss.4–5 Public Order Act 1986 being used to prosecute those engaging in racist, indecent, or threatening chants or displays, and Article 10(2) permits necessary restrictions to protect public safety, the prevention of crime or disorder, and the protection of the rights of others.

By extension, neither is Article 11 limited to protest assemblies, although the clarification of this by the courts has taken longer than in respect of Article 10. In terms of the applicability of Freedom of Assembly to football crowds, Article 11 has been held not to apply to purely social gatherings lacking "organised assembly or association",[39] but, "in view of its importance the right to freedom of assembly should not be interpreted restrictively". Strasbourg has recently stepped away from trying to formulate or exhaustively list the criteria necessary to define an assembly (CoE, 2021, para 12), but case law suggests that football gatherings would fall within the remit of Article 11. In the 2002 case of *Gypsy Council v United Kingdom*, Article 11 was applied a gathering at the Horsmonden Horse Fair, which was held to be a "significant cultural and social event in the life of Romany Gypsy community",[40] indicating the reach of this protection into the social and cultural realms. Further indication that Article 11 could apply to football fan gatherings came in 2007 from the House of Lords in *R (Countryside Alliance) v Attorney General*,[41] which debated gatherings of fox hunters. Here, only Lord Hope suggested that Article 11 was not applicable to social gatherings, with both Lady Hale (who later served as President of the UK Supreme Court) and Lord Bingham expressly in favour of this interpretation. When this case reached Strasbourg in *Friend and Countryside Alliance v the United Kingdom*,[42] the ECtHR dismissed the argument that the UK's recent ban on hunting

[38] *Vajani v Hungary* (2010) 50 EHRR 44; *Donaldson v United Kingdom* (2011) 53 EHRR 14.

[39] *Anderson v United Kingdom* (1998) 25 ECHRR CD172.

[40] *The Gypsy Council and Others v The United Kingdom* App. 66336/01. See also *Javit An v Turkey* App. 20652/92.

[41] [2007] UKHL 52.

[42] [2009] ECHR 2068.

foxes contravened the ECHR, but the court accepted the argument that both Arts. 10 and 11 were engaged by this activity:

> [The] primary or original purpose of art.11 was and is to protect the right of peaceful demonstration and participation in the democratic process … Nevertheless, it would, in the Court's view, be an unacceptably narrow interpretation of that article to confine it only to that kind of assembly, just as it would be too narrow an interpretation of art.10 to restrict it to expressions of opinion of a political character … [the] Court is therefore prepared to assume that art.1 may extend to the protection of an assembly of an essentially social character.[43]

Support for the ECtHR's position on the reach of Article 11 in *Friend* has subsequently come from Strasbourg in *Emin Huseynov v Azerbaijan*,[44] which concerned police intervention to suspend a party, and arrest participants of the 'Che Guevara Fan Club', who were celebrating the eightieth anniversary of the birth of the revolutionary, in a café in Baku. From these multiple ECtHR authorities, and the position of the majority of the House of Lords in *Countryside Alliance*, it is clear that football fans gathering together in the UK can rely on Article 11, as they can on Article 10. Once again, and reading the Articles together, the extent of the positive obligations of the police towards football fans under Articles 10 and 11 "should be assessed in the light of the subject matter of the assembly", particularly taking into account whether the views being expressed were minority views subject that were "vulnerable to victimisation".[45] It is therefore likely that football fan rights of assembly and expression would not be viewed as equally fundamental to the individual as rights relating to participation in political protest. Nevertheless, through the ECHR and s.6 HRA 1998, fan rights of expression and peaceful assembly require protection and, at the time of writing, also trigger positive obligations on the part of the police.

The decisions in *Gypsy Council, Countryside Alliance, Friend,* and *Emin Huseynov* effectively bring football policing operations into the same

[43] *Friend v United Kingdom* [2009] ECHR 2068.

[44] App. 59135/09.

[45] *Berkman v Russia* (2020) App. 46712/15, para 55.

sphere as protest policing. Following "Adapting to Protest" (HMIC, 2009), police forces are now expected to put human rights front and centre of their approach to policing protest crowds. HMIC reached this conclusion after noting inadequate training in, and attention to, human rights obligations at "more highly charged events, such as large-scale protests" (HMIC, 2009 p. 5). The report particularly focused on the need to "facilitate" peaceful protest and Martin's excellent study of the policing of protests and marches in Northern Ireland details how this enabled officers to create a "script" for human rights compliance (Martin, 2021). However, there is no equivalent to 'Adapting to Protest' for football fans. Furthermore, at the time of writing, the College of Policing APP on Public Order makes no reference to human rights in relation to non-protest forms of assembly such as football gatherings (College of Policing, 2013),[46] instead talking almost exclusively about this only in relation to protest. Neither does the new UKFPU (UK Football Policing Unit)-led APP on Football Policing refer to human rights. As we will see in Chap. 8 and elsewhere, our observations rarely found a "script" for human rights compliance in policing operations (Martin, 2021) in football, nevermind serious attempts to implement a rights-based approach on the ground. Indeed, travelling without tickets (which would engage Article 11) and use of banners or wearing of high-status fashion brands (Article 10) are still sometimes seen as indicators of risk by those managing football policing operations. Post-*Friend*, this is a potentially dangerous oversight that leaves those responsible for football operations at risk of litigation. During our observations, and sometimes because of our influence, Arts. 10 and 11 were referenced in some football policing briefings, but more commonly such reference was worryingly absent. Furthermore, even within forces where human rights-based approaches to football events were observed, these were sometimes inconsistently applied, depending on personnel, club, or importance of the fixture (see also Browne, 2021).

---

[46] It is hoped that the new Public Order Public Safety APP, expected 2022–2023, will remedy this gap.

Obligations on Police to Protect or 'Facilitate' Assembly

Although not expressly referencing football crowds, the ECtHR/Council of Europe Guide on Freedom of Peaceful Assembly (CoE, 2021) and the OSCE/ODIHR Venice Commission Guidelines (CoE, 2019) have drawn together Strasbourg jurisprudence and provide further detail and guidance on how police forces should look to apply Article 11 in this context. It is clear that non-violent, but disruptive, acts committed during an assembly remain protected by Article 11, particularly where roads may be temporarily blocked, and that "assemblies should be regarded as an equally legitimate use of public space as other, more routine uses of such spaces, such as commercial activity or pedestrian and vehicular traffic" (CoE, 2019, para 62), although there is a wider margin of appreciation for sanctioning intentional disruption of ordinary life and traffic when this is related to "conduct which cannot enjoy the same privileged protection under the Convention as political speech or debate on questions of public interest" (CoE, 2021, para 73). Non-violent but disruptive acts committed during an assembly remain protected by Article 11, meaning that police interventions must both fall under Article 11(2) and satisfy the proportionality test set out in *Bank Mellat*, above. Furthermore, the legitimate objectives under Article 11(2), in particular "the prevention of disorder", should be interpreted narrowly (CoE, 2021, para 59) and should go beyond the prevention of a "hypothetical risk" of public disorder (CoE, 2019, para 139). Restrictions on the visual or audible content of any expression of the assembly should only be imposed where necessary, and proportionate to a legitimate aim, and there is a "duty to facilitate assemblies at the organiser's preferred location and within 'sight and sound' of the intended audience" (ibid, para 22). As the ECtHR has noted, "the right to freedom of assembly includes the right to choose the time, place and modalities of the assembly, within the limits established in [Article 11(2)]."[47] Finally, disruption or dispersal of any gathering by police, "may only be justifiable on specific and averred substantive

[47] *Sáska v Hungary* App. 58050/08, para 21.

grounds, such as serious risks provided for by law … and only after the participants had been given sufficient opportunity to manifest their views", is not justified purely by non-compliance with formal assembly requirements, and "the use of force must remain proportionate to the legitimate aims of prevention of disorder and protection of the rights of others" (CoE, 2021, paras 81–83).

From this, it is clear that football policing operations have a duty to facilitate fan gatherings or marches in public spaces, even where these may interfere with traffic or commercial activity, and may only disperse or divert fan groups as a matter of last resort and following clear communication. Policing strategies focused on keeping rival fans apart must not go beyond what is necessary to prevent disorder, with fans allowed to gather together and express their identity within "sight and sound" of their target (rival fans and, where appropriate, television audiences). This does not, however, mean that fans have the right to gather exactly when, and where, they want if this would put public order at risk. If there is evidence that such a gathering will engage one of the reasons for interference with rights set out in Arts. 10(2) or 11(2), *and* such interference is proportionate to achieving that aim, then crowds can be corralled or dispersed. But the horizontal effect of the positive obligation also means that police have a duty to protect fan gatherings from intimidation or attacks by rival fan groups[48] and provide a relatively safe environment for people to assemble.[49] Even excessive or unnecessary surveillance of fan gatherings can be seen as having a "chilling effect" on the effective exercise of Article 11 (Ashton, 2017, pp. 13–14).

More complicated is the extent to which the police are expected to facilitate expression and assembly on private land, particularly in football stadia. There is no human right to attend a football match,[50] and no human rights obligation on football clubs, as private companies, to allow

---

[48] In *Redmond-Bate v DPP* [2000] HRLR 249 it was held that where there was a risk of public disorder between two groups expressing opposing views, the duty was to confront those posing the threat.

[49] *Christians against Racism and Fascism v United Kingdom* App.8440/78 (1980) 21 DR 138; *Identoba and others v Georgia* App. 73235/12; *Platfform "Ärzte für das Leben" v Austria* (1988) 13 E.H.R.R. 204.

[50] *Commissioner of Met Police v Thorpe* [2015] EWHC 3339 at 19.

particular individuals to attend matches or particular areas of the stadium, or allow them to remain if they have contravened terms and conditions. Neither Articles 10 nor 11 provide "an automatic right of entry" to private property (CoE, 2019, para 64),[51] and the difference in judicial approaches to public land in contrast to private land was recently illustrated in *DPP v Cuciurean.*[52] However, Freedom of Expression and Assembly "must remain practical and effective" (CoE, 2019, para 64), and in *Lashmankin v Russia*, the ECtHR noted that "the purpose of an assembly is often linked to a certain location and/or time, to allow it to take place within sight and sound of its target object and at a time when the message may have the strongest impact".[53] For fans protesting against club owners, often the stadium, and sometimes the pitch, is the best, if not only, way to get their voices heard. If a fan engages in chanting, or displays a banner, that breaches the terms and conditions of their ticket, then provided this power is set out in the terms and conditions, the club's security may eject them. However, police officers should be careful in the extent to which any assistance in ejecting spectators could be seen as infringing rights under Arts. 10 or 11. While police officers generally do not eject fans for breaches of ground regulations, they are sometimes called upon by clubs to disperse protests from club land or even the pitch.

As we saw in Chap. 3, encroachment onto the pitch is a criminal offence,[54] but if a peaceful protest is occurring on the field of play, conducting arrests or using dispersal tactics must be human rights-compliant. Officers should only break up a peaceful protest, even if it is unlawful, if they consider that the protesters' presence in that location is not necessary for them to get their point heard by their target.[55] Unpopular club owners that avoid fan forums and only attend matches, cannot avail themselves of police support to clear pitches until the protesters have

---

[51] See *Appleby v. United Kingdom* [2003] ECHR 222, para. 47.

[52] [2022] EWHC 736 Admin. This case concerned Aggravated Trespass under s.68 Criminal Justice and Public Order Act 1994. The s.68 offence does not include the "lawful/reasonable excuse" defence that is contained in FOA 1991, so its applicability for FOA convictions for protest is unclear.

[53] App. 57818/09, para 405.

[54] s.4 FOA 1990.

[55] *Appleby* [2003]; *Anderson and others v United Kingdom* (1998) 25 ECHRR CD172.

made their argument heard. Furthermore, in the protest case of *Director of Public Prosecutions v Ziegler and others,*[56] the Supreme Court, by a majority decision, set aside convictions for breaches of section 137(1) of the Highways Act 1980. The appellants had argued that their rights under Articles 10 and 11 ECHR counted as "lawful excuse", which was a statutory defence to the obstruction of the highway. The statutory defence of "lawful excuse" also exists in s.4 of the Football (Offences) Act 1991 and could potentially prevent convictions for fans who are lawfully in the stadium and who have invaded the pitch to take part in a protest because that is the only way they can be heard by their target(s).[57] However, once the protest has made its point, the Articles 10/11 defence will dissipate, allowing police, once they have communicated their intentions to the crowd, to disperse the crowd and charge any fans not cooperating under s.4 FOA. None of this, of course, prevents club security staff, who do not have the same obligations to facilitate assembly and expression under the HRA, from dispersing the protest and ejecting those involved from the stadium.

Between them, the judgments in *Ziegler*[58] and *The Mayoral Commonalty v Samede*[59] set out the factors that should be taken into account when determining whether a restriction on Articles 10 and 11 rights is likely to be proportionate. These include the extent of the breach of domestic law, the duration of the assembly, level of interference with the rights of others, the importance of the location of the assembly to its purpose, and prior cooperation with the police. While the two judgments focus solely on protest, they are also valuable to football policing operations. However, while protests on the pitch would probably receive some protection from unnecessary interference, it is unlikely that either the duty not to disperse peaceful assemblies or the FOA s.4(2) defence extends to other forms of assembly and expression—for example, pitch invasions to celebrate goals, promotions, or titles. The reason for this, as detailed earlier in this chapter, is that the court should take into account whether

[56] [2021] UKSC 23.

[57] Although they may also be committing Aggravated Trespass under s.68 Criminal Justice and Public Order Act 1994, which does not contain a "lawful excuse" defence.

[58] Paras 71–78.

[59] Para 39 Lord Neuberger MR.

the views pertaining to the Article 10/11 rights relate to "very important issues" and whether they are "views which many would see as being of considerable breadth, depth and relevance".[60] Protests against important issues such as a club's very existence, its ownership, the proposed sale of the stadium, or breakaway leagues would be likely to satisfy this test, but more frivolous protests or carnivalesque gatherings would probably not. Neither would these human rights protections prevent the police taking action against fans who unlawfully broke into a stadium in order to protest.[61]

Human Rights Compliance in Police Decision-Making Processes

It should be clear from the above that those responsible for the policing of football crowd events need to be aware of, and responsive to, a number of different human rights considerations. Disproportionate, arbitrary, or unnecessary breaches by the police of Articles 5, 10, and 11, or a failure to protect fans from interferences by others, particularly in relation to Peaceful Assembly and Expression, have the potential to result in legal challenges under s.6 HRA and substantial compensation claims. Further, where a court is satisfied that a human right has been restricted by police actions, the burden of proof will shift to the police to demonstrate that their limitation of the right in question was proportionate.[62] We cannot, however, expect those making key tactical decision on a matchday to be always able to make the correct human rights decisions, or to have immediate access to the expertise to assist them. Human rights-compliant decision-making in complex crowd situations, with numerous actors

[60] Ibid, paras 40–41. This judgment was upheld by the Supreme Court in *DPP v Ziegler and others* [2021] UKSC 23.

[61] In May 2021, around 2–300 Manchester United fans unlawfully gained access to the stadium and invaded the pitch hours before a planned match in order to protest against the club owners and their attempts to take the club into a "European Super League". As the invasion of the pitch took place more than two hours before the scheduled kick-off, FOA s.4 did not apply, but the fans could have been charged with Aggravated Trespass under s.68 Criminal Justice and Public Order Act 1994.

[62] *Jersild v Demark* (1995) 19 EHRR 1.

involved and many conflicting rights engaged, is complex and difficult. Fortunately for the police service, the courts have regularly been willing to give weight to the expertise of public officials when assessing whether a decision to restrict human rights is proportionate (Hickman, 2010, pp. 147, 175–7), and both domestic courts and the ECtHR have demonstrated considerable leniency, and been sympathetic, towards a police officer's belief that interferences with human rights are needed to prevent disorder in public order situations.[63] Further, the highest domestic appellate court has demonstrated a willingness to take into account the attempts of public authorities to apply human rights appropriately, and accepted human rights-compliant results even when the correct procedure has not been followed. In two key domestic human rights cases in 2006 and 2007 (neither unfortunately relating to football or the police), the House of Lords gave "a steer in the direction of a culture of rights, but refrain(ed) from imposing any prescriptive or legalistic requirements on public authorities" (Kavanagh, 2014, p. 258).

The starting point is that as human rights are ultimately substantive rather than merely procedural, unlike other areas of administrative law focused more on decision-making processes, if a football policing operation results in a human rights-compliant result, how they arrived at that outcome is much less significant.

> The role of the court in human rights adjudication is quite different from the role of the court in an ordinary judicial review of administrative action. In human rights adjudication, the court is concerned with whether the human rights of the claimant have in fact been infringed, not with whether the administrative decision-maker properly took them into account. If it were otherwise, every policy decision taken before the 1998 Act came into force but which engaged a Convention right would be open to challenge, no matter how obviously compliant with the right in question it was (Baroness Hale in *Belfast City Council v Miss Behavin' Ltd*).[64]

[63] See, for example, *The Queen (on the application of McClure and Moos) v Commissioner of Police* [2012] EWCA Civ 12, *Austin* (2012), and *S.V. and A. v Denmark* (2018).

[64] [2007] 1 WLR 1420, para 31.

As was set out in *R (Begum) v Governors of Denbigh High School*,[65] there is also no requirement that a public authority must adhere to a legally prescribed decision-making structure akin to that which a court would apply in a human rights case, and the failure by an authority to reason a decision that results in a human rights-compliant outcome in practical terms should not pose it a problem in the courts. This approach has been criticised for departing from Parliamentary intent and effectively watering down human rights protections (Mead, 2012), but the case law appears to provide some leeway for forces making key tactical decisions.

The flip side of the House of Lords's rulings in the *Miss Behavin'* and *Begum* cases is that where a public authority has restricted one of the ECHR rights, if that authority has attempted to apply human rights criteria correctly in its decision-making process, it is less likely to be found to be in breach of them. As Kavanagh points out, the test of proportionality is a combination of both the substantive and the procedural (Kavanagh, 2014, p. 249), and both House of Lords cases took into account the extent to which the public authorities genuinely considered the relevant ECHR issues when reaching their decision. In *Begum*, Lord Bingham stressed that it would be harder for complainants to challenge the decisions of public authorities if they had undertaken a "conscientious" consideration of human rights,[66] whereas in *Miss Behavin'*, Baroness Hale noted that a public body that had addressed its mind to the ECHR when arriving at a decision would have this taken into account by the court.[67] Similarly, Lord Neuburger stated that where a public authority has "properly considered" the relevant human rights, "the court is inherently less likely to conclude that the decision ultimately reached infringes the applicant's rights".[68] This leads Kavanagh to conclude that "If a public authority has conscientiously paid proper attention to the human rights considerations when making its decision, the task of the challenger is harder and there will be a greater likelihood that the authority's decision will be regarded as proportionate" (Kavanagh, 2014, p. 255).

---

[65] [2007] 1 A.C. 100.

[66] *Begum*, Para 31.

[67] *Miss Behavin' Ltd*, Para 37.

[68] *Miss Behavin' Ltd*, Para 91.

Moreover, recent case law developments seem to clarify the importance of the police carrying out their own proportionality considerations before interfering with Article 10 or 11 rights, rather than this merely being something for the courts to consider *post facto*. In *R (Leigh and others) v Met Police Commissioner*,[69] the Divisional Court considered the decision of the Metropolitan Police to inform organisers that their proposed vigil for the murdered Sarah Everard was unlawful under Covid-19 lockdown regulations. The court held that their failure "to carry out a fact-specific proportionality assessment in accordance with Ziegler" made their actions "legally flawed".[70] The implications for football policing, and the obligations on officers when making decisions about dispersal, escorting, and kettling, are clear. A "conscientious" and "fact-specific" proportionality assessment now needs to be part of the process of making strategic and tactical decisions in the event of a subsequent legal challenge. A consideration of all relevant human rights here is important, despite insufficient consideration being given to Articles 10 and 11 by the current APP guidance. Furthermore, a rigorous application of the *Bank Mellat* proportionality test (albeit mediated by *Pwr v DPP* and *Akdogan v DPP*) is essential when rights are to be interfered with. The force must be able to demonstrate that the restrictions arise from a legitimate objective (usually to avoid violence or disorder), that they are expected to meet that objective (i.e. that they are likely to achieve that aim), that there is no "less intrusive measure" that could be used, and, overall, that the infringement of the rights does not outweigh the benefit of the measure imposed.

Courts, guided by the text of the ECHR, are generally minded to accept measures directed towards preventing disorder and violence as being legitimate, and have also demonstrated that they are usually ill-equipped, or unwilling, to engage with evidence about the effectiveness and suitability of police tactics (Stott & Pearson, 2006). When it comes to the "less intrusive measure"[71] stage of the proportionality assessment, both domestic and Strasbourg case law illustrates that the senior officer

[69] [2022] EWHC 527 (Admin).

[70] *Leigh*, para 107. See also Tan (2022).

[71] Elsewhere referred to as the "least restrictive alternative" test or, in *de Freitas v Permanent Secretary of Ministry of Agriculture* [1999] 1AC 69, "the means used to impair the right or freedom are no more than is necessary to accomplish the objective".

making the decision is expected to consider alternative approaches to the challenge they are facing. 'Bubbles', 'kettles', coercive escorts, and 'hold-backs' that restrict the Articles 10 and 11 rights of supporters "should only be imposed by a senior police officer who reasonably believes that, based on the evidence available at the time, containment of the crowd is the least restrictive way of preventing an 'imminent' breach of the peace" (James & Pearson, 2015, p. 469), and any containment should be kept under constant review and removed at the earliest opportunity. For example, the Court of Appeal in *McClure* paid particular attention in its conclusion to the fact that the officer making the decision to kettle the protest crowd reasonably believed that "no less intrusive crowd control operation"[72] would have prevented mass disorder, having considered and ruled out the possibility of identifying and isolating those who were violent or disorderly.[73] Similarly, in the ECtHR ruling in *Austin,* the Grand Chamber placed great emphasis on the fact that the police continually reviewed their containment tactic and had adopted this because it was less intrusive than other more physically coercive measures.[74]

Most interesting for our purposes is how this played out in the more recent football case of *S. V. and A. v Denmark*,[75] concerning the preventative detention of fans suspected of attending a fixture to engage in violence and at which disorder had already occurred. In concluding that the breach of Article 5 was proportionate, the ECtHR observed that the policing operation had previously used "manoeuvre tactics to prevent such clashes" and had engaged "in proactive dialogue with the fans/spectators from 12 noon, when they started to arrive, and in the event of any clashes, to detain only the instigators".[76] In other words, the police were able to demonstrate that the restrictions had only been imposed due to the fact that the alternative, less intrusive, tactics had not fully succeeded. *S. V. and A. v Denmark* provides a clear indication that, aside from their evident value in reducing the risk of disorder set out in Chap. 6, proactive

[72] *McClure,* para 95 (Hughes MR).

[73] *ibid*, para 20.

[74] *Austin* (2012), particularly paras.66–67.

[75] *S. V. and A. v Denmark* (2018).

[76] Para 163.

liaison tactics can also assist a force that needs to escalate its response to violence at football, if it finds itself subsequently facing a human rights challenge in court.

Conclusions

This chapter has demonstrated that football policing operations need to take into account, not only the obligations not to breach the 'negative' rights such as the right to Life, Liberty, Privacy, and the prohibition on inhumane treatment, but need to more consistently and robustly adhere to their obligations to help fans secure their freedom of Assembly and Expression. Football fans have somewhat suffered here, with most case law in this area relating to protest, and neither College of Policing nor UKFPU APP currently mentioning peaceful assembly or free expression in relation to football policing. However, a series of ECtHR cases, and a strong lean by the House of Lords, clarify that football fan gatherings now engage Articles 10 and 11. This needs to be acknowledged by the College of Policing, UKFPU, and individual forces, to avoid putting the police at risk of successful litigation under the HRA (and probably any legislation that replaces it) in the event of a disproportionate breach of ECHR rights. As we will see later in the book, our observations indicated that forces generally achieved human-rights compliant results in their operations, which is sufficient to satisfy the current domestic legal position. However, in the event of a legal challenge, most forces would be in a weak position to defend their actions. With Arts. 10 and 11 rarely mentioned in match planning and operational documentation, it is both difficult for police decision-makers to be prepared to apply the proportionality tests to any restrictions, or to be able to demonstrate to a court that they were attempting to achieve a human rights-compliant result. In the next chapter we will critique several football policing case studies and identify the problems that approaches based on static understandings of dispositional risk can bring. This tends to overshadow one of the other genuine risks that every operation faces: the risk of litigation. Adopting a human rights-based approach to policing football crowds, or even a "script" for human rights-compliant operations (Martin, 2021), will ultimately mitigate this risk.

Moreover, we contend that applying a human rights-based approach to football policing is not only useful in protecting forces from potential litigation but also *strategically and tactically beneficial*. First, it serves to enhance the legitimacy of policing operations within the fan communities the police are serving. As we saw in Chap. 6, facilitating fan desires to engage in free expression and assembly, rather than a default position of containment and control, is much more likely to result in policing operations being seen as legitimate, and less likely to see resistance from fan groups. Second, from a tactical standpoint, prioritising human rights in decision-making can help ensure positive public order outcomes. In this sense, and regardless of the immediate political future of the HRA, in complex and challenging crowd situations, applying ECHR Article 11 could help to focus an officer's mind on what should be one of the key questions: "Is the assembly I am policing peaceful?" Further, applying the test of proportionality can encourage officers to consider whether tactics which restrict rights of assembly and expression are likely to be effective in achieving positive public order outcomes (as opposed to making disorder worse), and whether there are less restrictive, probably less confrontational, measures to achieve the same aim. As we move on to the core empirical part of this book, in the next chapter we will see how a failure to apply such a decision-making process can contribute to unacceptable public order outcomes.

References

Ashton, V. (2017). State Surveillance of Protest and the Rights to Privacy and Freedom of Assembly: A Comparison of Judicial and Protestor Perspectives. *European Journal of Law and Technology, 8*(1), 1–19.

Bromberger, C., Hayot, A., & Mariottini, J. (1993). Allez L'OM, Forza Juve: The Passion for Football in Marseille and Turin. In S. Redhead (Ed.), *The Passion and the Fashion: Football Fandom in New Europe* (pp. 103–151). Avebury.

Browne, M. (2021) *A Human Rights Approach to the Policing of Football Fans*, Unpublished PhD Thesis. The University of Manchester.

Bullock, K., & Johnson, P. (2012). The Impact of the Human Rights Act 1998 on Policing in England and Wales. *British Journal of Criminology, 52*(3), 630–650.

CoE. (2019). *OSCE/ODIHR Venice Commission Guidelines on Freedom of Peaceful Assembly* (3rd ed.). Strasbourg.

CoE. (2020). *Guide to Article 9 of the European Convention on Human Rights – Freedom of Thought, Conscience and Religion*. Council of Europe.

CoE. (2021). *ECtHR Guidelines on Freedom of Peaceful Assembly*. Council of Europe.

College of Policing Authorised Professional Practice. (2013). https://www.app.college.police.uk/app-content/public-order/policing-football/ (Updated 2018).

Dixon, D. (2007). Changing Law, Changing Policing. In M. Mitchell & J. Casey (Eds.), *Police Management and Leadership* (pp. 23–36). Federation Press.

Dyke, T. (2009). Focus on Article 11. *Judicial Review, 14*(2), 185–196.

Fenwick, H. (2009). *Civil Liberties and Human Rights* (4th ed.). Routledge.

Fenwick, H., & Masterman, R. (2017). The Conservative Project to "Break the Link between British Courts and Strasbourg": Rhetoric or Reality? *Modern Law Review, 80*, 1111–1136.

Fenwick, H., Phillipson, G., & Williams, A. (2017). *Text, Cases and Materials on Public Law and Human Rights*. Routledge.

Glover, R. (2018). Keeping the Peace and Preventive Justice - A New Test for Breach of the Peace? *Public Law, 3*, 444–460.

Her Majesty's Inspector of Constabulary. (2009). *Adapting to Protest: Nurturing the British Model of Policing*. HMIC.

Hickman, T. (2010). *Public Law After the Human Rights Act*. Hart.

Home Department White Paper. (1997). *Rights Brought Home: The Human Rights Bill, Cm.3782*. HMSO.

James, M., & Pearson, G. (2015). Public Order and the Rebalancing of Football Fans' Rights: Legal Problems with Pre-emptive Policing Strategies and Banning Orders. *Public Law, 3*, 458–475.

Kavanagh, A. (2014). Reasoning About Proportionality Under the Human Rights Act 1998: Outcomes, Substance and Process. *Law Quarterly Review, 130*, 235–258.

King, A. (2003). *The European Ritual: Football in the New Europe*. Ashgate.

Martin, R. (2021). *Policing Human Rights*. Oxford University Press.

Martyn, P., & Taylor, R. (1997). Something for the Weekend, Sir? Leisure, Ecstasy and Identity in Football and Contemporary Religion. *Leisure Studies, 16*(1), 37–49.

Mead, D. (2009). Of Kettles, Cordons and Crowd Control – Austin v Commissioner of Police for the Metropolis and the Meaning of "Deprivation of Liberty". *European Human Rights Law Review, 3*, 376–394.

Mead, D. (2010). *New Law of Peaceful Protest: Rights and Regulation in the Human Rights Era*. Hart.

Mead, D. (2012). Outcomes Aren't All: Defending Process-Based Review of Public Authority Decisions Under the Human Rights Act. *Public Law*, 63–87.

Morris, D. (1981). *The Soccer Tribe*. Jonathan Cape.

Neyroud, P., & Beckley, A. (2001). *Policing, Ethics and Human Rights*. Willan Publishing.

OSCE. (2016). *Human Rights Handbook on Policing Assemblies*. OSCE.

Pearson, G. (2012). *An Ethnography of English Football Fans: Cans, Cops and Carnivals*. Manchester University Press.

Pearson, G., & Rowe, M. (2020). *Police Street Powers and Criminal Justice: Regulation and Discretion in a Time of Change*. Hart.

Pearson, G., Rowe, M., & Turner, E. (2018). Policy, Practicalities, and PACE s.24: Police Understanding and Subsuming of Necessity in Decision-Making on Arrest. *Journal of Law and Society, 45*(2), 282–308.

Starmer, K. (1999). *European Human Rights Law*. Legal Action Group.

Stone, R. (2001). Breach of the Peace: The Case for Abolition. *Web Journal of Current Legal Issues, 2*(2).

Stott, C., & Pearson, G. (2006). Football Banning Orders, Proportionality and Public Order. *Howard Journal of Criminal Justice, 45*(3), 241–254.

Tan, G. (2022). An Obligation on the Police to Carry Out Proportionality Assessments? *Administrative Court Blog* 22/3/22. https://administrativecourt-blog.wordpress.com/2022/03/12/an-obligation-on-the-police-to-carry-out-proportionality-assessments/

8

Understanding Risk in Football

Introduction

In this chapter we return to the question of how 'risk' is understood and managed in football policing. In Chaps. 4 and 5 we considered the role that risk has played in the move to 'intelligence-led' football policing and in the criminal justice system generally, with an increasing reliance upon administrative processes and tools designed to pre-empt deviance and to control suspects, in contrast to post-offence legal measures. We also saw that 'risk' in football policing is predominantly understood as relating to predispositions towards, or intentions to engage in, violence against rival supporters. In this chapter, we will draw together six case studies from our fieldwork observations (the methodology is discussed in Chap. 1). Our data and analysis indicate that risk, with regard to whether football crowd disorder will develop, is a complex and nuanced *process*, where predisposition, or prior intentionality, plays only a minor role. The risk factors identified empirically through our research related more commonly to situationally embedded interactions, frustrated identity-related expectations, perceived legitimacy of policing, and a number of legal, structural, and geographical factors. The vast bulk of the empirical data we present in both this, and Chap. 9, has not been previously disseminated. It is important to note that the case studies we discuss here are

G. Pearson, C. Stott, *A New Agenda For Football Crowd Management*, Palgrave Studies in Risk, Crime and Society, https://doi.org/10.1007/978-3-031-16298-5_8

only a sample of the times these issues became apparent, but they reflect the more extreme examples of how risk tends to be misunderstood in football crowd policing, often with negative consequences for public order. As we will argue, a narrow dispositional understanding can lead to policing responses that *create* risk, not only of disorder at that fixture, but also risk for future fixtures, as well as financial risk, risk of reputational harm, and the risk of litigation.

The Importance of History in Assessing and Managing Risk

As we explained in Chap. 4, planning for football fixtures begins almost immediately following the announcement of the fixtures at the start of the season. Consequently, from the moment league fixtures are released (usually late June), the Dedicated Football Officers (DFOs) in the relevant police forces will have categorised every league fixture for that season in terms of the risk of violence and disorder occurring. As we have already discussed, this categorisation is to achieve two primary objectives. First, it is to predict, as far in advance as possible, the human resources that may be required to police it, so that force planning teams can understand when demand is likely to occur. Second, it is to predict the overall costs of policing football so, where possible, agreements can be reached with clubs about the payments they will make for every policed fixture under the Special Police Services arrangements. In these early stages of planning there will inevitably be little, if any, contemporary intelligence, so the assessments are based primarily upon historical factors, reputation of the visiting fans, and speculative assumptions about what might take place.

Case Study 1: A 'Regional Derby' in the North

The first case study was a regional derby in northern England in the early winter of 2019, between two teams in the lower leagues. It was identified as a risk fixture because it was expected to be one of the biggest attendances of the season for the host club, and both home and visiting clubs had relatively notorious, and active, 'risk groups'. Police planning had begun on the assumption that at least 100 'risk' supporters from the visiting club would attend, who it was understood would pose considerable challenges, both inside and outside the stadium. Correspondingly, from as early as July the previous year, police intelligence reports suggested that this fixture was to be one of the season's two "big days out" for the visiting club's risk groups. A more contemporary intelligence report noted the other identified high-risk fixture had already taken place and seemed to confirm this assessment; while it occurred in another police jurisdiction, the report noted that heavy policing resources had been required to "keep rival fans separated" (although no disorder had actually occurred).

In the days preceding the fixture, firmer intelligence was received by the host force suggesting that the rival risk groups had been in contact with each other (from which pre-planned disorder was inferred rather than stated), and that two 'rogue coaches' had been booked under the guise of a stag weekend and shopping trip by a 'risk fan' from the visiting team. This detailed intelligence stated that the coaches were scheduled to travel to a city proximate to the one hosting the fixture. It was suggested that the intention of those on board was then to travel from that city by rail to the match-city, deliberately to evade police. The intelligence overview in the Operational Order noted that these coaches would "have the older risk on, who are not too interested in the game, but are looking to attend for trouble". During the pre-match police officer briefing, it was also announced that the home 'risk group' would be 'turning out' in significant numbers and intelligence suggested that at least one of them was planning to deliberately provoke the visiting risk fans. All in all, this was clearly being flagged up to be a challenging day.

By the morning of the match, 120–140 visiting fans labelled as 'risk' were expected to travel, and the public order operation maintained its Category C classification, mobilising significant police resources into the city. The early stages of the operation revolved entirely around locating the two 'rogue' coaches, which were quickly identified, intercepted, and detained at a motorway junction close to the city where they were expected. The DFO from the visiting force boarded the vehicles and confirmed to the Bronze Commander that there were indeed between eight and ten 'Category C' fans on one of the coaches and several 'Category B' and 'hangers on' on both. However, further interrogation of the situation indicated more nuance. The coach organiser identified himself to the Bronze—he was a male in his early 20s and very deferent, polite, and compliant. He articulated to the Bronze Commander that both coaches simply wanted to travel to the nearby city centre so those on board could drink in pubs before travelling on to the match in the adjacent city. The organiser claimed that they were celebrating the 60th birthday of one of their number, were not seeking to cause problems, but did not want to travel directly to the match-city as they knew there would be nowhere comfortable to drink before the match that they would be allowed into. On that latter issue he was correct; the pub allocated to visiting fans was small, always overcrowded and—in our view—not particularly pleasant.

The football team in the adjacent city was playing away from home on that day, but the Bronze Commander was concerned that large numbers of fans from that club would be drinking in the city centre. His view was that the visiting 'risk' drinking in this city centre could lead to confrontations if the coaches were allowed to proceed. This was despite the organiser's assurances that they had no intention of seeking out confrontations, not least because of his claims of positive affiliations between the supporters of the two clubs. With the visiting fans planning to travel onwards by train to the match-city, this would inevitably have meant they would have also been required to walk through the host club's city centre, with its bars and pubs frequented by that club's 'risk'. With the identification of the coaches further validating the pre-match intelligence and with identified 'risk' fans on board, the commanders judged they had little option, but to use breach of the peace (BOP) powers and the Guidance issued by the Office of the Traffic Commissioner to compel the coaches to travel directly to the designated 'away pub' adjacent to the match venue. As the Bronze Commander explained in an interview a few weeks later:

> I'm conscious that we don't want to treat everybody with one approach, but you have to go off what your spotters are telling you. If they are saying

> six to eight of their top boys are on there, with another set of Cat B's and C's well that's giving me a problem. That's not a coach of law-abiding people. If it was, we would not have even pulled it over. So, you've then got a decision to make. I'm speaking to Silver Commander, and we are saying well if they go into [the other city], it's a massive city, and we lose them or they disperse, then they go on the train network [to the host city], then we've got no control have we, in what goes on. That's why you have to explain why you have to do what you have to do. I said to the organiser of those coaches: "I can't let you go into [the other city] because there will be an imminent breach of the peace."

This explanation suggests, at best, a stretching of the common law powers to breaking point, particularly with the lack of intelligence about the location of the 'risk' supporters from the city in which the fans wished to drink (and one would have expected them to have travelled away to their team's fixture). A hypothetical risk of disorder will struggle to be defined as 'imminent' for the purposes of detention to prevent a breach of the peace. But more clearly (as we saw in Chap. 7), the decision interfered with what appears to be a peaceful assembly, without any consideration of European Convention on Human Rights (ECHR) Article 10 or 11 freedoms, or an application of the human rights proportionality test. If there had been up-to-date intelligence that a rival risk group was awaiting the coach occupants, then the police could have argued either that the assembly was not peaceful by nature or that the restriction on their movements was a lawful (applying common law BOP powers) and proportionate (under ECHR Article 11(2)) restriction to prevent crime and disorder. But according to the Bronze Commander there was no express consideration of the key human rights questions, and furthermore, it was evident that preventing imminent confrontation was not the primary objective behind the decision:

> Bronze: I think it's about eliminating the opportunity for disorder. You think about (…) some of the barristers, they always ask you "could you have foreseen what was going to occur"? Now if you are sat in a witness box and giving evidence and somebody has said to you that they are all risk fans and they are going to a fixture in [one city] but they want to go and drink in [another] with [the football team in that city] playing down the road in

[a third city 70 miles away], why did you do that? And you said, "I want to give them the benefit of the doubt". You're going to struggle aren't you if there is mass disorder and there are windows going in and they are running amok, where there are big business paying big rates. It's a difficult one and you would have to be very brave to say let them get on with it and let's see what happens because you know the reputational risk you are taking.

Interviewer: Reputation for who?

Bronze: For us as commanders, for the organisation or the local authority.

It is evident from this account that, as we argued in Chap. 4, the 'risk' categorisation has a complex inter-relationship with accountability. Having detained vehicles containing fans categorised as risk, in this case at least, police decision-making revolved as much around the "in the job trouble" (Chatterton, 1979; Waddington, 1994) they might experience should they release their 'grip' on those fans. In this sense, the evidence the commander had about the potential for "on the job" trouble (ibid) was less important. As the Silver Commander later reflected on the decision to contain the fans,

There is a mantra from the College [of Policing] that a decision as to whether a course of action was reasonable will be taken by a group of peers with similar experience and qualification … in other words, they would have got 3 silvers with similar experience of policing big events as me and asked them what they would have done and then the likely outcome would be that I would have been served papers for Gross Misconduct. So, I'm struggling as to how I could do anything differently in the same situation due to the consequences for me.

Despite the legally dubious but practically real basis for the decisions, there were no individuals on the coaches willing, or able, to contest this outcome and the visiting fans were escorted directly to the nominated 'away pub'. However, the pub was not yet open, and it remained closed for another half-hour, as staff had yet to arrive. Consequently, there were immediately challenges for the police, particularly in terms of accessing alcohol and food for the fans. There were too few police resources present to corral the fans and it was unclear on what legal basis that could be achieved. The policing plan was meant to be based on facilitation of legitimate fan objectives, but so far, despite best intentions, police action appeared to us to have done the opposite. There was, however, an off-licence and supermarket across the road which became quickly overwhelmed as fans bought up cans and bottles and flowed back out into the road and congregated around the pub. In the melee, the small number of Category C fans, the 'top lads' identified earlier, slipped away and located themselves more comfortably into a nearby 'home pub', which was already open.

Sometime afterwards, their presence came to the attention of the police. Our observations confirmed they were sitting quietly and interrelating well with home fans inside, with no evident tensions. On interviewing one of the 'risk' and the visiting DFO, it became apparent their 'Category C' status was because several of them had been subject to football banning orders (FBOs) for activity decades ago, rather than a direct indication of the threat they posed on that day. The fans admitted to us they were not celebrating a birthday but were keen to point out that one of their number was 60 years old. All they were seeking to do, they claimed, was find a pub where they could drink in a relaxed atmosphere, which they knew was impossible in the away pub that, even when open, was notoriously bad, busy, and short-staffed. He pointed out how quiet they were being and how they were getting on well with the home fans around them; indeed, we observed home fans in the pub disputing the presence of the police rather than the visiting 'risk'. Nonetheless, the Bronze Commander was concerned that if left alone, home fans would attack them. He also explained that the landlady had complained about the visiting fans. She could, of course, have simply refused to serve them any further drinks, but the commander tasked one of his Operational Football Officers (OFOs) to go into the pub and persuade the fans to leave. Evidently lacking in good communications skills and having no prior relationship to these fans, the host force OFO was unable to achieve this, so the Bronze Commander re-entered, explained to the fans his rationale, and ordered (again, under what legal power was unclear) them to return to the designated away pub. Shortly afterwards the fans finished their drinks, left, and headed back to their designated venue.

In the end, while no home 'risk fans' materialised pre-match, the hundreds of away fans now gathered in the pub were corralled together and an attempt was made to escort them to the stadium. Throughout this last pre-match phase, it was evident that once the fans moved off, it was they, rather than the police, who were in control of their direction and pace of travel. It was also clear that several of the fans were walking well away from the 'escort' and readily capable of confronting others should the opportunity arise. The march down to the away turnstiles was enjoyable to the fans who, evidently empowered by walking *en masse*, were free to collectively chant their support for the visiting team and contempt towards their opponents. During the procession, it was reported that a window of a house was broken, a small group of Asian youths were racially abused, and a car was damaged. We were left asking whether any of this would have occurred if the fans had been left to make their own way to the stadium and contend that a human rights-based approach to the situation may have indicated a more sensible, proportionate, and legally robust way forward for the police operation. Certainly, there was no evidence or indication that the 'Category C' risk fans from the 'rogue' coach were involved in any of this criminality. The match itself passed off without incident, but post-match some away fans who had travelled by train were attacked as they sought to make their way home. But even here the conflict seems to have been situationally determined and interactional rather than merely about fan dispositions. The nearby railway station had been temporarily closed, forcing the away fans to walk to another station in the city, through the area populated by pubs frequented by home 'risk'. As they passed through that area, some home fans had confronted them, and police had been required to draw batons to keep the groups apart. It is reasonable to assume that had the rail network not been disrupted, the interactions that led to this post-match 'disorder' would simply not have occurred.

Case Study 2: A Historical Rivalry

Our second case study which highlights the complex situational and interactional nature of 'risk' in football policing relates to a midweek evening cup tie between two clubs meeting for the first time in over a decade. Although this was not a 'derby', the rival fans had been involved in a notorious riot around over three decades earlier and the visiting fans had a wider reputation for disorder and, on occasion, racism. The tie was a sell-out and given the notoriety of the visiting fan group, this was seen as a high-risk fixture and categorised as a Cat C-IR, despite the fact that the several previous fixtures between these clubs across the previous 30 years had not attracted any significant issues.

Our research team had the opportunity to engage with the Silver Commander in the weeks before the match. He was immediately candid about what he had experienced so far in the planning phase, describing several challenges that he believed were driving resources into the fixture unnecessarily. In particular, the notoriety of the fixture in the town made it a highly salient event for the local Police and Crime Commissioner (PCC). The home club's stadium was in the heart of a predominantly Asian and Muslim community, and both supporter groups were either stereotyped as being racist or had links to far-right political groups. Subsequently, the PCC put pressure on the Chief Constable, based on his judgement that there were concerns about violence, and to ensure that sufficient resources would be in place to protect the community. In response, the force conducted a community-impact assessment, but this contradicted the PCC assertions of significant community concerns and empowered the Silver Commander to try to avoid sucking unnecessary resources into the operation. However, the situation was then further complicated by intelligence reports that were feeding into the planning cycle. A report delivered by the visiting DFO indicated that around 150 Category B 'risk' fans affiliated to the visiting club would attend. The Silver did not trust the information and challenged the validity of this intelligence. Our view is that this was not an unreasonable assessment by the DFO for every away fixture involving the visiting fans, but we shared the Silver Commander's view that this reflected the ambiguity and 'catch all' nature of the risk categories, rather than being an accurate assessment of underlying risk these fans may pose.

The commander had also received a report by a pub landlady in the town which was known to be frequented by home 'risk'. She had contacted the police to inform them that three people, apparently affiliated to the visiting club, had entered her premises and declared that away fans intended to 'take-over' her venue on the day of the match. As we explained in Chap. 4, the source of this information should have led to it being classified as very low-grade intelligence (e.g. E4), but it had a very powerful impact, exacerbated by the fact that at a previous fixture, a group of visiting fans from a different club had taken over a 'home pub' by arriving early in the town centre. The Silver's assessment was that this would be a relatively low-risk fixture, but taking all the above into account, he felt he now had little choice but to classify it as their highest-risk match of the season.

Despite the evening kick-off, the intelligence about the pub 'takeover' also meant the Silver Commander had to bring a Police Support Unit (PSU) on duty at 11.00, before the main briefing. Both the main briefing and the Operational Order distributed at it communicated the intelligence picture discussed above, stating that large numbers of the visiting fans would arrive via rail to try and take over the home pub. The disseminated intelligence also suggested that visiting fans would be "grouping up before travelling" and may visit intervening towns on their journey. In the briefing, the DFO also showed pictures of knives disguised as credit cards that it was claimed the visiting fans tended to carry. The briefing concluded by focusing on five to six Danish 'ultras' from Copenhagen FC who were also expected to be attending. The Op Order stated that this was not unusual because the visiting club "do attract European Ultra supporters at various times in the season due to their reputation for football violence". The picture painted by the intelligence was therefore clear: the visiting fans posed a significant threat. Despite this overwhelming emphasis on the potential for disorder from the visiting fans, the summary in the Op Order concluded, somewhat bafflingly given what had just been described, that there "is no intelligence to suggest pre-planned disorder is likely at this fixture". At the same time, there was little to no information about the nature, intentions, or potential threats and risks posed to the away fans by home fans. This absence would prove to be very meaningful.

Once our fieldworkers were deployed on the matchday, it became clear that logistical issues lay at the heart of the challenges facing the host force. The stadium is a considerable distance from the town centre and not well served by transport links, parking, or public houses. Subsequently, the public order operation invariably relies upon a few pubs near the main railway station being prepared to host visiting fans. By nominating at least one of these as the 'away pub', the police 'encourage' (indeed often actually compel) visiting fans to gather there, and claim they are facilitating fan intentions. This enables the police to focus their resources onto the visiting fans, to control their movement as their main strategic approach, to try to prevent confrontations developing. However, this approach also means the police are then faced with the challenge of large numbers of visiting fans moving together from the pub to the stadium. Like many others across England and Wales, this host force work in partnership with a local bus company to provide free, or subsidised, transport from the nominated 'away pub' to the stadium. However, on this occasion, the notoriety of the visiting fans meant the management of the premises close to the station had refused to cooperate, so these were no longer available. Instead, the police operation had to utilise a pub that required visiting fans arriving by rail to walk across the town centre.

The aim of the operation was therefore to gather all the visiting fans into this nominated pub and encourage them to use the buses that had been organised to take them to and from the stadium. However, we could identify little, if anything, done to communicate this expectation to the fans. This was surprising, given that the visiting DFO had knowledge that these fans historically preferred to walk together to the ground. Bizarrely, this kind of identity or culturally relevant information was not included in the reports or briefings. 'Walk-ups' are complex issues; on the one hand, they are a cultural expression of power and identity (Pearson, 2012, pp. 117–121); visiting fans walking collectively through the 'home' territory is not just an opportunity for them to celebrate their identity and verbally denigrate their opposition, it is also a symbolic act often interpreted as a challenge to, and by, home fans. In response, home 'risk' fans often see the need to put on a show of strength in opposition; for some this is even seen as an obligation to retain cultural credibility. Equally, the collective nature of the walks can be seen as a defensive manoeuvre by the visiting fans, who know that if they gather and walk up together, they are less likely to get "picked off" by home fans who might see it as legitimate to attack them (see Stott and Pearson, 2007, Chap. 1). On the other hand, and as we shall see later in this chapter, what must also be considered is that these large walk-ups are almost invariantly the product of police tactics. After being encouraged, or even compelled, to gather in a single location, these are essentially people acting peacefully and compliantly, and in line with their ECHR of assembly and expression. Walk-ups are, in the main, populated by a broad constituency of the travelling fan base and the bulk, if not all, of them have no intention of proactively seeking out violent confrontation. They are attending to watch a sporting fixture, celebrate and express their identity, and wish to, or have been required to, walk to the event and simply want to do so without being violently assaulted, whatever the intention of a minority among them.

As the visiting fans began to arrive by train, their first encounter with police was a PSU from the British Transport Police (BTP), heavily kitted-out in protective equipment. This stood in stark contrast to the low-profile tone that the Silver Commander from the host force had stressed in the briefing he wanted to achieve. Yet with no control over BTP resources, and no-one from BTP present at the earlier briefing, it would have been unclear to them what the commander's objectives were. Stood across the road was a serial from the host force, dressed in normal uniform, tasked to try and deliver the Silver's engagement-led approach. As is often the case, the contrasts sent a confusing message about the kind of policing the fans were set to receive that day. As we will demonstrate in a theme of our empirical findings, none of the PSU officers present were verbally engaging with the fans, despite those from the host force having been explicitly instructed to do so. With each arriving train, visiting fans filtered out of the station. A few approached the police and asked for information about where to go, before walking in small groups through the now largely quiet and pedestrianised town centre towards the designated pub. As we shadowed one group, it was noticeable that despite the large number of police involved in the operation, there was not a single officer positioned in the considerable distance between the station and the away pub. This gap would later turn out to be significant.

By early evening, the attempted 'take-over' of the home pub had failed to materialise, and the designated away pub had become crowded with fans stood drinking and socialising inside and out. The situation was calm, and the Bronze Commander stood a little distance away, across the pedestrianised area in front of the pub, contemplating how he could grasp an opportunity to convince fans to board the buses to take them to the stadium. Darkness had fallen when it was announced on police radio that an altercation was occurring near to a burger bar just a few metres away. Suddenly three police carriers drove at speed, with sirens blaring and blue lights flashing, past the pub towards the incident. The sound and sight of the commotion alerted the visiting fans at the pub that something was taking place, so more fans gravitated outside. It was evident that many of the fans could see a large group gathered behind the police cordon that was now in place. Some outside the pub appeared to be mobilising to engage in—probably defensive—confrontation as if they were expecting to be attacked by the group on the other side of the cordon. The situation became increasingly tense. However, it soon became clear to the fieldworkers that no confrontation would occur as it became apparent that the group behind the cordon were not opposition, but fellow visiting supporters, who had presumably arrived on a later train and were merely seeking to access their allocated pub. Soon the police realised their mistake and the fans behind the cordon were allowed through. As they approached the pub, the visiting fans also realised what was happening, welcomed them, and the situation momentarily calmed.

Later, we interviewed one of the host force spotters about his experience of this incident. He explained that, during the early evening, he was undertaking surveillance of one of the pubs frequented by the home club's risk groups. A group had left the pub much earlier than would be normal on a matchday, and he immediately radioed this information in and requested that resources were applied to the group but had become frustrated because none materialised quickly enough to stop them walking into the town centre. He followed as they walked past a burger outlet, just as a group of visiting fans who had arrived by rail were leaving. His view was that at first the two groups did not realise they were opposing supporters, but when they did, an altercation quickly developed and equally quickly subsided, when the home fans dispersed. This was the altercation that provoked the PSU to respond, but what the PSU had not initially understood is that by the time they intervened, only the visiting fans remained. Nonetheless, the description of the incident again demonstrates how the conflict was more about circumstances and interactions than it was about intentionality. Moreover, more of a threat was being posed by the home 'risk' than those visiting fans, who had merely stopped to buy something to eat.

Nonetheless, the commotion had drawn most of the visiting fans outside, and since it was only about an hour before the match, several decided it was time to begin walking to the stadium. Others followed and quickly the entire contingent of several hundred visiting fans had left both the pub and the buses behind them and begun marching through the town centre towards the stadium. The rapidly developing situation left the police with little option but to try to keep up with the fans and attempt to marshal them and also control traffic as best they could. In a debrief with the senior commander a few days after the event, the senior commander clarified that during this walk-up, the bulk of police resources were deployed trying to control groups of home fans who made several attempts to evade police to try to reach the procession of visiting supporters. The PSUs successfully managed to keep the home fans away, and as a result, the visiting fans weaved their way through the streets and traffic without major incident. At one point an altercation did develop, but this was because a car became enclosed within the marching crowd. The driver apparently became stressed and tried to drive dangerously through the crowd, leading several fans to rebuke them. However, others quickly intervened, calmed the situation, and shepherded the car away. No serious confrontations developed, there were no racist incidents observed or reported, and the fans arrived at the stadium and were inside just in time for kick-off.

The match itself passed off without incident, ending in a draw, but after the match the police faced the same logistical challenge of large numbers of visiting fans needing to get back to the railway station. To achieve this, the host police used a BTP PSU to create a cordon to block the road outside the away exit, where they placed four buses. Conditioned to regular post-match holdbacks and other restrictions, many of the visiting fans began to filter out a few minutes before the end of the match to get away in good time. Those leaving early were allowed through the cordon, but as the match ended and fans began to flow into the street in larger numbers, it was closed off. This immediately created tensions, not least because the first to be stopped had just seen their fellow fans walk through the cordon. Once more, it was unclear what legal powers the police were using to contain the away fans at this point, but presumably they would have claimed common law BOP. While a few fans got onto the buses, the majority chose not to and abutted the cordon. There was little observable communication from the police, other than assertive instruction from the officers that fans could not move past. As those at the front verbally asserted their rights to walk to the station, large numbers of home fans were progressing into the busy street just a few metres on the other side. After a few minutes, several hundred visiting fans pushed collectively at the cordon, which was quickly overwhelmed, and then flowed into the roadway where they were almost immediately subjected to attack by large numbers of home fans who had made their way to the junction. While we saw no evidence of it, it could have been the case that the rival 'risk' fans had been communicating to arrange a confrontation. However, given this road junction is the first point at which home and visiting fans come into contact post-match, it is traditionally where disorder tends to occur so would hardly take much 'organising'. In any case, there followed around five minutes of serious disorder involving hundreds of people, which eventually subsided as the away fans coalesced into a single group that the police then managed to corral and escort on foot to the station, from where they departed, largely without further incident.

This observation demonstrates that the historical reputation of fan groups is meaningful but also that it is a very weak way of understanding and predicting the complex dynamics of risk that play out during match events. It is clear there are better ways to comprehend how the disorder we observed materialised. On the one hand, once again, our data suggests the threats to public order were less about disposition and intention and more about identity and interaction. In this case, the visiting supporters have an identity built around their local club and local geographical heritage. This enamours them with a strong sense of collective solidarity. Within their heritage and history, particularly from the 1970s and 1980s, they have developed a reputation and notoriety and like to celebrate this at away fixtures. This fan group have a consistent history of some very high-profile incidents of disorder occurring in every football season, but most fixtures they are involved in pass off without incident. The normative dimensions of this identity revolve around specific forms of behaviour. As with other fan groups, a significant number of them like to gather before their away matches to drink, socialise, and reconnect with friends, and wherever possible, they like to walk collectively to the ground if they can. These fans fully understand that their notoriety attracts attention, and that walking through home fan territory in this way is both an assertion of their identity, status, and power, but is also a means to protect themselves from attacks from anyone brave enough to confront them. While not necessarily seeking out confrontation, they will defend themselves and others in their group if they are attacked. But, if left unmolested, they will not generally seek to proactively attack others, not least of all because they feel they have nothing to prove.

It is important to reflect that none of this kind of 'identity' information made its way into the formal briefing. Yet our data suggests that by taking an identity-based perspective, the host force may have been better able to predict and manage what ultimately what might occur. Indeed, to some extent they did, because they had already tried to manage the expected walk-up, before singularly failing to solve that problem. Correspondingly, the overwhelming focus on the risk posed by visiting fans impacted directly on deployments in ways that appeared to have undermined the problem-solving capacity of the host force operation and potentially to have even contributed to the interactional and situational elements of risk that subsequently materialised.

What is evident from this case study, and a pattern repeated in almost all the fixtures we observed, is that the 'risk' posed pre- and post-match was little, if anything, to do with visiting fans organising to create conflict. Rather, it was more often linked to groups affiliated to the home team, who in this case had turned out in significant number. Yet, there was virtually no focus upon the home fans in the intelligence, pre-planning, or briefing. As with most of our other observations, the conflict we observed also appeared to have little relationship to the pre-event intelligence. Instead, it flowed out of identity-based interactions and from circumstances, often created by the police tactics themselves. Predicting and managing these conflicts based merely upon information about the movement and specific intentions of so-called risk fans, particularly those of the visiting club, appeared to us to be at best problematic and, at worst, entirely flawed and potentially counter-productive to the aim of protecting public order. In this sense, the quality and validity of the underlying intelligence, focused as it was almost entirely on away fans, was limited and often highly problematic in terms of the subsequent deployments.

And finally, what of the risk posed by Copenhagen 'Ultras' expected to attend this fixture? The following evening, FC Copenhagen were scheduled to play Malmo away in the Europa League, a fixture that would have undoubtedly been seen by the club's Ultra-groups as one of the most significant clashes in their history;[1] therefore, it was fanciful to believe that they would have travelled from Denmark to attend this match in the lower tiers of the English Leagues instead. We were able to establish that some Danish fans did attend, but these were a well-known group of 'ex-pats' who live in the UK and who have adopted and support the visiting team home and away. But, based on this intelligence, the host force deployed resources to a local airport all day, to monitor for potential arrivals that never materialised. This again demonstrates that while significant conflict did take place, and the police resources were ultimately required, the time, location, and cause of the confrontation had very little to do with the intelligence picture or assessments of risk that had been driving the planning and delivery of the operation from the start.

Case Study 3: A North Versus South Premier League Fixture

The next event we want to explore also highlights several issues about the complex relationships between risk assessment and operational deployments. The intelligence around this fixture was particularly interesting, not least of all because we had good access to it (and have discussed it in Chap. 4). As is normal, a feed was delivered into the host force around four weeks before the mid-January event, to assist in confirming the categorisation of the fixture, and the resource planning and mobilisations that will be required. In this case, a report in mid-December from the

[1] https://www.theguardian.com/football/2019/oct/03/battle-of-the-bridge-malmo-and-fc-copenhagen-collide-in-europe

visiting DFO indicated they had received information from "a sometimes-reliable source" that was not known to the DFO. This information was that the visiting club's notorious hooligan 'firm' had targeted the fixture to celebrate the anniversary of their formation. On closer inspection, we were able to determine that this was indeed an anniversary year of the group, but they were using this as a marketing device to sell their merchandise across the whole season, rather than an intention to target or attend any specific fixture. In effect, our judgement was that the intelligence was flawed because it was based on a misunderstanding and fundamentally flawed.

The report indicated that while there was no intention to cause "issues", their anniversary a decade previously was associated with 300 of their number travelling to attend a particular fixture. In other words, while the report was based only on weak and indirect information, it implied that hundreds of one of the most notorious groups of risk fans in the country would be descending on the host force for this fixture. Whether these fans intended to initiate disorder or not was seen as a relatively moot point. The report dated 12 December was in place to inform the Silver planning meeting that took place one week later. This meeting was critically important because it will have cemented the idea in the host force that this was indeed going to be a high-risk fixture that would require significant policing resources. The report certainly helps us to understand why the fixture was classified as a Category C operation, making it one of the most police resource-intensive fixtures of the season for that club. This classification was apparently quickly validated by a second intelligence report that was received dated 20 December. That report, based again only on an untested source not known to the DFO, confidently reaffirmed that the fixture "will be busy" because "everyone is going" and "some will be making a weekend of it".

Given this was now classified as a Category C fixture, it was the case that a force-wide mobilisation plan needed to be initiated. Consequently, a senior commander in the research team carried out analysis on the police officers involved, to try to understand the impact the operation may have had on the broader police capacity of the force. According to the Operational Order, this required the deployment of at least 177 officers from the Silver Commander downward. Of these, the force was able to track 138, mostly police constables, back to their source of extraction. Deducting the money the club paid for the police inside the stadium, we were able to estimate that the financial cost to public purse was £34,240.53. This made it the second most expensive fixture of the season for that venue. While it may not seem a fantastically large amount of money, when added to the cost of policing the other fixtures, it cost the force £600,000 to police just that one stadium that season. The force has several others under its jurisdiction, meaning that, in financial terms, the cost of policing football in that force area regularly reaches or exceeds £1.5 million per annum. Furthermore, we were also able to explore and understand some of the hidden or indirect costs. Of our sample of 138 officers, 48 were on cancelled rest days. This meant they had lost important opportunities to relax—at a very important time of year to reconnect with home life, friends, and family; significant lost opportunities in a highly stressful occupation like policing.

It is also important to recognise that most of the officers involved in the PSUs, as well as many of the commanders, had been abstracted from their 'day jobs' across every district within the force. This meant that the normal policing activity within those areas would have been undermined. Indeed, we were able to calculate that while the statutory minimum police requirements were not breached in any of those districts, this was only because an additional three sergeants and nine constables had their rest days cancelled to cover the divisional 'duty' resourcing precepts. What this suggests is that across the force, police capability in it at least some of its divisions was stripped to a bare minimum to populate the POPS (policing for Public Order and Public Safety) operation surrounding this fixture. Through interviews with some of these staff, we explored what they might have otherwise been doing. One PSU Inspector explained to us that if they had not been drawn into the football operation, his officers would have been tasked that day with arresting the multiple high-volume offenders they had on warrant but had yet to detain. In other words, given these officers were on football duty, several prolific offenders would have potentially been left to commit further crimes. This would have created both harms within the wider community and more demand for the police, who would then be required to respond to, and potentially investigate, any crimes that took place. These additional costs are not included in the above overall calculations, but perhaps more importantly they speak to us about the hidden costs of policing football, given such issues must be occurring week-in-week-out in almost every force across England and Wales during the football season.

The major logistical exercise of mobilising these officers was already well underway when a third intelligence log was submitted dated 3 January. This was the most confident assessment; it was classified as derived from a source that was "mostly reliable" and was information that "was known to be true without reservation" (i.e. B1). Contradicting the earlier reports, the DFO now reported that the fixture would *not* be targeted by the risk group, who had chosen instead another cup match with notorious local rivals that were apparently more attractive to them. Thus, ten days before the fixture, the host force was aware that the information informing their operation had changed fundamentally. Despite this new intelligence, at a final planning meeting held on 10 January, no decision to change the level of categorisation or resourcing was taken. Referring to the planned anniversary the subsequent log of the Silver Commander records that

> [T]here are groups of risk supporters from both clubs who it is anticipated will attend this game. The intelligence is not specific in terms of number of those risk supporters attending so professional assumptions have been made. It is believed that around 60-150 [visiting] risk supporters could attend this fixture and based on their previous behaviour if provoked will commit disorder … [A]rrangements have been made by local [home] risk supporters to identify a pub where the [away] supporters can meet and drink before the game. It is not clear at this stage what the intentions are but as the arrangements have been made to meet at a location outside of the Town Centre there is potential that it could be for the purposes of disorder. There is however further intelligence that this is usual practice for the [away] risk group.

It was unclear to us where this intelligence was derived from, or how it was rated, but taken together the Silver Log paints a confident picture of a significant underlying potential for disorder. Indeed, the Silver Commander concludes that

> [As] can be seen from the information and intelligence, both teams have risk groups who are capable of causing disorder. If a policing operation was not in place there would be an increased likelihood of serious disorder, damage, injury and disruption in [the town] and disruption to not only the public attending the event but also going about their general business in the locality.

Consequently, despite the fundamental change in intelligence, he evidently saw no justification to demobilise any of the planned resources.

On the day of the event, the policing operation began with a briefing that included all the PSU staff and which started by covering the intelligence. Delivered using a series of *PowerPoint* slides, the briefing informed all police staff that an unknown number of away risk fans were already on an identified train heading towards the town, and that the home team risk group had organised a pub for them. The implication was that this anticipated contact between the fan groups indicated threat and risk, but for us this was somewhat of a bizarre conclusion. The Silver plan stated that the assumption was that arrangements had been made by the home club risk group to identify a pub outside the town where the visiting supporters could meet and that this was for the purposes of disorder. However, at the briefing, the pub mentioned was not out-of-town but instead adjoined to the railway station so hardly needed any organisation for the away fans to gravitate towards it. Also, it was unclear why helping to organise a pub for visiting fans to gather in was being interpreted as a signal of a conspiracy to create disorder.

The slides then detailed information that the home risk fans would attend this fixture in significant numbers, that they 'often' sought out disorder and rather obviously, given they apparently had organised the pub, that the two risk groups had been "in contact with each other". There was then a full slide on the anniversary of the visiting club's "main risk group" and their apparent plan to attend the fixture. While it was noted they would not be "looking for disorder", it was also stated this was only "unless challenged" because "they will not back down if confronted". The slide concluded with the statement that the home risk element were aware of this large visiting contingent of away risk travelling to the fixture. There was no mention of the now-firm intelligence from the visiting

DFO that the anniversary group would not now be attending. Bearing in mind the early intelligence was only ever weak, the very clear picture of elevated-risk painted within the briefing did not seem to reflect the lower levels of risk the intelligence was now more confidently predicting.

The slides then set out the engagement-led approach the commander wanted his officers to deliver. He made clear he wanted them to "engage with members of the public, gather information and provide reassurance and support". The verbal briefing reaffirmed how the commanders wanted the officers to "actively engage with fans". The commander made clear this engagement was not just about being nice to people, but for the specific purpose of providing the operation with ongoing risk assessments about the identity, capability, intentions, and immediacy of any threats to public order. He also reminded officers of their dispersal powers under s.35 Anti-Social Behaviour, Crime and Policing Act 2014.

The operation itself took a relatively standard format of identifying premises within the town centre that were nominated by the police as 'away pubs'. Officers were positioned in and around the station, who informed anyone that asked where they could go to get a drink before the match. As a result, several hundred away fans eventually gathered inside and outside of these two adjacent pubs, drinking and socialising. Several PSU officers were deployed and stood on the opposite side of the road to the pubs while several Protest Liaison Team officers (PLTs) mingled within the crowd talking to the fans (we will discuss the use of PLTs in this fixture, and football operations more generally, in Chap. 9). We saw no evidence of any away fans showing any indication of actively seeking out confrontation. Indeed, one of our observers was positioned on the train that had been identified in the briefing as containing the unspecified number of away 'risk' fans that were on their way to the fixture. She walked up and down the carriages on several occasions during the journey assessing the situation and wryly concluded that the "only thing these fans were at risk of was a heart attack". Indeed, on arrival, our other observers saw no evidence of anyone on that train as fitting a risk profile and the fans dispersed into the town centre without incident. There was actually very little engagement from any of the police officer present outside the station and the fact that the intelligence picture painted at the briefing was proving to be less than correct did not appear to be communicated to the command team across the radio.

At the same time, a large group of around 100 home fans, some of whom were categorised as 'risk' by the home DFO, had gathered in a small bar close to the away pub. It was not unusual for these fans to drink in that venue before a match. Nonetheless, given some had been identified as risk, a PSU was deployed to the bar. On arrival, the officers simply sat inside their vans and made no attempt to verbally engage with anyone, as they had been instructed in the briefing to do, even though several fans were regularly standing outside the bar to smoke cigarettes, offering an easy opportunity for engagement. As time passed, it was evident to the Bronze Commander that a potential problem was developing. This relatively large gathering of home fans would inevitably have to walk to the stadium past the pub with the away fans. It would be likely, should they do so, that interactions with the away fans gathered outside their pub would develop, possibly escalating into confrontation. As a result, the commanders took the decision that the best course of action was to encourage the visiting supporters to leave their pub well beforehand, and to send officers with them. However, as the Bronze Commander was organising the escort, most of the visiting fans took it upon themselves to leave the pub and began walking towards the stadium. The police were then caught on the back foot and forced to run after the away fans, taking some time to catch up with them. Nonetheless, there were no issues and the fans arrived at the stadium without incident.

While all of this was occurring, a group of home fans left the nearby bar and began to walk towards the stadium past the pub which still had several visiting supporters gathered outside. There were now very few police outside the pub and an altercation developed, which escalated rapidly as the handful of officers remaining in the vicinity drew their batons to keep the opposing fans apart. While the situation quickly calmed, the police detained 16 home fans in that location and served them all with s.35 dispersal orders, requiring them to leave the town and preventing them from attending the fixture. There would have been clear grounds for challenging the legality of most of the dispersal orders, given the lack of individual consideration of the risk posed those served with them (not least by Pearson, who was in the process of being served an order before he could prove he was part of the observation team). Nonetheless, information about the identity of these fans was passed to the safety officer and they were subsequently banned from the stadium by the club, with several having their season tickets withdrawn. Some of these bans led to disputes arising; the fans claimed they merely happened to be in that location and were not involved in any aspect of the altercation, and two days later, the local newspaper ran a headline story questioning the legitimacy of the bans. The same news outlet also later that season ran headline stories questioning the high costs of policing at the stadium.

Case Study 4: A New 'Derby'

Our next two case studies continue to illustrate the complex nature of risk in football and the dangers of basing policing operations on relatively poor-quality, pre-event intelligence. However, on this latter theme, they introduce a different angle; in these case studies, the pre-event and early intelligence indicated that groups of travelling fans did *not* pose a risk of engagement in disorder, but subsequently, these groups caused significant problems on the day. Our research has suggested that it is more common for police to over-deploy because of weak intelligence, but these examples show that this is not always the case. Our fourth case study is that of what we have called a 'new derby', in that the two lower-league teams were from towns only a few miles apart, but who had historically not competed in the same league. The intelligence picture noted that while the visiting club's fans were keen to establish a rivalry with the home club, the home club viewed their own rivalries as existing with larger clubs that were at the time in higher divisions. The concern for the policing operation was whether the home club's risk groups, predominantly comprised of older fans, would be provoked by the expected behaviour of groups of mainly younger away 'risk' fans to a sufficient extent that they would be drawn into confrontation. As a result, the fixture was classified as a Category C, and our observations suggest this intelligence picture was broadly correct; groups of visiting supporters walking from the main transport interchange towards the stadium attempted to provoke groups of home fans engaging in pre-match drinking through derogatory chants, but the home fans, including those identified as 'risk', pointedly ignored this, to the extent that they responded by chanting that they only hated their more traditional rivals. However, ultimately significant disorder occurred in the stadium and on the pitch (which was highly unusual in our research), when a visiting supporter invaded the field of play. He evaded stewards trying to detain him and stood goading home fans, two of whom then ran on to the pitch to punch him, resulting in both sets of fans surging at the segregation line, requiring steward and police intervention to keep them separated as pyrotechnics were set off.

The police responded quickly and effectively to the incident inside the stadium, but what was interesting to the research team was not necessarily the incident of serious disorder, demonstrating once again, as it did, the idea that the ebb and flow of risk is the product of interactional dynamics. Instead, what we want to emphasise here is the fact that an OFO had earlier identified a group of younger fans from the visiting club (many dressed in styles commonly associated with 'hooligan' culture) in their own town centre. They had radioed in to the commander that this group were not 'risk'. Subsequently, the group was not followed by the police as they boarded public transport to the home club's town. Nonetheless, one of our observers travelled with the group and was able to identify them as they arrived into the host town centre. The next the police operation was itself aware of this group was when a security guard phoned to say that he had stopped a group of young fans entering an arcade. By the time this was radioed through, the group was only 100 yards away from the first of several 'home' pubs where home risk fans were gathered. The operation had sensibly deployed a serial outside that pub, but had the home fans been inclined to respond to any provocation of the visiting group, the serial would have struggled to prevent confrontation. Once the group were identified as posing a potential risk to public order, the operation quickly responded, forming loose cordons around home pubs, and blocking-off roads, to encourage the younger group of away fans towards the designated 'away pub' where most of the older visiting fans were gathered. However, once the group reached the pub, they were not permitted inside by the door staff, due to the obvious fact they were underage. As a result, they had to stand in the cold and rain for nearly an hour before the visiting fans were escorted to the stadium, by a route that avoided the two remaining home pubs.

The focus on a static definition of risk here dented what was an otherwise well-planned and well-informed operation. Regardless of whether the young fans had been involved in disorder before (and considering some appeared as young as 12 or 13, it would have been a surprise if they had an existing risk profile), their appearance as a group by the home club pubs was always going to require managing; not to prevent them attacking the pubs, but to protect them from the home 'risk', some of whom had considerable previous history of engagement in football-related violence. In fact, we would argue that the main concern for the host force should have been less about the idea of risks to public order and more about safeguarding vulnerable young people, who had travelled to a potentially high-risk location with no parental accompaniment, leaving them open to assault from others. The strategy of managing risk built around accessing public houses was clearly never going to be suitable and, as such, the policing operation merely left the group on the street with all the ongoing exposure to various risks (both shorter and longer term) which that implied.

Case Study 5: A New Rivalry?

Our fifth, and penultimate, case study relates to a match between two of the larger and more prestigious clubs in the Championship at that time. Although this was not a derby, as with the previous case study, the visiting supporters were viewed by the police as wanting to establish a rivalry with the home club's supporters, that the latter had little interest in reciprocating. The match was given the lowest-risk categorisation, but given this was a large club in a metropolitan area, this still attracted significant resources. Reflecting this, the host force adopted a hybrid classification of Cat A-IR. The match was scheduled for an early kick-off, and with no direct trains from the visiting club's city, it was anticipated that most visiting supporters would travel by coach to the match, meaning that most deployment would be around the pubs near the stadium, the coach park, and the visiting turnstiles. A serial was sent into the town centre to 'keep an eye on' a group of home fans identified as 'risk', and another to the train station, but no problems were anticipated here. As the morning progressed, it was reported back by officers at the station that, as the intelligence picture had suggested, no groups of visiting fans had arrived by train.

Pre-match passed off with no notable incident, and happy that they had the numbers to ensure the visiting supporters could safely get back to their coaches at the end of the match, the commander made the decision at half-time, after a one-sided 45 minutes dominated by the home team, to stand down one of the PSUs. Normally, this kind of flexibility in the light of available evidence is welcome, but unfortunately, on this occasion the matchday information on which it was based was flawed. Although not identified by the officers at the station, two of the observation team had identified a group of around 40–45 fans arriving by train and leaving the station by a side-exit. The observers were of the view that these fans were from the visiting team. Had the research team had the time to get together and share this information prior to the decision to stand down resources, this would have placed them in an interesting ethical position. However, generally this type of information-sharing only took place at the post-event debrief, and so it was as much a surprise to the fieldworkers by the away exits as it was to the police, when, following the full-time whistle, what was almost certainly the same group of visiting fans, started walking onto the main road full of home supporters, rather than into the coach park at the back of the stand. The situation was made potentially even more volatile by the fact that the visiting team had equalised with virtually the last kick of the match to secure a completely undeserved draw, which of course the visiting fans celebrated raucously, after being relentlessly goaded for most of the match by large sections of the home crowd.

By the time the group had been identified, it was too late to prevent confrontation. The Bronze Commander, who was present by the away exits, attempted to engage the visiting fans in dialogue to encourage them not to walk down the road, which is traditionally seen as the 'territory' of the home fans, and a frequent location of disorder when visiting fans appear there in numbers. However, although he succeeded in getting some of the fans to stop and listen, other visiting fans from this group outflanked him and walked into the road. The group, undoubtedly aware of the danger of their position, gathered close together, and when a handful started singing the name of their team, it was clear that disorder was inevitable. Several home fans in the crowd, angered by their presence and expression, attacked the group, throwing punches at the visiting fans, who were quickly pushed back against the side of the stand. As word spread about the perceived provocation, more home fans moved to attack the visiting group, who gathered close and attempted to defend themselves against overwhelming odds. The violence lasted several minutes before a PSU, stationed in the coach park, were able to run to the location of the fighting, cordon off the visiting fans and, as punches still rained down on them, shepherd them away from the road and into a location where they could be corralled until buses were arranged to take them back to the station. Once again, the fixture illustrated the limitations of pre-match intelligence, the lack and quality of comprehensive matchday information, as well as the interactional and place-based nature of much football-related disorder in England and Wales.

Case Study 6: A 'Regional Derby' in a Rural County

Usually, the most predictable 'high-risk' fixtures are local derbies. Such history and geography played a powerful role in planning and risk assessment for the final case study we will consider in this chapter, where both lower-league clubs were from cities within the same rural county. This was only formally classified as a Category B fixture, but had initially been, and still had the 'look and feel' of a Category C event, and was by far the largest public order operation the division would deploy that calendar year. Planning and resourcing were extensive with four PSUs, four Spotters, Evidence Gathering Teams (EGTs), Dog Units, Prisoner Transport, and a drone unit. In addition, the police innovated by using four PLTs and a deployment of additional OFOs (then still referred to as spotters) in a serial formation. The match was a ticket only sell-out, with around 1150 away fans expected to attend.

We outlined the intelligence report for this fixture in Chap. 4, which stated that the visiting club had a risk group that could number more than 100 for high-profile fixtures, but that they had not been 'active' at away fixtures for two years. Nonetheless, the extensive report detailed a catalogue of mostly minor incidents involving anti-social behaviour, homophobic chanting, provocation, and relatively low-level disorder at an array of fixtures across the last few seasons involving fans of both clubs across the country. Perhaps most seriously, there had been major disorder when these clubs last played each other three years previously. Buried in the detail was also information suggesting that visiting 'risk' fans would *not* be travelling to this match or to the host city. While hidden away in the intelligence report, this was apparently known to the host operation and helps explain why the match was reduced to a Category B.

None of this altered the fact that the problems faced by the host force were again logistical. A significant number of away fans were expected to travel to the host city by train and would therefore need to walk through the city centre, past pubs frequented by home fans including the home club's 'risk' groups. As is normative, the way this logistical challenge had been dealt with historically by the host force was to negotiate with the management of a pub near to the railway station that was prepared to host the visiting fans. If this could be achieved, the pub was then allocated to them, and when they arrived, they would be 'facilitated' into that pub and then taken under police escort, or by bus, to the stadium. The police have no legal power to directly enforce this, so often use a potential for BOP as their justification, when they judge it necessary, to prevent visiting fans from leaving. However, on this occasion, the historical notoriety of the derby meant the usual 'away' pub had decided not to open. Furthermore, the host force wanted to try to avoid undertaking an escort because of the way this impacted upon the normal life of the city centre by disrupting traffic and creating a high-profile spectacle that may concern (non-football-attending) members of the public and attract the attention of the home 'risk'. The strategic goal was to deploy to the station early, to monitor fan arrivals, identify and contain any risk fans, and encourage others to move into the city under their own volition to accommodate themselves in various pubs, before making their own way to the match.

As expected, the visiting fans began arriving in the city by train relatively early for the 13.00 kick-off. While there was no dedicated away pub, around 3–400 visiting fans quickly gravitated into a single city centre pub, which became the focus of police attention. Several carriers were parked in the roadway outside, with their officers deployed into the street, concentrated outside the pub in a quasi-cordon. While this was not tasked to prevent fans from leaving, it certainly had that effect. It was also raining heavily and the numbers of vehicles and police in the area caused traffic congestion and created something of the kind of disruption and spectacle the police had been hoping to avoid. We observed several examples of members of the public expressing concerns about whether it was safe to be there; after all, why would so many police be there if there was no threat? However, the visiting DFO and spotters were clear in their assessments that there were, as expected, no identified away 'risk' fans present in the pub.

At this time, a group of around 15 home 'risk' were detected in an adjacent street. With plentiful police resources available, they were quickly intercepted, corralled, and escorted by a PSU back into the city centre. It appeared to us to be more of a display by a handful of the home fans to 'show' that they had, at least, tried to confront the visiting group, rather than a genuine attempt to seek confrontation. As we have previously discussed, such 'shows' are an important dimension through which fans who identify with this aspect of football 'culture' seek to protect their reputation. Once forced back to the city centre, these fans were then allowed to disperse, surprising the observers who expected more of an active attempt by the police to disrupt these fans, for example, through use of s.35 dispersal powers preventing them from gathering again in the city centre. Perhaps unsurprisingly, we observed two of these individuals on the main street a little later in the day, outside a pub frequented by other home supporters. We surmised that they were 'spotting' other ways of reaching away fans and continued to pose a potential threat to them.

The relatively large numbers of fans now gathered in the 'self-appointed' away pub posed an increasing dilemma for the police commanders. Their view was the fans would be very likely to walk to the stadium collectively, or at least in large groups. With hostile home fans present in the city centre, they knew that allowing them to do so would present considerable risks, even if the away fans were unlikely to be actively seeking out confrontation. From what we could observe, the concerns here were more about protecting the away fans' safety as it was about protecting others from them. As a result, at around 11.20, the commanders decided to escort the away contingent to the stadium. This directly contradicted an earlier strategic commitment to try to avoid an escort, but the whole scenario had the increasing air of inevitability. Around this time someone inside the pub ignited a pyrotechnic, filling the upper floor with coloured smoke. This coincided with the away fans flowing out onto the street outside. Now corralled by the cordon that had closed in around them, it took almost half-an-hour to organise the escort. During that period, the main roadway through to the city centre was blocked by police vehicles, which, contrary to the strategic goal, caused considerable disruption to the otherwise busy city centre.

Eventually, the escort moved out into the roadway, which was evidently an intense moment of joy for the away fans. Having been corralled together, this was their opportunity to feel empowered. Now they were surrounded by police, they were able to express and celebrate their identity, and animosity towards their rivals, without fear of retribution from opposing fans. The escort then began the circuitous route around the city centre and the long march to the stadium, where they arrived just before kick-off. The only issues that developed were traffic-related as the police had to close off several roads *en route*. The away team suffered a heavy defeat, leading to several of the visiting fans leaving the match early. Those that remained, who had travelled by train, were then escorted back to the city centre again without incident, largely because the policing operation made considerable effort to prevent small groups of home fans, who were clearly seeking to, from confronting them.

There are several issues that arise from this final case study. The first is that it provides another example of where the history of clashes between the fan groups and their local proximity were primary drivers of the risk assessment, even in the face of information that suggested many 'risk' fans from the visiting club were not planning to travel. The second, once again, is that despite the operational focus on the visiting fans, it was home fans that presented the most obvious threats. However, a more unusual observation is that one of the major difficulties this force faced was with the accreditation of its public order commanders. At a national level, the senior commanders of public order operations must undertake a required amount of deployment in their roles to retain the certification they need to be able to perform that function. With so few major public order operations in this region, the opportunities for this accreditation are few and far between. In this sense, regardless of the underlying risk, the force was almost obligated to run the operation, as much to gain the necessary accreditation and experience for its staff, as it was to deal with any underlying threats to public order. In this sense, there appeared to be little desire to 'problem solve' a solution to the escort; the operation appeared to us to have deployed far more staff than were required and there was a surrounding air of predictability that events would play out in the way they did.

Conclusions

The six case studies set out above are the best examples, from many more, of the limitations of an understanding of risk that is based purely on disposition. Despite significant careful planning, intelligence-sharing, dialogue between forces representing home and away fan groups, and large deployments of police officers, incidents of disorder occurred, some of which were serious breakdowns of public order. Typically, risk is understood too much as being intentional rather than contextual, often with too much focus on historical issues which may not be relevant to the fans attending the current fixture. Although obviously, on occasion, groups of fans do attend matches with the express intention of violently confronting rival groups, our observations indicated that this was unusual. Given the mass surveillance around football events, the expertise of OFOs, and the operation of s.14A football banning orders, the relative lack of activity by 'hooligan firms' should probably not be too much of a surprise.

Instead, for most fixtures we observed, risk was driven by other factors, many of which we identified time and time again. Geographical risk factors such as the route between train station and stadium, the lack of attractive public houses or food outlets, and pinch points where home and away fans may come into contact post-match, were all better indicators of when, and where, disorder could occur, primarily because these were all issues that shaped the patterns of interaction that took place. Also cropping up all too often was the unfortunate consequences of the laws on alcohol consumption set out in Chap. 3; many fans arrived by rail rather than official coach because this enabled them to consume alcohol *en route*, and often 'rogue coaches' turned out simply to be full of fans wishing to drink pre-match somewhere that was not the 'designated' pub or away end concourse.

In Chap. 5, we set out some of the potential weaknesses in pre- and post-match dialogue with fan groups, but problems in dialogue between police officers and fans were also observed on the matchday. Another feature of all our observations was the almost-uniform failure of PSU officers in particular, to proactively engage with match-going fans. We encountered many good examples of DFOs, OFOs/spotters, PLTs, PSU inspectors, and Bronze Commanders proactively engaging with fans, and we will highlight some of the ways in which these interactions helped to prevent or defuse problems in Chap. 9. Unfortunately, this proactive communication was largely—although of course not entirely—absent from PSU officers, despite all pre-match briefings we observed emphasising the need for it. Most officers would respond pleasantly and helpfully to engagement by fans, but this was almost always fan-led (e.g. questions about directions or recommended pubs). Too often, officers simply watched as spectators walked past them or gathered in front of them. On some occasions they would even watch as problematic interactions between different fan groups escalated. It may be that this is a result of how PSUs are structured, with constables preferring to defer decisions to their sergeant or inspector, or it may be that there is insufficient focus in public order training on the value of interacting in crowd contexts. Alternatively, it may be that officers who often have had their rest days cancelled are simply less inclined to do the job well. Whatever the explanation is, it seemed strange to us that police officers who in their normal day-to-day activities will regularly engage in proactive dialogue with sometimes quite difficult members of the public, seem disinclined to do the same when faced with crowds of peaceful football supporters.

Our case studies also indicate the often very weak, and sometimes even fanciful, nature of football intelligence, particularly relating to visiting supporters and often, we suspected, gleaned from hearsay and social media rumour and bravado. Too often even DFOs demonstrated severe gaps in knowledge about the 'culture', or sub-cultural breakdown, of the fans they were tasked with managing, or they fell back on stereotypes that view supporters as a homogeneous entity and a problem to be controlled. We found evidence of poor handling, labelling, and dissemination of intelligence, and much was often treated at face value with little nuance, even when the intelligence picture started to change. The reputational and career risks of 'getting it wrong' meant that many match commanders preferred to play it safe and deploy resources 'just in case', and reducing match categorisations or numbers of officers deployed, even when the intelligence picture changed, was unusual. Sometimes deployments were even made that simply reflected police training needs, rather than the demands of the specific public order situation. At times it appeared that the real risk the police operation was managing was to its own reputation (and by implication the threat to the career of the relevant senior commanders), as much as it was to the risk of violence and disorder.

One thing was incontrovertible from our perspective: football policing operations across England and Wales are largely being over-resourced, leading to a great deal of redundancy (i.e. use of human resources that are not required). Moreover, the one-dimensional understanding of risk that dominated all the operations we observed failed, on many occasions, to identify the dynamics of changing risk and in some of the examples above, even created risks of disorder where there had previously been none. But it also created other problems. Delayed, or mistaken, responses to the risk of disorder had the potential to lead to litigation against forces, either for misuse of police powers (e.g. dispersal orders) or under human rights law. They also typically drew officers away from vital community policing work and potentially contributed to the chipping away of officer morale. We concluded that there must be a better way of understanding and managing risk at match events, and in the next chapter we turn our attention to some of the successes which we observed during our research that give an indication of a new way forward.

References

Chatterton, M. (1979). The Supervision of Patrol Work Under the Fixed Points System. In S. Holdaway (Ed.), *The British Police*. Edward Arnold.

Pearson, G. (2012). *An Ethnography of English Football Fans: Cans, Cops, and Carnivals*. Manchester University Press.

Stott, C., & Pearson, G. (2007). *Football Hooliganism: Policing and the War on the English Disease*. Pennant.

Waddington, P. (1994). *Liberty and Order: Policing Public Order in a Capital City*. UCL Press.

9

Dialogue-Based Approaches to Football Policing

Introduction

In April 2009, a newspaper seller called Ian Tomlinson was making his way home from work when he got caught up in a forceful police dispersal of a large-scale demonstration that was taking place in central London. As he tried to move down a narrow street, he walked into a serial of police officers. Assuming he was a protester, one of the officers struck him across his legs with a baton and pushed him to the ground. Only 30 minutes later, Ian Tomlinson lay dying from internal bleeding just a short distance away. The following day, Chief Constable Meredydd Hughes, then Association of Chief Police Officers (ACPO) lead for uniformed operations and who oversaw the public order policing portfolio, was interviewed on BBC radio. He claimed that the policing operation had been a great success, rejected the idea that Tomlinson's death was connected to police use of force and asserted he had died from an unrelated and coincidental heart attack. However, a campaign led by *The Guardian* the following week led to video footage emerging, which showed that Tomlinson had indeed been struck and pushed by a police officer just prior to his death. The investigation also categorically disproved claims that police medics had come under attack as they tried to save his life. The subsequent controversy led directly to a formal inquiry into the policing of the

G. Pearson, C. Stott, *A New Agenda For Football Crowd Management*, Palgrave Studies in Risk, Crime and Society, https://doi.org/10.1007/978-3-031-16298-5_9

protest conducted by the primary national police oversight body, HMIC, now Her Majesty's Inspectorate of the Constabulary and Fire and Rescue Services (HMICFRS).

The inquiry began with a relatively narrow focus on the policing of the protest on the day of Mr Tomlinson's death, but subsequently developed into a full review of public order policing in England and Wales, the outcome of which had far-reaching and widespread implications. The first of two reports from the inquiry concluded that there were substantial errors in police decision-making. Senior Metropolitan Police Commanders were criticised for paying inadequate attention to the European Convention on Human Rights (ECHR) and Human Rights Act (HRA) 1998. More specifically, it argued that the police had been groundless in their use of the Public Order Act 1986 as the justification to corral, and then subsequently disperse, otherwise peaceful protestors. It argued that this was because senior commanders had misunderstood the primacy of the HRA which, as we established in Chap. 7, created duties for police not to negatively interfere with, and also to positively protect, freedoms of peaceful assembly and expression (HMIC, 2009a), not only for protestors but also for football fans. Despite this, as we shall argue below, the subsequent, otherwise progressive, reforms to police policy, guidance, and practice are problematic because they have remained largely, if not exclusively, confined to the policing of protest (Stott & Gorringe, 2013). Indeed, the second, more comprehensive report, outlining a series of required reforms, was entitled "Adapting to Protest" (ATP), despite the fact these recommended changes related to the policing of public assembly more generally (HMIC, 2009b).

Criminal Intelligence Versus Dialogue

In combination, both HMICFRS reports were significant because they led to the most substantive reforms to public order policing in England and Wales since the 1980s. These developments can be understood to relate to three key areas, the philosophical and political perspectives of public order policing, the legal framework and scientific basis for policing crowds, and the strategic and tactical approaches that these perspectives and frameworks enabled (Stott & Gorringe, 2013). Turning to the first of these, ATP was subtitled "Nurturing the British Model of Policing" to give emphasis to one of its core arguments, that public order policing in England and Wales had begun to lose touch with a core Peelian principle of policing through consent. In the executive summary of ATP, HMICFRS argued that while, for most events, the so-called British Policing Model is deployed successfully, "at a small number of more highly charged events, such as large-scale protests, its core values are being tested and are in danger of being undermined" (HMIC, 2009b, p. 5). They concluded that the "British model is easily eroded by premature displays of formidable public order protective uniform and equipment" (HMIC, 2009b, p. 5). In other words, the kind of public order policing that is regularly deployed to police protest, and by consequence at football, is dangerous because it can undermine one of the basic tenets of democratic policing, public consent.

The report went on to expose several underlying problems that it judged were leading to this difficulty, such as a lack of national standards on the use of force, inconsistent approaches to tactics, lack of command capability, inadequate training, and poor understanding and application of both law and science among police commanders. Perhaps most relevant to the discussion here, ATP highlighted significant problems in respect of poor communication between police and crowd participants, and proposed ways of overcoming this through improving police capacity for dialogue. Indeed, it is significant that the report devoted a whole chapter to communication, making it the main tactical innovation proposed. Moreover, ATP highlighted the problematic use of specialised units referred to as Forward Intelligence Teams (FITs) who, it states,

> have become a regular feature of the policing of public [during demonstrations]. FITs are deployed in units of two or three uniformed officers. They are trained to gather intelligence and information on the changing mood, dynamics, and intent of crowds which is then passed back to the control room or intelligence centre to assist in the appropriate deployment of resources (HMIC, 2009b, pp. 126–127).

As this description should make clear, in many ways FITs are the 'spotters' of protest-related public order policing and have their origins in that football role, representing just one other example of the interchange between the domains. The report goes on to highlight that the ACPO Public Order Standards, Tactics and Training Manual defined that the FIT's primary role is "to identify individuals and groups who may become involved in public disorder" and to "establish a dialogue with individuals and groups to gather information and intelligence" that can then be used to "provide commanders with live updates in order that resources can be deployed efficiently and effectively".

What these descriptions highlight is the fact that a core aspect of the role of the FIT is to develop dialogue with protesters, particularly those who they suspect might become involved in confrontation. It is relevant to note that this operational remit is very similar to the Authorised Professional Practice (APP) guidance of the role of the spotter (now Operational Football Officer [OFO]):

> The spotter has two main roles:
>
> 1. Information and intelligence—to provide a football policing operation with live and relevant information and intelligence on supporters, ensuring appropriate resource deployments by POPS commanders. On occasions it may also be appropriate to deploy them to gather evidence in support of FBO applications.
> 2. Community engagement—to act as a link between the police and a club's supporter community, with a view to achieving increased trust and confidence between the football operation and supporter community.
>
> These two roles complement each other, e.g., a spotter is required to communicate to commanders both positive and negative information and intelligence associated with supporters during an operation (College of Policing, 2013).

Nonetheless, it was apparent to the HMICFRS that the role of FIT officer had shifted, and for various operational reasons they had begun to work primarily in a surveillance and criminal intelligence capacity, in a way that has been criticised as oppressive and constituting harassment of peaceful protesters by several protest groups (see HMIC, 2009b, pp. 126–127). Put differently, the FIT's role in gathering intelligence had led to a situation where crowd participants, in this case protesters, increasingly saw the role as illegitimate, which in turn undermined any capacity for those officers to deliver dialogue. Consequently, HMICFRS recommended that public order policing operations should develop a different kind of community engagement strategy focused more heavily on "identifying key stakeholders or influencers within the protest community, the wider community and any group(s) opposed to the protest event" (HMIC, 2009b, p. 163). Moreover, that having struck up these relationships, "ongoing communication should be maintained with all relevant stakeholders throughout the operational planning stages and during the event itself" (*ibid*, p. 164). As we shall see below, these recommendations were subsequently adopted by ACPO and still serve as a core guiding principle for all public order policing in England and Wales.

Human Rights, Science, and the Policing of Crowds

Central to ATP, and the subsequent statutory ACPO guidance, was an examination of the legal and scientific framework at work in contemporary public order policing in England and Wales. Indeed, as we have argued elsewhere, ATP can largely be understood as an analysis of the application of both the HRA and the implications of contemporary crowd psychology to the policing of protest (Stott & Gorringe, 2013), which has not until recently begun to be extended into the domain of policing football.

Turning first to the law, even though the HRA had at that time been in place for nearly a decade, it was evident to the HMICFRS that public order policing in England and Wales had not significantly adapted to accommodate the far-reaching implications of the new legislation. Rather, it was only in wake of a critical incident nine years after the statute's commencement that such analysis had taken place. This is just one example of how police reform, even at an international level, often operates in this domain; in the wake of a disaster, the subsequent political context drives an inquiry, and this analysis can then create change. A core ambition we have with our work, is to try at the very least, to get the learning and consideration into place proactively. Indeed, considering Ian Tomlinson's underlying health conditions and the relatively low levels of force that were involved, it is somewhat surprising to us that a similar critical incident has not already occurred in the context of football, where heavy alcohol consumption is a norm and police use of force is far more common than it is in the policing of protests.

Turning to crowd science, ATP was also important because it asserted a radical conceptual shift, in that it recommended that the prior mob-psychology approach should be formally rejected. It argued that it should be replaced by the social identity approach (SIA) to crowd behaviour (commonly referred to as Social Identity Model [SIM] or Elaborated Social Identity Model [ESIM]), which should serve as the knowledge base for all public order policing in England and Wales (see HMIC, 2009b, Chap. 4). While, in the context of our discussions in Chap. 6, this is a welcome development, it is important to acknowledge that this means that 'mob-psychology' was still being taught to public order commanders in England and Wales as late as 2010, even though it had been rejected by science decades before. As we set out in Chap. 6, the SIA is important for policing because it proposes that collective action in any crowd is both enabled, and constrained, by a shared social identity. In other words, such dynamics are not specific to political demonstrations, but universal to all crowd events, including football. As we have seen, the research work that had been conducted by the point had already begun to show that the form (i.e. who will or will not become involved in collective action) and normative content of these identities (i.e. what those involved will or will not do) is not fixed and static but dynamic and contextually defined, so can be shaped and reshaped through the patterns of policing that occur during crowd events (Reicher, 1996; Stott & Drury, 2000; Stott & Reicher, 1998). As we have already argued, this body of work has shown that where perceptions of police illegitimacy develop in a crowd, they often do so because policing itself is seen as disproportionate and indiscriminate. ATP was the point at which that science was formally accepted by the police in the UK, who began to acknowledge that such perceptions could unite crowd participants psychologically, both legitimising and empowering crowd participants to engage in conflict, particularly towards police.

This scientific position was subsequently adopted by ACPO and is currently taught in outline and hybrid form to all public order police commanders in the UK by the College of Policing. Correspondingly, ATP examined, and drew heavily on, the social identity-based research on the policing of football crowds at Euro2004 that we set out in Chap. 6. As we have explained, this work highlights how collective conflict is far less likely to occur and escalate where policing is based upon an awareness of these interactional social-identity based dynamics. The HMICFRS, and subsequently ACPO, therefore drew upon the principles of policing derived from this scientific work on football policing, and combined them with the positive and negative duties of the HRA, to recommend a facilitation and dialogue-based strategic and tactical approach for the policing of protest (i.e. peaceful public assemblies). While similar developments had been occurring for several years outside the UK, ATP drew three primary conclusions from this science. These were that:

> the most effective means of maintaining peaceful and consensual relations between the police and a dynamic crowd is through: (a) a strategic approach to policing protest which is centred upon the facilitation of peaceful behaviour within a crowd; (b) a tactical response which increases police capability for dialogue and communication with crowd members; and (c) a graded, differentiated and information led approach to police use of force (HMIC, 2009b, p. 89).

However, while these are very positive developments, as we saw in Chap. 7, there is an underlying problem with APP in that it implies these approaches apply merely to protest rather than the public order policing of crowds per se—including football. A key element of our argument about the future development of football policing is that there is no reason whatsoever why such an approach should be constrained merely to the policing of protest and should instead apply in every respect to those that populate other forms of peaceful assembly, including football crowds.

Dialogue Policing in Scandinavia

ATP acknowledges it was not the first to make these kinds of recommendations. Indeed, about a decade earlier, public order policing in Sweden and Denmark went through similar crises. Following serious riots in Copenhagen, the police in Denmark underwent reforms and began using what it refers to as the "Mobile Concept" for the policing of crowds. This approach has been in place since the late 1990s. Very similar to the Police Support Unit (PSU) formation in England and Wales that we discussed in Chap. 4, the concept, like those now used in several western democracies, revolves around squads of police officers with protective equipment (i.e. 'riot gear') using vehicles to provide the capability for rapid mobility. These units are designed to enable the coordinated, minimal, use of force to corral, disperse, or arrest people involved in crowd events that have already, or are expected to, become 'disorderly'.

Some years later in Sweden, another political crisis grew from several days of rioting surrounding an international summit in the south-western city of Gothenburg in 2001, where police fired over 150 rounds of live ammunition. Following a formal inquiry into the protests, the then autonomous police regions in Sweden developed and adopted the "Special Police Tactic" (SPT). Drawing heavily from the Danish Mobile Concept, the SPT focused on building a nationally coordinated approach to the policing of crowds by using squads of officers with similar equipment and vehicles, working to comparable command structures, all of whom were trained to similar standards in use-of-force tactics. In effect, Sweden developed its own form of 'Mutual Aid', where police officers from one city could work together in another in the event of large-scale demonstrations or riots. The Swedish Police rolled out the SPT via a nationwide training programme which, like the HMICFRS, adopted the social identity approach to crowds as its underlying conceptual rationale. The new approach began to be operational from around 2005 and remains to date the approach for managing 'high-risk' crowd events, both in protest and football, across the main urban centres of Sweden (Adang, 2012).

Unique to the SPT in Sweden are specialised units of 'Dialogue Police' who work as an integral part of the public order operation. While fully embedded, these squads were specifically developed to work independently from those units oriented towards coercion and criminal intelligence. As FITs in the UK were originally intended to deliver, their primary role is to build perceptions of police legitimacy upon which relationships of trust and confidence with crowd participants can be developed. In practice, these Dialogue Police offer public order commanders an opportunity to better understand the situation, to de-escalate and avoid any use of force. Yet, in contrast to FITs, it was recognised by the police in Sweden that this capacity could not be enabled or delivered if the dialogue units had any role in surveillance, intelligence, or enforcement. Instead, they have always operated with very high levels of integrity and discretion before, during, and after protest crowd events. In other words, even though they are police officers, they do not seek to detect or prosecute crime, but instead prioritise building effective working relationships with protest organisers and other influential people within related communities. It was recognised that these affiliations must be engineered over time and built upon transparency and mutual respect, not through fear of enforcement. Indeed, this in many ways was the problem HMICFRS had highlighted with FITs, that there had been a failure to recognise and retain clear operational distinctions between criminal intelligence and dialogue.

Through dialogue units, the police in Sweden were often able to open channels of otherwise unavailable two-way communication between public order police commanders and protesters. In the pre-event phases, the Dialogue Police began acting almost as 'third party' mediators in negotiations between the enforcement-focused public order police commanders and protesters, for example about sensitive timings, routes, and behaviours. On the day, they are ever-present on the ground, working within crowds and wearing uniforms that clearly identify them as Dialogue Police, often helping to broker new agreements when unanticipated difficulties emerged. The Dialogue Police then work after the event to address concerns and to build upon these relationships towards the next occasion when a public order policing response might be required. Dialogue policing in Sweden is therefore a specialised role, requiring unique skills, such as having a desire to develop background knowledge and to understand the issues driving protests, and requiring empathy and, obviously, good communication capabilities. To be clear, the Dialogue Police were often negotiating with police commanders on behalf of protesters perhaps more than they were with protesters on behalf of the police. It was for this reason that many of the original Dialogue Police in Sweden came from a background as trained negotiators. These are not skill sets that are necessarily normative in the enforcement-based world of public order policing and require good recruitment and retention strategies surrounding the role to remain effective. This is not least of all because of the way the role creates tensions between the dialogue units and their colleagues, who often feel they are violating core police norms. Nonetheless, it became quickly apparent that the method was highly effective in managing crowd events because the non-enforcement focus of the Dialogue Police helped secure fundamental rights, build police legitimacy, and avoid the need for coercion (Adang, 2012; Holgersson & Knutsson, 2011; Stott & Gorringe, 2013; Stott et al., 2013, 2019a, b).

Despite their apparent effectiveness and the underlying rationale for the SPT (i.e. to create a nationally coordinated approach to public order policing per se), the Dialogue Police in Sweden initially remained firmly embedded within the remit of policing protests. As a result, SPT commanders and operations were regularly facing relatively high levels of serious football-related public disorder without the forms of de-escalatory dialogue-based tactical intervention that they would have ready access to if they were policing a political demonstration (Stott et al., 2019a, b). In Sweden, as elsewhere, there were 'spotters'—or Supporter Police as they are colloquially referred to in Sweden—but relationships between these officers and the more problematic fans (i.e. 'Ultras' and 'hooligan' groups) were not good because of the former's role in gathering intelligence, arresting, prosecuting, and banning. To address this anomaly, in 2012 the Stockholm Police Department decided to split its Supporter Police unit. Some staff stayed as 'spotters', while others were redeployed to a new role—referred to then as *Evenemangs Polis* (which translates to 'Event Police') within which they functioned to all the same principles as the protest-related Dialogue Police. As with the success of the Dialogue Police in protest, this new *Evenemangs* role soon began to evidence success in building relationships with fan groups that had otherwise not been open to dialogue (e.g. the more radical Ultras that follow the three larger Stockholm clubs). The SPT commanders quickly began to recognise their value in helping to de-escalate and avoid conflicts prior to, during, and after events, and across the last few years these units have begun to roll out nationally (see Stott et al., 2019a, b).

In Denmark too, there was growing recognition of the dialogue limitations of the Mobile Concept. Supported by researchers, then at Aarhus University, the police across the country began developing new units of specialised Event Police. These took a different form to the *Evenemangs* Polis in Sweden, but there was still a significant focus on developing units specifically designated and trained towards improving dialogue with football fans during high-risk scenarios and, through this, to better manage crowd dynamics (Havelund et al., 2011). Correspondingly, over the next few years, Denmark experienced significant declines in the levels of football-related public disorder. Given the strong police interchange between the two Scandinavian countries, the Danish 'Event Police' approach then also found some traction with Swedish colleagues, who developed similar units in the southern cities of Malmo, Helsingborg, and Gothenburg, following police reforms flowing from the death of a supporter during football-related disturbances in Helsingborg in 2014. Thus, outside the UK there has been a strong trend of developing and enhancing dialogue-based engagement with so-called risk fans. This capacity has been delivered in large measure through separating out the criminal intelligence and coercive elements of public order policing from dialogue roles, and developing non-coercive 'community policing' oriented and dialogue-based primary tactical interventions.

Dialogue Versus 'Spotting' in England and Wales

After the publication of the HMICFRS report, ACPO revised its manual of guidance for policing public order in England and Wales to accommodate many of the core recommendations put forward in ATP (ACPO, 2010). At the strategic level, the new guidance made clear that public order commanders needed to recognise that they should never start their planning from the mob-psychology premise that crowds are inherently violent and dangerous, the latter assumption which remains endemic in the policing of football. Instead, it was formally acknowledged that conflict in crowd situations can emerge spontaneously from interactional dynamics, specifically the disproportionate and indiscriminate police use of force against crowds. We would of course argue these interactional dynamics can be between groups within the crowd (e.g. opposing fascist and anti-fascist groups, or 'risk groups') and as such are by no means isolated merely to interactions with police. They key issue is merely that the dynamics of risk during crowd events are interactional rather than merely dispositional.

Correspondingly, the guidance also acknowledged the primacy of the HRA and the positive obligations to proactively facilitate peaceful assemblies. Indeed, a core element of our arguments laid out in Chaps. 6 and 7 is that these legal duties and principles of crowd psychology apply as much to peaceful assembly in the context of a football event, as they do to a political demonstration. Let us remind ourselves, the science that underpins the ACPO 2010 guidance, and now APP, on policing protests was to a large extent based upon studies of the policing of 'hooliganism' involving English football fans travelling into continental Europe. The problem is that APP fails to make this generality clear, referring extensively and ubiquitously to policing protests, rather than to crowds or public assemblies more generically. This distorted focus in the guidance in turn appears to have led to a situation where most police commanders and organisations across England and Wales have assumed the guidance does not apply to football, and have thus not advanced their approaches as they have done regarding protest. It remains an ongoing problem that the guidance on public order policing in England and Wales, that should apply both to football and protest, is so heavily, and we assert erroneously, skewed towards the latter at the expense of the former, which is merely one sub-element of how, and where, the bulk of public order and public safety (POPS) policing is applied.

Nevertheless, following the new ACPO guidance, a progressive police commander in South Yorkshire Police, Martin Scothern, was working with Stott to develop a new specialist dialogue unit, with a view to the policing operation for the Liberal Democrat party conference, to be held in Sheffield in April 2012. These new specialist dialogue units were referred to initially as Protest Liaison Teams (PLTs) and their key role was to build relationships with demonstrators before, during, and even after the event. Their deployment was seen by the police as a huge success, with research suggesting the PLTs played a key role in the avoidance of any major disturbances throughout the three days of surrounding protest events, some of which became highly charged (see Gorringe et al., 2012; Waddington, 2012). Consequently, collaborating with Stott, similar units were rolled out in the Metropolitan Police Service (MPS) and Sussex Police. In parallel, ACPO and the new College of Policing, led on the development of 'Police Liaison Officers' or PLOs, based directly on the South Yorkshire PLTs that became operational nationally the same year. By 2015, most police forces in the UK had developed these new units and at the time of writing are deploying them to police protests mostly to good effect (Stott et al., 2013; Stott & Gorringe, 2013; c.f. Jackson et al., 2018).

It was evident that across England and Wales, public order Gold and Silver Commanders were changing their approaches to an array of protests to give much greater strategic focus to the facilitation of peaceful assembly. However, given the problematic emphasis on protest in the national guidance, as with Dialogue Police in Sweden, there was little, if any, corresponding uptake of these new strategic and tactical developments when the very same commanders and public order resources were applied to the policing of domestic football in England and Wales (Hoggett & West, 2018; Stott et al., 2019a, b). This lack of uptake was not because of an absence of evidence. Indeed, in 2005 ACPO and UK Football Policing Unit (UKFPU) commissioned a programme of work, to examine the extent to which a social identity-based approach could be constructed in the policing of the domestic leagues in England and Wales. The research focused on a series of recommendations that our work suggested would allow for a far more constructive, efficient, and effective football policing approach to develop (e.g. Hoggett & Stott, 2010a, b). In summary, these related to changes to how the police should understand risk: "the issue facing the police is not exclusively one of handling known prominents, but also of risk assessing and handling the dynamics of crowds within which prominents are present dynamics which, of course, the police are a component part" (Stott et al., 2008b, p. 277). Correspondingly, it was suggested that public order policing in football should shift towards a more facilitation- and communication-led approach, and we concluded that the national doctrine surrounding command and control should afford Bronze Commanders more efficacy and training in adapting pre-event tactical plans to meet these changing interactional dynamics of risk (ibid).

Central to these arguments was an analysis of the contrasting role of spotters and Dedicated Football Officers (DFOs). Our work shows that the management of interactional dynamics could be better achieved through a more advanced strategic approach to communication which would bring multiple benefits, such as providing the police with a platform for the efficient use of resources, accurate risk assessment, channels of liaison, and the opportunity to build and reinforce positive relations with even high-risk fan groups, a liaison and dialogue process within which Football Intelligence Officers (FIOs), Football Liaison Officers (FLOs), and spotters play critically important roles (ibid.). This efficacy is being potentially undermined by the dual 'criminal intelligence' and 'community policing' roles that underpin the function of spotters, within both ACPO football guidance and the operational theatre. We suggested that, as HMICFRS had identified with FITs, the former role is motivated by the requirement to gather evidence on crowd participants who are judged to be consistently posing risk, sometimes across several events. Hence, spotters are funded to travel with fans to away fixtures to maintain and develop this intelligence picture, primarily to obtain convictions and football banning orders (FBOs) to assist in the process of preventing 'risk fans' from attending events, essentially on the assumption their convergence is the primary cause of conflict.

Contrastingly, the community engagement role is motivated by a requirement for the spotters and DFOs to establish good links with their travelling fan base and to liaise in dialogue with them. Yet, over decades of observation, our research suggested that these contrasting roles leave some officers facing incompatible demands. As we noted in Chap. 5, for many spotters their roles in arresting, prosecuting, and banning fans left them faced with hostility and perceptions of illegitimacy, unable then to recraft relationships with those fans that are conducive to dialogue. In contrast, our research suggested that by developing a more distinct 'community' policing-oriented role, in line with the Swedish *Evenemangs Polis*, spotters and DFOs could go some way towards reconciling these objective tensions. Indeed, as we return to our ENABLE observations, we will demonstrate the key role that these 'community policing' roles can play in the effectiveness spotters/OFOs bring to football policing in England and Wales.

Effective DFO and Spotter Liaison

Our next case study relates to two matches in the English Football Championship between teams who have not had a historical rivalry. The first fixture, in 2018, was marred by an incident at half-time, when large numbers of the visiting supporters moved down into the concourse and several requested that stewards opened exit gates to allow them to move outside the stadium to smoke cigarettes. At their home venue, the gates are opened as a matter of routine so that fans can smoke without breaching laws prohibiting smoking in enclosed public places. The stewards refused and, because the fans felt this was an unreasonable restriction, the situation became tense and some attempted to open the gates. A PSU was quickly deployed to the concourse to support the stewards and serious confrontations developed when police officers used pepper spray against the crowd. At one level, the conflict once again reinforces the idea that an identity-based approach helps understand and predict circumstances that may evolve into disorder. Put simply, given it was normative for fans to be allowed to smoke at their home stadium, it is likely they may want to do so when travelling away. Had that been communicated, understood, and facilitated (e.g. by providing a smoking area), then it is highly unlikely the interactions that culminated in confrontation would have occurred.

Nonetheless, regardless of underlying cause, the key implication of this confrontation was that it fed forward to the following season and the next fixture between the two teams. Given that major confrontation had taken place, the pre-season risk categorisation planning classified it as high risk and therefore on a pathway to attracting significant police resources.

However, for several years, the home police force had been developing a new approach to policing this club, centred around a strategy of facilitation, and underpinned by dialogue and engagement, which was enabled to a significant degree by the DFO at the club. As a result of this, immediately following the disorder, the DFO set up a stakeholder debriefing, including senior police commanders, club security officials, and fan groups. Through this meeting, the force and the club were able to reflect on the underlying causes of the disturbance and recognised that it had arisen unintentionally through situationally determined, interactional, dynamics. Moreover, through the meeting, the DFO developed a working relationship with fan group representatives from the visiting club. Consequently, he was then able to set up dialogue with them around the second fixture, providing information that reassured the Silver Commander and planners that there was no need to categorise it as high risk and, subsequently, managed to get the assessment downgraded to a Category A fixture. The club also put in place arrangements for fans to be able to stand outside during the half-time to smoke and the event passed off without any confrontations.

Our fieldwork also identified many situations where spotters, operating in their dialogue, rather than their evidence-gathering role, were able to use their skill set to influence supporter behaviour and reduce the risk of disorder. At another of the ENABLE observations, for a high-risk, same-city derby, a group of around 200 visiting supporters who had been categorised as 'risk', were drinking by the main railway station prior to boarding the train to the stadium. 'Special' trains had been arranged for the visiting supporters, which went directly to the station closest to the away turnstiles. It was assumed that this information had been effectively disseminated amongst the travelling support, but when the group moved *en masse* towards a different platform, from which a scheduled service would stop first at a station by the home turnstiles, spotters intervened and negotiated with the fans, successfully encouraging them to wait for the special train. This prevented a potential confrontation with police who would have immediately mobilised to try to keep the fan groups apart and who would have assumed this was a deliberate attempt by them to evade security measures. But the intervention by the spotters also enabled information to be fed back to the operation that this 'risk' group were not intent on confronting the home supporters.[1]

It is clear from these two examples that many officers in specialist football policing roles have the skills and legitimacy necessary to intervene, negotiate, and de-escalate to reduce the risk of disorder even in high-risk situations or where trust has previously broken down. There are many other examples of this kind of work in our research that suggest that when spotters and DFOs are performing this community policing type of role (liaison with fan groups, shifting tolerance levels upwards regarding minor issues, seeking to ensure the early release of arrested fans, etc.), they often do a great deal to undermine the potential for conflict (and add tactical depth to the host force operations). Additionally, by being seen to act in the interests of the legitimate intentions of fan groups, such interventions could help to overcome the antagonistic and counter-productive polarity that can exist between police and high-risk fans. In short, it was evident that at times spotters are often acting much less like FITs and more in line with the operational approach of the *Evenemangs Polis* in Sweden (see Stott et al., 2008a, b). It is hoped this will become more apparent as the new OFO role becomes embedded, which we will consider later.

Policing High-Risk Fan Groups: An Evidence-Based Approach

Our work has delivered a wide range of empirical evidence which demonstrates that a social identity-based approach to public order policing applies not just to policing protests or English fans when travelling abroad, but also to the sometimes very challenging context of domestic football in England and Wales. It is key to illustrate that these approaches can work even when applied to situations where there are problematic fan groups who have a reputation for engaging in regular disorder. This was demonstrated most powerfully through ethnographic research conducted with fans of Cardiff City FC from 2006, who at the time were second

[1] This observation is discussed in more detail in Stott et al. (2019a, b).

only in number of FBOs to Leeds United. Twenty-three observations were conducted at Cardiff fixtures home and away across three seasons, collecting data from the fans, and a range of other groups with whom they interacted, across a series of events in the latter part of the 2000s. On many of these occasions we were able to secure good access to the related policing operations, so were able to access data on intelligence, operational approaches, and command decision-making (Stott et al., 2012).

Despite their notoriety, our analysis of this group was also motivated in part by statistics which suggested a decline in levels of collective conflict involving Cardiff fans across a period of five seasons, particularly at their old home stadium, Ninian Park, between 2002 and 2006. For example, in the season 2002/03, there were 194 Cardiff fans arrested (both home and away), but by 2004/05, this figure had declined by over 50%. Correspondingly, the South Wales Police (SWP) recorded fourteen 'significant incidents' of disorder involving Cardiff fans during the 2002/03 season, which, by 2004/05, had declined to a total of five, none of which occurred at Ninian Park, and only three of which, according to SWP, involved "major disorder". This reduction in the number of incidents was reflected in the scale of policing operations at Ninian Park, where the 2001/02 season saw the use of approximately 1716 police officers. By 2005/06, this had declined to 946 officers. This pattern of decline has continued year-on-year, currently making these fans, at the time of writing, one of the least problematic groups in the country despite the fact they have a sizable 'risk group' following.

Throughout this period of decline, our data also indicated there was still the sporadic re-emergence of 'major incidents' of 'disorder', primarily at away fixtures. We analysed this pattern from the perspective of the theoretical social psychological processes and policing approaches we had researched internationally (see Chap. 6) and concluded that the decline in collective conflict at and around Ninian Park occurred in parallel with a move away from a 'deterrence' towards a 'dialogue and facilitation' based policing approach by SWP, the local force with jurisdiction in Cardiff. Having recognised previous failures in their approach, in partnership with the club, SWP set about implementing a new way of policing football. On the one hand, they moved towards a facilitation strategy, seeking to focus less on merely trying to control negative behaviours and more on promoting the legitimate aspects of fans' identity-based actions. On the other hand, they began to improve dialogue with their large 'risk' following, by developing and refining the community policing approach among their spotters and DFOs. For example, the football unit began informally separating the criminal enforcement and fan liaison roles by allocating them to different members of the team, much like the Stockholm police had done with the development of the *Evenemangs* polis.

Our analysis suggested this change in policing had a dramatic effect on the intergroup relationships between SWP and Cardiff fans. The data suggested that shared perceptions of the legitimacy of the police and club security officials began to develop among the more problematic elements of the fan base (i.e. those fans who would be frequently categorised by police as 'risk'). This, in turn, appears to have impacted upon both the inter- and intra-group dynamics of multiple crowd events involving these fans at home and away fixtures across following seasons. While our evidence suggested that there were increasing levels of perceived legitimacy, as we would expect in such social contexts, fans also appear to have 'self-regulated' in situations of potential intergroup conflict. In effect, our research suggested that while so-called hooligans were often present, they were increasingly disempowered, apparently as a direct result of a growing inability to influence the wider body of fans (cf. Stott et al., 2001). This change in the internal dynamics of the fan group appears to have impacted back upon the intergroup context over time. The reducing levels of 'hooliganism', and increasing levels of 'compliance', then led to improved trust between the fans and the 'spotters', which improved the quality and flow of information and intelligence. Over time this allowed SWP to feel confident enough to withdraw resources from fixtures they had historically policed heavily. Within two seasons of implementing the new approach, 'significant' incidents of 'disorder' all but disappeared from home fixtures and policing costs, and resource demand for SWP had reduced by half.

Further evidence supporting our contentions regarding the centrality of social identity and intergroup interaction in the context of domestic football in England and Wales was reinforced through our analysis of fixtures away from Ninian Park. In these situations, there was more evidence of the key roles played by perceptions of legitimacy and important episodes of 'self-regulation', all of which coincided with the policing approaches adopted by the host force of the clubs they were visiting. Where those host forces also adopted 'dialogue and facilitation' policing, events were likely to pass off without significant conflict. It was apparent that, in turn, episodes of 'self-regulation' had resulted in several examples of the psychological and physical marginalisation of those seeking conflict. If incidents did still develop, they remained small-scale and localised, and, given the marginalisation of those involved, were easier to detect, detain, and prosecute. These processes coincided with a marked reduction in conflict in those force areas compared to previous fixtures, often at the same stadiums where, in preceding seasons, serious rioting involving Cardiff fans had occurred. This transformation in fan behaviour then enabled resource- and cost-reduction for that host force at subsequent Cardiff fixtures across the following years. It was evident that this downward trajectory was not an accident but a strategically engineered outcome of partnerships between the stakeholders involved, including the fans themselves.

Conversely, almost polar-opposite group-level processes were apparent in situations in which major collective conflict and tensions did still take place. As we have noted, despite the transformations achieved in some locations, sporadic, sometimes major, incidents of disorder involving Cardiff fans still occasionally took place. In other words, risk was consistently present among the fan base, but evidently required certain situational conditions, to manifest as collective conflict. During our observations of some of these incidents, we noted that the host police force was less willing and capable of engaging in dialogue with either the fans or SWP, and as a result was far more reliant on a 'deterrence'-based strategic approach towards their public order policing. Correspondingly, such policing coincided with perceptions of police illegitimacy, an increased level of the apparent appropriateness of confrontation among the fan base, and less self-regulation (cf. Stott & Reicher, 1998). In this sense, the data from this study further reinforced our theoretical view that interactional dynamics were central to understanding the drivers of 'risk' and that a 'deterrence' policing approach was both inefficient, and often ineffective, at managing them. Our empirical work also demonstrates that such coercive policing can be counter-productive, because not only is it associated with these major escalations of collective conflict, it is also, according to our observations, potentially one of its primary causes.

It is evident from this ethnographic work that the empirical relationships between legitimacy, intergroup interaction, and 'self-regulation' corresponded with the research on how public 'disorder' in the context of international football tournaments is both created (Stott & Reicher, 1998; Stott et al., 2001) and avoided (Reicher et al., 2004, 2007; Stott et al., 2007, 2008a, b). But, until the Cardiff study, there had been little systematic empirical exploration of these 'conflict reduction' approaches in any domestic football context. As we discussed above, the small body of SIA research that did exist focused on developing models of effective police practice and exploring the relationships between police understanding of crowds and their strategic and tactical responses. That work already suggested the importance of a consent-based approach (Alderson, 1984; Hough, 2007) to the policing of football (Stott et al., 2008a, b). Moreover, this work argued that an understanding of social identity processes was being under-utilised operationally by the police commanders in domestic football contexts, which was, and we contend still is, leading to missed opportunities for conflict-reduction, particularly across the longer term (Hoggett & Stott, 2010a, b). The study on Cardiff fans empirically bolstered these initial contentions but added further evidence of the underlying interactional and psychological processes that are mediating the relationships between policing and public order outcomes.

PLTs in Football: A Model of Good Practice?

As it was with protest following the publication of ATP, based on our research the question became, how it is best to achieve police dialogue in football? We have already identified the potential role that 'spotters' can play if they can overcome the limitations introduced by their parallel focus on intelligence-gathering, prosecutions, and banning. Our evidence is consistent with the idea that confrontation within domestic football crowds is often an outcome of the way dynamic intergroup interactions feed into the 'identity information' that fans use to understand themselves and their social relationships which, in turn, govern the form of their collective action. In this respect, our analysis increasingly suggests that the route to conflict-reduction in domestic football—at least in England and Wales—is not through 'deterrence' policing based upon 'instrumental' models of social compliance (cf. Harcourt, 2001). Rather, our data and theory are more closely aligned, to Tyler's 'process based' policing model, which proposes that reductions in criminality reside in generating policing responses that are perceived as legitimate (Sunshine & Tyler, 2003; Hough et al., 2010; Radburn et al., 2016; Radburn & Stott, 2018).

In this respect we would assert that a key measure of the effectiveness of a football policing operation lies in its ability to effectively manage these interactional social psychological processes. Furthermore, what we also demonstrate is the historical dimension to these social psychological processes and their relevance to understanding 'hooliganism' within domestic competitions in England and Wales. Since the group-level processes we have identified occur across multiple events and locations, our analysis points towards the need for a more integrated approach to the policing of high-risk fan groups as they move from one jurisdiction to another. As our work on Cardiff fans demonstrated, a 'dialogue and facilitation' approach will only be effective if both visiting and host forces adopt it, and do so across the longer term. In other words, the piecemeal, localised, and short-term 'one-off event' approach to the policing of football crowd events may be a root cause of the enduring nature of the problem. The logic of accountability for public order means commanders are often too focused on securing positive outcomes only for the event for which they hold responsibility. During our observations they rarely, if ever, have an eye on how this fan group will behave in two weeks' time at another location, or indeed how this group may behave if, and when, they returned to the same stadium or same police jurisdiction next season (Leach, 2021). We would contend that such 'short-termism' prevents the effective management of the historical group-level processes that, if successfully harnessed, as they were with Cardiff, can deliver longer-term conflict, and therefore cost, reduction. Indeed, Cardiff City now have some of the lowest arrest figures of all the major clubs in England and Wales year-on-year and have done so more or less over the last decade. While they are impossible to measure, we would estimate that the savings to policing costs from the work invested in the first decade of the 2000s will by now have been worth millions of pounds. Put differently, policing football in England and Wales is intractable because it is a long-term process, the group-level dynamics of which are spread across time and police jurisdiction. Addressing football-related disorder therefore requires a much more effective, and nationally coordinated, approach to its public order operations. However, in the absence of this coordination (given APP's current focus on protest) a key objective must be to encourage individual police forces across England and Wales to proactively motivate and mobilise change. In other words, to build change from the bottom up.

There have already been some important successes in this regard that further exemplify the value of a dialogue-based approach (e.g. Stott et al., 2016), but often these drives towards innovation have also exposed some of the underlying problems that need to be addressed before coordinated successes can be meaningfully achieved. As we have discussed, the changes flowing from ATP have to date made no reference to police obligations to facilitate peaceful assembly in relation to football. In Chaps. 4 and 8, we identified that football policing often sets its strategic ambitions around maintaining the so-called Queen's Peace, in a manner that is then largely achieved through surveillance and the subsequent categorisation, containment, and escorting of risk fans as the primary tactics. In this respect, football policing strategies and tactical approaches often stand in stark contrast to those created for protests, often by the very same Gold and Silver Commanders, where detailed attention is invariantly paid to the guidance reforms and police obligations under the HRA, and where dialogue is used as a primary tactic. As we asserted in Chap. 7, both domestic and European Court of Human Rights (ECtHR) jurisprudence suggests that football fans should enjoy comparable rights of assembly, association, and expression as those who engage in political protest. Thus, we propose that there is a clear and obvious need for police forces in England and Wales to revisit and update their strategic intent for policing football to ensure that it accommodates a facilitation- and dialogue-based approach.

There have been police forces that have sought to innovate, some notable examples being Staffordshire, Sussex, Lancashire, West Yorkshire Police (WYP), and West Midlands Police (WMP), and both WYP and

WMP have trialled the use of PLTs in football. Our research on these trials identified both key advantages and limitations. Turning to the latter first, it was evident from these trial deployments that they struggled to become established in football policing operations in the longer term because, without changes to the underlying strategy, their deployment lacked obvious function and struggled to integrate with the more established and orthodox roles of PSUs, dogs, Evidence Gathering Teams (EGTs), and spotters. As a result, they were often assigned to the operations on an *ad hoc* basis and were neither properly nor formally integrated into the Op Order; this is to a great extent the result of the orders usually being 'off-the-shelf' plans that are often difficult to change (see Chap. 4).

In one trial, senior commanders took the decision that PLTs would deploy without the customary blue bibs that visually differentiate them from their yellow-jacketed PSU colleagues. The subsequent lack of clarity concerning their role and function among fans was then amplified by sometimes inappropriate allocation of tasks by public order commanders who were unclear, and sceptical, about how and if they could be usefully deployed. On occasion, their presence also meant they were replacing, rather than supporting, PSU staff, who would have otherwise bolstered the coercive capabilities of the operations. These factors appear to have led to an insecurity, ambiguity, and even antagonism, regarding the PLT role and function among some other police colleagues who, from the outset, essentially felt that they were imposed by senior commanders in ways that were undermining 'tried-and-tested' ways of delivering football-related public order operations. This was particularly evident among spotters, many of whom interpreted the innovation as a threat to their own role. In this respect, the PLTs encountered the same issues of hostility from public order colleagues that they have experienced during their introduction into protest policing (Stott et al., 2013) and which have been encountered during the introduction of other forms of liaison-based policing elsewhere (Havelund et al., 2011; Holgersson & Knutsson, 2011). Our analysis here also resonates with a broader issue of the potential resistance to, and the importance of, managing progressive evidence-led change in the police service as whole (Hoggett & Stott, 2012).

Nonetheless, the evidence produced during these trials (and our observations of them) suggests that PLT deployment can play a role in improving the effectiveness of football policing operations. Through their proactive approach, PLTs were often the first to engage with, and evaluate, the nature and dynamics of 'risk' fan groups as they arrived onto the operational footprint, for example by assessing who was influential and how these groups interacted with the wider fan base (see Stott et al., 2016). In line with their mandate, the PLTs did not seek to assertively impose restrictions on these fans, rather to liaise with them. These concentrated interactions appear to have been important in terms of opening a process of dialogue and positive influence around the 'risk fans' throughout the events. The continued engagement across time by PLTs allowed for 'limit setting', which appeared to undermine attempts by the 'risk' fans to agitate others, and to promote 'self-regulation' among the fans. The PLTs' positive interaction with the fans also apparently helped promote police legitimacy and potentially helped avoid circumstances where otherwise peaceful supporters could have been drawn into conflict. Furthermore, their proximity and ongoing interactions empowered police capacity to understand situations of emerging risk and to react quickly, and proportionately, to emerging conflict, thereby avoiding escalation. Neither spotters nor PSUs were in any position to deliver such functions, and it was our judgement that if PLTs had not been involved, these positive outcomes would simply not have been achieved.

Through their deployment within football crowds, PLTs were also better suited to quickly identify developing conflict and were observed directly intervening to prevent problems escalating. We can briefly revisit Case Study 3 from Chap. 8 to illustrate this. Following matches, home and visiting supporters typically take the same path or road from the stadium back to the centre or train station. It is common for PSU officers to line the road, usually at quite wide intervals, to be able to respond quickly to any disorder. However, during our observations, as people in the crowd walked past them, all they were able to pick up were snippets of conversation or gesticulation and were not able to identify interactions that were—from our perspective—building up towards conflict. At this match, the PLTs instead split up and walked back to the train station *with* the crowd. Due to their position within the crowd, and their movement with people in it, they had the ability, in contrast to their static PSU colleagues, to observe how interactions were developing between two small but vocal groups of rival supporters. It was clear to the observer that this interaction was becoming increasingly, if subtly, heated and that conflict was becoming likely. The same conclusion had obviously been reached by the pair of PLTs a short way behind them, because the moment that there was movement by two of the fans towards the others, the PLT officers stepped in and physically prevented confrontation, pushing one group of fans away, and remonstrating with the others. It was our view that without their intervention, violent conflict, albeit probably involving only a handful of fans, was almost certain.

Our observations demonstrated that PLTs were also capable of 'problem solving'. For example, in another case study, we observed that PLTs were able to facilitate the movement of fans towards the stadium by organising taxis. This intervention removed the need for a resource-heavy police escort that the Silver Commander was already setting in motion. This facilitation had the effect of leaving a 'risk' group—who we judged had come to the fixture to seek out opportunities for confrontation—relatively marginalised, physically isolated, and small enough to be effectively managed. It also had the corresponding effect of avoiding the otherwise inevitable escort of a large crowd of fans through the city centre, the majority of whom had no intention of engaging in confrontation, and that the Gold Commander had wanted, as a key strategic goal, to avoid. These outcomes are all entirely in line with those 'de-escalatory' functions associated with PLT deployment in the context of protest and reflect their underlying utility in this context.

The current orthodoxy in protest policing is for PLTs not to become involved in the use of force, through fear this might compromise their capacity to negotiate with protesters. Indeed, the doctrine is for PLTs to withdraw at the point at which conflict begins to emerge (and as such PLTs do not have access to protective equipment). The colloquialism is that PLTs do not go 'hands on'. However, during our observations in the football policing context, we identified issues in relationship to the use of force. Given PLTs often found themselves mixing within crowds, rather than standing outside them, which is the norm for most of their PSU policing colleagues, situations did develop where use of force was necessary and required to de-escalate the situation (e.g. to push away an opposing fan who was being provocative). Given the PLTs were in the direct vicinity of the rapidly developing incident, and fully aware of what was going on, as police officers it is not immediately clear to us why they should not intervene. Indeed, such intervention was often seen as entirely appropriate and legitimate by everyone present, given the cultural norms at work. And, as we saw from Case Study 3, PLTs did on occasion use proportionate force to intervene and prevent the escalation of conflict where they were best placed to do so. Nevertheless, the orthodoxy around PLTs not using force is a barrier to their effectiveness, and we would suggest that achieving liaison-based approaches in football may require some adaptation of the PLT concept, to bring them more into line with the dialogue-oriented 'Event Police' developed in Denmark, who do exercise low-level use of force if necessary (Havelund et al., 2011).

A good example of this was a specialised unit that was developed by West Midlands Police to manage a specific problem at one of their major football clubs. It was evident to some of the operational commanders that disorder at this venue was predominantly occurring post-match in the area immediately outside the stadium. They were able to determine that this was often the result of a group of fans that gathered in one specific section of the stadium adjacent to the area containing the away fans. Several of their 'youth risk' fans watched the match from this section. Across the course of fixtures, they observed that this group would goad and insult the visiting fans, leading to tensions both inside and outside the stadium. In partnership with the club, the force developed what they referred to as the "ENABLE unit" to deal with the problem. As with any standard POPS deployment, the unit was a serial of six police constables (PCs), a sergeant, and a vehicle with a driver. However, officers populating these units were recruited, rather than merely selected, and as such it was possible to ensure a mix of skills. In the ENABLE unit we observed the serial was a mix of Level One-trained Operational Support Unit (OSU) officers, as well officers trained as PLTs and spotters. All the officers were therefore highly experienced in working in both POPS and football, so understood the 'culture' well. Their mixed skill sets combined well and helped them manage the interactions across the segregation lines during the fixtures; without necessarily making arrests or pursing banning orders, instead they would focus on using dialogue to de-escalate, and set behavioural limits.[2] After just a few months of deploying the ENABLE units, the DFO reported to us that post-match arrests declined by over 80%.

Conclusions

The example from Case Study 3 of the effectiveness of PLTs in football again reinforces our contention that 'risk' is not primarily about the presence, or indeed absence, of fans categorised by the police as 'risk' but is instead predominantly interactional. Clearly, the underlying identities and 'culture' of fans play a role, but the extent to which this manifests as 'disorder' is situation-specific and highly mediated by interactions that revolve, as with all crowd events, around dynamics of legitimacy and power. Dynamics that, in policing parlance, might be translated as identity, capability, intent, and immediacy (or ICII). In other words, fan 'disposition' is just one element of a broader array of factors that need to be considered and managed within the complex group-level dynamics of a crowd event. As we have argued, what also needs to be considered is that the 'risk' the police are exposed to in policing football does not simply relate to the presence and absence of 'disorder'. Equally, 'risk' relates to the potential reputational damage and loss of public confidence, often to individual Silver Commanders, that can flow from accusations of excessive expenditure and the infringement of rights protected under the law, both of which are high-profile challenges that have been levied at police because of their policing of football. This returns us to our earlier discussions about the definitions, assessment, and management of 'risk' in the context of the domestic leagues of England and Wales. The evidence and theory arising through our work, both in terms of the law and crowd psychology, suggests that a route to efficient and effective football crowd

[2] It is important to acknowledge that WMP also had a parallel deflection programme in operation at this club. Instead of applying FBOs, the force would first refer 'risk' fans to the programme to try to dissuade them from engaging in further offending https://www.independent.co.uk/sport/football/news/football-trouble-violence-west-midlands-police-jack-grealish-aston-villa-vs--birmingham-a8821226.html

policing, even in high-risk scenarios, is through implementing a graded, facilitation, and dialogue-based policing approach.

In this respect we welcome the fact that in the summer of 2021, the UKFPU issued new outline guidance on the policing of football that we believe offers some considerable opportunities to advance the agenda for the police both strategically and operationally. First and foremost, the new guidance brings 'engagement' front and centre to the proposed approach. In addition, the new guidance has replaced the role of the spotter entirely and replaced it with the Operational Football Officer or OFO. We believe these changes, which we will discuss more in Chap. 10, open new concrete opportunities for police forces across England and Wales to forge a more nationally coordinated approach to fan engagement. To achieve this, we would suggest that it is important, perhaps more than ever, to embed the national strategic framework for policing football into practice. But alongside this, for present purposes, we suggest that football strategies need to operate around three simple but fundamental objectives: first, the prevention of crime, disorder, and anti-social behaviour; second, the protection of police legitimacy and human rights; and third, ensuring a safe environment for all members of the public. It will be this facilitation, safety, and rights-based strategy that in turn will then enable a more dialogue-focused tactical capability, through which it will be possible to not only address any increase to, but also significantly reduce, the levels of disorder in football.

References

Adang, O. (2012). Reforming the Policing of Public Order in Sweden: Combining Research and Practice. *Policing and Society, 7*(3), 326–335.

Alderson, J. (1984). *Law and Disorder*. London: Hamish Hamilton.

Association of Chief Police Officers (ACPO). (2010). *Manual of Guidance on Keeping the Peace*. NPIA.

College of Policing. (2013) *Authorised Profession Practice: Policing Football* (updated 2020). https://www.college.police.uk/app/public-order/policing-football

Gorringe, H, Stott, C., & Rosie, M. (2012). Dialogue police, decision making and the management of public order during protest crowd events. *Journal of Investigative Psychology and Offender Profiling*. https://doi.org/10.1002/jip.1359

Harcourt, B. (2001). *Illusion of Order: The False Promise of Broken Windows Policing*. Harvard University Press.

Havelund, J., Ilum, J., Jensen, M., Nielsen, B., Rasmussen, K., & Stott, C. (2011). Event Policing - Dialogue in the Policing of Mass Events in Denmark. *European Police Science and Research Bulletin, 4*, 3.

Her Majesty's Inspector of Constabulary. (2009a). *Adapting to Protest*. HMIC.

Her Majesty's Inspector of Constabulary. (2009b). *Adapting to Protest: Nurturing the British Model of Policing*. HMIC.

Hoggett, J., & Stott, C. (2010a). Crowd Psychology, Public Order Police Training and the Policing of Football Crowds. *Policing: An International Journal of Police Strategies and Management, 33*(2), 218–235.

Hoggett, J., & Stott, C. (2010b). The role of crowd theory in determining the use of force in public order policing. *Policing and Society, 20*(2), 223–236.

Hoggett, J., & Stott, C. (2012). Post G20: The Challenge of Change, Implementing Evidence Based Public Order Policing. *Journal of Investigative Psychology and Offender Profiling*. https://doi.org/10.1002/jip.1360

Hoggett, J., & West, O. (2018). Police Liaison Officers at Football: Challenging Orthodoxy Through Communication and Engagement. Policing, 1–17. doi:https://doi.org/10.1093/police/pay032.

Holgersson, S., & Knutsson, J. (2011). Dialogue Policing: A Means for Less Crowd Violence? In T. D. Madensen & J. Knutsson (Eds.), *Preventing Crowd Violence*. Lynne Rienner Publishers Inc.

Hough, M. (2007). Policing New Public Management and Legitimacy. In T. Tyler (Ed.), *Legitimacy and Criminal Justice*. Russell Sage Foundation.

Hough, M., Jackson, J., Bradford, B., Quinton, P., & Myhill, P. (2010). Procedural Justice, Trust, and Institutional Legitimacy. *Policing, 4*, 203–210.

Jackson, W., Gilmore, J., & Monk, H. (2018). Policing Unacceptable Protest in England and Wales: A Case Study of the Policing of Anti-Fracking Protests. *Critical Social Policy, 38*(1), 22–43.

Leach, I. (2021) "It's on My Head": Risk and Accountability in Public Order Policing. *The Police Journal: Theory, Practice and Principles*. doi:https://doi.org/10.1177/0032258X211041021.

Radburn, M., & Stott, C. (2018). The Social Psychological Processes of 'Procedural Justice': Concepts, Critiques and Opportunities. *Criminology and Criminal Justice*. https://doi.org/10.1177/1748895818780200

Radburn, M., Stott, C., Robinson, M., & Bradford, B. (2016). When Is Policing Fair? Groups, Identity and Judgements of the Procedural Justice of Coercive Crowd Policing. *Policing and Society*. https://doi.org/10.1080/10439463.2016.1234470

Reicher, S. (1996). "The Battle of Westminster": Developing the Social Identity Model of Crowd Behaviour in Order to Explain the Initiation and Development of Collective Conflict. *European Journal of Social Psychology, 26*, 115–134.

Reicher, S., Stott, C., Cronin, P., & Adang, O. (2004). An Integrated Approach to Crowd Psychology and Public Order Policing. *Policing: An International Journal of Police Strategies and Management, 27*(4), 558–572.

Reicher, S., Stott, C., Drury, J., Adang, O., Cronin, P., & Livingstone, A. (2007). Knowledge-Based Public Order Policing: Principles and Practice. *Policing, 1*, 403–415.

Stott, C., & Drury, J. (2000). Crowds, Context and Identity: Dynamic Categorization Processes in the "Poll Tax Riot". *Human Relations, 53*, 247–273.

Stott, C., & Gorringe, H. (2013). From Sir Robert Peel to PLTs: Adapting to Liaison Based Public Order Policing in England and Wales. In J. Brown (Ed.), *The Future of Policing: Papers Prepared for the Steven Independent Commission into the Future of Policing in England and Wales* (pp. 239–251). Routledge.

Stott, C., & Reicher, S. (1998). How Conflict Escalates: The Inter-Group Dynamics of Collective Football Crowd "Violence". *Sociology, 32*, 353–377.

Stott, C., Hutchison, P., & Drury, J. (2001). "Hooligans" Abroad? Inter-Group Dynamics, Social Identity and Participation in Collective "Disorder" at the 1998 World Cup Finals. *British Journal of Social Psychology, 40*, 359–384.

Stott, C., Adang, O., Livingstone, A., & Schreiber, M. (2007). Variability in the Collective Behaviour of England Fans at Euro2004: Public Order Policing, Social Identity, Intergroup Dynamics and Social Change. *European Journal of Social Psychology, 37*, 75–100.

Stott, C., Adang, O., Livingstone, A., & Schreiber, M. (2008a). Tackling Football Hooliganism: A Quantitative Study of Public Order, Policing and Crowd Psychology. *Psychology Public Policy and Law, 14*(2), 115–114.

Stott, C., Livingstone, A., & Hoggett, J. (2008b). Policing Football Crowds in England and Wales: A Model of "Good Practice"? *Policing and Society, 18*, 258–281.

Stott, C., Hoggett, J., & Pearson, G. (2012). 'Keeping the Peace': Social Identity, Procedural Justice and the Policing of Football Crowds. *British Journal of Criminology, 52*(2), 381–399.

Stott, C., Scothern, M., & Gorringe, H. (2013). Advances in Liaison Based Public Order Policing in England: Human Rights and Negotiating the Management of Protest? *Policing: A Journal of Policy and Practice, 7*(2), 212–226.

Stott, C., West, O., & Radburn, M. (2016). Policing Football "Risk"? A Participant Action Research Case Study of a Liaison-Based Approach to "Public Order". *Policing and Society*. https://doi.org/10.1080/10439463.2015.1126267

Stott, C., Havelund, J., & Williams, N. (2019a). Policing Football Crowds in Sweden. *Nordic Journal of Criminology, 1*, 35–53.

Stott, C., Pearson, G., & West, O. (2019b). Enabling an Evidence-Based Approach to Policing Football. *Policing: A Journal of Policy and Practice*. https://doi.org/10.1093/police/pay102

Sunshine, J., & Tyler, T. (2003). The Role of Procedural Justice and Legitimacy in Public Support for Policing. *Law and Society Review, 37*, 513–548.

Waddington, D. (2012). A "Kinder Blue": Analysing the Police Management of the Sheffield anti-"Lib Dem" Protest of March 2011. *Policing and Society, 23*(1), 46–64.

10

The New Agenda: Proposals for Reform in Law and Policing

Introduction

In this chapter we put forward our recommendations for combined legal and policing reforms to football crowd management in England and Wales. In part 1, we will suggest several proposed legal reforms, and in part 2, we will propose corresponding reforms to policing operations. As we have explained from the outset of this book, we believe that reforms to only one or the other, while undoubtedly beneficial, will be limited in their overall impact. We contend that the legal reforms proposed will result in a statutory framework that would be seen as more legitimate by match-going supporters, would provide greater tactical options for police, and would reduce conflict and be more widely beneficial for public order and public safety. But alone, they will not prevent the problems in terms of football policing based on set categories of dispositional risk that we have identified in Chap. 8 and elsewhere. Similarly, we will argue the proposed reforms to policing will make considerable improvements in terms of understanding risk in football events, improving dialogue, and being more responsive and adaptable to public order challenges. But ultimately, without legal reform, the police will still be obligated to enforce laws that are often seen as illegitimate, can be practically unenforceable, and can be counter-productive to public order.

G. Pearson, C. Stott, *A New Agenda For Football Crowd Management*, Palgrave Studies in Risk, Crime and Society, https://doi.org/10.1007/978-3-031-16298-5_10

Part 1: Legal Reforms

In Chap. 3, we saw that some legislation has proven to be ineffectual, difficult to enforce consistently, and even counter-productive to public order in and around stadia. Other legal powers sit uncomfortably with human rights protections. Moreover, because of a combination of these factors, the powers we identify for reform are also seen as illegitimate by many fans. This has the effect of making it increasingly likely that police interventions based upon these powers will also run the risk of being seen as illegitimate. We have criticised some of these legal powers elsewhere, but this chapter provides our first attempt to put forward comprehensive and detailed proposals to remedy these problems. We make no recommendation for reform of many of the specific legal offences; to be perfectly clear, we do not consider that it is necessary to make changes to powers to deny drunken football fans entry to stadia, or to prohibit ticket touting, or to criminalise missile throwing in the stadium. Neither do we argue here for a relaxation of the law on indecent chanting, despite the creep of this offence. Nor do we support a relaxation on the law on pyrotechnics, although we do believe that the authorities need to engage more constructively with fans to negotiate an acceptable compromise in this domain. Further, for the powers that we focus on in this chapter, we argue that many of the reforms can be carried out at a judicial level without requiring legislative change. It is only regarding some offences under the Sporting Events (Control of Alcohol) Act 1985 (SECAA) that we believe significant statutory reform is necessary.

Stadium Safety

In Chap. 3, we considered the problems with the stadium safety legislation, including the Safety at Sports Grounds Act 1975. Throughout this book, the problems relating to stadium safety have arisen in the context of the engagement between police and stewards and the spectators they are managing. In Chap. 5 we also considered the importance of liaison between fans and those responsible for ensuring their safety, particularly through Independent Advisory Groups. The interim Taylor Report recommended that representatives from recognised supporters' clubs should be participants in stadium Safety Advisory Groups (SAGs) to determine key issues in relation to safety at the stadium they are responsible for. This recommendation was scaled back in the final report, which recommended that representatives of a recognised supporters' organisation should be consulted on matters of safety, "but they should not be full members of the team" (Taylor, 1990, Para 152). Currently, fan groups do not possess standing positions on Safety Advisory Groups and at most clubs there is no formal route through which fan concerns are heard by the SAG. The recommendations of the Taylor Report in this instance have clearly not been followed and we are of the view that this can lead to safety concerns being overlooked, and interventions by stewards being seen as inappropriate and illegitimate, potentially leading to resistance and sometimes disorder.

Our recommendation here is in line with the interim report, that representative(s) from match-going fan groups should be given standing positions on SAGs. This is particularly salient at the moment, with the recent recommendation that 'safe standing' should be rolled out across England and Wales, but that supporter groups should be involved in decisions about where it should be introduced (Welford et al., 2022). This, of course, raises questions of how to determine which fans should attend, or which groups should be represented, which may vary depending on the club in question. Ultimately, what is key is that representation is not limited only to 'official' or club-recognised groups, that those who attend are broadly representative of regular match-going spectators, and that there are structures in place for input and feedback from SAGs across the wider match-going community. Supporters are the key stakeholders in stadium safety, being those ultimately with the most to lose should another fatal disaster occur. As even the watered-down recommendation from the Final Taylor Report has been ignored, this requirement needs to be placed on a more formal footing. One option would be to amend s.3 of the Safety at Sports Grounds Act 1975 to specifically include a requirement for consultation with fan groups. However, this is probably overkill, and the same outcome could be achieved through amending the next edition of the Green Guide to include a requirement that SAGs invite fan representatives to attend. The Sports Grounds Safety Authority (SGSA) could police this requirement through threat of requiring the local authority to withhold a safety certificate where such consultation does not take place.

Invading the Pitch

In Chap. 3 we also discussed s.4 of the Football (Offences) Act 1991, which criminalises invading the pitch. The intention behind this offence was to deter spectators encroaching "onto the playing area, or any area adjacent to the playing area to which spectators are not generally admitted" in the absence of the high perimeter fencing that the Taylor Report recommended be removed. Once an individual's presence in this area has been established, the offence is made out without any *mens rea* requirement; the Crown does not need to prove intent or recklessness on the part of the defendant, but instead, s.4 provides a statutory defence of "lawful authority or lawful excuse". In the context of post-Taylor all-seater stadia with the problems of migration identified in Chap. 3, "lawful excuse" should include the fairly common situation where a fan standing in the front few rows is physically pushed forward by fans behind, usually following a goal (typically a decisive goal where players celebrate in front of the stand). This type of short-lived and minor encroachment onto the area between the stand and the pitch is not the type of pitch invasion envisaged by the legislation (and LJ Taylor tantalisingly suggested the police should not charge traditional and harmless celebrations, particularly after the conclusion of the match),[1] but many fans have been convicted for them.

Further, the defence set out in s.4, provides little practical assistance in this situation as it takes the form of an express reverse burden of proof. Reverse burdens are controversial; they are a departure from the presumption of innocence, the "golden thread" of the English criminal justice process,[2] that is protected by Article 6(2) of the European Convention on Human Rights (ECHR). However, reverse burdens which fall *within* an offence for which the ultimate or persuasive burden rests with the state

[1] Taylor, 1990, para 301.

[2] *Woolmington v DPP* [1935] UKHL 1.

have been supported by the European Court of Human Rights (ECtHR),[3] and they are increasingly common in low-level offences, particularly regulatory ones.[4] Nevertheless, Strasburg jurisprudence has been clear that reverse burdens should be confined to within "reasonable limits which take into account the importance of what is at stake and maintain the rights of the defence".[5]

> From this [ECtHR] body of authority certain principles may be derived. The overriding concern is that a trial should be fair, and the presumption of innocence is a fundamental right directed to that end .... Relevant to any judgment on reasonableness or proportionality [of a reverse burden] will be the opportunity given to the defendant to rebut the presumption, maintenance of the rights of the defence, flexibility in application of the presumption, retention by the court of a power to assess the evidence, the importance of what is at stake and the difficulty which a prosecutor may face in the absence of a presumption.[6]

Although the leading domestic case of *Sheldrake* does not provide clear and unequivocal guidance to magistrates and judges considering the human rights compliance of statutory reverse burdens, it seems to be established that there should be "compelling" reasons for a reverse burden and that "making a case easier for the prosecution to prove is not a major reason for upholding a reverse onus" (Ashworth, 2005, p. 220). The key question is whether there is a "real risk of unfair conviction" resulting from the reverse burden.[7] Would requiring the reverse burden allow a conviction where reasonable doubt of commission of the offence exists, thereby curtailing the presumption of innocence? And for offences where the defence has a "direct bearing on the moral blameworthiness of the accused", such as the s.4 offence, the House of Lords has held that there

---

[3] *Salabiaku v France* (1988) 13 EHRR 379.

[4] Lord Clyde differentiated between regulatory and "truly criminal" offences re reverse burdens (*R. v. Lambert* [2002] 2 AC 545 para 38). In the mid-1990s, Ashworth and Blake (1996) estimated around 40% of offences contained some departure from the presumption of innocence.

[5] *Salabiaku*, para 28.

[6] *Sheldrake v Director of Public Prosecutions Attorney General's Reference (No 4 of 2002)* [2005] 1 A.C. 264, Lord Bingham, para 21.

[7] *Sheldrake*, para 51.

is "an inroad into the presumption of innocence".[8] This consideration should take into account how onerous the burden to prove or disprove the defence would be upon the parties[9] and the difficulties a defendant may have in proving the defence, including the difficulty in getting witnesses to come forward.[10] A defence that is "readily provable" by the defendant will be more likely to be considered human rights-compliant.[11] The judge should also consider the severity of the mischief the reverse burden is seeking to counter and the consequences of the conviction.[12] Currently, where a court considers that a reverse burden is disproportionate, it should utilise s.3 HRA (Human Rights Act) 1998 to 'read down' the provision into a less-onerous evidential burden instead (Dennis, 2005).[13]

Where, then, does this leave the human rights compliance of s.4 Football (Offences) Act? As with most of the legal provisions regulating football fan behaviour, the legality of the s.4 reverse burden has not yet been tested in a reported case. On the one hand, while not a purely regulatory offence, s.4 applies only to a certain category of potential defendants who make a choice to enter a regulated environment and it could be argued from this that spectators need to be aware of the risks of entering a stadium to watch a regulated match.[14] As Dennis (2005, p. 920) states,

> Individuals who voluntarily participate in a regulated activity from which they intend to derive benefit accept the associated burden. This burden is the risk that they may have to account for any apparent wrongdoing in the course of that activity, even where the liability involves an adverse moral evaluation of their conduct.

We do not feel that this argument is compelling with regard to s.4. The risk of being pushed onto the pitch in a crowd surge only applies to those who

[8] *Lambert*, Lord Steyn para 35.

[9] *R v Clarke* [2008] EWCA Crim 893.

[10] Sheldrake, para 51.

[11] R v *Johnstone* [2003] UKHL 28, Lord Nicholls, para 50.

[12] *Sheldrake*, para 51.

[13] Meaning that instead of being asked to prove on a balance of probabilities that the defence applies, the defendant is merely asked to adduce evidence to raise the defence, which the prosecution will then have to rebut beyond reasonable doubt.

[14] *Johnstone* paras 52–3.

find themselves in the front few rows of stands, and in most situations where such surges occur, fans have little to no choice of where in the stand their ticket is located; they do not usually choose to accept that risk. Moreover, the importance of the regulatory environment consideration appears to be reduced by *Sheldrake*, which on our reading prioritises the outcome of the trial and overall ECHR Art. 6 considerations over the form of the offence.

We therefore need to consider several separate but interlinked issues in assessing whether the reverse burden in s.4 satisfies Art. 6(2), drawing upon the ECtHR and domestic case law identified above. First, we need to consider what the 'compelling' reason for including the reverse burden is. The offence arises from the Taylor Report (Taylor, 1990), which recommended removing or lowering perimeter fences. The Report speculated that this could lead to more pitch invasions[15] and noted that "running on the pitch often provokes and is a prelude to disorder".[16] Taylor considered that a separate offence of invading the pitch was needed to deter the conduct rather than just provide an avenue for retrospective punishment.[17] The need for a defence for lawful incursion in the case of emergency was considered in the Taylor Report,[18] and the section was amended with emergency situations in mind.[19] However, we could find no justification in Hansard for the reverse burden instead of a *mens rea* requirement of intention or recklessness. Neither could we find any discussion of the risk of fans being pushed onto the pitch or encroaching onto it to escape a crush. It appears that the inclusion of the reverse burden is merely to make it easier to gain a conviction, rather than to respond to any particular challenge in proving the guilty mind of the suspect.

The seriousness of the mischief is the second issue we need to consider. While 'hooliganism' has (rightly or wrongly) long been considered a serious societal problem, was running on the pitch really a social problem

[15] Para 300.

[16] Para 289.

[17] Para 299. The earlier Poppelwell report had recommended "creating an offence of disorderly conduct at a sports ground" that would include missile throwing or running on the pitch. However, it was considered at the time that s.5 of the Public Order Bill would suffice (Popplewell, 1986, Para 290).

[18] Para 301: "the offence should be aimed at prohibiting invasion of the pitch without good reason or reasonable excuse." This paragraph also noted the need for the police "to exercise sensible discretion and judgment" in charging.

[19] Hansard, Standing Committee C, 27/03/91.

that required a deviation from the presumption of innocence? We need to remember that running on the pitch in a threatening or distressing manner was already a criminal offence, so s.4 really only criminalises invasions that were not threatening or distressing. And, of course, at the time it was enacted, pitch invasions were not an ongoing or intractable problem—the request of the Taylor Report, while sensible, was largely speculative.

Third, we need to consider both the likelihood and the seriousness of the defendant being the victim of a miscarriage of justice. As we have argued elsewhere, crowd surges, migration, and poor stewarding can lead to innocent fans stood at the front of stands being pushed over the barriers or having to hurdle the barriers to avoid injury. It is probable that the introduction of rails for safe-standing purposes will reduce these occurrences (Welford et al., 2022), but the extent and effect of the roll-out has yet to become apparent. And, as we will see, the difficulty of obtaining evidence of lawful excuse to encroach on the pitch means that an unfair guilty verdict in this situation for a *blameworthy* pitch invasion which is prosecuted is very high. Further, if the victim of a miscarriage of justice, the penalty placed upon the defendant is potentially very severe. While this is only a summary offence with a maximum sentence of a level-3 fine,[20] s.4 convictions regularly also lead to s.14A football banning orders (FBOs), which the Court of Appeal has already ruled have a severe punitive effect.[21] Recent changes to the operation of s.14A, making FBOs easier to obtain (see Chap. 3), make this even more problematic.

Fourth, given that the mischief behind the offence is *deliberately* encroaching on the pitch in a way that could provoke other fans, questions need to be asked of why a *mens rea* requirement is not included. As Dennis (2005 p. 922) argues,

> If an offence is widely defined so as to include conduct which is not presumptively blameworthy a reverse onus provision which requires the defendant in effect to prove that he was not blameworthy infringes the presumption of innocence and is unlikely to be justifiable.

[20] s.5(2).

[21] *Gough and Smith v Chief Constable of Derbyshire* [2002] EWCA Civ 351, para 90 (Lord Phillips).

This is precisely what is occurring here; should a fan run on to the pitch to escape a crush, fire, or terrorist attack, they would need to prove the existence of that event or their belief it had occurred, despite that fact that the police would be in a far better position to show this.

This leads us onto the final problem with the reversal, the difficulty in practical terms of the defendant (in contrast to the ability of the prosecution) being able to prove they had lawful authority or excuse to be present in the prohibited area. Proof of lawful authority will most likely only be obtained through the testimony of stewards or police officers, the latter raising legitimate concerns for a case brought by the state. A more usual defence would be lawful excuse, typically that the fan was pushed from behind in a crowd surge, or had to escape from a crowd crush, usually following a goal. Here, testimonial evidence could be provided by other fans, but given that fans are regularly stood amongst supporters who they may not know, or know only in a matchday context, securing witness testimony poses considerable challenges to the defendant. Witness testimony could also be gained from a steward or a police officer, but given that the police will have charged the defendant and that close relationships typically exist between clubs and police forces, this also poses obvious challenges. Evidence could also come from closed-circuit television, but again it is the club and the police who have access to the CCTV footage, not the fan. The difficulty for the defendant discharging the burden of proof, in contrast to the prosecution, is the strongest argument that the reverse burden is not compliant with Art.6(2).

In our view, should the s.4 reverse burden be challenged in court, particularly where a defendant struggled to obtain evidence of lawful excuse, an application of *Salabiaku*, *Lambert*, *Sheldrake*, and *Johnstone* would lead to the judge bring required to read down the reverse burden into an evidential burden. Where evidence is difficult to obtain, this reading down would still not remove the risk of a miscarriage, but a fan who had failed to secure CCTV footage pertaining to a crowd crush or surge could produce evidence of blockages to obtaining the evidence, which may be sufficient to raise the defence for the prosecution to then disprove. We do not believe that such a reading down of s.4 would prevent successful prosecutions against those invading the pitch without lawful excuse or reduce the deterrent value (such as it is) of the legislation.

An alternative approach to reforming s.4 would be to amend the statute. One approach to this could be to limit its reach from “any area adjacent to the playing area to which spectators are not generally admitted” to just the pitch itself, which would solve the problem of the accidental fall over the barrier. Alternatively, and more radically, the statutory offence could be replaced by a *mens rea* requirement of intention or recklessness that would be for the prosecution to prove. This approach would, however, also prevent potential defences to convictions for pitch invasions carried out as part of protest action that may arise as a result of the *Ziegler*[22] decision discussed in Chap. 7.

Football Banning Orders

In Chaps. 3 and 5, we identified the legal and practical problems with FBOs, along with the many explicit and implicit criticisms of s.14 of the Football Spectators Act 1989 by the Court of Appeal. To summarise the practical issues, there is some anecdotal evidence from self-confessed ‘former hooligans’, match-going fans, and football intelligence officers that FBOs have played a positive role in helping to break down some of the more organised groups of violent fans and reducing instances of premeditated football-related violence. The evidence is by no means robust, and more research is needed as to the extent of this impact (e.g. on whether FBOs on conviction have been more useful than those on complaint), but we consider that it is highly probable that s.14A FBOs at least have had a positive impact domestically. Further, we consider it eminently sensible that where an individual has been convicted of committing a violent or disorderly offence, and it is likely that they may reoffend in this context, a ban enforced by criminal sanction is an appropriate response. We also believe this is likely to be considered as proportionate and legitimate by most fans. However, there is a lack of evidence that the threat of a FBO acts as a deterrent for most fans, many of whom are simply unaware of how serious the implications of being served with one is, both financially and in terms of free movement. Equally, on the other side of the

[22] *DPP v Ziegler and other* [2021] UKSC 23.

argument, we have not seen any robust evidence to suggest that any fans see FBOs as a 'badge of honour', thereby encouraging them to engage in violence or disorder.

Further, in terms of their effectiveness in reducing violence or disorder involving English and Welsh fans *abroad*, we see little evidence that FBOs have had a significant direct impact upon levels of disorder. As we saw in Chap. 6, there is now a robust and coherent cannon of research, predominantly but not exclusively from social psychology, that suggests that major disorder abroad involving English fans is *not* predominantly caused by those with a predisposition towards engaging in violence or disorder. There is strong evidence that the major incidents of collective disorder abroad involving England fans, from Stockholm in 1989 through to Marseille in 2016, were spontaneous events that escalated from minor incidents, due largely to inappropriate and disproportionate police interventions. In all the major incidents, it was not those with previous convictions, or who were 'known' to the authorities, that were typically involved. In short, the existence of FBOs cannot be shown to have a direct impact upon reducing disorder abroad involving English fans, whose travel abroad continues to pose a risk, particularly in countries with traditional 'show-of-force' policing strategies. We are aware of the argument expressed that FBOs have been useful in encouraging local forces to police the English fans more leniently because they believe the 'hooligans' are not present. But our evidence suggests this argument is over-stated—throughout this book we have constantly shown that it is the lack of correspondence between the police risk assessment and the actual risk posed that can lead to football-related disorder. Believing that there is a reduced threat because of FBOs is simply not beneficial to those tasked with managing the visiting fans, because it plays down the need for interaction with those fans who do attend.

We have also revisited the human rights arguments that cast into doubt the legality of the current operation of both s.14A and 14B banning orders. To summarise, even if we agree with the Court of Appeal in *Gough* that FBOs in the early 2000s were analogous to a civil injunction, and therefore appropriate to fall under a civil court procedure, the development of the FBO into a "super banning order" (James & Pearson, 2018), particularly through the typically unchallenged imposition of far-reaching and standardised conditions, under s.14G, that do not take into account the context or nature of the initial offence or complaint, makes this judgment largely irrelevant to the current operation of s.14 FSA (the Football Spectators Act 1989) 1989. Under the current HRA regime, it is very likely that the current operation of FBOs would be found wanting if challenged in the appeal courts on the grounds of Arts. 6 and 7 of the ECHR. Further, the use by some police applicants of evidence of little other than guilt by association with 'risk groups' casts doubt on whether the higher standard of proof required in FBO cases by Lord Phillips is being followed.

Ultimately, despite the many criticisms of s.14 FSA, these legal problems could be remedied without the need for legislative reform. Many of the issues, in terms of evidence adduced and conditions imposed, have resulted from the reliance by many defendants upon criminal law legal representatives for what is a civil law application. Improvements in appointment of, and preparation by, defence counsel would mean defendants are better placed to challenge what, in some examples, has simply been sharp practice by FBO applicants. Those contesting applications need to remember that the decision of a court to impose an FBO only indicates the battle for their client is half-lost. District Judges and lay magistrates hearing s.14 cases also need to be better informed as to the operation of the FBO scheme, the civil nature of the hearing, and the elevated standard of proof. They need to remember that for s.14B FBOs in particular, their guiding authority in *Gough* hinges on the analogy with civil injunctions, which simply does not hold water where standard overarching conditions are applied uncritically to individual cases. Judges should insist that each condition requested by the applicant is necessary, in light of the specific circumstances of the case, and should not uncritically agree to all conditions simply because the defendant has not contested the order or attended the hearing. Judges also need to be wary of 'guilt by association' evidence and bear in mind (as is required of them by HRA and likely by any 'Bill of Rights' replacement), that accepting such evidence may have a chilling effect on rights of assembly and association under ECHR Art. 11.

If reform is not possible through changes to legal procedure, then legislative reform will be required, and we believe that what was proposed in

Public Law in 2018 is still the minimum required to ensure fairness, legitimacy, and human rights compliance:

> We propose that s.14B be amended to ensure that individuals are not served with FBOs on complaint merely by virtue of guilt by association or failing to distance themselves quickly enough from 'risk' individuals or instances of disorder. To achieve this, the test in s.14B(2) that, 'the respondent has at any time caused or contributed to any violence or disorder' should be amended to reflect its original aims to capture those who have, 'organised, caused, or actively engaged in' violence and disorder. Further, to rein in the 'super-FBO', s.14G also needs amending to ensure that courts tailor all FBOs to meet the threat posed by the specific respondent. Currently, courts must provide reasons for not imposing a FBO following conviction for a football-related offence. A corresponding duty to state in open court the reasons for imposing each condition attached to a FBO under s.14G, whether imposed on complaint or conviction, would provide an appropriate safeguard (James & Pearson, 2018 p. 61).

Further to these legal reforms, it is time that the Home Office supported research into the effectiveness of s.14A and 14B FBOs, considering both their value in reducing domestic football-related violence and disorder, and that engaged in by fans of British club and national teams abroad.

Reform to Alcohol Legislation

The Sporting Events (Control of Alcohol, etc.) Act 1985 is by far the most ineffective of the statutes seeking to regulate football crowds. It has failed in its overarching aim of reducing alcohol consumption around football matches and needs urgent and extensive reform. At numerous times in this book, we have discussed its failings, and its unintended consequences, which endanger fan safety, increase the risk of disorder in and outside stadia, and can make effective dialogue policing more difficult to achieve. As a result, it should be little surprise that our calls for reform here are the most far-reaching and require the most significant parliamentary attention. We propose two statutory amendments to SECAA which, in effect, would strip away two of the current offences. The first proposed reform is that s.2 of the Act should be amended to no longer make it a criminal offence to consume alcohol purchased inside the stadium within sight of the pitch.[23] We believe this change would alleviate the congestion within concourses, make it easier for police officers to engage in these spaces, and reduce the risk of non-consenting fans being caught up (and soaked) in 'concourse parties'. Over a longer period, it is possible that this may also start to alter collective behaviour, by encouraging fans to enter the stadium and go to their seats earlier, which would alleviate congestion at turnstiles, entrances, and radial stairways. Football stadiums in Britain have developed post-Hillsborough, into safe, tightly regulated, well-segregated, and surveillance-heavy spaces. It seems remarkable to us that we still have pre-Hillsborough legislation in place which effectively discourages many fans from entering those spaces until as late as possible.

It has been suggested that allowing the consumption of alcohol in sight of the pitch could lead the throwing of beer and cups in the air. This is, however, speculative. Many English football supporters already have experience of drinking in sight of the pitch, without such misbehaviour occurring. The 2006 World Cup in Germany, for example, permitted the consumption of alcohol within sight of the pitch, and in 2019, UEFA relaxed their ban on alcohol consumption at their club matches, meaning that in countries with no domestic ban (including Germany and Italy), English fans can consume alcohol in the stands. Furthermore, under s.2 of the Football (Offences) Act 1991, throwing beer would be a criminal offence, and individuals could be identified through CCTV, and banned, as they are able for other football-specific offences. But, moreover, nothing in our recommendation would force clubs or event organisers to allow the consumption of alcohol in these areas. The ban could still be upheld by terms and conditions of entry and the threat of ejection. In this way, clubs would be able to pilot a slow reintroduction of alcohol consumption within sight of the pitch, and, in stands where problems occur, stop its sale. Local police would also retain the ability to prevent

[23] This also reflects the proposal for a trial of the relaxation of this provision by the 2021 'Fan Led Review' led by Tracey Crouch MP (DCMS, 2021).

the consumption of alcohol in sight of the pitch if problems (such as missile throwing) increased, through their role on SAGs. Effectively, such a move would not remove the ability to ban alcohol within sight of the pitch but would change it from a criminal law issue to one of contract and licensing, empowering clubs, police, and local authorities.

Secondly, we propose a reform to s.1 SECAA, to no longer make it a criminal offence to consume alcohol on chartered trains and coaches. This would, we believe, have several positive impacts upon football spectator management. It is likely to make official coaches, along with chartered trains and coaches, more attractive to those fans who wish to drink *en route* to matches, thereby taking many fans off the crowded day-to-day rail network, in turn reducing the risk of conflict with other fans, and complaints from members of the public travelling on the same trains for non-football reasons. Greater numbers of fans on official or charter transport would also potentially be beneficial to liaison-based policing approaches, allowing an opportunity for greater use of dialogue officers and also ensuring that the local force can plan more effectively for when, where, and how many visiting fans are arriving. Once again, the suggested reform does not force coach or train operating companies to serve or permit the consumption of alcohol, it merely gives them the choice as to whether to permit alcohol consumption.

Part 2: Reforms to Football Policing

Having considered potential changes to the law, we now move on to discuss different ways of thinking about policing football in England and Wales, based on our research both domestically and internationally. While we make these recommendations specifically with football policing in England and Wales in mind, these proposals have their roots in research from across Europe and principles of crowd psychology that make similar proposals useful far beyond these shores.

Integrated Guidance and Human Rights

As we argued in Chap. 4, football policing in the UK is public order and public safety policing (POPS), applied to football. Put differently, a security arm of the British state, initially designed by police and government to respond to mass urban rioting, is deployed on an almost-weekly basis during the football season to regulate the behaviour of hundreds of thousands people attending sporting events. It is relevant in this sense that within the National Police Chief's Council (NPCC), the portfolio for football sits separately from that for other sporting events like cricket, rugby, and athletics. This seems to be a direct legacy of the evolution of the national policing response to the public disorder of the 1970s and 1980s that we discussed in Chaps. 2 and 4. It was in the 1990s, following Hillsborough, that a related football arm of ACPO developed within the 'public order policing' portfolio. This led eventually to a 'stand-alone' manual of guidance. It was not until both the public order and football manuals were incorporated, under the College of Policing's Authorised Professional Practice (APP), that the two began to become more formally merged. But even with this incorporation, the two sections still sit as relatively uncomfortable bedfellows, that rarely speak to, or cross-reference, one another. For example, as we have argued above, APP on POPS still makes ubiquitous and invariant references to protest rather than to crowd events in general and the football section, at time of writing, makes little, if any, reference to its public order precursor.

One obvious recommendation we therefore make is that APP is further updated to ensure statutory guidance for football and POPS sits much more firmly and explicitly together. In this way, the principles of community engagement, human rights, intelligence, national decision-making models, and the policing approaches applied to protest, will more easily be related by police commanders and their colleagues to football, rather than being seen as unrelated, perhaps even separate, domains. A key outcome of this could, and should, be a change in the nature of the strategies used to police football that are developed by Gold Commanders. Specifically, the guidance as it relates to core principles, legislation, command, planning, and deployment which underpin POPS policing needs to be more explicitly understood to apply equally to policing crowds at football as well as demonstrations. Arguably most important here is the section in APP POPS on legal frameworks, which deals with the positive and negative duties created by the ECHR and is given direct effect upon the police, as public authorities, by the s.6 HRA, in relation to public assembly and freedom of expression.

More specifically, at the time of writing, the sub-sections in the POPS APP on the legal framework in England and Wales are variously titled the "starting point for policing public protest: the presumption in favour of peaceful assembly" and "restricting the right to peaceful protest". As we established in Chap. 7, the implication currently is that these rights apply to protest, but not to other forms of public assembly. This wording is both misleading and confusing for those commanders looking to craft their strategies for managing non-protest crowd events, including football matches. When the POPS APP was originally drafted, the position that Article 11 did not apply to other crowd gatherings arguably reflected the position under domestic and European law at the time (although this was not the case for Article 10). However, the law has developed since then, extending the Article 11 protection to social and cultural assemblies, and POPS APP has been out-of-date in this respect for over a decade. Correspondingly, at a strategic level in football there also needs to be a greater focus on the facilitation of human rights under ECHR Articles 10 and 11. The future legal status of domestic protections for ECHR rights is currently unclear, with a proposed "British Bill of Rights". If implemented in anything approaching its current form, this will reduce the ability of citizens to challenge policing operations that potentially infringe their human rights. In particular, it is likely to dilute, possibly to a homeopathic extent, the positive obligations to facilitate assembly and expression. However, the new Bill, if enacted, looks likely to retain the duty on public authorities not to infringe the ECHR, and of course positive obligations to protect Arts. 10 and 11 freedoms will still exist on behalf of the British state and could still be accessed through a successful ECHR challenge. Moreover, our contention is that not only will our proposal reduce the likelihood of football policing operations being found in breach of their human rights obligations, but that a human rights-based approach to football policing is a useful tool for facilitating the legitimate aims of fans, making proportionate tactical decisions, and subsequently reducing the risk of conflict between police and fans. A human rights-based approach to football policing should be embedded not only to reduce the risk of a force being sued, but because it aligns with the dominant crowd science on how to achieve more positive public order outcomes.

PSU and the Problem of Verbal Engagement

As we have demonstrated throughout this book, the PSU has been a central tool in the tactical armoury of POPS policing since they were developed in the 1970s and 1980s. It is not just a tactic, of course, but the process through which police officers transform from their normal roles into tactical formations capable of confronting situations involving high-end collective violence, such as urban riots and civic disorder. More broadly, this capacity to mobilise and deploy police staff into POPS formations is one of the reasons why the UK does not have a standing gendarmerie and in this sense is a fundamentally important structural component—and extension—of the so-called British Policing Model, that revolves around doctrines of consent and minimal use of force. In other words, the PSU is the primary nationally standardised mechanism through which police forces across England and Wales mobilise staff into POPS specialist operations. Put differently, in the context of football, POPS operations mobilise highly trained staff capable of restoring public order in the context of a potentially lethal riot but uses them to manage largely peaceful football fans. To us this seems somewhat of a juxtaposition, where there is not much in the way of a 'middle ground'. Of course, it is necessary for police forces to retain POPS capacities and to train them for events like the 2011 English riots, but at the same time it is important to recognise that such riots have only ever happened every few decades and, in the main, these highly trained POPS resources are, for the vast bulk of their time, a contingency used week-in-week-out as a primary tactic to police football.

As we highlighted in Chap. 8, throughout our decades of observation there has been at least one issue that has confronted us ubiquitously. PSU officers struggle to proactively engage in verbal interaction with fans. In the main, these officers, when they get out of their carrier vehicles, tend to stand observing the situation around them. When we do see them engaging, it is more often when they have been approached by fans (e.g. to ask directions) or when they are talking with their colleagues. If they walk alongside fans they are escorting, they often do not take the many opportunities this affords them to strike up conversations. In such circumstances, when verbal interaction takes place, it is more often assertive than it is friendly 'banter'. While, of course, some PSU officers are excellent communicators, and the levels do vary from force to force, the majority invariantly and ubiquitously do not engage proactively. This is even though, at almost every briefing we have observed for these very same operations, the senior police commander explicitly briefs them to engage with fans proactively, recognising their responsibilities to be "friendly but firm". Equally, during our research, senior commanders have expressed, on many occasions, frustration about their failure to ensure PSU staff deliver this stated operational goal. They even described to us how many of these officers have day-to-day roles in which they are understood to be effective communicators, but when deployed within a PSU, these skills appear to evaporate.

This problem frustrates many commanders because it is explicitly recognised in policing that verbal engagement is a key tool in helping to manage crowd events effectively and that such interactions deliver several inter-related operational benefits. First, these commanders understand that good verbal engagement helps manage police legitimacy, in that by being friendly to members of the public from the outset, officers can build positive relationships and improve police legitimacy. Second, through such interaction, officers can get a clearer sense of the situation in front of them and whether those who they are policing have peaceful intent. In other words, verbal engagement increases the depth and quality of information and intelligence that the police can draw upon to make their decisions. Third, through this verbal engagement, officers can build social capital with people in the crowd. If situations subsequently become tense, officers can often draw upon these earlier interactions to help de-escalate the situation and negotiate strategically positive outcomes (e.g. encourage fans to join an escort or remain behind a cordon without having to resort to threats or use of coercion, or to help calm a situation where force has been used).

In this sense, we are not alone in acknowledging what we observe empirically. The ongoing debate, for us, is not so much that this difficulty exists but how it can be resolved. Most of those commanders we speak to hold the view that verbal engagement with members of the public is a fundamental of ordinary policing and officers can, and should, carry this basic skill set with them, even when they are deploying within a PSU. For them, the solution lies in improving the quality of the briefing these officers receive. From our fieldwork, what this argument fails to acknowledge is that no amount of briefing seems to make any difference. Instead, we argue that the low levels of engagement are an outcome of *organisational identity*. The PSU (or at least the serials within it) has a group-based identity and is a formation designed to exercise a monopoly on the use of force as, and where, the circumstances dictate. The national minimum standards for PSU training revolve almost entirely around tactics used to exercise force and the very reason these officers have been deployed is because the operational leadership has judged that their skills might be necessary. Indeed, one of the aims of PSU training is to remove the discretion that these very same officers are often required to exercise in their normal duties. Instead, within a PSU, officers are obligated to work as a unit under stress, following the direction of their superiors. It is discipline and cohesion that is required to make them effective as a PSU. As such, the organisational context is one where verbal engagement is not normative to PSU group-level identity.

In this respect, we suggest the solution lies in creating new groups and identities, where verbal engagement is the norm, to work alongside PSUs. As we have discussed in Chap. 9, there have already been some innovative attempts to try to address the issue in Scandinavia. As we illustrated, in Denmark, and later in Sweden, specialised units referred to as 'Event Police' were developed. These units still operate in the same formations as their 'public order' colleagues (i.e. in squads moving around in vehicles) but wear slightly different uniforms to signify their distinctive function. In Denmark, the Event Police also have a deeper level of understanding of football 'culture' and, in both countries, hold the specific remit of verbal engagement rather than use of force. In effect, they are trained and deployed specifically to verbally engage with fans, which they achieve. If the situations remain broadly calm, these units are the primary tactic and, because of their training, officers are not risk-averse, even when situations become apparently difficult. If situations do become confrontational, these Event Police will tend to fall back to be replaced by their more assertive public order colleagues. As we have also explored, in England, some police forces have trialled the use of Police Liaison Officers to try to plug that engagement gap, and to reasonably good effect. These PLOs were developed precisely to improve police capacity for verbal engagement with protesters but are still rarely used in policing football.

Engagement and the Operational Football Officer

Through our co-production approach we have, through the latter stages of our work, been focused on driving research-based reform in football policing. As such, our work has often been conducted in partnerships with various police organisations and specific commanders who have by-and-large taken a constructive attitude towards our reform agenda. Indeed, in early 2020 we were included in consultations by the UK Football Policing Unit (UKFPU) in their role of leading on redrafting the College of Policing APP for football. Several of the recommendations we make here were also central to our feedback to them, some of which have already been incorporated into new draft guidance, distributed by UKFPU to police forces across England and Wales in the summer of 2021. For example, in Chap. 5, we discussed the new definitions of 'risk supporter'. What is genuinely exciting to us about this new draft guidance, is the opportunity it now affords to bring significant change, where we can convince police forces and other stakeholders to recognise and embrace this.

First, and perhaps foremost, the new guidance brings a stronger emphasis to the importance of engagement with fans and the need to manage social influence processes among them, via dialogue and engagement. We have already discussed, in Chap. 5, how the new football

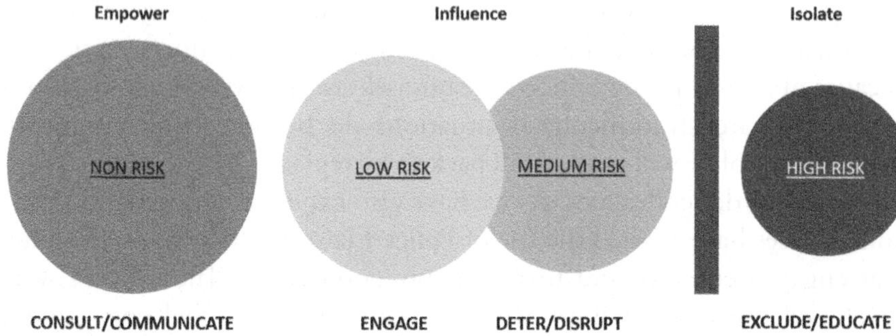

Fig. 10.1 New risk fan categorisation from the revised Football Policing APP (UKFRPU 2021). Non risk: There is no current intelligence or information that the supporter intends, or is likely, to engage in disorderly, anti-social or criminal behaviours. Low risk: Current information or intelligence that they may engage in low level anti-social behaviour or commit minor criminal offences often influenced by alcohol and/or drug use. Medium risk: Current information or intelligence that they have the potential to escalate to violence or disorder. High risk: Current information or intelligence that may actively seek involvement in violence or disorder or influence others to do so

policing APP redefined individual categorisation of risk. The following diagram from that guidance illustrates how these new risk categorisations map onto the stronger strategic emphasis on engagement and dialogue, as a tool to empower "non risk" fans, isolate "high risk" fans, and influence the behaviours of those in the middle from the "medium risk" to the "low risk" (Fig. 10.1).

Encouragingly, this brings football guidance much closer into line with some of the underlying principles of community engagement central to POPS APP. Correspondingly, the new guidance adopts the strategy developed following Euro2004, and in the run up to the 2006 World Cup, by the Home Office to manage England fans travelling to international football fixtures, which we outlined in Chap. 6. In this sense, the focus on excluding 'risk fans' (e.g. via the use of arrests and FBOs) has been supplemented with the important goal of managing the circumstances through which more confrontational elements of the fan base influence the wider fan community during crowd events. Further, the adoption of this strategy for policing the domestic leagues of England and Wales now also falls into line with the basic conceptual principles of crowd psychology that already underpin the APP guidance on POPS more generally and therefore opens the door for a more facilitation-led, and dialogue-based, policing approach for football.

Second, the new guidance has disbanded the long-standing role of the 'spotter' and replaced it with the 'Operational Football Officer' or OFO. For us, this opens a whole raft of further opportunities for tactical innovation. As we have discussed (Chaps. 4, 5, and 9 in particular), the role of the spotter carries with it clear connotations that the primary objectives of the role are the surveillance of football crowds, the identification and categorisation of 'risk' fans, and ultimately the development of portfolios of intelligence and evidence designed primarily to exclude 'troublemakers' from the game. The new role of the OFO still carries this function with it, but also creates new opportunities to create different ways of confronting the problems of football-related disorder. The change of name is significant for a start, as this indicates to both officers and fans the expanded remit of the role. Additionally, the role descriptors now include greater emphasis on engagement (both pre- and post-event), 'developing relationships', 'influencing behaviour', and diverting and educating, as well as just securing convictions and FBOs. The change in emphasis is perhaps best illustrated in the new graphic setting out the OFO role. Whereas previously this had been a linear list, starting with engagement and ending in the securing of FBOs and convictions, now the graphic is circular, encouraging OFOs making decisions about convictions and FBOs (or diversion or education), to consider how this will impact upon the next step of helping to "build trust and confidence" within fan communities (Fig. 10.2).

Some of the new opportunities arising from the reform of the old role of 'spotter' to the new OFO are already being grasped by some police forces, who are creating serials of highly experienced football officers, with knowledge of football fan 'culture' and identity, and skills of proactive engagement, meaning they, operationally at least, are akin to the Scandinavian 'Event Police'. For us, the best example of how to utilise this opportunity in football policing in England and Wales is to build serials of OFOs like the so-called ENABLE unit we discussed in Chap. 9, developed by West Midlands Police. At the time of writing, we are engaged in trying to encourage other forces to develop similar units

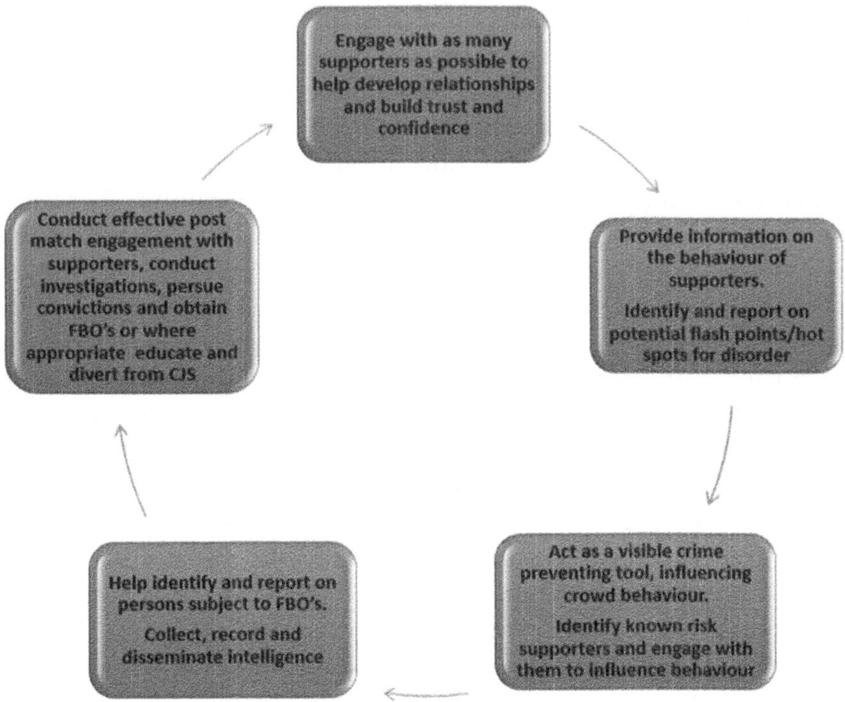

Fig. 10.2 New OFO role descriptor, revised football policing APP (UKFPU 2021)

which, if developed, could then be evaluated and measured in terms of their effectiveness in managing the interactional dynamics of football crowds in ways that reduce disorder.

Specialist Engagement and the Role of the Clubs and Supporters

As we described in Chap. 1, the problems associated with disorder at football are not going away and appear, at least in the short term, to be amplified in the post-Covid-19 lockdown environment. We have stressed that there is, in our view, a very real danger that this drives a retreat into outdated modes of reactionary, resource-heavy, policing and 'knee jerk' legislation and policy, in a flawed attempt to try to be seen to be dealing with the problem. Instead, we would encourage that authorities, now more than ever, turn to the research and theory to generate solutions. One of the key challenges they will face in developing the dialogue-led solutions we propose will be in reaching new groups of match-going fans that are unfamiliar with, and antagonistic towards, the police. Reaching these, predominantly young, people will be challenging and requires significant long-term investments in skills, time, and energy. In short, it will require what we would refer to as 'specialist engagement' of the kind that can currently only be delivered by Dedicated Football Officers (DFOs) and OFOs, who will be regularly policing these fans both home and away. To develop this dialogue, these officers will have to take every opportunity to show discretion and achieve outcomes that help them to cement effective working relationships with these fans, so that they can help create positive group-level influence among them. This may require sophisticated deployments that are likely to need different OFOs adopting different roles, some more focused on evidence-gathering and enforcement, and others concentrating on dialogue and engagement. We would also encourage police forces to think about mutually exchanging serials of OFOs, so that a larger contingent can travel from the visiting force to replace a serial or perhaps even two from the host force, on a reciprocal—and relatively cost neutral—basis.

One of the issues that will also need to be confronted is also the idea that this is merely a police problem. As we discussed in Chap. 9, in Sweden and Denmark these specialist engagement roles within the police are complemented by a very specific 'conflict management' form of Supporter Liaison Officer (SLO; Stott et al., 2018). These roles developed because UEFA obligated every club that competes in its competitions to create at least one. The idea was that the SLO would act as a bridge between supporters and both the club and police. Football clubs across England and Wales who have participated in European competition should all have invested financially in a SLO. However, in contrast to most of Europe, in the main these roles in the UK have been created or filled by staff from the marketing or communications teams at clubs and deal predominantly with ticketing issues. In Sweden, the *Allsvenskan*, the top league within Swedish football, worked with their clubs to create a different approach that located SLOs within their club's safety and security operations. Clubs also ensured these SLOs were credible among the more difficult to reach fans, such as the 'Ultras'. As a result, genuine dialogue between fans and police was more realistic and achievable, and the SLOs have become an important conduit through which dialogue between police and fans takes place. One of our recommendations is also, therefore, that the Football Leagues and clubs in England and Wales follow a similar route and equally recognise their own responsibilities to facilitate engagement and dialogue with their supporters. There are a few clubs that have already taken this approach, such as Cardiff City F.C., and we would go as far as to argue that it is a failure of clubs to invest in this way that continues to embed problems, and forces the police into situations where they must respond by ploughing expensive human resources into managing the resultant public order issues surrounding the game. Let us be clear, dialogue with fans is not merely a matter for the police.

We would also suggest that the DFOs and OFOs take a far more community policing-based approach. Instead of seeing football fans merely as crowds, they should be seen as a moveable community. Moreover, it is evident to us that many of the 'youth risk' are merely young people from the neighbourhoods surrounding football clubs. In this sense, the place to engage with these young people is not merely on matchdays through a POPS operation, but in their day-to-day lives through, and in partnership with, their local neighbourhood policing teams. If this is done in partnership with the clubs, programmes could be developed to draw these young people into forms of engagement that act like multi-stakeholder violence reduction initiatives, similar to those that already operate across England and Wales to reduce knife crime.[24] It seems odd to us that the lessons from the acknowledged successes of these proactive violence reduction initiatives do not more readily translate into the policing of football where the main and ongoing challenge is the reduction of violence![25]

[24] https://www.gov.uk/government/publications/violence-reduction-unit-evaluation-2019-to-2020

[25] This may again speak to the rather siloed nature of football policing units and operations, which tend to operate independently of other force initiatives or priorities. Another example is the tension between the desire of some football units to avoid late kick-offs in an attempt to reduce disorder around grounds and data which suggests that domestic abuse tends to increase when matches kick off early (Ivandić et al., 2021).

Intelligence and Resourcing

A key feature of our analysis has been the relationships between intelligence, risk categorisation, and operational planning. It was evident across all the ENABLE observations we have discussed, as well as earlier fieldwork, that the intelligence picture underpinning football policing operations is often very weak and bears little relationship to the behaviours that subsequently emerged. In addition, we noted very little critical analysis of this intelligence. Our analysis demonstrates that intelligence is focused primarily upon categorising 'risk' fans. While such an approach is in line with APP guidance and has proven to be of value, our analysis also suggests such a narrow conceptualisation of risk is highly problematic. Pre-event intelligence on whether a specific number of fans posing 'risk' were likely to attend was of limited use, not least of all because it failed to recognise the fluidity of fan subcultures (Pearson, 2012) and the context-specific, dynamic, and interactional nature of 'risk' as it subsequently materialised.

In other words, police concepts of intelligence often revolved merely around imposing the category 'risk fans', who in turn would be seen as 'the problem' because it was assumed they were predisposed towards conflict. Such risk assessments provided little, if any, information beyond this, in terms of heterogeneity of composition or variability of intent. In this sense, it was evident that the police forces were working with a relatively limited and under-developed understanding of the identities, 'cultures', and likely behaviour of the fan groups they were managing. In turn, this undermined the quality of the information they could utilise to predict the level and dynamic nature of threats that were subsequently posed, and therefore how to best deploy proportionately and efficiently to them. A second drawback of this limited categorisation approach appeared to be that some police forces could miss opportunities for more meaningful and productive engagement with fans they categorised as 'risk' (Hoggett and Stott 2010a, b).

Often, in contrast to police expectations, we also often found little evidence of any major underlying threat that was brought about by 'risk' groups travelling to these events who were conspiring to precipitate disorder. The tensions and conflict we did observe were largely the result of patterns of intergroup interaction, that were mostly unexpected and developed during the event itself. It was also evident that it was the capacity of the policing operation to proactively manage these interactions, primarily through facilitation and a graded tactical approach based upon communication, that was a primary correlate of operational success (see also Stott et al., 2008, 2012, 2016; Hoggett and Stott 2010a, b; Hoggett & West, 2018). Where the intelligence changed to suggest lower risk, there was a tendency toward the retention of the earlier reports, even if the latter intelligence was of higher quality. It seems to us, given the complexity of operational mobilisation, host forces get 'locked in' to the recruitment of human resources, with senior commanders then keen to embrace weak intelligence to legitimise the heavy level of resourcing that has been applied. To address this, we suggest that the intelligence reports provided by police move beyond a focus merely on the number of risk fans likely to attend, towards a more comprehensive analysis of their identity and behavioural norms. This fuller intelligence picture would focus as much on the legitimate and lawful intentions of the fan base as it would on any underlying intentions towards criminality. This would then enable police commanders to explicitly plan for how to facilitate these legitimate intentions and manage any underlying sensitivities that might be likely to emerge.

References

Ashworth, A. (2005). Burden of Proof. *Criminal Law Review* 218.

Ashworth, A., & Blake, M. (1996). The Presumption of Innocence in English Criminal Law. *Criminal Law Review, 306.*

DCMS. *Fan-Led Review of Football Governance: Securing the Game's Future*, 24 November 2021. https://www.gov.uk/government/publications/fan-led-review-of-football-governance-securing-the-games-future/fan-led-review-of-football-governance-securing-the-games-future

Dennis, I. (2005). Reverse Onuses and Presumption of Innocence: In Search of Principle. *Criminal Law Review, 901.*

Hoggett, J., & Stott, C. (2010a). Crowd Psychology, Public Order Police Training and the Policing of Football Crowds. *Policing: An International Journal of Police Strategies and Management, 33*(2), 218–235.

Hoggett, J., & Stott, C. (2010b). The Role of Crowd Theory in Determining the Use of Force in Public Order Policing. *Policing and Society, 20*(2), 223–236.

Hoggett, J., & West, O. (2018). Police Liaison Officers at Football: Challenging Orthodoxy Through Communication and Engagement. *Policing, 1–17*. https://doi.org/10.1093/police/pay032

Ivandić, R., Kirchmaier, T., & Torres-Blas, N. (2021) *Football, Alcohol, and Domestic Abuse*. Centre for Economic Performance Discussion Paper No. 1781. London School of Economics.

James, M., & Pearson, G. (2018). 30 Years of Hurt: The Evolution of Civil Preventative Orders, Hybrid Law, and the Emergence of the Super-Football Banning Order. *Public Law, 1*, 44–61.

Pearson, G. (2012). *An Ethnography of English Football Fans: Cans, Cops, and Carnivals*. Manchester University Press.

Popplewell Committee of Inquiry into Crowd Safety and Control at Sports Grounds Final Report. (1986). HMSO Cmnd. 9710.

Stott, C., Adang, O., Livingstone, A., & Schreiber, M. (2008). Tackling Football Hooliganism: A Quantitative Study of Public Order, Policing and Crowd Psychology. *Psychology Public Policy and Law, 14*(2), 115–114.

Stott, C., Hoggett, J., & Pearson, G. (2012). 'Keeping the Peace': Social Identity, Procedural Justice and the Policing of Football Crowds. *British Journal of Criminology, 52*(2), 381–399.

Stott, C., West, O., & Radburn, M. (2016). Policing Football "Risk"? A Participant Action Research Case Study of a Liaison-Based Approach to "Public Order". *Policing and Society*. https://doi.org/10.1080/10439463.2015.1126267

Stott, C., Khan, S., Madsen, E., & Havelund, J. (2018). The Value of Supporter Liaison Officers (SLOs) in Fan Dialogue, Conflict, Governance and Football Crowd Management in Sweden. *Soccer and Society, 2*(2), 196–208.

Taylor, L. J. (1990). *The Hillsborough Stadium Disaster: Final Report*. HMSO.

Welford, J., Bowes, L. Stutz, A., & Pearson, G. (2022). *Early Adopters of Licensed Standing Areas in Football Stadia: Report for the SGSA on the Findings from the Independent Evaluation (CFE/SGSA, July 2022)*. https://sgsa.org.uk/wp-content/uploads/2022/07/Early-adopters-of-licensed-standing-areas-CFE-Research-evaluation-July-2022.pdf

11

Conclusions

'The Perfect Storm': Revisiting Euro Sunday

We start this conclusion by returning to the events of 'Euro Sunday' that we used to introduce this book. The Casey Review into the disorder called the combination of factors in the build-up to the day "the perfect storm" (Casey, 2021), and we would concur that this metaphor has merit in depicting the complex nature of the interacting factors that produced the collective behaviours witnessed on that day. The context and situation were unprecedented in several ways, mostly related in one way or another to the period of strict Covid-19 'lockdowns'. Given those circumstances, it is our view that incidents of disorder and successful 'jibs' of Wembley stadium were inevitable. However, applying the findings of our research into the management of football crowds, we can also see that several opportunities to deflect, reduce, or mitigate the scale of the problems that ultimately did occur on that day were missed. Euro Sunday therefore provides us with an excellent opportunity to pull the various arguments we have made within this book together to demonstrate how the New Agenda for football crowd management could have worked.

G. Pearson, C. Stott, *A New Agenda For Football Crowd Management*, Palgrave Studies in Risk, Crime and Society, https://doi.org/10.1007/978-3-031-16298-5_11

Understanding Fan Behaviour and 'Cultures'

The first lost opportunity occurred during the planning stage for the tournament. Without any large area to locate a fan park or other places where the thousands of fans can gather safely in the period before these kinds of fixtures, regardless of whether they have tickets for the match, was a major oversight. Bearing this in mind, a few months before the event, the British Government made the decision that Covid-19 restrictions on gathering and social distancing could be relaxed inside stadiums but made no provision beyond this. What this meant was that while crowds could gather inside, significant restrictions would be in place outside. Not for the first time in the handling of the pandemic, this overlooked or downplayed the significance of the journey to the match and the pre-match festivities. It ignored what we already knew about fan behaviour during the pandemic from other major football events; the breaches of Covid-19 restrictions from non-socially distanced gatherings that were the result of title or promotion celebrations in Coventry, Leeds, and Liverpool, as well as the anti-Super League protests, particularly at Arsenal, Chelsea, and Manchester United. Once the original, and strictest, "Stay at Home" restrictions were lifted, fans had demonstrated that they would travel to, and gather in, public spaces to express their identity, and engage in transgressive, carnivalesque, and sometimes disorderly or criminal behaviour.[1] More generally, we also know how international football tournaments work; that provision for non-ticket holders in the form of fan zones and other experiences is now an essential part of the planning. With Covid restrictions still in place, the authorities were unable to facilitate such gatherings, but their failure to do so seemed to be based on an expectation that football crowds would simply return to norms of experiencing international tournaments that have not existed since the early 1990s, if not before. The central government decision to allow the European Championship matches to proceed despite the ongoing pandemic, but at the same time not to consider the need for fan

---

[1] Other groups had also gathered together during this time, including protesters ('Black Lives Matter', anti-vaccination, and those supporting key workers), 'VE Day' celebrants, those participating in the Sarah Everard vigil, and clubbers gathering for illicit dance music events.

zones, demonstrated a startling naivety about English fan 'culture' and behaviours.

Once England qualified for the Euro2020 final, large gatherings of ticketless fans were inevitable, and yet the plans put in place to manage this were piecemeal. Aside from one small fan zone in Trafalgar Square, there were no serious plans to accommodate the thousands of ticketless fans who were to descend on London, or those local fans who wished to gather to celebrate England's first appearance in a major final since 1966. And we should remember that the bulk of the ticketless fans *did not* attempt to enter the stadium: around 25,000 of the estimated 33,000 fans left the environs of Wembley as kick-off approached of their own volition. We assume the rationale for the decision not to plan for ticketless fans was that, due to Covid-19 restrictions, the authorities wanted to discourage fans from travelling and gathering in the city. Indeed, it is difficult to see how the football or local authorities could have provided such venues with these government regulations in place. Nonetheless, while the establishment of fan parks with big screens would have encouraged some fans to leave their homes to watch the match, open air fan zones in London and around the country would have also provided an opportunity for fans to express their identity and celebrate England's success more locally, almost certainly keeping some fans out of London and more fans away from Wembley. In short, the government decisions over Euro2020, and its position on health restrictions nationally, set the wheels in motion for the outcome that was the disorder at the Euro2020 Final. It was a failure to learn from experience, and to facilitate the realities of modern football fan 'culture', that formed the first gathering clouds of the perfect storm.

So, the first item on our New Agenda is for a greater understanding and knowledge of dominant football fan behaviours and for this to be the primary basis for informing pre-event risk analysis. Pushing aside the uniqueness of situation at Wembley, as we saw in Chap. 5, there is already a great depth of research-based knowledge about British fan behaviour from a large body of ethnographic work with fans. This knowledge of 'cultural' and 'subcultural' norms should always form the foundation of plans and strategies to manage football crowds more generally (Reicher et al., 2007). Furthermore, clubs, governing bodies, local authorities, and police need to engage to a far greater extent, and on a routine basis, with their regular match-going support, to understand not only their dominant norms of behaviour and legitimate desires but also the challenges that are in the way of realising these intentions. Some clubs and police forces are already ahead of the game in this respect, with some excellent Dedicated Football Officers (DFOs) and Operational Football Officers (OFOs) engaging in the type of long-term dialogue, communication, and negotiation, that helps to build knowledge that prevents unnecessary interference with fan intentions, reduces conflict, and enables the planning of more effective and proportionate crowd management. Other clubs and forces have been less impressive, focusing their attentions on deterrence-based communications, excluding all those categorised very broadly as 'risk supporters', or building links merely with 'official', but broadly unrepresentative, fan organisations.

Intelligence, Infrastructure, and Risk

The Casey Review's investigation into the police intelligence picture ahead of the Euro2020 Final noted that those who became involved in the disorder were not typically known to the police as 'risk supporters'. As we saw in Chap. 6, this is in common with most large-scale disorder abroad involving English fans historically, and this background knowledge should have provided the template for the policing response on the day. While the Metropolitan Police were correct in their assessment that the major risk on the day would come in the form of spontaneous disorder, rather than planned violence, the intelligence clearly did not predict a mass gathering so early in the day. Perhaps based on their Covid-19 assumptions, their deployments indicate they treated the fixture more as a typical evening match, rather than an international tournament event of national significance. The behaviour of England fans on the day was also reflective of that at major tournaments abroad, and as a result, it was largely predictable that gatherings would require proactive policing interventions from mid-morning onwards. These gatherings also necessitated the type of policing that was shown in Chap. 6 to be successful in managing England fans at tournaments abroad: early intervention, the setting of tolerance limits, and—most importantly—dialogue to both communicate with fans and inform police commanders about the emerging and evolving risks. There was little evidence, for example, that at any stage on the day the police—or anyone else—made any more than a piecemeal effort to try and communicate to fans about the lack of venues to watch the final in the vicinity of Wembley, or to try and encourage fans to move away from the stadium environs in time to watch the kick-off elsewhere. As we have argued above, with government restrictions and the Metropolitan Police Service (MPS) strategy for managing public assembly during Covid in place, combined with the lack of provision for ticketless fans, it is difficult to see how the police could have actively adopted the necessary facilitation-focused approach.

Much of the risk, therefore, was contextual—situational, geographical, and infrastructural—rather than being linked merely to 'troublemakers' attending with a predisposition towards engaging in violence or disorder. In this sense, it was arguably the way in which the area around Wembley stadium has been designed and developed, with alcohol outlets, shopping outlets, and small public gathering spaces near to an unsuitable temporary Outer Security Perimeter that provided the greatest risk on the day. And that risk turned out not just to be of anti-social behaviour, criminality, and violence, but also of a potentially fatal crowd crush. The environment around Wembley enabled large numbers of increasingly intoxicated fans to gather near the OSP, with nowhere to watch the match for a significant number. In this sense, reflecting many of this book's core arguments; 'risk' in football crowds is typically less about predispositions and more about context. In our experience, at planning and briefing stages, the latter is all too frequently overlooked as attention instead focuses primarily on the former. Furthermore, the risk of violence is often given more attention than the risk to the safety of fans, as was clearly the case once again at the Champions League final in Paris in 2022.

Therefore, the second item of our New Agenda for football crowd management is the need for a fundamental rethink of what 'risk' is in football, where it arises, and how it can be managed. It is clear from our research that the current focus on pre-dispositional 'risk' is of little help in predicting when, where, and to what extent disorder, violence, or criminality occur. This is despite the vast amount of time and resource dedicated to gathering information, and categorising and monitoring fans. As we have consistently shown, the risk of disorder is primarily interactional and is often influenced by geographical and infrastructural factors, or how relationships between different groups (including the police) develop over the course of the event. Furthermore, there needs to be a recognition that disorder, criminality, and violence are not the only risks that a police force needs to manage; it must also consider the reputational risks—to both police commanders and their organisations—and the risk of litigation. But above and beyond all of these dangers, we propose that safety should be the most important, overarching strategic aim of event planning, which should also consider how the layout of turnstiles, stadium approaches, alcohol outlets, and transport hubs can lead to potential congestion and risk to life.

Policing and Dialogue

In the previous two sections, we have set out how contextual, geographic, infrastructural, legal, and 'cultural' factors all combined to create 'the perfect storm' at Wembley. While these factors meant that some anti-social behaviour, disorder, criminality, and congestion were inevitable on the day, even with the bad hand the police had been dealt, there were still numerous ways in which interventions could have been made to mitigate the situation and reduce problems. As we have established, dialogue and relationship-building are fundamental to successful football policing operations, and yet in the build-up to the Euro2020 Final, this appears to have been largely absent. Indeed, a feature of responses to the Casey Review's fan survey were views expressed by fans about the general lack of police in the build-up to the match, particularly on the route to the stadium via Wembley Way and the areas around it.

This absence can be partly explained by the late deployment of the bulk of resources, which were not available until nearly 15.00. We suspect this late arrival was also a cost issue; ensuring that officer deployments corresponded with shift patterns in the late afternoon would have reduced the financial and human resource burden of policing the event considerably for the MPS. But by this time, the areas where problems were occurring were already congested, and there had been many instances of pyro and bottle-throwing. Reactively deploying officers into densely crowded areas without any of the prior 'limit-setting' and dialogue work would likely have provoked confrontation and set in motion escalatory crowd dynamics. Forming 'a ring of steel' around the stadium at this point to try to prevent further mass breaches was probably the only option left to the MPS. However, from CCTV footage and the fan survey, there was little evidence of intervention from police spotters (OFOs). The records indicate that three vans of OFOs were present at Wembley from 12.00, well before the area had become too congested or disorderly to deploy into, and we have subsequently established that some DFOs/ OFOs were engaged in the crowd, responding to issues of disorder, and interacting with fans. It may have been that they were simply overwhelmed by the size of the crowd or were pulled in too many different directions on the day to have been more effective.

In any case, in Chaps. 9 and 10 we reflected on the value that specialist officers, be they DFOs, OFOs, or Protest Liaison Team Officers (PLTs), can have intervening in football crowds. Their knowledge and expertise of football crowd behaviour, their willingness to proactively engage in communication (in contrast with the bulk of Police Support Unit [PSU] resources), and their confidence to challenge behaviour and take positive action, make them the key tactical resource in football policing in England and Wales. The Casey Review made no direct recommendations aimed at the police service, despite the frequently expressed concerns about the late deployment of resources, nor does it appear the views of DFOs/OFOs were canvassed. However, it is possible that a more visible—and better resourced—deployment of OFOs into the crowd gathered close to the OSP could have played an important role in improving dialogue with crowd members, communicating intelligence about the number of ticketless fans present and their likely intentions. These officers could have intervened in incidents of low-level criminality or disorder and, in so doing, set down tolerance limits much earlier in the day. As we have argued in this book, such dialogue-based approaches to football policing have proven effective, so there is no reason to assume they would not have been a helpful tool in preventing the clouds becoming the storm. In this sense, 'Euro Sunday' reflects how there are key opportunities ahead in the development of the OFO, moving it away from a predominantly reactive intelligence-gathering and football banning order (FBO) securing-and-enforcing role, towards one focused on proactive dialogue and de-escalation functions. Such changes are the third element of our proposed New Agenda for football crowd management.

The Law and Criminal Justice System

The final point to make as we revisit the Euro2020 Final is the way in which the laws designed to regulate football crowds fundamentally failed on the day. We have already noted how law and policing need to work in tandem for effective crowd management, and how for high-risk football events, decisions need to be made by forces about what offences will be enforced and to what extent. The above-mentioned absence of policing from the pre-match crowd meant that there was little, if any, setting down of tolerance limits on behaviour, and as the day wore on and members of the crowd became more intoxicated, criminal behaviour such as open drug-taking, pyrotechnic use, and bottle-throwing started to become normalised behaviour. Furthermore, there is no suggestion that the wealth of football-specific laws played any positive role in managing crowd behaviour on the day. For example, the Sporting Events (Control of Alcohol, etc.) Act (SECAA) 1985's prohibition on drunken entry to the stadium appears both unenforced and unenforceable. What is more, that Act once again may have played a role in contributing to the levels of disorder, by both encouraging fans to drink outside the stadium rather than inside it, and then contributing to crushes and misbehaviour in the concourses pre-match and at half-time.

Moreover, it remains remarkable that the bulk of legal tools currently available to the police to help manage football crowds were enacted during, or at the end of, what we might consider to be the era of 'hooliganism', when violence and disorder in and around football stadia in England and Wales was occurring with relative regularity. In 2021, the Law Commission noted that the legal framework around football had not been revisited since 2006 (Law Commission, 2021), but in reality, this overplays the extent to which successive governments have been willing to revisit the operation of the law in the context of football crowds. Some offences have remained untouched since they were enacted in the 1980s or early 1990s. Moreover, while other offences have been modified to close loopholes and encapsulate more behaviour than before, there has been little attempt to consider the regime in a wholesale manner, look to reduce little-used, ineffective, or out-of-date offences, or consider how new legislative tools could be used to confront the problematic behaviours that can cause challenges in football crowds.

There is an almost palpable fear amongst many legislators, and some elements of the police, that to reform laws that were created to confront problematic behaviour in the 1970s and 1980s will in some way lead to a return of that type of behaviour. Conversely, there also seems an unwillingness to accept that when crowd disorder incidents do occur, they may indicate failures of the current legislative regime, rather than providing an argument for why such laws should remain. This is illustrated by the response to the Euro2020 Final disorder and the role played by the SECAA's restrictions on the consumption of alcohol within sight of the pitch. While an amendment of that legislation would not have prevented many of the problems that presented themselves that day, it would probably have had a positive impact upon levels of disorder.

In Chaps. 3 and 10 in particular, we drew attention to the problems with the drafting of much of the legislation, demonstrating the failings of many antiquated laws, some of which were never especially suitable for managing football crowds in the first place. In the previous chapter in particular we made recommendations for reform of these laws, to increase the relevance of the law to contemporary football crowd behaviours and take into account the radically changed environment in which they are now expected to operate; in which infrastructure, technology, and fan 'cultures' have fundamentally changed, as well as the way in which the role of the police themselves has altered as a result of challenges such as austerity. We have also, in our empirical chapters, detailed many observed incidents of when the existing laws created problems for the effective and legitimate policing of challenging football match events, as well as incidents where a failure by police to apply a human rights-based approach to football policing related to damaging and sometimes violent outcomes. In this book we have therefore attempted to demonstrate the damaging effect that poor laws can have upon the legitimacy and effectiveness of football policing. While, as we will summarise in the next section, we have uncovered plenty of evidence of poor public order policing in football, we need to remember that "[f]ront-men like the police become the 'fall guys' of the legal system" (McBarnet, 1981, p. 156).

It is therefore not enough that police operations are reformed, when they will still be required to enforce laws that are seen as unjust, illegitimate, or arbitrarily enforced. The meaning of law is, after all, not abstract, but an aspect of the social experience (Cotterrell, 2006, p. 25) of those against whom it is enforced. And an important narrative within match-going communities, which we have shown to be true, is that the law is discriminatory against football fans in contrast to those of other sports. The legal framework, supported by the policing and criminal justice systems and structures, is set up with football fans in the crosshairs. The statutory safety framework ensures that police will be present at matches and that CCTV will be operational keeping fans under surveillance. Many police policies, agreed with clubs, will be to arrest for even minor infringements and the Crown Prosecution Service (CPS) policy for offences committed at the football is to prosecute. The football-specific offences themselves are set up to be easy to secure prosecutions and convictions, employing strict liability and reverse burdens of proof rather than the requirement to prove intention or recklessness on the part of the fan. Finally, the Football Spectators Act 1989 places an onus on magistrates and judges to impose FBOs with conditions which are often wildly disproportionate to the transgression which has led to it. For a football fan committing a minor offence, in contrast to most other areas of society, the opportunities for deflection from the criminal justice system, community resolution, or restorative justice are substantially diminished, without there being any justification for why this should be the case.

As we noted in the preceding chapter, one problem for football crowd management arises from the rather siloed nature of football policing operations when considered alongside other force-wide policies or priorities. This is exacerbated by the existence of football-specific offences, the list of FBO-qualifying offences set out in Schedule 1 Football Spectators Act 1989, and the funding regime for football policing units. Those tasked with policing football have their use of this limited array of legal measures monitored nationally and are effectively encouraged to rely on these. Local football policing operations have, to differing extents, become reliant upon central funding secured through the pursuit of FBOs, and all local football policing units are measured against the extent to which they are able to secure FBOs. This has the effect of narrowing the focus of both specialist football officers and PSU officers towards those offences that fall under Schedule 1. It is therefore effectively more beneficial for football policing operations to secure convictions for some offences than others, which means that local football units may not always be using the most appropriate legal tools to confront the misbehaviour they are faced with. It also means that the UK Football Policing Unit (UKFPU) are naturally more inclined to look for solutions to arising problems through the means of Schedule 1 offences and FBOs.

Consequently, there is little encouragement for operations to look for other solutions to the misbehaviour they are challenged with, such as through using existing Violence Reduction Units or other educational or criminal justice deflection programmes. There is also little evidence that football policing operations are considering the use of other forms of preventative civil orders, such as Criminal Behaviour Orders. The best example of how this unfortunate relationship between law and policing has become problematic is illustrated by the response to online racist abuse faced by England players, particularly following the Euro2020 final. The typically knee-jerk response was, in a rather contrived and convoluted manner, to add this type of abuse to the schedule of offences which could lead to a s.14A FBO, and tinker elsewhere with the legislation to make it easier to impose FBOs even without proof they would prevent future misbehaviour. The change will require specialised football officers to essentially police online behaviour, and the movements of individuals who may not even attend live matches. But it is far from the best way to reduce the likelihood of a repetition of the problematic behaviour. Securing a Criminal Behaviour Order, which could impose conditions not to engage in certain online activity associated with such abuse, would be much more appropriate.

Procedural Justice

The existence of this siloed legal system, and lack of alternative criminal justice approaches to low-level or first-time offending in football, leads us on to the question of procedural justice. The processes we identified throughout this book expose the relationship between a social-identity based approach and procedural justice theory (PJT). In this respect, both the Social Identity Approach (SIA) and PJT provide a consistent and far-reaching theoretical case that the route to police legitimacy, and therefore conflict-reduction during domestic football crowd events, resides not merely in excluding 'risk' fans but in developing police capability to act proportionately through 'dialogue'-based interventions. Our data is increasingly consistent with the idea that this is because, in so doing, police are (1) more likely to maximise normative consent within the crowd and (2) maintain or even build legitimacy for the entire policing operation (even if more 'robust' tactics are subsequently required). In this respect, we suggest that the evidence increasingly supports the assertion by Hough et al. that "normative compliance is economically more viable and is more stable over time than instrumental compliance which … carries a growingly unaffordable social and fiscal cost" (Hough et al., 2010, p. 205). There are evident advantages in football policing operations adopting some of the key tenets of PJT, which emphasise the importance of communication (i.e. giving voice) and treating citizens with respect. And a poor adherence to procedural justice from the police can certainly exacerbate problems within a football crowd and increase the risk of disorder. However, when we dig deeper, our research in this area also highlights some of the limitations of PJT in its applications to public order policing (cf. Radburn & Stott, 2018).

Laws that are seen by those against whom they are enforced, or through the way that the CPS or the courts treat them, as being in their nature illegitimate or unfair, challenge the concept of procedural justice. In effect, it matters little whether a law seen as *substantively* unjust is being enforced in a manner that is compliant with *procedural* justice; it will inevitably cause tension and potential conflict between the police and the policed. In the same way as 'zero tolerance' or 'broken windows' models of policing can backfire, many of the laws discussed in Chap. 3, particularly prohibitions on indecent (but not racialist) chanting and entering a football ground while drunk clash with dominant forms of behaviour in English and Welsh football crowds which, in and of themselves, are seen as being legitimate forms of fan identity and expression. To try to take action against fans exhibiting these behaviours would therefore be seen as inherently illegitimate, regardless of how the law was enforced. In other words, a procedurally fair enforcement of either law would be impossible, without provoking significant resistance and disorder, and would inevitably lead to the long-term damaging of relationships between fans and those policing them.

In addition, football policing questions any assumptions of a mechanical link between procedurally fair treatment and perceptions of procedural justice (c.f. Worden & McLean, 2017). PJT has received specific criticism for failing to account for situations or contexts where legal, societal, or structural imbalances mean the law is applied more rigorously to different demographics, or where different laws apply to different people (see Kyprianides et al., 2021; Shaap & Saarikkomäki, 2022). To take an obvious example, regardless of how procedurally fair a stop and search of a young man from an inner-city black community is, they are unlikely to see either the law or the individual stop as legitimate if it is the fifth time that week it has occurred and their white compatriots never get stopped at all. Moreover, for our purposes, PJT reveals its limitations in public order situations where the breaking of laws is seen, within the policed community, as legitimate or accepted, such as protest, festival, or football crowds. As we set out in Chap. 5, for a large sub-culture of 'carnival fans' who attend matches, *transgression* from the norms of everyday life is a key driving factor, and this departure regularly means engagement in the committal of minor offences, many of which only exist in the context of football. Successful football policing operations understand and adapt to this reality, establishing clearly communicated and understood tolerance limits. These red lines are, however, rarely drawn where low-level, and low-harm, offences start.

In contrast to traditional understandings of procedural justice, many of the most successful football policing operations we observed contained a considerable element of negotiation and compromise, some of which required the police operation to turn a blind eye to minor offences in order to reduce the risk that serious disorder would occur. This also meant that there were occasions where laws that were enforced in a procedurally fair manner (e.g. equally across fan groups, with prior warning and respectful communication) caused conflict, because in other forces, they were not enforced so rigorously. Furthermore, classical understandings of PJT also struggle to account for the kind of human rights-led proportionality decision-making requirements that we have championed in this book, which again may lead to activity which *prima facie* is a breach of the criminal law but complies with ECHR Art. 10/11 freedoms of expression or assembly. It is the tension between effective (in terms of protecting public order, and safety, and satisfying human rights obligations) football policing and the rigours of unenforceable laws that may be seen as illegitimate in fan communities, that lead us to the fourth item on the New Agenda. There is need for a wholescale reform of the statutory framework around football, and the attitudes of organisations like the CPS towards minor offences committed in this context, carried out in consultation with the supporters. Until the legal framework around football reflects the genuine concerns of the fan community, and is seen as *substantively* fair, effective, and proportionate, both the law and the police operations enforcing it will always struggle to be seen as legitimate.

The Direction of Travel

In addition to putting forward the theoretical and empirical arguments about how law and policing of football can be improved, in this book we have also mapped the positive developments in policing that have already taken place and the ongoing changes. It is important to note that despite the problems we have identified, the broad direction of travel in terms of football policing in England and Wales is a positive one. Some police forces have engaged in evidence-based approaches to football policing for many years, applying innovative approaches to solving specific problems, and developing good practice, some of which we identified in Chaps. 9 and 10. Furthermore, in 2021, as we have discussed, the authors contributed to the review of the existing national guidance on football policing and the development of a new edition of the Authorised Professional Practice (APP) produced by the UKFPU and College of Policing. The new policy brings statutory guidance more in line with established crowd management theory. In particular, in giving greater strategic emphasis to engagement, and re-titling the role of police spotter to 'Operational Football Officer', it places greater emphasis on their role in dialogue and long-term relationship-building with supporters. Potentially of equal significance, the new APP also redrafts the definition of 'risk supporter', placing greater emphasis on the importance of 'current' intelligence of likely behaviour, rather than historical expectations, and the way in which police intervention can help direct the behaviour of fans in the middle-risk categories. The new APP is a significant step forward in promoting an evidence-based approach to football policing on a national—and indeed international—level and we hope it will genuinely influence the strategies and tactics used by all police forces across England and Wales in their football policing operations. Furthermore, we have also been involved in conversations with the College of Policing about the content of their forthcoming, revised, POPS APP, and are hopeful that this will reflect, for the first time in national guidance, that football fans possess equivalent freedoms of assembly and expression to protesters.

In law, unfortunately, the direction of travel is less clear. In 2021, four reports independent of each other criticised the current legislative regime around football as being out-of-date, disproportionate, or piecemeal.[2] This was welcome recognition of the deficiencies we also identify in this book, and we welcome the calls for reform. However, unfortunately there have also been knee-jerk calls for more football-specific offences, extension of existing offences, and an expansion of the qualifying offences for football banning orders. These proposed changes are likely to have, at best, a marginal effect upon effective football crowd management and also have the potential to undermine the legal operation of the entire FBO regime. Perhaps more significantly, the proposal to repeal the Human Rights Act 1998 (HRA) and replace it with a Bill of Rights that

[2] The SGSA/CFE Report into Persistent Standing at Football (SGSA, 2021), the Casey Review, (Casey, 2021) the Fan-Led Review into Football Governance (Crouch, 2021), and the Law Commission's Final Report on Hate Crime (Law Commission, 2021).

imposes fewer obligations on police forces to protect the rights of citizens (particularly through watering down their positive obligations) threatens to undermine the progress that POPS operations have made in facilitating the legitimate expectations of both protest and football crowds. We can only hope that the case made for facilitation through the overwhelming evidence from crowd science is strong enough to encourage football policing operations to continue with this approach, even if a change to human rights law no longer requires it as a domestic legal obligation.

Overall, however, at the time of writing, the direction of travel for football crowd management in England and Wales is positive. Furthermore, given that many countries with more serious problems of football-related violence and disorder often look to Britain for lessons in how to overcome seemingly insurmountable problems in this area, this may also bode well for the outlook internationally. But there is no room for complacency that past failures are behind us. It is certainly not guaranteed that this positive direction of travel will continue, especially when confronted with apparent rises in instances of disorder such as those that followed the release of the Covid-19 lockdown restrictions, and the increasingly authoritarian restrictions of freedoms of assembly and expression in many areas of society that we are seeing in the UK and elsewhere.

Research Co-production and Knowledge-Exchange

Ultimately, the key for successful management of football crowds depends on those responsible for introducing legislation, writing policing policy and guidance, and organising and implementing crowd management strategies and tactics, understanding both the groups they are managing and the complexities of crowd interactions. Central to this, as we have argued throughout this book, is that risk needs to be understood as not to be purely the result of predisposition by individuals towards violence, disorder, or criminality, but as an outcome of the interactional dynamics of crowd events, often shaped by historical, contextual, and infrastructural factors. Engagement by legislators, police, and security personnel with up-to-date theory and empirical research is therefore key to reducing the risks to public order and safety at and around football events.

We have set out in this book a series of arguments pointing towards the importance of academic research and theory in this domain and shown how productive it can be when police and universities work together in a partnership of knowledge co-production, in order to address important social issues. We would argue that the successes in the area of football crowd management provide a valuable case study for how this kind of collaboration might work in other areas of society where there is conflict between communities and authority. We have put forward an alternative evidence- and theory-based framework to the orthodox position on controlling football crowds, which we argue will remedy many of the problems we have identified and should lead to sustainable and proportionate football crowd management practices fit for the twenty-first century. But it is not a case that following these recommendations will future-proof us from crowd disorder or violence. We need to engage in a continual programme of co-produced research, knowledge-building and sharing, innovation, and testing, to ensure that our football crowd management strategies remain up to date with changing environments, laws, technologies, and behavioural norms. The fifth, and final, part of our New Agenda is therefore that we must acknowledge that managing football crowds is not simply about applying rigid and static, recommendations, but that it should also involve committing to a process of continual learning.

References

Casey, L. (2021). *The Baroness Casey Review: An Independent Review of Events Surrounding the UEFA Euro 2020 Final 'Euro Sunday' at Wembley.*

Cotterrell, R. (2006). *Law, Culture, and Society: Legal Ideas in the Mirror of Social Theory*. Ashgate.

Crouch, T. (2021). *Independent Report of the Fan-Led Review of Football Governance: Securing the Game's Future*. DCMS. https://www.gov.uk/government/publications/fan-led-review-of-football-governance-securing-the-games-future/fan-led-review-of-football-governance-securing-the-games-future

Hough, M., Jackson, J., Bradford, B., & Myhill, A. (2010). Procedural Justice, Trust, and Institutional Legitimacy. *Policing, 4*(3). https://doi.org/10.1093/police/paq027

Kyprianides, A., Stott, C., & Bradford, B. (2021). "Playing the Game"': Power, Authority and Procedural Justice in Interactions Between Police and Homeless People in London. *The British Journal of Criminology, 61*(3), 670–689.

Law Commission. (2021). *Hate Crime Laws: Final Report.* HC942 Law Com No 402.

McBarnet, D. (1981). *Conviction: The Law, the State and the Construction of Justice* (p. 156). Palgrave Macmillan.

Radburn, M., & Stott, C. (2018). The Social Psychological Processes of "Procedural Justice": Concepts, Critiques and Opportunities. *Criminology and Criminal Justice.* https://doi.org/10.1177/1748895818780200

Reicher, S., Stott, C., Drury, J., Adang, O., Cronin, P., & Livingstone, A. (2007). Knowledge-Based Public Order Policing: Principles and Practice. *Policing, 1*, 403–415.

Shaap, D., & Saarikkomäki, E. (2022). Rethinking Police Procedural Justice. *Theoretical Criminology.* https://doi.org/10.1177/13624806211056680

Sports Ground Safety Authority/CFE. (2021). The Management of Persistent Standing at Football Matches. https://sgsa.org.uk/wp-content/uploads/2021/06/The-management-of-persistent-standing-Final-report.pdf

Worden, R., & McLean, S. (2017). *Mirage of Police Reform: Procedural Justice and Police Legitimacy.* University of California Press.

Appendix

Table of Cases

G. Pearson, C. Stott, *A New Agenda For Football Crowd Management*, Palgrave Studies in Risk, Crime and Society, https://doi.org/10.1007/978-3-031-16298-5

De Freitas v Permanent Secretary of Ministry of Agriculture [1999] 1 AC 69, p. 29, 229.
Donaldson v United Kingdom (2011) 53 EHRR 14, p. 219.
DPP v Cuciurean [2022] EWHC 736 Admin, p. 223.
DPP v Stoke on Trent Magistrates' Court and Another [2003] EWHC 1593, p. 73.
DPP v Ziegler and other [2021] UKSC 23, p. 76, 217, 225, 226, 229, 312.
Eiseman Renyard and Others v United Kingdom App 57884/17 5 March 2019, p. 213.
Emin Huseynov v Azerbaijan App 59135/09 7 May 2015, p. 220.
Friend and Countryside Alliance v United Kingdom [2009] ECHR 2068, pp. 219–220, 221.
Gough and Smith v Chief Constable of Derbyshire [2001] EWHC Admin 55, p. 87.
Gough and Smith v Chief Constable of Derbyshire [2002] EWCA Civ 351, p. 82, 88, 310, 314.
Greater Manchester Police v Wigan Athletic FC [2008] EWCA Civ 1449, p. 106.
Harris v Sheffield United Football Club Ltd [1988] 1 QB 77, p. 105.
Identoba and others v Georgia App 73235/12 12 May 2015, p. 223.
Kharaahmed v Bulgaria, App 20587/13 21 February 2015, p. 216.
Kudrevicius and Others v Lithuania App 37553/05, p. 216.
Kuznetsov v. Russia, App 10877/04 23 October *08*, p. 214.
Javit An v Turkey App 20652/92 20 February 2003, p. 219.
Jersild v Demark (1995) 19 EHRR 1, p. 226.
Lashmankin v Russia App 57818/09 7 February 2017, p. 223.
Leeds United Football Club v West Yorkshire Police [2013] EWCA Civ 115, p. 106.
Mail v McDowell [1980] 6 WLUK 302, p.86.
McCartan Turkington Breen v Times Newspapers Ltd [2001] 2 AC 277, p. 218.
Miller v College of Policing [2020] EWHC 225 (Admin), p. 216.
Miranda v Secretary of State for the Home Department and Ors. [2014] EWHC 255, p. 218.
Moss v MacLachlan [1985] IRLR 76, p. 67.
Muller and Others v Switzerland [1988] ECHR 5, p. 214.

Öllinger v. Austria App 76900/01 29 June 2006, p. 214.
Osman v United Kingdom (2000) 29 EHRR 245, p. 211, 217.
Ostendorf v Germany App 15598/08 7 March 2013, p. 209, 213.
Özgür Gündem v. Turkey [*2000*] ECHR 104, p. 216.
Perinçek v Switzerland (2016) 63 EHRR 6, p. 214, 215.
Plattform "Ärzte für das Leben" v Austria (1988) 13 EHRR 204, p. 216, 223.
PWR v DPP; Akdogan and another v DPP [2022] UKSC 2, p. 209, 229.
Redmond-Bate v DPP [2000] HRLR 249, p. 223.
R (Begum) v Governors of Denbigh High School [2007] 1 A.C. 100, p. 228.
R (Laporte) v Chief Constable of Gloucestershire [2006] UKHL 55, p. 209, 215.
R (Leigh and others) v Met Police Commissioner [2022] EWHC 527 (Admin), p. 229.
R (on the application of Bridges) v Chief Constable of South Wales [2020] EWCA Civ 1058, p. 211.
R (Prolife Alliance) v British Broadcasting Corporation [2003] UKHL 23, p. 217.
R (Countryside Alliance) v Attorney General [2007] UKHL 52, pp. 219–220.
R v Arbery [2008] EWCA Crim 702, p. 90.
R v Boggild and Others [2011] EWCA Crim 1928), p. 90.
R v Clarke [2008] EWCA Crim 893, p. 308.
R v Curtis [2009] EWCA Crim 1225, p. 89.
R v Doncaster Justices ex parte Langfield QBD 149 JP 26, 22 Oct 1984, p. 61.
R v Doyle (Ciaran) and Others [2012] EWCA Crim. 995, p. 89, 90.
R v Elliott [2007] EWCA Crim 1002, p. 90.
R v Hughes [2005] EWCA Crim 2537, p. 89.
R v Jelf [2020] EWCA Crim 631, p. 90.
R v Johnstone [2003] UKHL 28, p. 308, 311.
R. v. Lambert [2002] 2 AC 545, pp. 307–308, 311.
R v Mabee [2007] EWCA Crim 3230, p. 90.
R v Rogers-Hinks (1989) 11 Cr App R (S) 234, p. 87.
R v Smith [2003] EWCA Crim 2480, p. 90.
R v Stamford [1972] 2 QB 391, p. 73.
R (White) v Blackfriars Crown Court [2008] EWHC 510 (Admin), p. 89.

Table of Legislation

Criminal Justice and Police Act 2001, p. 101.
Criminal Law (Consolidation) (Scotland) Act 1995, p. 61.
Equality Act 2010 s.4, p. 74.
European Convention on Human Rights.

Article 1, p. 216, 220.
Article 2, p. 209, 211.
Article 3, p. 209.
Article 5, p. 154, 209, 211, 212–213, 226, 229.
Article 6, p. 76, 83–84, 89, 306–312, 314.
Article 7, pp. 83–84, 89, 314.
Article 8, p. 154, 211–212.
Article 9, p. 215, 216
Article 10, p. 11, 76, 154, 203, 213–226, 229–232, 239, 319, 346.
Article 11, p. 11, 76, 154, 203, 213–217, 219–226, 229–232, 239, 319, 346.
Protocol 4 Article 2, p. 212.

EU Council Resolution OJC/322 2006, p. 147.
Fire Safety and Safety of Places of Sport Act 1987, p. 53.
Football (Disorder) Act 2000, p. 41, 80.
Football (Offences) Act 1991, p. 57, 71–76.

s.1, p. 71.
s.2, pp. 71–72, 316.
s.3, pp. 72–74, 75, 219.
s.4, pp. 74–76, 224, 225, 306–312.
s.5, p. 310.

Football (Offences) (Designation of Football Matches) Order 2004, p. 71.
The Football (Offences) (Designation of Football Matches) (Amendment) Order 2022, p. 71.
Football (Offences and Disorder) Act 1999, p. 73.
Football Spectators Act 1989 p. 7, 55, 80–86, 89, 312–315, 342.

Glossary and Acronyms

ACC Assistant Police Constable
ACPO Association of Chief Police Officers
APP The College of Policing's Authorised Professional Practice
ATP Adapting to Protest (HMIC Report 2009)
BOP Breach of the Peace
BTP British Transport Police
CPS Crown Prosecution Service
DFO Dedicated Football Officer (working with a particular club)
DOT Divisional Observation Team
ECHR European Convention on Human Rights
ECtHR European Court of Human Rights
EGT Evidence Gathering Team
ENABLE The programme of research work (Enabling an Evidenced-Based Approach to Policing Football)
ESIM Elaborated Social Identity Model
Euro Sunday The European Championships (Euro2020) Final at Wembley, 11 July 2021
FBO Football Banning Order (under s.14A and B of the Football Spectators Act 1989)

G. Pearson, C. Stott, *A New Agenda For Football Crowd Management*, Palgrave Studies in Risk, Crime and Society, https://doi.org/10.1007/978-3-031-16298-5

FBOA Football Banning Orders Authority
FIT Forward Intelligence Team (Protest Policing)
FOA The Football (Offences) Act 1991
FSA The Football Spectators Act 1989
GMP Greater Manchester Police
HMICFRS Her Majesties Inspectorate of the Constabulary and Fire and Rescue
HRA Human Rights Act 1998
Jib/Jibbing/Jibber The practice of entering a stadium (or accessing another service) without paying for entry.
MPS The Metropolitan Police Service for London
NCIS National Criminal Intelligence Service
NPIA National Policing Intelligence Agency
NPoCC National Police Coordination Centre
NFIU National Football Intelligence Unit (now UKFPU)
NPT National Police Training
OFO Operational Football Officer (previously called 'spotters').
OSP Outer Security Perimeter, used to keep ticketless fans away from the turnstiles
OSU Operational Support Unit
PAR Participant Action Research
PC Police Constable
PCC Police and Crime Commissioner
POPS The responsibility of policing for Public Order and Public Safety
PSP Polícia de Segurança Pública
PSU Police Support Unit. A PSU contains 22 officers, Level 2+ Public Order trained.
SAG The local authority's Safety Advisory Group for stadia
SECAA Sporting Events (Control of Alcohol, etc.) Act 1985
Serial A group of officers comprising a sergeant, six constables, and a driver
SGSA The Sports Grounds Safety Authority
SIA Social Identity Approach
SLO Supporter Liaison Office
SPS Special Police Services
SPT Special Police Tactic (in Swedish Policing)
SSGA Safety at Sports Grounds Act 1975
SWP South Wales Police

Rogue Coach An unofficial coach of travelling supporters which has not complied with Traffic Commissioner Guidelines to inform the police of its route and destination.

UKFPU The UK Football Policing Unit

WMP West Midlands Police

WYP West Yorkshire Police

Index[1]

[1] Note: Page numbers followed by 'n' refer to notes.

G. Pearson, C. Stott, *A New Agenda For Football Crowd Management*, Palgrave Studies in Risk, Crime and Society, https://doi.org/10.1007/978-3-031-16298-5

L

M

N

O

P

The manufacturer's authorised representative in the EU is Springer Nature Customer Service Centre GmbH, Europaplatz 3, 69115 Heidelberg, Germany. If you have any concerns regarding our products, please contact ProductSafety@springernature.com

Printed and bound by CPI Group (UK) Ltd, Croydon, CR0 4YY

30/09/2026

02225243-0014